AF716498

THE INSTITUTIONAL PROBLEM IN MODERN INTERNATIONAL LAW

Modern international law is widely understood as an autonomous system of binding legal rules. Nevertheless, this claim to autonomy is far from uncontroversial. International lawyers have faced recurrent scepticism as to both the reality and efficacy of the object of their study and practice. For the most part, this scepticism has focused on international law's peculiar institutional structure, with the absence of centralised organs of legislation, adjudication and enforcement, leaving international legal rules seemingly indeterminate in the conduct of international politics. Perception of this 'institutional problem' has therefore given rise to a certain disciplinary angst or self-defensiveness, fuelling a need to seek out functional analogues or substitutes for the kind of institutional roles deemed intrinsic to a functioning legal system. The author of this book believe that this strategy of accommodation is, however, deeply problematic. It fails to fully grasp the importance of international law's decentralised institutional form in securing some measure of accountability in international relations. It thus misleads through functional analogy and, in doing so, potentially exacerbates legitimacy deficits. There are enough conceptual weaknesses and blindspots in the legal-theoretical models against which international law is so frequently challenged to show that the perceived problem arises more in theory than in practice.

Volume 11 in the series Hart Monographs in Transnational and International Law

Hart Monographs in Transnational and International Law

Series Editor: Craig Scott, Professor of Law, Osgoode Hall Law School of York University, Toronto

The objective of this series is to publish high-quality scholarship in public international law and private international law, as well as work that adopts 'transnational law' as its thematic, theoretical or doctrinal focus. The series strives to be a leading venue for work of the following sort:

* critical reappraisals of foundational concepts and core doctrinal principles of both public and private international law, and their operation in practice, including insights drawn from general legal theory;

* analysis and development of conceptions of 'transnational law', including in relation to the role of unofficial law and informal processes in transnational regulation and in relation to theories and studies of 'governance' in transnational spheres; and

* empirical studies of the emergence, evolution and transformation of international and/or transnational legal orders, including accounts and explanations of how law is constructed within different communities of interpretation and practice.

The series will also be home to monographs that explore the interactions between the ever-integrating fields of public and private international law. Of special interest are explorations of the extent to which these interactions are structured by higher-order principles and policies, on the one hand, and by politics and the exercise of various forms of power, on the other hand.

The series is open to work not only by law scholars but also by scholars from cognate disciplines.

Recent titles in this series

Volume 6: The Payment Order of Antiquity and the Middle Ages: A Legal History
Benjamin Geva

Volume 7: The Concept of Unity in Public International Law
Mario Prost

Volume 8: Interlocking Constitutions: Towards an Interordinal Theory of National, European and UN Law
Luis I Gordillo

Volume 9: Transnational Terrorism and State Accountability: A New Theory of Prevention
Vincent-Joël Proulx

Volume 10: Transconstitutionalism
Marcelo Neves translated by Kevin Mundy

The Institutional Problem in Modern International Law

Richard Collins

•HART•

OXFORD • LONDON • NEW YORK • NEW DELHI • SYDNEY

HART PUBLISHING
Bloomsbury Publishing Plc
Kemp House, Chawley Park, Cumnor Hill, Oxford, OX2 9PH, UK

HART PUBLISHING, the Hart/Stag logo, BLOOMSBURY and the Diana logo are trademarks of Bloomsbury Publishing Plc
First published in Great Britain 2016

First published in hardback, 2016
Paperback edition, 2019

Copyright © Richard Collins 2016

Richard Collins has asserted his right under the Copyright, Designs and Patents Act 1988 to be identified as the Author of this work.

All rights reserved. No part of this publication may be reproduced or transmitted in any form or by any means, electronic or mechanical, including photocopying, recording, or any information storage or retrieval system, without prior permission in writing from the publishers.

While every care has been taken to ensure the accuracy of this work, no responsibility for loss or damage occasioned to any person acting or refraining from action as a result of any statement in it can be accepted by the authors, editors or publishers.

All UK Government legislation and other public sector information used in the work is Crown Copyright ©. All House of Lords and House of Commons information used in the work is Parliamentary Copyright ©. This information is reused under the terms of the Open Government Licence v3.0 (http://www.nationalarchives.gov.uk/doc/open-government-licence/version/3) except where otherwise stated.

All Eur-lex material used in the work is © European Union, http://eur-lex.europa.eu/, 1998-2019.

A catalogue record for this book is available from the British Library.

Library of Congress Cataloging-in-Publication Data

Names: Collins, Richard, 1979– author.

Title: The institutional problem in modern international law / Richard Collins.

Description: Oxford ; Portland, Oregon : Hart Publishing, An imprint of Bloomsbury Publishing Plc, 2016. | Series: Hart monographs in transnational and international law ; volume 11 | Based on author's thesis (doctoral)—University of Sheffield, 2011. | Includes bibliographical references and index.

Identifiers: LCCN 2016021697 (print) | LCCN 2016022053 (ebook) | ISBN 9781849465229 (hardback) | ISBN 9781509900442 (Epub)

Subjects: LCSH: International law.

Classification: LCC KZ3410 .C655 2016 (print) | LCC KZ3410 (ebook) | DDC 341—dc23

LC record available at https://lccn.loc.gov/2016021697

Series: Hart Monographs in Transnational and International Law, volume 11

ISBN: HB: 978-1-84946-522-9
PB: 978-1-50992-792-0
ePDF: 978-1-50990-043-5
ePub: 978-1-50990-044-2

Typeset by Compuscript Ltd, Shannon

To find out more about our authors and books visit www.hartpublishing.co.uk. Here you will find extracts, author information, details of forthcoming events and the option to sign up for our newsletters.

Acknowledgements

This book began life as a doctoral thesis, which was considerably shorter and slightly different in focus (though no less demanding and time-consuming to write). I owe thanks to many individuals during that earlier writing process, not least of whom was my supervisor, Nigel White, whose patience, encouragement, academic engagement and good humour were much appreciated as my focus shifted and ideas developed. I am also grateful to my two PhD examiners, Patrick Capps and Rob Cryer, not only for their thorough treatment of the thesis, but in helping shape the direction that this book has taken since. I am particularly indebted to Patrick Capps, whose friendship, academic engagement and support since has been particularly helpful in sharpening the focus of my work to get it ready for publication. I am also extremely grateful to Duncan French, who was not only the kindest and supportive of colleagues in the final stages of completing the PhD and in preparing for its defence, but also agreed to chair the viva itself (and did so in the best of spirits), and has since remained a good friend, not to mention a critical sounding board as the book manuscript took shape.

During the writing process, I have been fortunate enough to work at two great institutions, the University of Sheffield and, more recently, University College Dublin. I would like to thank friends, colleagues and former colleagues at both institutions for their support and encouragement. I am also grateful to have been accepted to spend part of my sabbatical semester at the University of Amsterdam and remain thankful to colleagues there for engaging in debate on many of the ideas developed here.

In addition to those named above, amongst others who contributed, either directly or indirectly, to the writing process, my thanks go to Silvia Cecchia and family, Paul James Cardwell, Etienne Dunant, Matthew Hall, Matthew Saul, Richard Kirkham, Dimitris Kyritsis, Dimitris Tsarapatsanis, Tawhida Ahmed, Harriet Godfrey, Sarah Beedham, Tammy Hervey, Cormac Behan, Russell Buchan, Mike Giudice, Marieke de Hoon, Marija Bartl, Anne van Mulligen, Ingo Venzke and Catherine ('Kiki') Brölmann. I would particularly like to thank Ali Bohm, who not only proofread chapters for the PhD thesis and, more latterly, for the book, but has been the kindest, most supportive and generous of friends throughout the whole writing process. Others to whom I owe a particular gratitude include Margaret Martin, who not only provided friendly advice and encouragement but also spent a considerable amount of time reading and commenting on drafts of many of the chapters, as well as Jean d'Aspremont, who has been an excellent friend and academic colleague throughout the writing process, and whose ideas and approach have had a considerable impact in shaping (and sharpening) my own approach.

I also owe thanks to Richard Hart for his enthusiasm and support upon reading the initial proposal, and of course for accepting its publication. I would also like to thank Rachel Turner and, more recently, Emily Braggins for support and, most of all, much patience during the (long!) writing process.

I was fortunate enough to publish parts of what follows in some (albeit often quite modified) form elsewhere. Accordingly, Part I is based, to varying degrees, on the following: R Collins, '*Modernist-Positivism* and the Problem of Institutional Autonomy in International law' in R Collins and ND White (eds), *International Organizations and the Idea of Autonomy: Institutional Independence in the International Legal Order* (Abingdon: Routledge, 2011) 22–47; R Collins 'Classical Legal Positivism in International Law Revisited' in J Kammerhofer and J d'Aspremont (eds), *International Legal Positivism in a Post-modern World* (Cambridge, Cambridge University Press, 2014) 23–49; and R Collins, 'The Progressive Conception of International Law: Brierly and Lauterpacht in the Interbellum Period', in R McCorquodale and J-P Gauci (eds), *British Influences on International Law 1915–2015* (Leiden, Brill, 2016, forthcoming). In Part II, Chapter 4 is based substantially on R Collins, 'The Problematic Concept of the International Legal Official', which is forthcoming in *Transnational Legal Theory* (2016); and parts of Chapters 5 and 6 draw from R Collins, 'No Longer at the Vanishing Point? International Law and the Analytical Tradition in Jurisprudence' (2014) 5 *Jurisprudence* 265–98. Sections of Part III are based upon or have been influenced by R Collins, 'The Rule of Law and the Quest for Constitutional Substitutes in International Law' (2015) 83 *Nordic Journal of International Law* 87–127; R Collins, 'Non-state Actors in International Institutional Law: Non-state, Inter-state or Supra-state? The Peculiar Identity of the Intergovernmental Organization' in J d'Aspremont (ed), *Participants in the International Legal System: Multiple Perspectives on Non-state Actors in International Law* (Abingdon, Routledge, 2011) 311–25; R Collins, 'Between Contract and Constitution: International Organisations and the Protection of Global Public Interests' in C McCorkindale et al (eds), *The Public in Law* (Farnham, Ashgate, 2011); and R Collins, 'Mapping the Terrain of Institutional "Lawmaking": Form and Function in International Law' in E Fahey (ed), *The Actors of Postnational Rule-Making: Contemporary Challenges of European and International Law* (Abingdon, Routledge, 2015) 27–46.

Finally, I extend my broadest gratitude to Carolyn Brock, not only for her love, good humour, support and reassurance over the period of completing both the doctorate and the book, but without whom what follows would not have been possible.

Richard Collins, Dublin, 16 January 2016

Contents

Part III: Effect

Introduction

> To the innocent eye, the formal structure of international law lacking a legislature, courts with compulsory jurisdiction and officially organized sanctions, appears very different from that of municipal law. It resembles ... *in form though not at all in content*, a simple regime of primary or customary law. (emphasis added)
>
> HLA Hart, *The Concept of Law*[1]

IN AN ESSAY published at the beginning of the new millennium on the role of law in international politics, the distinguished international lawyer, the late Sir Arthur Watts, posed the rather bold question of whether international law was important—and if so, *how and why*?[2] In many ways this is a peculiar question for, as he noted:

> [W]e would not ask the equivalent question: 'is English law important?' ... We assume, rightly, that an effective legal system in our own countries *is* an important element in the fabric of society; we take it for granted that such a system, and the rule of law generally, do exist in practice; and we are generally confident that, given our democratic systems, the rules of law which go to make up those systems reflect a fair balance between the competing interests which exist within our own societies ... But at the international level there is a sufficient measure of doubt about each of these three elements to raise questions about the importance of international law.[3]

One can certainly question whether all of these assumptions about state-based legal orders are as widely shared as Watts claimed, particularly outside of the Anglo-American world, but in other respects his observation is an astute one. Whilst few international lawyers today would doubt the reality of international law as a legal system in the sense described, there remain persistent doubts and anxieties over the quality of this system, its overall autonomy from the political realm, and hence its capacity to secure the rule of law at the global level.[4]

[1] HLA Hart, *The Concept of Law*, 3rd edn (Oxford, Clarendon Press, 2012) 232.

[2] A Watts, 'The Importance of International Law' in M Byers (ed), *The Role of Law in International Politics: Essays in International Relations and International Law* (Oxford, Oxford University Press, 2000) 5–16.

[3] ibid 5.

[4] See, eg, A Somek, 'From the Rule of Law to the Constitutionalist Makeover: Changing European Conceptions of Public International Law' (2011) 18 *Constellations* 567. And see recently many of the contributions to C Ryngaert, EJ Molenaar and SMH Nouwen (eds), *What's Wrong with International Law?: Liber Amicorum A.H.A. Soons* (Leiden, Brill, Nijhoff, 2015).

These sorts of concern are pathological in the modern discipline—understandable, perhaps, bearing in mind the long-standing scepticism that has surrounded international law. For as long as it has been thought of as a legal system on broadly similar terms to domestic law, international lawyers have had to defend the reality, efficacy and, indeed, *importance* of international law in the conduct of international politics.[5] Primarily, this scepticism has focused on international law's peculiar institutional structure, which, when compared to more 'developed' domestic legal orders, lacks any authoritative, centralised means of law-creation, adjudication and enforcement. It was the recognition of this structural difference during the early nineteenth century, for instance, that led the English legal philosopher John Austin to dismiss the rules of international law as a form of 'positive morality',[6] just as it caused the German public lawyer Georg Jellinek, some years later, to re-imagine international law instead as a form of 'external public law' based solely on states' self-imposed restraint.[7] Insofar as twentieth-century theorists have been able to move past these reductionist accounts in order to defend international law on the same terms as municipal law, their efforts have still tended to point towards international law's 'primitive' institutional structure (eg, Hans Kelsen)[8] or, more damningly, have denied it the status of a legal *system* altogether (eg, HLA Hart).[9]

In response, of course, the discipline has grown to develop something of a thick skin, presenting a number of well-rehearsed (though often also somewhat pragmatic) defences: for example, by paraphrasing Louis Henkin's oft-quoted observation that nearly all states obey nearly all of the rules of international law nearly all of the time[10] or, more persuasively

[5] A Carty, 'Why Theory?—The Implications for International Law Teaching' in P Allott et al, *Theory and International Law: An Introduction* (London, British Institute of International and Comparative Law, 1991) 75, at 80. See further discussion in S Besson and J Tasioulas, 'Introduction' in S Besson and J Tasioulas (eds), *The Philosophy of International Law* (Oxford, Oxford University Press, 2010) 1, at 6–13.

[6] J Austin, *Lectures on Jurisprudence or the Philosophy of Positive Law*, 4th edn, revised and edited by R Campbell (London, John Murray, 1873) 188 and passim.

[7] G Jellinek, *Die Rechtliche Natur der Staatenverträge* (Vienna, A Hölder, 1880). However, I borrow the term 'external public law' from Koskenniemi's reading of Jellinek: see M Koskenniemi, 'Legacy of the Nineteenth Century' in D Armstrong (ed), *Routledge Handbook of International Law* (Abingdon, Routledge, 2009) 141, at 145.

[8] For Kelsen's views on the primitiveness of international law, see H Kelsen, 'Théorie du droit international public' (1953) 84 *Recueil des Cours* 1, at 31–34 and 131. He expressed this view most explicitly, perhaps, in his political writings: see, eg, H Kelsen, *Law and Peace in International Relations: The Oliver Wendell Holmes Lectures* (Cambridge, MA, Harvard University Press, 1942), especially at 51–55.

[9] See Hart's discussion of international law in Ch 10 of Hart (n 1) 213–37. The perception of international law as a primitive or otherwise deficient legal order has been a recurring theme in international law scholarship. See, eg, A Campbell, 'International Law and Primitive Law' (1988) 8 *Oxford Journal of Legal Studies* 169.

[10] L Henkin, *How Nations Behave: Law and Foreign Policy*, 2nd edn (New York, Columbia University Press, 1979) 47.

perhaps, by drawing upon Hart's empirical claim that, regardless of such compliance, no state actually denies the binding force of international legal rules per se.[11] Furthermore, with the significant material expansion and growing institutional complexity of international law witnessed from the latter half of the twentieth century onwards, it has become very difficult to describe the modern international legal system as in any sense 'primitive'.[12]

Nevertheless, it is hard still not to note the remnants of doubt and anxiety as to the coherence and effectiveness of international law as a legal system. In comparison to a well-functioning rule of law state, the decentralised institutional architecture of international law appears to leave it structurally indeterminate: its rules seemingly more malleable, more open and, overall, more difficult to disentangle from underlying political forces.[13] One need only open any contemporary international law textbook to be told, on the one hand, of the significant growth and expansion of international law in recent years, only then to be warned, on the other, not to expect too much from a decentralised legal order with its inherent structural weaknesses.[14] In fact, this very expansion, or 'maturation', of the international legal order seems, if anything, to have heightened such concerns, as anxieties over the proliferation of increasingly autonomous institutional structures, regimes and dispute settlement bodies are expressed increasingly through the 'post-modern' leitmotifs of 'deformalisation' and 'fragmentation' of international law.[15]

None of the above would matter, of course, if all that was at stake was a purely conceptual, even semantic debate concerning the reality of something called 'international law'—as Glanville Williams once claimed, 'a verbal dispute, and nothing else'.[16] However, it is clear that this is not the case. International lawyers have, in the main, not remained content to simply defend

[11] This, of course, is building on Hart's simple recognition of the 'internal point of view' of international legal participants themselves. See Hart (n 1) 89–91 (on the internal point of view) and 231 (applied to international law).

[12] See, eg, Besson and Tasioulas (n 5) 8–13.

[13] See, principally, M Koskenniemi, *From Apology to Utopia: The Structure of International Legal Argument* (Cambridge, Cambridge University Press, 2005).

[14] See, eg, M Shaw, *International Law*, 7th edn (Cambridge, Cambridge University Press, 2014) 4–8; and see in particular M Dixon, *Textbook on International Law*, 6th edn (Oxford, Oxford University Press, 2007) 13, under a section on the 'weakness of the international system': 'International law lacks many of the formal institutions present in national legal systems. There is no formal legislative body, no court machinery with *general* compulsory jurisdiction and no police force ... While this may not be a serious defect because of the different purpose of international law, there will always be some difficulties, especially if malefactors are perceived to be able to violate the law with impunity.'

[15] See, eg, M Koskenniemi and P Leino, 'Fragmentation of International Law? Postmodern Anxieties' (2002) 15 *Leiden Journal of International Law* 553; or M Koskenniemi, 'Global Governance and Public International Law' (2004) 37 *Kritische Justiz* 241.

[16] G Williams, 'International Law and the Controversy Concerning the Word "Law"' (1945) 22 *British Yearbook of International Law* 146, at 146.

the reality of international law as a rhetorical practice or specialised form of political discourse. Rather, as I argue in this volume, they have attempted to defend its reality as an autonomous system of rules capable of cohesively regulating international relations and pre-empting the political freedom of states.[17] This is not just to say that they place value on the ideal of the rule of law (though clearly many do).[18] Rather, my claim is that this kind of rule of law idealism is implicit within the conceptual models of law or legal order against which international law is commonly compared and found wanting. On these terms, it becomes almost impossible to avoid the conclusion that international law is somehow deficient or defective at a constitutional level,[19] thus confirming its status as a 'poor relation of domestic law'.[20]

This, in short, is the 'institutional problem' in modern international law. This book is an attempt to engage with this problem: to better understand why it arises, upon what assumptions it is premised, and what effect it has had on our thinking about the nature and potential of legal norms to structure or regulate international politics. However, my aim in engaging with the structural peculiarities of a decentralised legal order is, ultimately, to argue that this condition should not be thought of as a 'problem' at all. In that sense, the word 'problem' in the title, if not exactly a misnomer, carries a certain ambiguity as to exactly what this problem is and where it lies. In fact, I will argue that the view that international law is somehow 'constitutionally deficient' arises only because of the rather incoherent and unrealistic expectations that we have of the international legal order. This is not an argument born from realism or pessimism, suggesting the need to 'water down' our expectations or ideals; rather, I argue that these ideals themselves are premised on an assumed paradigm of legality drawn from domestic experience which itself is increasingly subject to theoretical challenge and contestation. As Samantha Besson and John Tasioulas have acknowledged, 'if international law does not fit the criteria of the concept of law used at the domestic level, it may not (only) be a problem for the legality of international law, but (also) for those criteria themselves and hence for a given legal theory'.[21] In a broader sense, therefore, this book is an engagement between international law and analytical legal theory, aimed

[17] See Koskenniemi (n 13) passim.

[18] Indeed, as Blum claims, for many diplomats and international lawyers, the rule of law appears as 'the single most important goal of the international system'. See G Blum, 'Bilateralism, Multilateralism, and the Architecture of International Law' (2008) 48 *Harvard International Law Journal* 323, 331–2; and see further below in Ch 7.

[19] Somek (n 4). On the perception of 'constitutional deficiency', see also A Somek, 'Kelsen Lives!' (2007) 18 *European Journal of International Law* 409, at 432–34.

[20] As Tasioulas notes, if 'it belongs to the essence of law to claim authority, and if the authority claimed by [international law] is a diluted version of that claimed by domestic law', then it seems that international law's 'status as a poor relation of domestic law is confirmed'. J Tasioulas, 'The Legitimacy of International Law' in Besson and Tasioulas (eds) (n 5) 97, at 98.

[21] Besson and Tasioulas (n 5) 8.

at demonstrating that if the institutional problem is a problem at all, it is one that inheres more in theory than in practice. Let me now explain this problem further.

I. THE INSTITUTIONAL PROBLEM: AN EXPLANATION

To say that international law can be understood as an autonomous legal order begs the obvious question of what one means by law's autonomy in this respect. The claim is certainly not without ambiguity.[22] However, it is within this ambiguity that I can perhaps best explain the nature of the institutional problem (as I have termed it). From one perspective, to recognise the autonomy of international law is to say simply that the international legal order possesses the qualities of a legal system.[23] Despite the evident scepticism noted above, the idea that the international legal order can be thought of as a system in this sense might (now) appear obvious and self-evident,[24] encapsulated in key aspects of the modern discipline such as the doctrine of sources,[25] the idea of 'secondary' rules of responsibility[26] or conflicts of norm principles such as *lex specialis derogat legi generali* or *lex posterior derogat priori*.[27] In its recent study report on the perceived problem of 'fragmentation' in international law, the International Law Commission (ILC) has explicitly confirmed such a systemic reading. As the ILC's Special Rapporteur, Martti Koskenniemi, has stated:

> It is often said that law is a 'system'. By this, no more need be meant than that the various decisions, rules and principles of which the law consists do not appear ... randomly related to each other. Although there may be disagreement among

[22] See, eg, BH Bix, 'Law as an Autonomous Discipline' in P Cane and M Tushnet (eds), *The Oxford Handbook of Legal Studies* (Oxford, Oxford University Press, 2003) 975–87; and R Unger, *Law in Modern Society* (New York, Free Press, 1976) 52–54. I discuss the ambiguities surrounding the idea of the autonomy of law at length at the start of Ch 6.

[23] See generally E Benvenisti, 'The Conception of International Law as a Legal System' (2008) 50 *German Yearbook of International Law* 393, particularly at 394–95. On the concept of a legal system generally, see J Raz, *The Concept of a Legal System*, 2nd edn (Oxford, Clarendon Press, 1980).

[24] See, eg, V Lowe, 'The Politics of Law-Making: Are the Method and Character of Norm Creation Changing?' in Byers (n 2) 207, at 207–12.

[25] See further below in Ch 3, in section IV in particular.

[26] See, eg, International Law Commission, *Draft Articles on Responsibility of States for Internationally Wrongful Acts, with Commentaries* (2001), particularly at 31–32, paras 1–5; available at: http://legal.un.org/ilc/texts/instruments/english/commentaries/9_6_2001.pdf. On the technical and somewhat artificial nature of this distinction in international law, see E David, 'Primary and Secondary Rules' in J Crawford, A Pellet and S Olleson (eds), *The Law of International Responsibility* (Oxford, Oxford University Press, 2010) 27–33.

[27] For an in-depth discussion of the ordering effect of these principles, see Ch 7 of J Pauwelyn, *Conflict of Norms in Public International Law: How WTO Law Relates to Other Rules of International Law* (Cambridge, Cambridge University Press, 2003) 327–439.

> lawyers about just how the systemic relationship between the various decisions, rules and principles should be conceived, there is seldom disagreement that it is one of the tasks of legal reasoning to establish it.[28]

Accordingly, to recognise that international law can be understood as a system—and in that sense demonstrates a certain autonomy—is to acknowledge the simple, *though no less important*, point that international legal rules are not just 'rules of thumb' or—as Tom Franck put this—'ad hoc reciprocal arrangements'.[29] Rather, they derive their validity from source-based criteria endogenous to, and determined by, the system itself.[30] As self-evident as this understanding might appear, however, the important point is that this systematicity is not something in-built or intrinsic to the very nature of international legal relations. Like any legal system, international law is a social construct and has come to be understood in this way because this systemic understanding is deemed meaningful and important to international legal participants—states, lawyers, diplomats and other actors—as a basis of association in their mutual relations.[31] Indeed, insofar as international society is very much defined by moral agnosticism and political pluralism, the international legal system can be seen to provide an inter-subjective framework—a language or lexicon—by which states and other actors are able to pursue their often varied, though sometimes also more coordinate, objectives through the imprimatur of the legal form.[32] It is this form which provides a stable set of objective standards, allowing a basis of common association (as well as a peaceable means for critical engagement) in the absence of moral and political agreement. In other words, the apparent objectivity of the legal framework allows one to identify 'content-independent' reasons for action (or inaction)—reasons which necessarily claim to displace or exclude any other reasons we might have to act, or refrain from acting, in any given set of circumstances.[33]

[28] International Law Commission, 'Fragmentation of International Law: Difficulties Arising from the Diversification and Expansion of International Law: Report of the Study Group of the International Law Commission, Finalized by M. Koskenniemi', UN Doc A/CN.4/L.682, 13 April 2006, at 23, para 33 (footnotes omitted). Available at: http://legal.un.org/ilc/documentation/english/a_cn4_l682.pdf.

[29] TM Franck, 'Legitimacy in the International System' (1988) 82 *American Journal of International Law* 705, at 752.

[30] The sources thesis is a key component of the validity of law under theories of legal positivism, but this view is also shared more broadly amongst a range of contemporary theoretical perspectives. See, eg, the various contributions to RP George (ed), *The Autonomy of Law: Essays on Legal Positivism* (Oxford, Oxford University Press, 1996).

[31] See, generally T Nardin, *Law, Morality, and the Relations of States* (Princeton, Princeton University Press, 1983).

[32] Koskenniemi (n 13) 563–89 and passim.

[33] See, eg, N Gur, 'Are Legal Rules Content-Independent Reasons?' (2011) 5 *Problema* 175, at 178–81 in particular; and see also the discussion in A van Mulligen, 'Framing Deformalisation in Public International Law' (2015) 3–4 *Transnational Legal Theory* 635.

Insofar as states and other participants place value on this kind of legal objectivity, it is possible to say that there is, at least at some level, a broad commitment to the rule of law as a governing principle in international relations.[34] Indeed, as Besson has argued: 'To identify a society as having a system of law, as opposed to some other sort of order, is to identify it as satisfying some or all of the requirements associated with the Rule of Law.'[35] Nevertheless, just like the notion of legal autonomy that it presupposes, the rule of law itself is also a notoriously ambiguous, somewhat amorphous concept.[36] Most often, the ideal of an international rule of law is applied in a more critical, evaluative sense, suggesting the need for law's autonomy in a much stronger form, that is, to require legal rules to objectively restrain or pre-empt the exercise of arbitrary political power.[37] This seems to be particularly the case insofar as international law has increasingly come to be thought of less as a neutral framework for societal co-existence and more as a means to secure the realisation of certain agreed-upon goals, for instance, peace, order, human rights and so on. To speak of the autonomy of law on these terms, then, is to agree with Oscar Schachter that international law should function as 'a means of independent control that effectively limits the acts of the entities subject to it'.[38]

Perhaps unsurprisingly, this more demanding rule of law vision seems perpetually frustrated by the decentralised institutional architecture of the international legal order, which, as Koskenniemi has most famously argued, appears largely *indeterminate* in impacting the political choices of states and other powerful actors.[39] Acknowledging this indeterminacy is not simply to point to the obvious 'open texture' of law generally, as Hart had occasion to discuss and distinguish some years previously.[40] The indeterminacy of international law is rather more *structural* in nature: fundamental to its very nature as a decentralised legal system. In other words, the system is deliberately constructed so as to defer back to states on questions of

[34] Nardin (n 31) passim.

[35] S Besson, 'Theorizing the Sources of International Law' in Besson and Tasioulas (eds) (n 5) 163, at 172.

[36] See, perhaps most extensively, BZ Tamanaha, *On the Rule of Law: History, Politics, Theory* (Cambridge, Cambridge University Press, 2004) 91–113; and see the discussion below in Ch 7, section II, at nn 46–47 in particular.

[37] As Hurd argues, whether applied in a domestic or international setting, it is commonly assumed that 'the rule of law is an alternative to the arbitrary exercise of power; and that the ultimate product of a rule-of-law system is the choice by the law's subjects to *comply* with the rules'. I Hurd, 'The International Rule of Law and the Domestic Analogy' (2015) 4 *Global Constitutionalism* 365, at 367.

[38] O Schachter, 'The Nature and Process of Legal Development in International Society' in R St J Macdonald and DM Johnston (eds), *The Structure and Process of International Law: Essays in Legal Philosophy, Doctrine, and Theory* (The Hague, Martinus Nijhoff, 1983) 745, at 747.

[39] Koskenniemi (n 13) passim.

[40] ibid 36–41, making reference to Hart (n 1) 124–28.

the existence, validity, applicability and, ultimately, enforceability of legal norms. Thus, in the absence of any 'single legislative will' behind international legal rules, the 'conflicting motives and objectives' of states cannot be resolved definitively. Indeed, such particular purposes may very well be *advanced* through the legal framework, which provides a means of legitimising as much as condoning state behaviour.[41] As Colin Warbrick has commented:

> The very lack of density to the rules of international law ... their uncertainty, their incompleteness and ... sometimes their incoherence one with another, increases the opportunity for imaginative interpretation for *whoever takes on the task*. The line between the legal and the political is drawn in a different place in the international legal system than it is in a developed, domestic legal order.[42] (emphasis added).

How should we respond to this apparent structural indeterminacy? It is certainly not self-evident that it should be treated as a problem as such—a fault, defect or deficiency—so much as a central aspect of international law's legitimacy and acceptability for states and other legal participants. Indeed, in the context of the kind of political relations that pertain at the international level, any other view of legal order would not only appear conceptually problematic, but arguably also empirically unrealistic and politically divisive.[43] Nevertheless, structural indeterminacy *will* necessarily (and logically) appear problematic if one presumes that international law must secure *determinate* resolution of particular normative problems or disputes. The problem—the *institutional problem*—therefore arises specifically not only because this kind of presumption is pervasive in the modern discipline, but, more critically, because it is arguably implicit within many of the most dominant modes of conceptual and normative enquiry about law and legal systems more generally—that is, exactly the kind of paradigmatic understandings against which international law is held up to such anxious scrutiny. As I will show at length in Part II, in fact, the dominant analytical approach to jurisprudential enquiry has helped to sustain a view of law which presumes a certain structural hierarchy and functional purport to legal systems, which one might plausibly describe as 'governmental' in character and which therefore appears prima facie incompatible with a decentralised legal system such as international law.[44]

Recognising the pervasiveness of this mode of thinking about law does not, of course, demonstrate that this kind of presumption is wrong.

[41] International Law Commission (n 28) para 34.

[42] C Warbrick, 'Brownlie's *Principles of Public International Law:* An Assessment' (2000) 11 *European Journal of International Law* 621, at 626–27.

[43] Koskenniemi (n 13) 591.

[44] I comment on this specifically in Ch 4, and elsewhere in R Collins, 'The Problematic Concept of the International Legal Official' (2015) 3–4 *Transnational Legal Theory* 608. However, a similar concern to some degree propels Brian Tamanaha's work: see, eg, B Tamanaha, *A General Jurisprudence of Law and Society* (Oxford, Oxford University Press, 2001).

However, it should at least cause us to question the coherence of this paradigm when confronted with clear evidence of international law's existence and operability as a functioning legal system. Furthermore, bearing in mind many of the developing internal debates, critiques and 'globalising' trends witnessed in contemporary analytical legal philosophy,[45] it seems that many of these presumptions, even in the domestic context, are now themselves subject to internal disciplinary critique.[46] In this respect, in what follows I want to argue that much of what is often deemed general and universal about the nature of law is not only inadequate and misleading when applied to make sense of international law as a legal system, but is also methodologically problematic and conceptually incoherent on its own terms. Specifically, in Part II, I will argue that legal theory has essentially fixated on the historically and socially contingent problems of state-based authority, thereby co-opting state institutional features as necessary (rather than contingent) aspects of law in general.

I mount this challenge as I believe that rather than challenge jurisprudential paradigms, international lawyers, in the main, have most often attempted to try to make international law fit this incoherent structural mould. This tendency has resulted in a rather unconvincing and, I believe, self-defeating effort to explain how, despite its apparent weaknesses, international law can nonetheless function as a coercive legal order capable of effectively regulating the conduct of international relations. Most often, this kind of defence has involved 'co-opting' states themselves, or—now more likely—the institutions, courts and other bodies they have created, as functional 'organs' of an increasingly organised (though partly imagined) international community. This response is, I believe, deeply problematic. It not only risks distorting understanding of the peculiar institutional characteristics of international law, but it also potentially bestows a legitimacy and authenticity on state actions and intergovernmental institutional structures which extends well beyond their rather more limited, delegated legal form. In doing so, as I now further explain, this response only serves to further exacerbate or intensify already-existing rule of law concerns.

II. THE LIMITS OF FUNCTIONAL ANALOGY

The argument (or, at least, part of the argument) that I pursue in this book then is that the effort to explain the autonomy of international law as a means of restraining political power typically leads international lawyers

[45] See, eg, Tamanaha (n 44); W Twining, *General Jurisprudence: Understanding Law from a Global Perspective* (Cambridge, Cambridge University Press, 2009); K Culver and M Giudice, *Legality's Borders: An Essay in General Jurisprudence* (Oxford, Oxford University Press, 2010).

[46] I discuss this trend further in R Collins, 'No Longer at the Vanishing Point? International Law and the Analytical Tradition in Jurisprudence' (2014) 5 *Jurisprudence* 265, at 274–75.

into what we might term a form of 'functional compensation'. This form of response to the institutional problem has a descriptive and a normative element: on the one hand, suggesting ways in which contemporary international law functions to compensate for its *formally* decentralised structure, whilst, on the other hand, arguing for necessary institutional reforms in order to strengthen the autonomy of international law in opposition to state sovereignty. This type of argument is, I believe, not only theoretically problematic, but in its dislocation of function and form, it also overlooks the structural and constitutional limitations imposed on the functioning of the international legal system by its purposefully decentralised legal form. In other words, the attempt to overcome decentralisation by 'reading in' a constitutional or institutional hierarchy, or to simply bestow a greater authority on certain bodies, processes or institutions than they otherwise possess, can only serve to highlight, or further exacerbate, certain legitimacy deficits. This is what Alexander Somek means when he describes a 'chain of substitutions' arising out of the desire to respond to the apparent weaknesses of a decentralised legal order, as each attempt to circumvent the problem actually only causes it to resurface in a slightly different form elsewhere.[47] This claim might sound somewhat ambiguous, so an explanation and some examples may help to better illustrate what I mean.

One means of response to international law's perceived deficiency has been to explain how in a decentralised legal order, states themselves can be understood as fulfilling necessary 'constitutional functions' in order to sustain the coherence of the system overall. Relying on a conceptual device like Georges Scelle's notion of *dédoublement fonctionnel*, or 'role-splitting', this argument would suggest that states are able to act both as subjects and 'officials' of the system at the same time.[48] Accordingly, not only can we picture states as bound by the law, but also as being tasked with the role of sustaining and administering the system overall—authoritatively determining its meaning, policing potential breaches and ensuring its enforcement in the last measure. However, this kind of reading only seems to re-describe the structural condition of international law, highlighting its inevitable indeterminacy, as it is precisely because the system defers back to states as authoritative actors in this way that concerns have arisen over the openness and malleability of international legal rules in the first place. As Terry Nardin has argued, whilst states may have an 'authoritative' role in applying, interpreting or enforcing the law, they cannot be seen as authoritatively representative—as 'organs'—of the system in any meaningful sense, that is, in the sense that their determinations would be opposable to all other

[47] Somek (n 4) 568.

[48] See, eg, G Scelle, 'Essai de systématique de droit international (Plan d'un cours de droit international public)' (1923) 30 *Revue Générale de Droit International Public* 116.

international actors (including other states).[49] Antonio Cassese makes a similar point, noting how the effort to bestow functional 'officialdom' on states is something of a misleading analogy:

> Clearly, in relation to the international community, one cannot speak of functions proper: when making law, settling disputes, or enforcing the law, States do not act in the interest and on behalf of the international community; they do not fulfil an obligation, but primarily pursue their own interests ... Of particular significance is the fact that each State has the power of 'auto-interpretation' of legal rules, a power that necessarily follows from the absence of courts endowed with general and compulsory jurisdiction.[50]

For this reason, then, it is hardly surprising that the costs or externalities of this kind of state-based 'administration' are usually seen to be compensated for, to some degree, by the development—or potential development—of authoritative international institutions, dispute settlement bodies or other regimes, which together impose certain compliance pulls on states. From the very beginning, particularly since the 'move to institutions'[51] in the wake of the First World War, intergovernmental institutions have often been seen as a means to compensate for the perceived inadequacies of a decentralised legal order, not necessarily mirroring precisely the kinds of constitutional organs found at the state level,[52] but certainly seen to be 'gap-filling' in their absence.[53] Again, however, the functional analogy is misleading. Whilst undoubtedly the effect of international law's institutionalisation has been to radically transform the day-to-day functioning of the international system—particularly in terms of how norms are created, compliance with the law is secured etc—to read these institutions as fulfilling the kind of constitutional roles which, in the state context at least, are seen as having a certain a priori authority over legal subjects seems inherently problematic.[54] Of course, it may well be the case that we need to look beyond the intergovernmental treaty form of the institution to make sense of the contemporary role and functioning of universal organisations such as the United Nations (UN), but this is quite different from suggesting that these institutions can be described in terms of the kind of official roles one commonly finds at the

[49] Nardin (n 31) 162–63.

[50] A Cassese, *International Law*, 2nd edn (Oxford, Oxford University Press, 2005) 6.

[51] D Kennedy, 'The Move to Institutions' (1987) 8 *Cardozo Law Review* 841.

[52] See, eg, J Crawford, 'The Charter of the United Nations as a Constitution' in H Fox (ed), *The Changing Constitution of the United Nations* (London, British Institute of International and Comparative Law, 1997) 3–16; or ND White, 'The United Nations System: Conference, Contract or Constitutional Order?' (2000) 4 *Singapore Journal of International and Comparative Law* 281.

[53] Cassese (n 50) 21.

[54] Arangio-Ruiz makes this point most critically in G Arangio-Ruiz, *The UN Declaration on Friendly Relations and the System of the Sources of International Law* (Alphen aan den Rijn, Sijthoff & Noordhoff, 1979) 199.

state level. The inherent constitutional limitations in any *intergovernmental* organisation suggest limits to such functional expressions of authority in international law. Unlike at the state level, the authority of international organisations remains ultimately grounded in the inter-state constitution, therefore deliberately limiting their capacity to act authoritatively, either on behalf of the international community as a whole or as agents or organs of the international system.

As such, and as I will outline at length in Chapters 8 and 9, whilst there has been an undoubted transformation in international law in recent years, brought about largely, even if not exclusively, through the 'institutionalisation' of the international legal system, it seems increasingly that this kind of 'global governance' has given rise to quite serious accountability deficits and legitimacy concerns. With a clear preponderance and proliferation of increasingly centralised and autonomous regimes, introducing innovative compliance mechanisms and dispute settlement bodies, one witnesses growing anxieties over the impact of institutionalisation on the overall systemic coherence of international law.[55] Not only does this kind of functional authority appear inadequate to effectively uphold and protect global public goods or community interests, suggesting a certain level of 'ad hocism' in global governance,[56] but any claim to authoritatively represent these interests seems precluded by the underlying (pluralist) tenets of the international legal order.[57] Institutionalisation has thus not resulted in any enhanced hierarchy or authority of international law overall, but an increasingly disordered array of non-state and inter-state regimes competing for authority with states, and with their own structural biases and political preferences. The rule of law concern resurfaces again in another form; Somek's chain of substitutions moves on another step.

III. OVERVIEW OF THE ARGUMENT AND STRUCTURE OF THE BOOK

Ultimately, I will show how the failure of this form of response to the institutional problem stems from the falsity of the presumption upon which it is based—a presumption, as I have suggested, widely shared by legal theorists and international lawyers alike—that international law *should* act to somehow 'govern' the conduct of the international community overall. I maintain instead that the purpose of any legal order has to be understood within the context of the kinds of political relations which pertain in the

[55] Compare JHH Weiler, 'The Geology of International Law—Governance, Democracy and Legitimacy' (2004) 64 *Zeitschrift für Ausländisches Öffentliches Recht und Völkerrecht* 547 and M Koskenniemi, 'Global Governance and Public International Law' (2004) 37 *Kritische Justiz* 241.

[56] Cassese (n 50) 66–67.

[57] See, eg, M Koskenniemi, 'International Law in Europe: Between Tradition and Renewal' (2005) 16 *European Journal of International Law* 113, at 116.

society or community in question. To see the purpose of international law as one of *regulating* or *governing* international politics is to misconstrue the nature of the political relations which pertain at the international level, which are fundamentally different from the relations of political subordination that exist within the state. The overall 'institutional purpose' of law within a plural, 'horizontal' society (such as arguably exists at the international level) must instead be understood in a way which is meaningful to the participants in that society. As such, by engaging head-on with these presumptions from a legal-theoretical perspective, I show how if the *international* rule of law, and the autonomy of law it presupposes, has meaningful explanatory purchase, it must at the very least presuppose a formal, institutional framework capable of securing a non-arbitrary means for mutual co-existence and cooperation under conditions of political plurality. Rather than reflecting any kind of constitutional deficiency, therefore, the decentralised legal form of the international legal order can be seen as both reflective and protective of this fundamental purpose and as a key aspect of the legitimacy of international legal rules.

To reach this conclusion is not at all to suggest that states and other actors cannot create ambitious hierarchical institutional forms within the international legal order, or that international law itself is incapable of change—this is not a position of conservatism or overtly realist scepticism. In fact, as the argument of the book progresses, I will explain how the international legal order has transformed itself quite dramatically, in both substantive and structural terms, as a result of the proliferation of a range of increasingly powerful institutions and regimes. However, my argument is also that a great deal of the legitimacy concerns that have arisen as a result of this transformation, where the kinds of functional autonomy and authority exerted by many global regimes seems to largely escape accountability, can be explained by the inherent—*and important*—tension this functional autonomy creates in its relation to international law's decentralised legal form. The system overall and the institutions created on its terms have to be understood at least in part by reference to their legal form, which in turn is justified as important and meaningful due to the kind of legitimacy pulls inherent within the international community.

My argument therefore follows from a view of the task of legal theory, and of the legal theorist specifically, which begins from the need to develop, understand and, ultimately, defend a view of law or legal order that is meaningful to international legal participants.[58] However, in beginning in this way, I will suggest that such an approach still requires informed moral

[58] In that sense, my argument and methodology have been greatly influenced by Patrick Capps' recent work. See P Capps, *Human Dignity and the Foundations of International Law* (Oxford, Hart Publishing, 2009). It should be noted, however, as will be clear in Ch 6 in particular, that Capps and I part company on the ultimate function of law and international law in particular.

judgement from the legal theorist: we cannot simply *presume* that certain institutional structures or functions of law are universally shared, based simply on shared legal and political experience of the state context. Any claim to understand what is important and necessary about law, in general or in particular contexts, must seek to understand, evaluate and defend the importance of law's key institutional features in a way which is defensible from the point of view of the kind of political and social relations in which law is present and from within which it takes on specific meaning. As such, whilst the question of international law's meaning and potential in the context of contemporary international relations remains somewhat controversial, the legitimacy of the system overall potentially pulling in different directions, I will seek to defend a view of international law's necessarily decentralised institutional architecture that remains meaningful precisely in its ability to facilitate more ambitious cooperation at the international level. This defence does not seek to present a complete account of the nature of contemporary international law—or, indeed, of the myriad, more specialised forms of 'global law' now arguably in existence[59]—but it does act as a clear normative defence of the international legal system's core structural architecture, understood as a necessary framework upon which much of this more ambitious global governance activity finds some foundation, and against which some form of legal accountability can be secured.[60]

Accordingly, in developing this argument, my aim in this book is to make an important intervention in methodological debates in legal theory as much as an interjection into contemporary debates about the evolving character of international law and global governance. I have divided the book into three discrete parts, each of which is further divided into three chapters. Whilst there is clearly narrative continuity between the three parts, each has a somewhat distinct focus, method and ambition. I have labelled them in turn—perhaps over-enigmatically—'Origins', 'Cause' and 'Effect'.

Part I (*Origins*) is historical, sociological and, to some degree, deconstructive in focus. It explains the emergence of the 'modern' discipline (in Chapter 1) in terms of a collective ambition to reconstruct or re-invent international law from a philosophical to a broadly institutional practice. I explain this transformation in terms of a broad disciplinary effort to account for international law as an autonomous system of positive legal rules on similar terms to state-based legal orders. In charting the scepticism that international lawyers have faced in explaining international law on these terms

[59] See, eg, recently N Walker, *Intimations of Global Law* (Cambridge, Cambridge University Press, 2014).

[60] Here, I have been greatly influenced by the work of Terry Nardin in *Law, Morality, and the Relations of States* (n 31).

(in both Chapters 1 and 2), I aim to illustrate the kind of presumptions, tensions and ambitions underlying this view of modern international law. I do so in order to explain the difficulties that international lawyers have faced in giving a coherent account on these terms—that is, in explaining this kind of autonomy in a decentralised legal system—and thus (in Chapter 3) I argue that this problem has left an overall impression of international law as essentially deficient at a constitutional level.

Part II (*Cause*) is more broadly theoretical and analytical in approach in an attempt to re-orient the focus of the 'institutional problem', specifically by considering and critically engaging with certain presumptions about law perpetuated by dominant ('descriptive-explanatory') approaches to analytical legal enquiry (in Chapter 4). In considering the methodological weaknesses of these approaches in adequately accounting for forms of law and legality beyond the state, I will ultimately advocate (in Chapter 5) the need to take a distinctly evaluative, more normative approach in order to understand law in its many guises. In doing so, my ambition is to defend a 'practically reasonable' concept of law which remains meaningful in a general (or universal) sense, but which can be applied in particular circumstances as a critical tool for engaging with the necessary institutional architecture of non-state legal orders such as international law. On these terms, I will argue (in Chapter 6) that law's empty, abstract autonomy—its formal, systemic character—should alone be seen as its most central (and most important) contribution to any society or political community. This normative idealism thus purposefully blurs the boundary between the *concept* and the *rule* of law, but does so conceiving of the latter as a somewhat abstract ideal that resists any specific institutional form.

Part III (*Effect*) reverts back to questions of international legal theory specifically, and does so primarily to show why the effort to explain international law's autonomy in any stronger, more pre-emptive sense necessarily leads to dangers of distortion and methodological confusion. As such, I first (in Chapter 7) explain why the attempt to apply any more ambitious kind of rule of law ideal to international law is necessarily problematic due to the importance of its decentralised legal form. Whilst I will (in Chapter 8) argue that the ambitious models of institutional cooperation, dispute settlement and innovative international 'governance' arrangements developed since the start of the previous century necessarily compliment *and complicate* the functioning of contemporary international law, I cast doubt on the (increasingly pervasive) view that such changes can be seen to transform or even centralise the nature of international 'legality' at the broadest systemic level. Nevertheless, in Chapter 9, I will go on to show a necessary and growing tension between the functioning of international law in practice, dispersed between increasingly complex sites of institutional and regulatory authority, and its continuing existence, in more formal terms, as a system of decentralised, non-hierarchical legal relations. I will argue, ultimately, that to understand the ideal of the international rule of law in contemporary international society is to appreciate the necessary *and important* tension between these *functional* and *formal* modes of international legality. In fact, I will show how a number of recent trends in international law scholarship, essentially advocating a less formal concept of international law in order to capture and constrain much of this 'deformalised' and 'fragmented' global governance activity, fail to grasp the continued structural importance of international law's legal form from a rule of law perspective, and thus potentially further exacerbate existing rule of law concerns.

Part I

Origins

1

A Fragile Autonomy: International Law at the Turn of the Twentieth Century

That law is an effect of lawyers' imagination is nowhere clearer than in the development of international law from the isolated diplomatic practices of the nineteenth century into a legal order sometime early in the twentieth. Professional jurists took it upon themselves to explain international affairs in the image of the domestic State, governed by the Rule of Law.

Martti Koskenniemi, *The Gentle Civilizer of Nations*[1]

SOMETIME BETWEEN THE mid-nineteenth and the early twentieth centuries, the older, philosophical tradition of the *Law of Nations* was made over into the kind of systemic, institutional practice familiar to us as modern 'international law'.[2] This transition was almost entirely complete by the turn of the twentieth century,[3] as (European) jurists gave shape to international law as an autonomous system of positive legal rules binding upon states in much the same way as they saw law regulating the conduct of public affairs within the state.[4] That nineteenth-century diplomatic practice did not automatically present itself as an autonomous legal system, in this

[1] M Koskenniemi, *The Gentle Civilizer of Nations: The Rise and Fall of International Law 1870–1960* (Cambridge, Cambridge University Press, 2001) 361.

[2] Bentham is said to have coined the term: see J Bentham, *An Introduction to the Principles of Morals and Legislation* (JH Burns and HLA Hart (eds), London, Athlone Press, 1970; first published in 1789) 293–300; and see further MW Janis, 'Jeremy Bentham and the Fashioning of 'International Law'' (1984) 78 *American Journal of International Law* 405, at 408–10 in particular.

[3] On this transition generally, see P Guggenheim, 'The Birth of Autonomous International Law' in *International Law in a Changing World* (Dobbs Ferry, NY, Oceana, 1963) 80; R St J Macdonald and DM Johnston, 'International Legal Theory: New Frontiers of the Discipline' in R St J Macdonald and DM Johnston (eds), *The Structure and Process of International Law: Essays in Legal Philosophy, Doctrine, and Theory* (The Hague, Martinus Nijhoff, 1983) 1, at 6–7; G Schwarzenberger, 'The Rule of Law and the Disintegration of the International Society' (1939) 33 *American Journal of International law* 56, at 65–66; R Pound, 'Philosophical Theory and International Law' (1923) 1 *Bibliotheca Visseriana* 1, at 73.

[4] See, eg, M Koskenniemi, 'Legacy of the Nineteenth Century' in D Armstrong (ed), *Routledge Handbook on International Law* (Abingdon, Routledge, 2009) 141, at 142–43.

sense, is a point often overlooked in modern doctrine and practice, which tends to take such a structural understanding for granted. In fact, until the middle of the nineteenth century, few areas of state relations were deemed to be regulated by law, at least in the sense of an overarching legal order structuring and governing relations between states.[5] Still, it is hard to refute the reality of the transformation which had occurred by the early twentieth century, by which time international law had come to be widely accepted as a legal system—similar in function, *if not necessarily in structure*, to domestic law—as academic method and legal reasoning itself became similarly systematic, inductive and institutional.[6] As Patrick Capps notes, international lawyers 'began to think of their subject *almost* as if it stood up by itself … that it could be disconnected from issues concerning philosophical method; that international law was an autonomous discipline of study'.[7] (emphasis added)

Nevertheless, Capps' equivocation with the word 'almost' is telling for, as the concerns in the Introduction revealed, from the outset, this understanding of international law as an autonomous legal system was critically received due to the obvious structural differences between international and domestic legal orders. In the absence of centralised institutions akin to those commonly found at the domestic level, international law appeared less certain and effective in actually regulating the conduct of international politics. The modern discipline was thus born with a persistent sense of its own structural weaknesses and a constant need to prove its own relevance in the conduct of international affairs. This is what I will come to term the 'institutional problem' in modern international law. I will say more about this problem in Chapter 3, but before doing so, my aim in the current chapter is to attempt to give an account of the origins of this problem, and specifically the difficulties facing late nineteenth and early twentieth-century international lawyers in giving a persuasive account of international law as an autonomous system of positive legal rules. To the extent that jurists from this time could be described as successful in ushering in such a transition in understanding of international law, this would prove to be a rather fragile autonomy, which, as I will show in Chapter 2, would not survive the First

[5] A Carty, *The Decay of International Law: A Reappraisal of the Limits of Legal Imagination in International Affairs* (Manchester, Manchester University Press, 1986) 14–15.

[6] See A Carty, 'Why Theory?—The Implications for International Law Teaching' in P Allott et al, *Theory and International Law: An Introduction* (London, British Institute of International and Comparative Law, 1991) 75, at 80–82; and generally Carty (n 5). By 'institutional' here, I refer to the social and artificial quality of law as a man-made artifice; for a fuller explanation of this quality of law, see Ch 6 of J Raz, *The Authority of Law: Essays on Law and Morality*, 2nd edn (Oxford, Oxford University Press, 2009).

[7] P Capps, *Human Dignity and the Foundations of International Law* (Oxford, Hart Publishing, 2009) 10.

World War unscathed and which would leave a perpetual sense of structural or constitutional deficiency which still haunts the modern discipline.

The chapter is structured as follows. In section I, I consider the almost universal shift away from a naturalist towards a positivist understanding of international law that occurred towards the end of the nineteenth century. Contrary to some contemporary reflections on this period, though, I argue that this transition should not be understood as a kind of apologetic concession to state power or the raison d'etat, but as part of a modernist renewal of the discipline attempting to give an account of international law as an autonomous system of rules capable of acting as a persuasive restraint on sovereign freedom. Nevertheless, in section II, I will then show the difficulties jurists faced in accounting for international law's autonomy in this respect, particularly in the face of recurring scepticism over whether such a law could be anything other than self-imposed political prudence on the one hand or moral utopianism on the other. I then take this analysis forward in section III, where I will note how the coherence of this systemic understanding had to depend upon assumptions about the inevitable evolution of international law towards the development of an institutional structure that more readily reflects the kind of model of law familiar from domestic legal experience.

I will say more about the coherence of this domestic paradigm itself in Part II. My immediate concern in exploring this transformation is more to demonstrate the particular theoretical difficulties that have faced international lawyers in accounting for the reality of the object of their study on these terms. Before moving on, one caveat should be noted at the outset. My ambition in Part I is certainly not to give a full chronological reflection of the recent history of modern international law.[8] Rather, by showing the recurrence of certain argumentative patterns, I aim to illustrate the inevitability of certain theoretical problems which emerge from the assumption that international law could be explained by reference to a domestic legal paradigm, which itself relies on a (rather unrealistic) rule of law ideal

[8] For a classic account of the history of international law presented in this style, see WG Grewe, *The Epochs of International Law* (Berlin, Walter de Gruyter, 2000). Whilst unsurpassed in many respects, there are limitations to presenting the history of a discipline, which shifts between theorisation, idealism and the practice of inter-state politics, in this way. As Ingo Hueck notes, the 'observation of the development of the theory of international law should possibly take place without focusing on specific historical turning-points or events', but rather 'the reconstruction of the development of the theory … [should] focus on the spirit of the time, and the social and political contexts respectively'. IJ Hueck, 'The Discipline of the History of International Law—New Trends and Methods on the History of International Law' (2001) 3 *Journal of the History of International law* 194, at 198–99. See also, for similar concerns, M Koskenniemi, 'Why History of International Law Today?' (2004) *Rechtsgeschichte* 61. Whilst space necessarily precludes elaboration of such social context beyond some generalities, I try to take account of the kinds of political and social contexts which prompted different conceptualisations of the nature of international law in different periods.

that stresses the importance of legal autonomy in securing the restraint of political freedom. I will assume for current purposes that this is a widely shared view of the nature of law in general, but, as noted above, I will return to consider this view, and the jurisprudential models that sustain it, at some length in Part II.

I. FROM PHILOSOPHY TO LEGAL SCIENCE

By the nineteenth century, international law was increasingly understood as a science, taught and studied separately from ecclesiastical or civil law, philosophy or theology—areas within which it had previously formed a coherent part. This understanding arose specifically from a growing 'professional' ethos or disciplinary self-consciousness to defend the coherence and efficacy of the law as a system of norms that could operate as an effective restraint in international politics—in particular, as law was understood to operate within the confines of the (European) state.[9] In the last third of the century, much of this professional spirit emerged as a desire to rid the discipline of its grounding in the metaphysics of natural law and instead to concentrate on 'systematising and interpreting' the century's limited multilateral treaty practice, giving shape to the idea of European diplomacy as 'a working system of largely customary law'.[10]

Depictions of the transformation of international law occurring towards the end of the nineteenth century tend to describe this era as the high-point of legal positivism,[11] often criticising this doctrinal approach as overly formalistic, abstract or even ideologically dangerous (for justifying the unrestrained sovereignty of states).[12] However, as a number of

[9] M Koskenniemi, *From Apology to Utopia: The Structure of International Legal Argument* (Cambridge, Cambridge University Press, 2005) 122–23; A Anghie, *Imperialism, Sovereignty and the Making of International Law* (Cambridge, Cambridge University Press, 2005) 48–52.

[10] Koskenniemi (n 4) 146. For a more detailed overview of this transition, see Ch 1 of Koskenniemi (n 1).

[11] See, eg, R Ago, 'Positive Law and International Law' (1957) 51 *American Journal of International Law* 691, at 699.

[12] See D Kennedy, 'International Law and the Nineteenth Century: History of an Illusion' (1997) 17 *Quinnipiac Law Review* 99, at 100–01. For examples of this kind of criticism, see, most famously, H Lauterpacht, *Private Law Sources and Analogies of International Law (with Special Reference to International Arbitration)* (London, Longmans, 1927) 43–44 and passim. I consider, and critically reflect on, this more in R Collins, 'Classical Legal Positivism in International Law Revisited' in J d'Aspremont and J Kammerhofer (eds), *International Legal Positivism in a Postmodern World* (Cambridge, Cambridge University Press, 2014) 23–49. I pick up on the rejection of 'classical' doctrine in *inter-bellum* jurisprudence specifically in the following chapter.

critical voices have recently begun to recognise,[13] this portrayal is arguably an overly simplistic representation of the disciplinary transition that occurred at this time.[14] Insofar as the critique stretches back into the mid- to late nineteenth century, it tends to ignore 'persistent strands of "naturalism" in that century's legal doctrine, constantly referring back to the moral and civilizing forces of European law and practices',[15] particularly in British and French works.[16] Such narratives also tend to neglect the more eclectic approach to theory discernible at this time (whether or not natural law is retained explicitly),[17] not to mention the fact that, by the beginning

[13] See, inter alia, Kennedy (n 12); Anghie (n 9); Koskenniemi (n 1); Koskenniemi (n 4); Koskenniemi (n 9) 71–157; C Sylvest, 'International Law in Nineteenth-Century Britain' (2005) 75 *British Yearbook of International Law* 9; M Lobban, 'English Approaches to International Law in the Nineteenth Century' in M Craven, M Fitzmaurice and M Vogiatzi (eds), *Time, History and International Law* (Leiden, Martinus Nijhoff, 2007) 65–90; and A Lev, 'The Transformation of International Law in the 19th Century' in A Orakhelashvili (ed), *Research Handbook on the Theory and History of International Law* (Cheltenham, Edward Elgar, 2011) 111–42.

[14] As Kennedy continues: 'This image, of a method before frustration with formalism, a doctrine before the erosion of sovereignty, and a legal philosophy before the pragmatic flight from theory, remains an active part of twentieth century disciplinary argument, although it reflects only dimly the actual doctrine, method or philosophy of the field before the First World War.' See Kennedy (n 12) 100. See further Collins (n 12) 29–36; and T Skouteris, *The Notion of Progress in International Law Discourse* (The Hague, TMC Asser Press, 2010) 117–20.

[15] Koskenniemi (n 4) 14. Stephen Neff has made similar claims, even if overall he paints a picture of the century as still, in the main, dogmatically positivist. S Neff, 'A Short History of International Law' in M Evans (ed), *International Law*, 4th edn (Oxford, Oxford University Press, 2014) 3, at 13–15. See also J von Bernstorff, *The Public International Law Theory of Hans Kelsen: Believing in Universal Law* (Cambridge, Cambridge University Press, 2010) 26–27.

[16] In terms of British approaches, the attachment was quite explicit. See, eg, R Phillimore, *Commentaries upon International Law*, 3rd edn (London, Butterworths, 1879), particularly at 14–29; T Twiss, *The Law of Nations Considered as Independent Political Communities* (Oxford, Oxford University Press, 1861), particularly at 110–11. See also the work of the more eccentric Scottish jurist, James Lorimer: *The Institutes of the Law of Nations: A Treatise on the Jural Relations of Separate Political Communities*, vol II (Edinburgh, William Blackwood and Sons, 1884). In French scholarship, the continued attachment to naturalism is evident in particular in the doctrine of the fundamental rights of states; see, eg, A Pillet, 'Recherches sur les Droits Fondamentaux des États dans l'Ordre des Rapports Internationaux et sur la Solution des Conflits qu'ils Font Naitre' (1898) 5 *Revue Générale de Droit International* 503–32. For a general overview, see E Jouannet, 'A Century of French International Legal Scholarship' (2009) 61 *Maine Law Review* 83, at 94.

[17] See generally, Collins (n 12) 31–32. This point applies particularly to the 'historical' jurisprudence which influenced figures such as Johann Caspar Bluntschli or Henry Summer Maine. See in particular JC Bluntschli, *The Theory of the State*, English translation from the 6th German edn (Oxford, Clarendon Press, 1885); JC Bluntschli, *Le Droit International Codifié*, 5th edn (Paris, Guillaumin, 1895); and HS Maine, *Ancient Law: Its Connection with the Early History of Society, and its Relations to Modern Ideas* (London, John Murray, 1861). For a detailed exposition of Maine's theory in this respect, see the arguments of Sylvest (n 13) 42–46, 54–56.

of the twentieth century, positivism itself had come to represent an umbrella term for a broad spectrum of quite diverse theoretical approaches.[18]

At the same time, insofar as there was still a discernible and definite shift towards the dominance of positivist method by the beginning of the twentieth century, two points should be made with regard to the ideological underpinnings and methodological consequences of this transition. First, this disciplinary shift needs to be placed in its historical context and understood for what it was: an attempt to find a more persuasive, more legitimate basis for the law of nations as a real restraint on the sovereignty of states. In particular, in a post-revolutionary Europe increasingly hostile to a priori or essentialist philosophical claims, public opinion had already turned against the naturalist idea of sovereignty as personal and divine right, a notion which had previously sustained the patrimonial legitimacy claims of the *ancien régime*.[19] Furthermore, at a time that saw the growth in prominence of empirical science generally, natural law argument was increasingly seen not only as illegitimate and speculative, but also as 'a set of excessively abstract (and in this sense arbitrary) maxims that could not form part of a practical *Jus publicum Europaeum*'.[20] For instance, the English jurist Thomas Lawrence claimed that natural law 'was false historically, and untenable philosophically' for it 'confound[ed] together the actual and the ideal'. He asserted confidently that state officials no longer appealed publicly to 'innate principles and absolute rights, but to rules which can be proved to have been acted upon previously in similar circumstances by all or most civilised nations'.[21]

Nineteenth-century international lawyers thus sought new means for legitimising as well as new ways of understanding the legality of inter-state relations. To construct a more convincing vision of an international public order under law, they sought insights from domestic experience, where sovereignty was seen as having already been reconstructed in more relative terms, tamed and harnessed by principles such as the rule of law. As Christian Reus-Smit notes, modern doctrine took shape under the influence

[18] S Neff, *Justice among Nations: A History of International Law* (Cambridge, MA, Harvard University Press, 2014) 226 ff.

[19] This was a common reflection amongst many European jurists writing towards the end of the nineteenth and in the early twentieth centuries: see, eg, G Rolin-Jaecquemyns, 'De l'étude de la législation comparée et de droit international' (1869) 1 *Revue de Droit International* 11, at 256–57; P Fiore, *International Law Codified and its Legal Sanction; or the Legal Organization of the Society of States* (translated from the 5th Italian edn by Edwin M Borchard) (New York, Baker, Voorhis & Company, 1918) 8–9; and TJ Lawrence, *Essays on Some Disputed Questions in Modern International Law* (Cambridge, Deighton, Bell and Co, 1885) 236–37; TJ Lawrence, *The Principles of International Law*, 7th edn (London, MacMillan, 1923) 132.

[20] Koskenniemi (n 4) 146.

[21] TJ Lawrence, *A Handbook of Public International Law* (Cambridge, D Bell & Co, 1898) 6.

of principles such as juridical equality, non-discrimination and self-legislative justice. These principles were seen as already delineating the allocation of political power within the state and, in this spirit, international law also came to be perceived increasingly as an institutional practice structured on the basis of mutual consent and reciprocal equality (at least in a formal sense).[22]

By the turn of the twentieth century, the reality of this transition—in both theory and practice—had become abundantly clear. One need only compare the reactionary and conservative legitimising principles and purposes underpinning the Vienna Settlement of 1814–15 with the more liberal purposes and multilateral ordering principles of the 1899 and 1907 Hague Conferences to see the reality of this changed understanding.[23] From a more doctrinal perspective, the repercussions of this change are clearly spelt out in Lassa Oppenheim's famous 1908 essay on the task and method of international law. Oppenheim begins—perhaps more charitably than Lawrence (above), though no less forthright—by dismissing natural law as an 'epoch in the evolution of human reason'. Natural law's importance in this respect was in having helped to spread liberal principles of constitutional legitimacy. Having now taken hold, however, such principles had shown the necessity of a clear demarcation of the legal and political realms:

> We know now-a-days that it is impossible to find a law which has its roots in human reason only and is above legislation and customary law ... Nobody denies the right of an author to criticize the existing legal rules, to condemn the prevailing social conditions, and to construct a body of rules which, when accepted, would constitute an improvement. But such rules, although ever so much supported by reason, justice, and equity, *would not be rules of law before they were either by custom or by legislation* adopted for the future conduct of those concerned.[24] (emphasis added)

[22] C Reus-Smit, *The Moral Purpose of the State: Culture, Social Identity, and Institutional Rationality in International Relations* (Princeton, NJ, Princeton University Press, 1999) 129–32, 134–35, 153; and see C Reus-Smit, 'The Constitutional Structure of International Society and the Nature of Fundamental Institutions' (1997) 51 *International Organization* 555, at 578, on how later in the century, the principle of 'rule determination' began to impact in inter-state relations. As he claims, the principle that 'social rules should be authored by those subject to them came to license multilateral forms of rule determination, while the precept that rules should be equally applicable to all subjects, in all like cases, warranted the formal codification of contractual international law, to ensure the universality and reciprocity of international regulations'.

[23] Reus-Smit (n 22) 131–32, 153.

[24] L Oppenheim, 'The Science of International Law: Its Task and Method' (1908) 2 *American Journal of International Law* 313, at 329. See also discussion in Sylvest (n 13) 43, where he reflects on the reaction to an 'unhistorical and a priori' natural law, which to jurists of this era 'might ... [have been] important for understanding a trajectory of evolution, but ... [was] incapable of guiding civilization in its advanced stages'.

Oppenheim was certainly not alone in espousing such a view of international law by this time.[25] By the early years of the twentieth century, few international lawyers thought of the object of their study as anything other than an artificial construct derived at some level from the will of states,[26] and the role of the international jurist as concerned with anything more than an 'analysis of the practice of the institutions of the State'.[27] As Carty notes, Oppenheim's approach signifies international law's almost total transition to a purely 'institutional' view of international law: it was seen as an autonomous legal order, grounded in state practice, where the validity of norms would derive from their conformity with conditions endogenous to the legal order itself rather than any a priori philosophical commitments.[28]

This conviction and methodological approach might strike contemporary international lawyers as 'naively positivistic' in many respects,[29] but it is important to understand the normative ambition underpinning this methodological commitment. For Oppenheim, in particular, international law was 'merely a means to certain ends outside itself', ends which were simply posited as crucial to the very idea of international law, chief among them being 'peace among the nations and the governance of their intercourse by what makes for order and is right and just'.[30] However, in order to realise these ends, it was crucial to maintain in existence the autonomous domain of the law. As Benedict Kingsbury has argued, persuasively, there is a barely concealed ethical commitment underpinning Oppenheim's positivism in this respect:

> Oppenheim's commitment to a positivist approach to international law was not simply an assertion that a positivist concept of law was the only coherent one, but also embodied a normative or ethical view that a positivist understanding of international law was best able to advance the realization in international society of a higher set of values to which Oppenheim adhered.[31]

[25] Already by 1894, in fact, Oppenheim's predecessor at Cambridge, John Westlake, could confidently claim that it was with 'law as an institution or a fact that the legal student has to deal'. See J Westlake, 'Chapters on International Law' in L Oppenheim (ed), *The Collected Papers of John Westlake on International Law* (Cambridge, Cambridge University Press, 1914, originally published in 1894) 13.

[26] Carty (n 5) 1–11 and passim. Whilst many jurists reserved a place for natural law argument, this normally had to be 'positivised', that is, manifest in the practices and usages of states. See Koskenniemi (n 9) 137–38.

[27] Carty (n 5) 8. As he continues: 'In this context there is no significant difference between the common law and civil law jurisdictions in so far as concerns legal method. Study of the "practice" of judicial institutions follows the same analytical, i.e. above all logical, conceptual method, as study of the "emanations" of the will of the State.'

[28] See Carty (n 6) 80–82.

[29] B Kingsbury, 'Legal Positivism as Normative Politics: International Society, Balance of Power and Lassa Oppenheim's Positive International Law' (2002) 13 *European Journal of International Law* 401, at 402, though it should be noted that Kingsbury himself challenges this view.

[30] Oppenheim (n 24) 314.

[31] Kingsbury (n 29) 431. See also Capps (n 7) 83.

Again, Oppenheim was clearly not alone in holding such opinions. As Anghie recognises, from the late nineteenth century onwards, jurists increasingly began to see the role of legal science as 'a struggle against chaos which could be won only by ensuring the autonomy of law, and establishing and maintaining the taxonomies and principles which existed in fixed relations to each other'.[32] In line with the prevalent liberalism of the times, any underlying commitment to international justice was thus expressed in procedural rather than substantive terms. The validity of legal norms would stem from their place within an objectively verifiable legal order, not from inherently subjective and dangerous moralism.[33]

However, it is precisely this point which brings me to the second, more methodological consequence of this shift. It is perhaps unsurprising that constructing a legal system from a basis of state practice and sovereign will is no easy feat. As Koskenniemi notes, it was far from a straightforward enterprise 'to imagine diplomatic correspondence and a few arbitration cases as manifestations of an autonomous legal order'.[34] Compared to more 'developed' domestic legal systems, international law appeared substantively and institutionally primitive. Far from being dogmatically positivist *in terms of method*, therefore, jurists of this era tended to be very creative in their attempt to account for international law's autonomy as a system of positive legal rules. They had to compensate for gaps and deficiencies in the law through, for example, moral argument, domestic analogy and historical reflection. As noted above, many retained arguments derived from natural law (even if not expressly couched in these terms) which, 'though usually termed "secondary" to positive law, fulfilled the important function of offering arguments when positive ones were not available'.[35] Meanwhile, their resort to domestic analogy not only helped to flesh out important substantive rules in areas such as the laws of territory, treaties and warfare,[36] but also—and perhaps more importantly—allowed jurists to make sense of the development of international law through teleological assumptions about its progressive evolution mirroring the constitutional development of (European) nation states.[37]

If nineteenth-century jurists had therefore succeeded in divorcing international law from its foundation as an expression of enlightenment philosophy and re-imagining it as an autonomous legal order, it could be portrayed

[32] Anghie (n 9) 51.
[33] Koskenniemi (n 9) 53–54.
[34] Koskenniemi (n 1) 362.
[35] Koskenniemi (n 9) 131.
[36] Koskenniemi (n 4) 150–51. See also, eg, J Westlake, *Chapters on the Principles of International law* (Cambridge, Cambridge University Press, 1894) 9–11 and later in Ch 9 on the title to sovereign territory.
[37] See generally Ch 1 of Koskenniemi (n 1); and Koskenniemi (n 9) 53, 143–54.

as such only by re-introducing principles, assumptions and teleological arguments that seemed to sit uncomfortably with the claimed scientific objectivity that had driven the quest for legal autonomy in the first place. As we will see in the sections that follow, it was only by creatively filling in the gaps in the law in this way that turn-of-the-century jurists were able to explain international law as autonomous in this respect—that is, as something more than, and set apart from, states' self-imposed restraint—but it was precisely their efforts in doing so that seemed to threaten that very same autonomy. The international legal system bestowed upon twentieth-century jurists seemed embryonic and fragile at best.

II. A FRAGILE AUTONOMY: THE SOVEREIGNTY PROBLEM

Insofar as the growing dominance of legal positivism resulted in a view of international law grounded in state sovereignty, this shift was certainly not therefore intended to construct barriers towards legal order. Rather than seeing the foundational idea of the sovereign equality of states as a form of deference to the raison d'etat, we can understand it as a constitutive organising principle, a necessary construct for the possibility of legal order in a decentralised political space. In other words, a formalised idea of sovereignty as a delineated order of absolute competence provided a procedural grounding for the law, an explanation of the possibility of autonomous law in the absence of an overarching moral consensus or centralised authority at the global level.[38] As Koskenniemi observes:

> From the late nineteenth century onwards, international lawyers have been critics of 'sovereignty' as egoism, arbitrariness, and the absolutism of state power. The contrary to sovereignty was international law ... The legacy of the nineteenth century was not excessive deference to sovereignty (arguments against such deference were common then as they are today) but rather the emergence of 'sovereignty' as the key *topos* of international law, leading the law into a formal and procedural direction, away from views about the substantive rightness or wrongness of particular types of behavior.[39]

David Kennedy makes a similar point:

> [F]rom the standpoint of international law, the sovereignty consolidated in the late nineteenth century was a very secular matter, a doctrinal project of practicality in a broader legal fabric whose existence, in turn, was simply obvious.

[38] An idea clearly expressed by the Permanent Court of International Justice (PCIJ) four years before its *Lotus* decision, in the *Wimbledon* case, claiming that the right to enter into legally binding agreements should be seen as an attribute of state sovereignty rather than resulting in its diminution. See *Case of the SS Wimbledon* (1923) PCIJ Ser A No. 1, 25; and discussion in J Klabbers, 'Clinching the Concept of Sovereignty: Wimbledon Redux' (1998) 3 *Austrian Review of International and European Law* 345; as well as Koskenniemi (n 4) 146.

[39] Koskenniemi (n 4) at 150.

> *If nineteenth century international lawyers had a blind faith, it was in law, not sovereignty.* Sovereignty was their construct, their response, a project of earnest doctrinal elaboration, opening a space for a new form of statecraft in an ancient legal fabric.[40] (emphasis added)

Nevertheless, whilst it might not have been the intention to erect a barrier to the possibility of legal order, doubts would soon emerge over the coherence of a positive system of rules grounded in the concordant wills and social practices of sovereign-equal states. In particular, the question arises as to how purportedly legal 'rules' could be anything other than self-imposed political prudence on the one hand or unenforceable moral speculation on the other.

A. Deriving Law from Sovereignty

The first form of scepticism relates to the idea that through their agreements—whether tacit or explicit—states might somehow be able to bind each other through their reciprocal promises, seemingly relying on some form of self-imposed restraint or mutual respect. Many critical reflections on this period relate this problem specifically to the oft-derided theory of *Selbstverpflichtungslehre* ('auto-limitation'), as emerged from the influence of neo-Hegelian jurisprudence, particularly from German public law theory from the mid-nineteenth century. This approach was applied to international law most famously, though by no means exclusively, by Georg Jellinek.[41] Essentially, we might understand international law under this model as a kind of 'external public law',[42] though such an understanding is more often than not caricatured and misunderstood, ignoring its underlying philosophical commitment. Certainly, and particularly prior to Jellinek's work, there was a distinctly 'voluntarist,' even nationalistic strand of thinking that used insights from historical jurisprudence and the philosophy of Hegel to justify a state-centric, monist account of legal obligation.[43] Nevertheless, the influence of such ideas outside of Germany was limited.[44] In any event, the much more influential account of the *Selbstverpflichtungslehre* developed by Jellinek is difficult to characterise in these terms[45]

[40] Kennedy (n 12) at 121.

[41] G Jellinek, *Die Rechtliche Natur der Staatenverträge* (Vienna, A Hölder, 1880) 2, 42–49, 56–58.

[42] The term 'external public law' comes from Koskenniemi's reading of Jellinek: see Koskenniemi (n 4) 145. The idea of 'äußeres Staatsrecht' can, however, be found much earlier in the work of Hegel himself: GWF Hegel, *Grundlinien der Philosophie des Rechts* (Georg Lasson (ed), Leipzig, Felix Meiner, 1911, originally published in 1821) 266–71 (paras 330–40).

[43] See the discussion in Koskenniemi (n 1) 179–265.

[44] Neff (n 18) 236–39.

[45] See, eg, Koskenniemi (n 9) 128.

and is perhaps more neo-Kantian than Hegelian in outlook.[46] In particular, Jellinek's position was underpinned by a distinctly objectivist account of state purpose, which was coupled with an acceptance of the constraining influence of social interaction.[47] In that sense, as Jochen von Bernstorff has recently argued, Jellinek's legal positivism was progressive and internationalist in outlook,[48] acting as a clear precursor to the more communitarian, constitutionalist international law scholarship to emerge out of Germany in the twentieth century.[49] As he puts it:

> While acknowledging the importance of the sovereign will of the State as the formal basis of all law, the binding nature of these fundamental rules in Jellinek is ultimately based on the notion of shared fundamental interests in a historically created international community of States. State sovereignty is understood as being defined and thus limited by the proto-constitution of this assumed international community.[50]

What ultimately counts here is the presumption of sociability that gives meaning to the interactions between states and which does not itself have to be accounted for within the system of law which it sustains.

As such, insofar as the idea of the *Selbstverpflichtungslehre* was influential after Jellinek, most sought to avoid the kind of philosophical account of inherent state purpose that underpinned his approach.[51] For instance, the influential early twentieth-century international lawyer Heinrich Triepel sought to qualify and improve upon Jellinek's approach by relying on a more socio-empirical basis for international law's validity, deriving the binding force of the law from a common will (*Gemeinwille*) which found expression within, and could be derived from, express (treaties) and tacit (custom) agreements between states (*Vereinbarung*).[52] Triepel aimed to highlight the different bases for international law in comparison to domestic law—an avowedly dualist approach which tried to overcome the shortcomings he saw in a (monist) theory of auto-limitation.[53] A similar approach

[46] Neff (n 18) 240.

[47] See Koskenniemi (n 1) 201, where he notes how criticisms of Jellinek's position 'fail … to address [his] move away from a pure voluntarism into a more genuinely sociological understanding of the law in terms of the structural constraints imposed on State will by the environment'.

[48] Von Bernstorff (n 15) 27–28.

[49] See further in Ch 7.

[50] J von Bernstorff, 'Georg Jellinek and the Origins of Liberal Constitutionalism in International Law' (2012) 4 *Goettingen Journal of International Law* 659, at 662.

[51] M Schmoekel, 'The Internationalist as a Scientist and Herald: Lassa Oppenheim' (2000) 11 *European Journal of International Law* 699, at 707. Though, as a counterpoint, see the work of Alfred Lasson, *Princip und Zukunft des Völkerrechts* (Berlin, Hertz, 1871), discussed in detail in Koskenniemi (n 1) 32–33.

[52] See generally H Triepel, *Völkerrecht und Landesrecht* (Leipzig, CL Hirschfeld, 1899); and H Triepel, *Droit international et droit interne* (Paris, A Pedone, 1920) 27–61.

[53] Triepel (n 52) 77.

found favour, at least initially, in the work of the Italian international lawyer Dionisio Anzilotti,[54] though in later years he would move to a more explicitly normative-conceptual framework, influenced by the work of Hans Kelsen.[55] As critics were soon keen to point out, however, the problem with all of these accounts, insofar as they try to ground the binding force of the law in agreements between states (*pacta sunt servanda*), is that they ultimately have to presume a kind of ethical sociability amongst states which sits outside of the system of international law, preceding it and giving it overall normative force.[56]

To the extent that Jellinek's approach had some influence beyond continental legal positivism, particularly through the German *émigré* Oppenheim,[57] this idea of an underpinning community will would surface again, albeit this time in a distinctly more pragmatic, Anglo-Saxon form. Oppenheim grounded the binding force of international law in what he referred to as the 'family of nations': a concept that was not merely an aggregation of the particular interests of states, but again existed as a kind of a priori assumption about their inherent sociability.[58] As Schmoekel claims:

> [Oppenheim] did not have to adopt Jellinek's theory of self-restraint as the foundation of law … Law was not forced on states because they live in a society, *but living in society causes the will to consent*. Both seem very close in theory and may have been influenced by the same sources, yet they formed distinct approaches.[59] (emphasis added)

Oppenheim's approach therefore needs to be distinguished from the more normative, scientific positivism developed by Triepel and Anzilotti (above). He was certainly sympathetic to Triepel's dualism, for instance, particularly in emphasising the specific purpose and institutional structure of international law in comparison to domestic law. However, his more pragmatic approach to theory gave a more sociological explanation of what was necessary for a community's survival and progressive development

[54] D Anzilotti, *Corso di Diritto Internazionale*, 4th edn (Padua, CEDAM, 1955) 82–85. See further G Gaja, 'Positivism and Dualism in Dinisio Anzilotti' (1992) 3 *European Journal of International Law* 123, at 127.

[55] See discussion in Gaja (n 54).

[56] See, eg, D Anzilotti, *Scritti di Diritto Internazionale* (Padua, CEDAM, 1957) 57; and see the remarks of Gaja (n 54) 127. For examples of these kinds of critiques, see Lauterpacht (n 12) 43–50; and A Verdross, 'Le fondement du droit International' (1927-I) 16 *Recueil des Cours* 247, at 262–86.

[57] Though, as Schmoekel notes, there was an important difference between their theoretical approaches in this respect: '[Oppenheim] did not have to adopt Jellinek's theory of self-restraint as the foundation of law … Law was not forced on states because they live in a society, but living in society causes the will to consent. Both seem very close in theory and may have been influenced by the same sources, yet they formed distinct approaches.' Schmoekel (n 51) 707; see also Carty (n 6) 81.

[58] Kingsbury (n 29) 409.

[59] Schmoekel (n 51) 707; see also Carty (n 6) 81.

rather than trying to conceptualise or reflect any form of actual or tacit agreement.[60] Kingsbury describes this well:

> His exposition and development of the idea [of the 'family of nations'] was not simply a description of a concept that everyone agreed upon, nor was it merely the postulating of a logical necessity for international law. He believed, it is suggested, that, in the circumstances then existing, this particular conception of international society was required for the effective development of international law.[61]

Although there were clear methodological differences between continental and Anglo-American approaches to international law, this shared emphasis on the need for a societal or community will underpinning the law still seemed a necessary construct in order to explain international law as an autonomous, objective system of rules. The close connection between law and society—*ubi societas ibi ius est*—was in fact a recurring rhetoric from the late nineteenth century onwards, with each concept mutually supporting the other. It was only by differentiating the whole from its constituent parts in this way that jurists from this era were able to sustain the coherence of the idea of international law as an autonomous normative order that was binding upon states.[62] We can see this close connection between law and society particularly in the work of Westlake, who saw international law as underpinned by an underlying social interest or a collective will opposable to that of the individual state[63]—or, as he put this himself, law could be found and enforced through the 'general consensus of opinion within the limits of European civilisation'.[64]

Sovereignty may have provided the foundation to explain the binding force of international law, but, as Anghie argues, to maintain the coherence of this view, a conception of a higher societal will had to be introduced:

> [S]ociety, rather than sovereignty, is the central concept used to construct the system of international law … Despite the positivist claims that the sovereign was the exclusive basis for the international system, it was only if society was

[60] L Oppenheim, *International Law: A Treatise*, vol 1, 3rd edn (London, Longmans, Green & Co. 1920) 14–15.

[61] Kingsbury (n 29) 409.

[62] Anghie (n 9) 47: 'sovereignty is important, inasmuch as society is constituted by sovereign states. Equally, however, it is because these states exist in society that international law can claim to be law. The interaction of the members of this society gives rise to rules *which are regularly observed and which are enforced by sanctions.* Consequently, society constituted law and law constituted society. It is through a complicated inter-play between law and society that the result is circularly achieved, that international order is maintained and international law is created'. (emphasis added)

[63] J Westlake, *International Law: Part I, Peace* (Cambridge, Cambridge University Press, 1904) 16.

[64] Westlake (n 36) 78.

> introduced into the system that positivists could approximate the idea of 'law' to which they urged adherence. Society, then, provides the matrix of ideas, the analytical resources which allied with sovereignty, could establish a positivist international legal order.[65]

Nevertheless, by placing emphasis on this idea of a society or international community, the reconciliation seems to raise a new problem. As soon as the whole (international society/community) is differentiated—*and abstracted* – from each of its constituent parts (states), the obvious difficulty became how to defend the coherence of this seemingly progressive, solidarist underpinning to the law from those sceptical that such a construct could be anything other than a form of disguised naturalism or moral abstraction. As I will now go on to show, in fact, this charge would grow to be a particular sting for jurists, particularly in Anglo-American works, due to the growing influence of the analytical positivism developed by the English legal philosopher John Austin.

B. Avoiding the Charge of Moral Utopianism

Austin's legal philosophy had essentially developed the political theory of Thomas Hobbes into an analytical model of jurisprudence which sought to make generalisable claims about law. The key to this understanding was the claim that the central normative aspect of legal rules was their ability to be enforced through the sanctioning power of a sovereign authority.[66] In the absence of such an overarching sovereign or political superior at the international level, Austin famously claimed that international law enjoyed, at best, the status of 'positive morality'.[67] Whilst the deficiencies of Austin's command-based approach to legal normativity were convincingly demonstrated some years later by Hart, amongst others,[68] by the late nineteenth century, his theory had begun to exert a significant influence, and became a principal cause of existential doubt in the professional self-consciousness of international lawyers in their efforts to defend both the reality and efficacy

[65] Anghie (n 9) 48.

[66] J Austin, *Lectures on Jurisprudence or the Philosophy of Positive Law*, 4th edn (R Campbell (ed), London, John Murray, 1873).

[67] Austin arrived at the notion of 'positive international morality' as he thought it impossible that a state could will an obligation into existence and retain its sovereignty: 'The so called law of nations consists of opinions or sentiments current among nations generally. It therefore is not law properly so called.' ibid 188.

[68] See, eg, Ch II of HLA Hart, *The Concept of Law*, 3rd edn (Oxford, Clarendon Press, 2012) at 18–25 in particular. See further my own discussion on this point in Ch 3 below.

of international law from critical attack.[69] In fact, a review of some of the key treatises from this time demonstrates how many international lawyers sought to explain how international law could be maintained as a positive legal order through the means of collective enforcement, despite its decentralised organisation.

Oppenheim's treatise was typical in this respect. He argued, *contra* Austin, that the law's binding force encompassed three aspects, none of which depended on the need for an overarching sovereign in the international sphere:

> There must, first, be a community. There must, secondly, be a body of rules for human conduct within that community. And there must, thirdly, be a common consent of that community that these rules shall be enforced by external power. It is not an essential condition either that such rules of conduct should be written rules, or that there should be a law-making authority or a law-administering court within the community concerned.[70]

Whilst Oppenheim clearly saw it as unnecessary for a decentralised legal order such as international law to be organised in the same way as the constitutional structure of a state, he clearly saw enforcement as a necessary condition for a state of legality, even if international law had to be enforced in a different way—primarily through reprisals and other mechanisms of 'self-help'.[71] In a sustained critique of Austin's approach, Oppenheim commented how:

> [M]unicipal law, constitutional law, ecclesiastical law, and international law are all branches of the same tree of law in general as a body of rules for the conduct of the members of a community, which rules shall by *common consent of the community* be eventually enforced by external power, in contradistinction to rules of morality which by common consent of a community concerned are to be enforced by conscience only.[72] (emphasis added)

Again, it is the common will of the 'family of nations' to enforce the law which gives normative force to international legal rules under Oppenheim's approach. Others went further in their criticism of Austin, whilst still accepting the need for some form of sanction in the law. For instance,

[69] Whilst I will principally refer here to British texts, the problem was felt in similar terms in American texts at this time (see, eg, FA Boyle, *World Politics and International Law* (Durham, NC, Duke University Press, 1985) 18–20), not to mention also, as Koskenniemi observes, that 'similar ideas had surfaced in *Staatslehre* and French jurisprudence as well': Koskenniemi (n 1) 48. On the Austinian influence generally, see also JE Nijman, *The Concept of International Legal Personality: An Inquiry into the History and Theory of International Law* (The Hague, TMC Asser Press, 2004) 111–14; Anghie (n 9) 44–45. On the effort amongst nineteenth-century British jurists to distinguish the autonomy of international law against Austin's criticisms, see also Sylvest (n 13).

[70] Oppenheim (n 60) 7.

[71] ibid 11.

[72] Oppenheim (n 24) 331.

Lawrence claimed that the kind of 'command theory' expounded by Austin had already been discredited, even at the national level, with the recognition that public opinion had replaced the need for physical force as the core of juridical sanction.[73] Similar arguments were advanced by others, particularly the staunchly positivist jurist WE Hall, who saw international public opinion as outweighing the necessity for organised force.[74]

Others accused Austin of taking a far too narrow approach in assessing legality. Westlake, for instance, claimed that Austin had not exactly erred, jurisprudentially speaking, but had narrowed down his enquiry too far by ignoring, as Oppenheim had also maintained, the fact that the ultimate binding force of law depended on the willingness of any society to ensure its enforcement.[75] A variation of this argument, developed by Thomas Holland, was to claim that Austin had ignored the different forms of law within the state. For Holland, international law was simply 'private law writ large', which, though commonly backed by the sanction of public authority in the domestic sphere, could nonetheless be conceptualised as sufficiently coherent in the absence of any external sovereign authority.[76] Westlake made a similar point:

> [S]tates live together in the civilised world substantially as men live together in a state, the difference being one of machinery, and we are entitled to say that there is a society of states and a law of that society, without going beyond reasonable limits in assimilating variant cases to the typical case.[77]

In making these kinds of defence in an attempt to 'correct' Austin's theory (just as Triepel and Anzilotti attempted, in their own way, to correct Jellinek's), Westlake and his contemporaries only really perpetuated the idea that international law was a less perfect form of a domestic paradigm. Specifically, in making the comparison between international and domestic legal orders and accounting for the difference between them, these jurists set international law up as necessarily inferior to a command-based domestic law paradigm. They might have argued that Austin had misunderstood the basis of sanction in

[73] Lawrence (n 19) 20–23.

[74] WE Hall, *A Treatise on International Law*, 2nd edn (Oxford, Clarendon Press, 1884) 14–15. See also a similar view espoused by the American jurist Elihu Root: E Root, 'The Sanction of International Law' (1908) 2 *American Journal of International Law* 451. On the presumption of an inherent sociability underlying Hall's position, see also Koskenniemi (n 1) 82–83.

[75] Westlake (n 36) 11–15; Westlake (n 63) 7–8.

[76] TE Holland, *Elements of Jurisprudence*, 9th edn (Oxford, Oxford University Press, 1900) 372. Whilst he could justify positive international law as law in this way, this still led him to demote its importance or its level of 'perfection' when compared to domestic law. As he concluded in an earlier essay on the 'systemic' features of positive international law: 'It is not reasonable to undervalue the services rendered by International Law, because it is not precise enough to supply a rule for every new case that arises, or strong enough to restrain from collision nations whose passions are once fully roused.' See TE Holland, *Studies in International Law* (Oxford, Clarendon Press, 1898) 167.

[77] Westlake (n 63) 7.

international law (eg, Hall, Lawrence and Oppenheim), confused a condition of the possibility of international law with the current state of international organisation (eg, Westlake) or just thought him overly pedantic in what could constitute law in the first place (eg, Lawrence and Holland). But for all concerned, a collective anxiety remained as to the fragility of the edifice of international law as a fledgling order of positive law. The lack of organised and centralised mechanisms for enforcing, adjudicating upon or developing the law appeared—whatever way they could justify it—as international law's distinct structural weakness: its institutional problem.[78]

III. 'AT THE VANISHING POINT': INTERNATIONAL LAW AS PRIMITIVE LAW

In all, therefore, however crude Austin's command theory might have been, in their attempts to refute him, many late nineteenth and early twentieth-century jurists also subtly reinforced his argument. By accepting a broadly hierarchical paradigm of legality (however much modified or qualified) based on domestic experience, most late nineteenth-century jurists dealt only with the empirical observations underpinning Austin's claim, often over-simplifying the central point of his theory in the process, and thereby missing its overall conceptual weakness too.[79] As Anghie notes, Austin had already anticipated, for example, Oppenheim's argument as to the common basis of custom in all forms of law; his point was merely that it would remain a form of positive morality, rather than law, until it had been recognised in common law (by a court) or statute (by a legislature).[80] That it would be better if international law evolved to introduce centralised organs designed to enhance this element of legal certainty was rarely contested, if at all.

The point is not that Austin's conceptualisation of domestic law's binding force was correct or indeed that all international lawyers felt the force of his critique to the same degree, but only that if one sought to prove that international law could exist as a positive legal order on the same terms as (yet despite its differences from) domestic law—as Oppenheim and others suggested—then something like the Austinian challenge revealed the weaknesses of international law thus conceived. It may belong to the same genus of law, but it is a genus which, in Oppenheim's words, had to 'be eventually enforced by external power'.[81] Whilst, as we saw above, jurists from this

[78] See Lawrence (n 19) 252 and passim.

[79] On the idea that Austin was set up as a 'straw-man' in this way, see Lobban (n 13) 80.

[80] Anghie (n 9) 46, referring to J Austin, *The Province of Jurisprudence Determined* (London, John Murray, 1832) 31.

[81] Oppenheim (n 24) 331. Similarly, Lawrence saw it as inevitable that international law would eventually develop an organised, centralised international tribunal to peacefully deal with international disputes on the basis of law. Lawrence (n 19) 252 and passim.

time had answers as to how international law could be enforced in lieu of centralised authority (either through the sanctioning 'force' of organised public opinion or by states themselves through mechanisms of self-help), these approaches were accepted as, at best, 'gap-filling' measures, making up for the lack of centralised force found within domestic legal orders.

Accordingly, the kind of scepticism which denied the binding force of international law is merely transferred to the law's institutional condition. It was only by assuming that it would evolve to become more like domestic law that international law could be reconciled on the same terms. This assumption is particularly evident, again, in Westlake's conceptualisation of the difference between domestic and international legal orders, which he saw as arising primarily because of international society's stage of development, not the existence of law within that society, which he took as a given:

> Since a loosely organised society can give less protection than a highly organised one, and its rules are not ascertainable with equal precision, it may have less claim to the obedience of its members. But the obligation of law on the conscience is a question of ethical philosophy different from that of the objective existence of law in a society, and lying deeper.[82]

On this basis, there was still a sufficient similarity between domestic and international legal orders in order to make the comparison, the difference being 'one of machinery', such that they could still be compared and contrasted 'without going beyond reasonable limits in assimilating variant cases to the typical case'.[83]

Nevertheless, the problem here is that rather than being theorised or understood on its own terms, international law is conceived precisely as a less perfect or incomplete variant of a hierarchical paradigm of legality drawn from domestic experience. By claiming that international law's structural dissimilarities compared to domestic law related merely to the law's material or institutional under-development, international law emerges only as a primitive version of domestic law, awaiting an as-yet-unattained stage of societal development and institutional maturity—the achievement of which could only but be a speculative (and ultimately theoretically self-destructive) assumption. In fact, it was the troubling nature of this position which pushed the noted Oxford scholar Thomas Holland (a prominent international lawyer as well as analytical legal philosopher) to describe international law as being at the 'vanishing point of jurisprudence'—his point being that to require international law to have a centralised organisation would either make it vanish into existing domestic law or else require some kind of overarching supra-state.[84]

[82] Westlake (n 36) 12.
[83] Westlake (n 63) 7.
[84] Holland, *Elements of Jurisprudence* (n 76) 369.

Accordingly, modern international law emerges from these accounts with an inherent constitutional weakness, which can be addressed only through a teleological assumption that as a legal order it necessarily must evolve to develop an (arguably unachievable) institutional architecture akin to domestic law.[85] This teleological argument underpins the sociological claim. The two rely on each other: it was only by acknowledging international society as similar to domestic states that turn-of-the-century jurists could sustain the idea that it was binding as law in the same way, but it was only in assuming that international law would necessarily develop in the future to more fully approximate this domestic paradigm that they could sustain the basis of the comparison in the first place. By introducing teleology into the argument, Austin's criticism can be turned on its head as a means of response: *international law's weaknesses help prove its similarity to the more 'typical' case*. In fact, Westlake takes this kind of reasoning further, justifying the creative role of the international jurist precisely because of the want of an institutional power 'to define and develop' international legal rules.[86] Accordingly, this lack of legislative and judicial machinery made it imperative for lawyers to take a progressive stance in order to develop the law to better reflect the underlying needs of international society.[87]

There is a certainty of conviction here that assumes international law's necessary evolutionary development and puts paid to the idea that this was an era mired in state-centric legal positivism. By looking at the development of other societies, one could by analogy explain international law's apparent defects as merely reflecting international society's early stage of development. Oppenheim, for instance, pointed out how custom had played an equally important part in the development of the legal orders of domestic states prior to their embracing centralised legislative machinery.[88] In fact, there is an obvious influence here from the kind of 'historical jurisprudence' developed by Westlake and Oppenheim's predecessor in the Whewell Chair at Cambridge, Henry Summer Maine.[89] The use of such evolutionary

[85] Oppenheim (n 24) 317–18.

[86] Westlake (n 36) 8. In fact, in a critical engagement with the achievements of the second Hague Conference in 1907, he dismissed the conference arrangements as a 'parody of a parliament' and a 'phantom of a legislature'. J Westlake, 'The Hague Conferences' reproduced in Oppenheim (n 25) 531, at 532.

[87] Westlake (n 36) 273–74; and see his 'Introductory Lecture on International Law, 17 October 1888', reproduced in Oppenheim (n 25) 393, at 409–10. See also Sylvest (n 14) 63–64.

[88] Oppenheim (n 60) 14–15.

[89] As Berman notes, this historicist approach seemed primarily to be aimed at tempering the more nihilistic implications of Austin's claims, but without 'recourse to the more murky [sic] (and less legitimate) forms of natural law thinking'. HJ Berman, 'World Law Transcendent' (2005) 54 *Emory Law Journal* 53, at 55. In this respect, the historical approach could support both conservative and progressive causes. See, eg, Neff (n 15) 17–19; and Koskenniemi (n 1) 42–47.

argument allowed lawyers to dismiss Austin without undermining the basis of the comparison between international and domestic legal orders. Looked at in this evolutionary perspective, it appeared only natural that international law had developed 'by help of fiction' and only later, in the nineteenth century, with the advent of 'scientific jurisprudence', that there was a real prospect of improving international law from its primitive state.[90] In fact, simply by placing Austin's command theory on such a linear historical trajectory, Maine was able to account for the imperfections of international law's current institutional structure as merely one stage—following on progressively from the naturalist, 'law of nations' paradigm that had preceded it—in an ongoing evolution of international society through law.[91]

As certain as the jurists from this era were about the necessity of international law's institutional development, it was nonetheless clear that the structure of the international legal order as it then stood seemed to be a clear barrier towards progress. As Maine was ultimately forced to conclude:

> The want of coercive power is, in fact, the one important drawback which attends all attempts to improve International Law by contrivances imitated from the internal economy of states, by something like legislation, and by something like the administration of law by organised tribunals.[92]

In all, therefore, there was an overwhelming sense of international law's structural weakness as an autonomous legal system. It was still at the vanishing point of jurisprudence, still craving the certainty of a more centralised institutional architecture.

IV. CONCLUSION

There is no doubting the reality of the transformation in understanding of international law which occurred between the mid- to late nineteenth and early twentieth centuries. As equally demonstrated in this chapter, however, there is also no escape from the implications of this transformation to the extent that international law began to be held up to comparison against an idealised version of domestic law, against which it seemed institutionally under-developed, immature or primitive as a system of law. From the assumption that international law could exist as a body of rules

[90] The quotations are taken from Vinogradoff's summation of Maine's position: P Vinogradoff, *The Teaching of Sir Henry Maine: An Inaugural Lecture* (London, Henry Frowde, 1904) 16–17.

[91] Maine (n 17) 53. For a detailed exposition of Maine's theory in this respect, see the arguments of Sylvest (n 14) 42–43.

[92] HS Maine, *International Law*, 2nd edn (London, John Murray, 1894) 213.

capable of instigating a means of social order, restraining the passions of states, came—as the next chapter will show—the crushing disappointment associated with the outbreak of the First World War. The apparent naiveté of the pre-war jurists, with their ambition to carve out an autonomous international legal order, was an easy target for *inter-bellum* jurists. The still embryonic professional practice and academic discipline of international law would again become beset by scepticism and self-doubt.

2

Scepticism and Renewal: International Law in the Inter-bellum *Period*

THE PROCEDURAL ENTHUSIASM of the late nineteenth-century jurists—their belief in codification, systematisation and inter-state arbitration—would not survive the outbreak of the First World War unscathed. The existential shock of the war had a profound effect on the future development of international law in the twentieth century. More particularly, the idea that international law could, or should, have been able to prevent the war but had demonstrably failed in this respect was a recurring rhetoric from this period, prompting inter-war jurists to stress the need for renewal and reconstruction in the law.[1] Already by 1917, prior to the end of the war, the German-Swiss jurist and noted pacifist Ottfried Nippold went so far as to admonish his own foolhardiness in believing in the abstract autonomy of law alone in the absence of any real juridical sanction. With the outbreak of the Great War, however, this faith had been substantially undermined:

> The war has brought us face to face with the relentless fact that international treaties have been broken ... faith in the moral power of international law has thereby suffered a shock from which the civilized world will not very quickly recover. This enables us to understand why, to-day, the call for more real sanctions for the international legal order has been heard on every hand.[2]

[1] See, inter alia, M Koskenniemi, *From Apology to Utopia: The Structure of International Legal Argument* (Cambridge, Cambridge University Press, 2005) 159; A Anghie, *Imperialism, Sovereignty and the Making of International Law* (Cambridge, Cambridge University Press, 2005) 124, 127–31; T Skouteris, *The Notion of Progress in International Law Discourse* (The Hague, TMC Asser Press, 2010) 103–20.

[2] O Nippold, *The Development of International Law after the War* (Oxford, Clarendon Press, 1923, originally published in German in 1917) 35. Lassa Oppenheim's approach also shifted subtly towards the end of the war, as he welcomed the development of collective security through the League of Nations as leading towards a more centralised enforcement mechanism for international law. See, inter alia, L Oppenheim, *International Law: A Treatise*, vol 1, 3rd edn (London, Longmans, Green & Co, 1920) 7, 10–11; and on the changed position of both jurists, see H Suganami, *The Domestic Analogy and World Order Proposals* (Cambridge, Cambridge University Press, 1989) 80–81.

Initially buoyed by the founding of the League of Nations and the development of the PCIJ—even if the League would eventually disappoint in this respect—jurists of the *inter-bellum* period quickly turned on their pre-war forbearers. The effort to explain international law as a functioning legal system in the absence of institutions capable of securing some form of juridical order in international relations seemed now either too fanciful and divorced from the realities of international politics, or else overly deferential in being too closely wedded to state sovereignty. That these criticisms seem somewhat contradictory only highlights the difficulties facing modern international lawyers—to some extent already outlined in the previous chapter—in explaining international law as a decentralised system of positive legal rules. Indeed, as Koskenniemi has most famously demonstrated, the modern discipline seems constantly plagued by critique from either side, as the openness of its rules leaves them always vulnerable to being put to use for seemingly opposed political purposes.[3] Indeed, the sense of frustration at the openness and malleability of international law is well-captured in the following critical remarks from the famous American jurist Manley O Hudson writing in 1923:

> As each belligerent nation sought in vain for a law which would restrain its enemies, as each neutral nation sought in vain for a law which would relieve it of the burdensome incidents of the struggle, the insufficiency of our pre-war law came to be felt in every part of the world. Its principles seemed inadequate, its limitations ineffective, and its bases insecure. In many quarters, belief in the utility of a law of nations was weakened, and faith in the efficacy of any effort to increase its authority was lost. Even our legal profession failed to withstand the effect of the general scepticism, and we allowed to be revived the futile discussions of the Austinian era as to the existence of a law of nations which might properly be called law.[4]

Foremost amongst the targets of the *inter-bellum* jurists was the theory of legal positivism, which, as already noted, had largely prevailed over naturalist theories by the end of the nineteenth century. By the late 1920s, this 'classical' legal positivism had become irrevocably associated with the kind of voluntarist logic expounded by the PCIJ in the infamous *Lotus* case, where the Court claimed that 'The rules of law binding upon States ... emanate from their own free will' and that: 'Restrictions upon the independence of States [could not] therefore be presumed.'[5] This kind of reasoning not only seemed theoretically flawed, being unable to account for international law as an autonomous system opposable to the will of the state, but also ideologically

[3] As he notes, both types of criticism can be levelled at naturalism and positivism: the former reduced either to unverifiable moral commands or related too closely to the idea of natural rights of sovereigns; the latter either too analytical and abstract or too closely related to state will or practice. Koskenniemi (n 1) 164 and passim.

[4] MO Hudson, 'The Development of International Law since the War' (1928) 22 *American Journal of International Law* 330, at 330–31.

[5] *The Case of the SS Lotus* (1927) PCIJ Series A, No 10, at 18. For a typical criticism, see JL Brierly, 'The "*Lotus*" Case' (1928) 174 *Law Quarterly Review* 154.

dangerous, underpinning the kind of nationalist ideology which was thought to have been directly causative of the First World War.[6] In a series of lectures on the 'new aspects of international law' delivered around the same time as the PCIJ's judgment, the Greek jurist Nicolas Politis stressed the poverty of this kind of positivist reasoning, 'for if a rule of law is merely the product of free will it is not really binding, but remains at the discretion of the States which created it'.[7] Already before the PCIJ's decision, writing in his first English-language publication in 1925, Hersch Lauterpacht decried the limits of legal positivism in even more forceful terms, arguing that it was 'fraught with danger', in particular due to the possibility 'that not only will the practice of states be taken as an unquestionable rule of law, but that the philosophy underlying this practice will be regarded as a true expression of the tendencies and the possibilities of the international society'.[8]

Nevertheless, if the shock of the war united *inter-bellum* jurists around the perceived failure of pre-war international law, their prognoses for its renewal or resuscitation varied widely and, in one sense at least, sharply divided the discipline. As Astorino notes:

> [The war was] viewed by all sides as an unequivocal moral failure. The sides, however, differed in their analysis of the war's causes. To the orthodox, the outbreak of war simply affirmed the absolute necessity of future adherence to law as the alternative to war. To the critics of orthodoxy, the war signalled the bankruptcy of toothless appeals to law; reality meant the objective fact, as could be demonstrated by empirical social science, of a balance of power politics.[9]

With no going back to an older, metaphysical naturalism, the priority for the modern era was thus how to re-imagine a more persuasive, more objective international law. The problem, however, was that there were quite widespread divergences over how to achieve—and, indeed, the likelihood of achieving—this ambition. As such, in the current chapter, I will outline three forms of response to this challenge.[10] These are not suggested as

[6] N Berman, '"But the Alternative is Despair": European Nationalism and the Modernist Renewal of International Law' (1993) 106 *Harvard Law Review* 1792, at 1800–08.

[7] N Politis, *The New Aspects of International Law* (Washington DC, Carnegie Endowment for International Peace, 1928) 5.

[8] H Lauterpacht, 'Westlake and Present Day International Law' (1925) 5 *Economica* 307, at 323–24. Similar criticisms are developed in his first monograph on international law: H Lauterpacht, *Private Law Sources and Analogies of International Law* (London, Longmans, 1927), especially 43–44.

[9] S Astorino, 'The Impact of Sociological Jurisprudence on International Law in the Inter-War Period: The American Experience' (1996) 34 *Duquesne Law Review* 277, at 280.

[10] Morgenthau, in fact, notes that pre-war positivism was attacked from 'three sides'. H Morgenthau, 'Positivism, Functionalism, and International Law' (1940) 34 *American Journal of International Law* 260, at 262. This tripartite response arguably over-simplifies the range of perspectives that characterised this era of disciplinary renewal. Nevertheless, my own structure of this chapter is influenced by this characterisation—relying on sociological approaches, neo-positivism and new natural law approaches in sections I, II and III respectively—less to give a comprehensive overview of theory from this period, and more to highlight possible disciplinary positions in response to classical positivism and to show the limitations of each.

empirically exhaustive positions, but in their juxtaposition they illustrate logically exhaustive alternatives, as well as illustrating the influence of somewhat opposed jurisprudential traditions emerging on both sides of the Atlantic. In other words, contrasted in this way they reveal the contours of the challenge *inter-bellum* jurists faced in accounting for the autonomy of international law as a persuasive restraint on the conduct of international politics.

The first, outlined in section I, reflects the growth of legal realism and, more generally, the influence of the social sciences in American jurisprudence.[11] These influences led many international lawyers towards a more empirical, sociological approach, which downplayed the importance of formal legal rules.[12] In its most critical form, this would eventually lead to the establishment of a new discipline of International Relations (IR), which was in many ways born out of the rejection of the possibility of the kind of legal autonomy pursued by classical positivists.[13] The second, outlined in section II, also sees the weakness of pre-war doctrine in its lack of scientific objectivity, but understands the notion of objectivity in a radically opposed way. This more scientific or 'pure' form of legal positivism—championed by the Viennese jurist Hans Kelsen and broadly influential in continental-European jurisprudence at this time—sought instead to isolate law's autonomy from political, social or ethical inputs precisely in order to guarantee its counterfactual normativity and thus its influence in shaping the relations between states.[14]

Both of these responses can be understood as an effort to take forward and correct the positivist project started in the previous century, as outlined in the previous chapter, but each also remains vulnerable to critique from the

[11] Sociological jurisprudence was also influential in France: see R Kolb, 'Politis and Sociological Jurisprudence of Inter-War International Law' (2012) 23 *European Journal of International Law* 233; and M Koskenniemi, *The Gentle Civilizer of Nations: The Rise and Fall of International Law 1870–1960* (Cambridge, Cambridge University Press, 2001) at 266–352, though in particular at 302 ff. On the Scandinavian Legal Realism movement and its influence on the international legal theory of Alf Ross, see also, inter alia, AL Escorihuela, 'Alf Ross: Towards a Realist Critique and Reconstruction of International Law' (2003) 14 *European Journal of International Law* 703.

[12] Compare, for instance, Astorino (n 9) with Kolb (n 11). See also C Landauer, 'J. L. Brierly and the Modernization of International Law' (1993) 25 *Vanderbilt Journal of International Law* 881, at 884–99 in particular.

[13] See, eg, the critical remarks of one of the founding figures of IR scholarship, Morgenthau (n 10) at 263–73 in particular. On the birth of international relations as a rejection of the autonomy of international legal rules, see M Koskenniemi, 'Carl Schmitt, Morgenthau, and the Image of Law in International Relations' in M Byers (ed), *The Role of Law in International Politics: Essays in International Relations and International Law* (Oxford, Oxford University Press, 2000) 17–34.

[14] For a contemporaneous overview of Kelsen's work, and of the 'Vienna School' more broadly, see J Kunz, 'On the Theoretical Basis of the Law of Nations' (1924) 10 *Transactions of the Grotius Society* 115; and for a more retrospective overview, see more recently Chs 3 and 4 of J von Bernstorff, *The Public International Law Theory of Hans Kelsen: Believing in Universal Law* (Cambridge, Cambridge University Press, 2010).

alternative position: one arguably unable to adequately explain law's normativity in a counter-factual sense; the other arguably too far removed from the underlying social facts of international relations. Accordingly, in section III, I outline the necessary contours of a 'middle way' between these two positions, illustrated by reference to the work of the popular jurists James Brierly and Hersch Lauterpacht. I show how both were able to move with more ease between sociological realism and normative idealism, in particular by showing how institutional developments of their time were helping to reveal the ethical foundation of international law whilst also encouraging its structural evolution towards a more centralised, institutional architecture. This kind of reconciliation comes at a price, however, as—just as for the generation before them—it premises the objectivity of international law on its necessary evolution, thus also revealing its constitutional weaknesses as currently structured. On this account, international law can only fully actualise itself, or so it seems, by developing the kind of overarching sovereign authority it purports to reject.

I. THE CALL FOR RELEVANCE: HANS MORGENTHAU AND THE REALIST TURN

One of the most significant influences on international law in the *interbellum* period stemmed from the rise of legal realism, as well as the broader sociological turn in American jurisprudence. Whilst early realists like Karl Llewellyn did not occupy themselves much beyond the practices of US law, the more sociological approach that he and others championed would come to have quite a considerable influence on American international law scholarship.[15] One of the leading proponents of the new sociological jurisprudence, Roscoe Pound, did briefly turn his attention to international law, and in doing so launched a scathing attack on the kind of legal positivism which characterised pre-war international law. Writing in 1923, shortly after the end of the First World War, he made this point most clearly, castigating legal positivism for believing in the progressive potential of an autonomous international law, divorced from actual social practices:

> [I]t is not hard to see why the nineteenth-century achieved so little in international law … [Nineteenth century positivists] did not seek to be active agents in legal development. *They expected legal development to operate itself from some international momentum.* The jurist was able to follow, arranging and ordering and systematizing or observing and verifying and thus discovering the foreordained lines of growth.[16] (emphasis added)

[15] See discussion of Astorino (n 9).

[16] R Pound, 'Philosophical Theory and International Law' (1923) 1 *Bibliotheca Visseriana* 1 at 88; also cited in Astorino (n 9) 287.

Pound wrote little on international law, but this critique, as well as the sociological approach he espoused more generally, was particularly influential in shaping a more pragmatic, realist and inter-disciplinary turn in US international law scholarship—an influence which continues to the present day. As diverse as the approaches of Pound, Llewellyn, and other key figures in this movement were amongst themselves, they were united in their disavowal of the formalism that was seen as prevalent in positivist jurisprudence since the end of the nineteenth century,[17] which, as Anghie notes, asserted the autonomy of legal reasoning from the fields of ethics and sociology.[18] Even if, for many of these jurists, legal positivism had rightly replaced an overtly metaphysical naturalism, this had become 'an outdated formalistic positivism that in its petrified form was simply incapable of responding adequately to the political and social realities of the times'.[19]

As a result of these concerns, it is easy to see how a new discipline of IR could emerge from the inter-war years, as a group of avowedly 'realist' scholars attempted to apply something like a sociological jurisprudence to the field of international law.[20] Prominent early figures in the IR movement, such as EH Carr and Hans Morgenthau, were essentially opposed to the legal-moralism and formalism of classical positivist jurisprudence, favouring instead a more thorough empiricism focused on the realities of state interactions and power politics.[21] For Carr, the idea that positive law possessed some autonomous normativity, that is, an ability to constrain the political realm, was deeply misguided.[22] Similarly, for Morgenthau, legal positivism's stress on the conceptual autonomy of law at the expense of the material factors that actually influenced state behaviour meant that it failed to live up to the scientism which had inspired it in the first place.[23] The unfolding events of the *inter-bellum* years, the failure of the League of Nations and the outbreak of the Second World War, would only help to solidify and add weight to these views.[24]

The emergence of realism and IR scholarship from this time thus has to be understood as a distinctly modernist reaction to, and attempt to further, the positivist transition begun in the previous century.[25] The criticism directed at pre-war international law is not so much concerned with its ambition—that

[17] Astorino (n 9) 282.

[18] Anghie (n 1) 128.

[19] Astorino (n 9) 277.

[20] On this transition generally, see Koskenniemi (n 13) 17.

[21] FA Boyle, *World Politics and International Law* (Durham, NC, Duke University Press, 1985) 11–13.

[22] EH Carr, *The Twenty Years' Crisis 1919–1939: An Introduction to the Study of International Relations*, 2nd edn (London, MacMillan, 1946) 229–31.

[23] Morgenthau (n 10).

[24] Much of Morgenthau's and Carr's most critical output came around the time of the outbreak, or in the aftermath of, the Second World War.

[25] Carty makes this point explicitly: A Carty, 'Why Theory?—The Implications for International Law Teaching' in P Allott et al, *Theory and International Law: An Introduction* (London, British Institute of International and Comparative Law, 1991) 75, at 83.

is, striving towards scientific objectivity in order to enhance the relevance of international law in the relations between states. Rather, the criticism comes precisely from the failure to live up to this ambition; the tendency to engage in unverifiable (that is, unscientific) doctrinal metaphysics.[26] We can see this criticism running through Morgenthau's seminal article in the *American Journal of International Law* from 1940: 'Positivism, Functionalism, and International Law'.[27] Morgenthau was persistent in his criticism of legal positivism and its stress on the law's conceptual autonomy because he saw that it required international lawyers to fall back on precisely the kind of naturalist assumption of objective purpose which positivists themselves had sought to remove from the law.[28]

Morgenthau therefore shared the aspiration of pre-war jurists like Oppenheim to make the study of law more realistic and therefore more persuasive. Unlike Oppenheim, however, he did not see the legal as something *conceptually* autonomous from the political. The autonomy of law was guaranteed domestically through the centralised institutions of the state, which enjoyed a monopoly on the use of force. The decentralised nature of the international legal order, on the other hand, meant that international law was ultimately dependent on unorganised, fluctuating and unstable political forces:

> In the domestic field, legal rules can be imposed by the group which holds the monopoly of organized physical force, that is, the officials of the state. The international sphere is characterized by the absence of such a group. International law owes its existence to identical or complementary interests of states, backed by power as a last resort, or, where such identical interests do exist, to a mere balance of power which prevents a state from breaking these rules of international law. Where there is neither community of interest nor balance of power, there is no international law.[29]

The pre-war jurists had erred, therefore, by not taking seriously this critical difference between the institutional structures of international and domestic legal orders. For Morgenthau, this had two particular consequences: in the absence of centralised machinery for legal compliance, adherence to international law would depend on a coincidence of interests or a balance of power; and in the absence of efficient mechanisms for legal development and change, pressure for change would precipitate an inevitable breakdown in social order at the global level.[30]

Morgenthau's realism is easily misunderstood. His critique of positivism came from both sides: in its divorce from sociological and empirical reality,

[26] D Kennedy, 'International Law and the Nineteenth Century: History of an Illusion' (1997) 17 *Quinnipiac Law Review* 99, at 113.
[27] Morgenthau (n 10).
[28] ibid 262–63.
[29] ibid 275.
[30] ibid 275–76; Koskenniemi (n 13) 22.

and in its disconnection from social mores and philosophical goals. On the one hand, he insisted that the broader social and political context could not be excluded from the processes of legal reasoning. On the other hand, he also saw the importance of giving law shape and direction through philosophical deduction as an integral part of juristic method. In fact, he argued that the 'intelligibility of any legal system depend[ed] upon the recognition of such a set of fundamental principles which constitute the ethical substance of the legal system'.[31] Nevertheless, it seemed that the fundamental structural differences between domestic and international legal orders created difficulties in giving this kind of moral shape to the law:

> This recognition is relatively easy to perform in the domestic field, where the constitution codifies the main bulk of those fundamental principles, and a highly integrated public opinion provides supplementary moral guidance. The task is much more difficult with respect to international law. Here there is no body of such principles separate from the ordinary rules of law. Some of those principles may be only partly expressed in these rules; others may not be expressed at all, and hence have to be detected, in a dangerously uncertain procedure, in the general moral ideas underlying the international law of a certain time, a certain civilization, or even a certain nation.[32]

As such, he argued that the attempt to account for international law as a system in the same way as within the domestic state would be simultaneously under- and over-inclusive: including rules which did not reflect the prevailing social conditions of the time, whilst ignoring those material factors which actually were determinative in shaping the behaviour of states.[33] What mattered, ultimately, was the *material* ability of a legal order to channel politics through legal institutions and monopolise the use of force—conditions which were patently missing at the international level, therefore requiring international lawyers to engage in a more rigorous empirical enquiry, looking beyond or behind the formal rules.[34]

Morgenthau was thus not simply denying the reality of international law, but rather was recognising the problem of its apparent autonomy from politics and morality—a condition which could only be guaranteed at the domestic level because of the structural, institutional conditions of state-based law. For Morgenthau, inter-state relations were therefore inherently more unstable, but this instability was caused by this structural difference,

[31] Morgenthau (n 10) at 268. He described the difference in the organisation of international and national systems in more detail, though from a more distinctly political perspective in H Morgenthau, *Scientific Man vs Power Politics* (Chicago, University of Chicago Press, 1946) 50–51 and passim.

[32] Morgenthau (n 10) 268.

[33] ibid 265–66, 273.

[34] ibid 274; see also Koskenniemi (n 13) 19–20.

not by the nature of international law per se. Essentially, he saw a condition of peace or order in international relations as only realisable through the development of something akin to a global state, though he thought that this goal was unrealisable due to the prevailing social and political conditions of international relations in his time.[35] This led him to suggest, though never fully develop, what he termed a 'functionalist' theory of international law, which stressed the materiality rather than formality of law.[36]

That Morgenthau therefore embraces an ideal of legal autonomy in theory—specifically through the determination of centralised officials—but denies its application to international law in practice reveals a fatal contradiction in his position, however. As Koskenniemi explains:

> [This] argument is curious because it both maintains and denies the law/politics distinction. The distinction is maintained through the assumption that law can be separated from non-law through a criterion (the likelihood of sanction). But the distinction is denied as the question of the likelihood of sanction becomes a sociological one. Binding force emerges with factual coercion. Law is merely a division of power politics ... What is binding is determined by what is politically effective.[37]

Ultimately, here, Morgenthau falls foul of the same critique that Hart would later direct against Austin. In his stress on empirical observation at the expense of conceptual enquiry, he leaves himself with no means of distinguishing legal from non-legal behaviour (the aim of the enquiry to begin with). Consequently, when taken to its logical conclusion, this argument either ends up denying international law's existence as law or—as has been argued by realists since Morgenthau—sees it as only of marginal or contingent relevance, being ultimately subservient to power politics.

The realist-functionalism underpinning Morgenthau's account therefore invokes the second, opposing critique that inter-war jurists aimed at the prewar professionals: the problem of how a law based on the concordance of separate wills could be anything more than a lowest common denominator of agreement, a simple gloss on the realities of state power. A purely empirical, behavioural or 'external'[38] theory of law ends up as pure apologism;[39] or worse, with Morgenthau, it results in the prevailing political conditions being seen as 'eternal laws by which man moves in the social world'.[40]

[35] Insights he develops more fully in H Morgenthau, *Politics among Nations* (New York, Knopf, 1949) 398–406. See also Suganami (n 2) 99–100.

[36] Morgenthau (n 10) 274.

[37] Koskenniemi (n 1) 199.

[38] On the internal-external distinction, see generally HLA Hart, *The Concept of Law*, 3rd edn (Oxford, Clarendon Press, 2012) 88–90 and passim. On the importance of the internal aspect of rules as described by Hart, see below in Ch 3, at nn 68–72.

[39] Koskenniemi (n 1) 160.

[40] Morgenthau (n 31) 220.

II. KELSEN AND THE NEO-POSITIVIST REVIVAL

If Morgenthau's approach can be understood as a rejection of the uneasy amalgamation of empiricism and conceptual abstraction one finds in prewar international jurisprudence, then a similar ambition underlies the broader jurisprudential agenda of Hans Kelsen. Like Morgenthau's realism, Kelsen's pure theory of law, developed during the early decades of the twentieth century, can be seen in this historical context as 'a modernist rebellion against the uncritical synthesis of traditional positivism'.[41] And again like Morgenthau, Kelsen's approach is aimed at isolating a more objective law, and is in many ways therefore a continuation of the nineteenth-century positivist project. Crucially, however, Kelsen takes the critique in the opposite direction with a quite rigid commitment to conceptual purity—to legal autonomy in an absolute sense. What mattered for Kelsen was not mapping law onto prevailing social conditions, but the need to separate out and clearly define the 'ought' claim of law; its normativity in the sense of it being opposable to sociological fact.[42] In applying his approach to international law in particular, Kelsen saw it as crucial to be able to determine international legal rules in isolation of the subjective social forces inherent in international politics.[43] To put this another way (and in contrast to Morgenthau), Kelsen saw that deriving international law simply from what states actually did, or said, risked destroying 'the autonomous integrity of the legal order'.[44]

This neo-positivist perspective thus takes an entirely different approach to understanding the 'objectivity' of law. A legal system did not depend for its coherence on being embedded in any particular institutional structure—it had to be systemically autonomous in a purer sense, regulating its own means of creation, mediation and enforcement.[45] A legal institution must logically take its identity from a pre-existing legal order: it is the legal order which bestows juridical identity and authority upon such institutions (eg, the state).[46] Taken to its logical extreme, this showed the necessary primacy of international law over domestic law, with the internal validity of domestic legal orders necessarily dependent upon the pre-existence of the international legal system.[47]

[41] N Berman, 'A Perilous Ambivalence: Nationalist Desire, Legal Autonomy, and the Limits of the Interwar Framework' (1992) 33 *Harvard International Law Journal* 353, at 363.

[42] H Kelsen, *General Theory of Law and State* (Cambridge, MA, Harvard University Press, 1945) 29–40 and passim; and see also Koskenniemi (n 1) 226–28.

[43] H Kelsen, *Principles of International Law* (New York, Rinehart & Co, 1952) 3–5.

[44] Berman (n 41) 363.

[45] H Kelsen, *Pure Theory of Law* (Berkeley, University of California Press, 1967) 71.

[46] ibid 285–86. On this point, see in particular M Prost, *The Concept of Unity in Public International Law* (Oxford, Hart Publishing, 2012) 73.

[47] Kelsen (n 45) 336 ff.

Kelsen's view of normativity distinguished so-called 'static' from 'dynamic' normative orders: the normative claim of the former, synonymous with morality, was clearly content-dependent, whereas for the latter, a dynamic normative order such as a legal system, the claim must be *content-independent*.[48] Accordingly, Kelsen's concept of a legal system outlined how norms are validated (and therefore binding) through their conformity with higher legal rules within a kind of hierarchical pyramid of norms, at the top of which stood Kelsen's well-known *grundnorm* (or 'basic norm'): an a priori hypothesis or supposition giving validity to the legal order as a whole.[49] Accordingly, the validity of international law rested precisely on such a 'foundational assumption', that is, 'on the hypothesis that international custom is a law-creating fact'.[50] Conceived in such conceptual-systemic terms, Kelsen had no problem in defending the objective reality of international law as a juristic fact.

Although the differences between their theories could not be greater in this respect, it is still important to reiterate that Kelsen begins from similar premises to Morgenthau, seeing law as a means of coercion aimed at instigating behavioural change. In this sense, what differentiates law from other forms of social order, according to Kelsen, is its capacity to coerce through the ultimate threat of sanction.[51] Both Kelsen and Morgenthau therefore shared the same normative starting point in the idea that this kind of order is beneficial and something akin to this form of law exists in well-functioning domestic systems. Where they (quite fundamentally) parted company, however, is that Kelsen thought that the lawyer should not be concerned with whether there was actual regularity of behaviour following from legal command, only that a legal norm *be capable of* coercive application through the sanction of another person 'designated by the legal order' itself.[52] As he claims:

> Law … is a coercive order not because the idea of the legal norm induces men to proper behaviour, but because the legal norm provides a coercive measure as a sanction. *The element of coercion is of the substance of the legal norm, not in the soul of the man subject to the legal norm.* Whether or not men do actually behave in such a manner as to avoid the sanction threatened by the legal norm and whether or not the sanction provided in the legal norm is actually carried out are issues totally irrelevant to the concept of law.[53] (emphasis added)

Again, the contrast to Morgenthau could not be starker. Legal *efficacy* and legal *validity* are sharply contrasted. This is not to suggest that Kelsen

[48] ibid 70–71.

[49] See, generally, Kelsen (n 42) 110–15 and passim.

[50] Kelsen (n 43) 314.

[51] H Kelsen, *Law and Peace in International Relations: The Oliver Wendell Holmes Lectures, 1940–41* (Cambridge, MA, Harvard University Press, 1942) 7.

[52] ibid 9.

[53] ibid 15.

was unconcerned with the efficacy of law or of international law more particularly—far from it. Like Morgenthau, Kelsen saw the potential solution to the problem of order in international affairs in the formation of something like a world state and, similarly again, admitted that as the international legal order was presently constituted, such an ambition could only be a utopian aspiration.[54] However, unlike Morgenthau, he accounted for the difference between national and international legal orders in a fundamentally different way. His monist conceptual approach presupposed both as part of the same genus of law, differentiating international law solely on the basis of its *current* lack of centralisation. The difference is one of degree, not kind. On this basis, Kelsen could, on the one hand, account for the reality of international law as a system of norms, seeing a coercive sanction in state reprisals and other forms of self-help (authorised by the legal order itself),[55] whilst, on the other hand, explaining the difference between legal orders simply in terms of the extent or their centralisation. In other words, he saw international legal order as capable of progressive evolution towards more centralised sanction (particularly through the regulation of the use of force in universal institutions such as the League of Nations and later the UN).[56] In this respect, Kelsen explained international law essentially as a primitive legal order in comparison to the domestic state, though, at the same time, the latter's jurisdictional sphere was validated and circumscribed by the former. The two were seen in monist terms as a conceptual whole.[57]

Nevertheless, his attempt to explain the autonomy of international law in a similar manner to domestic law also revealed a fundamental weakness in his position. In his stress on mechanisms of self-help as explaining the coercive sanction of international law, Kelsen relied upon the idea of the *bellum justum* (the just war). However, he freely admitted that his choice to conceptualise the international legal order in this way was an entirely *political decision*. Kelsen's need for systemic unity pushed him into a juristic hypothesis not only in the foundation of the law (the concept of the *grundnorm*), but also in terms of making sense of the conduct of international relations as a coercive legal order overarching and in that sense regulating state behaviour. He deliberately chose this interpretation, 'hoping to have recognized the beginning of a development of the future and with the intention of strengthening as far as possible all the elements of present-day international law which tend to justify this interpretation and to promote the evolution we desire'.[58]

[54] ibid 28.

[55] ibid 33–38; Kelsen (n 43) 20–34; H Kelsen, 'Théorie du droit international public' (1953-III) 84 *Recueil des Cours* 1, at 31–34.

[56] Kelsen (n 51) 48–55, 83–86, 145–51.

[57] See principally Ch VII of Kelsen (n 45) 320–47; and Ch V of Kelsen (n 43) 401–47.

[58] Kelsen (n 51) 54–55.

In admitting this choice in this way, he undermines the idea of international law as an autonomous legal order, as politics become again infused with legal analysis. In fact, Kelsen admitted at a number of points that the decentralised international legal order was fundamentally 'primitive' compared to the domestic ideal,[59] and thus had to presuppose the law's evolution in order to explain the differences between international and domestic law. However, by removing any moral or political considerations from within the pure theory of law, he was unable to justify his vision of international law as anything other than his own political preference: that which allows him to explain international law as inevitably moving towards a more centralised organisation similar to that existing within the state. This explanation allows Kelsen to account for international law as a conceptually complete legal order, but at the price of opening up his theory to the same critique which drove his quest for a pure theory in the first place, ie, the rejection of the subjective, arbitrary viewpoint.

Consequently, this conceptual completeness comes at a price. By divorcing the law from any overriding moral considerations or sociological context, Kelsen's theory leaves him unable to critique precisely the kind of behaviour he wished to condemn. By relegating law to coercive norms backed by sanction, he was unable to find an objectively verifiable distinction between valid resort to war or reprisal as a form of law enforcement, and precisely the kind of unilateral, arbitrary state behaviour that his theory aimed to restrict. The structure of the system again undermines the practical utility of the theory. International law and politics again become infused in an attempt to overcome this apparent institutional problem.

III. A MIDDLE WAY? LAUTERPACHT, BRIERLY AND THE RENAISSANCE OF NATURAL LAW

Taken on their own, both Kelsen's and Morgenthau's positions can be understood as attempts to fix the apparent failings of nineteenth-century positivism, to explain the autonomy of law in different ways and, thereafter, either to justify or deny this condition in international law as a matter of fact. For both, what mattered was the objective 'validity' of legal norms, but they understood validity in opposing ways—one conceptual, the other material.[60] However, both arguably failed to provide a fully convincing account of legal normativity in a decentralised legal order like international

[59] ibid 48–55. See also the discussion in C Leben, 'Hans Kelsen and the Advancement of International Law' (1998) 9 *European Journal of International Law* 287, at 289–92; and D Zolo, 'International Peace through International Law' (1998) 9 *European Journal of International Law* 306, in particular his criticisms at 314–15.

[60] On this point, see Koskenniemi (n 13) 22.

law. Both approaches can therefore be taken, illustratively rather than literally, as two polar alternatives to the unconvincing synthesis of classical positivism, with each in a way acting as a convincing critique of the other. Morgenthau's prioritisation of function over legal form arises precisely from a view that normativity derives from factual constraint, which means he is unable (just like Austin before him) to provide a criterion capable of isolating the distinctive compliance pull of legal rules. Kelsen, more persuasively perhaps, sees law's counter-factual normativity as key, but in trying to isolate law as a system that can function coercively in the absence of the institutional context of the state, he ends up reading into international law precisely the kind of creative functional distinctions which reveal the progressive liberal politics that drove his pure theory of law in the first place.

In both cases, then, each theorist fails to provide a convincing account of international law and each leaves himself open to critique from the other perspective: Morgenthau misses the importance of law's normativity in a conceptual sense, but in trying to compensate for this absence also undermines its social-factuality. Kelsen's stress on legal form over function distances law from the actual practices and motivations of states, but in doing so also undermines law's normativity by relying on *functional* postulates, which remain unverifiable other than by reading the subjective motivations of states. Not only is each a valid criticism of the other, but each also collapses into the other: the claimed objectivity of Morgenthau's functionalism is haunted by the subjective nihilism that arises in the absence of any recognisable legal form; Kelsen's legal formalism relies on an unverifiable functional distinction.

Between these two positions, we see the elements of what is required, conceptually speaking, to give a convincing account of international law as an autonomous legal order that is binding over states. In other words, following the conceptual schema set out by Koskenniemi (above), we can say that the task is to account for the law's autonomy in both a material (its concreteness) and a conceptual (its normativity) sense.[61] The problem is that a positivist account of law which is not already enmeshed in the institutional context of the state seems—at least on a surface level—incapable of offering up a plausible means of balancing the two demands. To be convincing in this respect, one has to re-introduce an element of progressive interpretation, a normative viewpoint which sits outside of the practices of states, and orders and arranges those practices into a coherent normative order opposable to state practice. From the *inter-bellum* period onwards, this has been the challenge facing international lawyers, but the problem is that it seems

[61] Koskenniemi refers to this not as 'autonomy', but alternatively as 'objectivity' or 'relevance', though the starting point is the same: a feeling that the consensual, voluntarist explanation of international law is incapable of accounting for the law's ability to restrain political choice. See Koskenniemi (n 1) 171–82. I return again to this problem in Ch 3, section I, below.

difficult to introduce such a perspective without it falling foul of the kind of critiques levelled against the pre-war positivists. I will say more about this structural tension in Chapter 3. Here, my concern is to demonstrate how modern perspectives attempt to move between these twin demands, but do so in a way which leaves a perennial sense of structural deficiency in the law.

To illustrate this point, I will draw on the approach of two prominent and extremely influential twentieth-century jurists, James Brierly and Hersch Lauterpacht, both of whom sought to re-introduce natural law argument as critical to accounting for the autonomy of international law in international politics. However, in line with the transition begun in the previous century, they sought to do so in a distinctly 'modernist' way—tying moral values and social ends back to an underlying community will rather than simply positing them a priori. Although Lauterpacht and Brierly were certainly not identical in their respective approaches—the former perhaps more forthrightly communitarian and progressive, and the latter perhaps more pragmatic, continuously stressing the need to relate the law to the 'facts' of international relations[62]—both move within a mutually reinforcing frame that relates the need for such facts to be interpreted according to progressive aims, aims which in turn are seen to be buttressed by the facts.[63]

One can see this reconciliation straight away in Brierly's first major essay from 1924, where he sets out the 'shortcomings' of international law in the wake of the kind of criticisms levelled at it above. In fact, he quotes directly from Pound, underlining the need for international law to respond better to the changing interests of international society as a whole.[64] He stresses the need for the law to be based on ethical principles, to take account of higher values, yet following Pound, he adopts a modern, sociological discourse in order to tie those values to the evolving needs of the international community.[65] In fact, he notes how such enquiry is all the more essential in international law, for it lacks the necessary institutions capable of responding to these changing needs:

> Within any well-ordered modern state the process of adapting the law to new conditions is perpetually going on. In part, in modern times, it is a conscious process operating through legislation, through judicial decisions, or through juristic interpretation; in part it is a more subtle process. But international law lost the most fruitful seed of development that it has ever had when, far too early for the

[62] Landauer (n 12) 885.

[63] I discuss the similarities and differences between the two jurists' approaches more in R Collins, 'The Progressive Conception of International Law: Brierly and Lauterpacht in the *Interbellum*' in R McCorquodale and J-P Gauci (eds), *British Influences on International Law 1915–2015* (Leiden, Brill, forthcoming, 2016).

[64] JL Brierly, 'The Shortcomings of International Law' in H Lauterpacht and CHM Waldock (eds), *The Basis of Obligation in International Law and Other Papers by the Late James Leslie Brierly* (Oxford, Clarendon Press, 1958) 68, at 72–74 (originally published in the *British Yearbook of International Law* in 1924).

[65] ibid 78–80.

> health of the system, though doubtless inevitably, its foundation in natural law was undermined. With the triumph of the positive school the problem of development became immensely more difficult, for the system possesses hardly any of the apparatus of change that exists within a municipal system. Not only has it no legislature, and until recently no courts; but even the spontaneous growth of a new customary rule is incomparably more difficult than it is within the community of a state. For the society of states is numerically small; the bonds between them are still much weaker than those between individuals in a state.[66]

It is no coincidence that this argument has much of the same structure as that of Westlake, described in the previous chapter,[67] essentially emphasising the progressive stance of the international jurist to compensate for the inadequacies of the institutional structures of the international legal order. Lauterpacht followed a similar course. In fact, in one of his earliest essays in which he paid tribute to Westlake's contribution to international law, he lambasted the inadequacy of prevalent positivist explanations of the binding force of international law and argued for the need to re-engage with natural law, but did so again in distinctly modern, sociological terms:

> The 'Renascence of natural law' has found its way from legal philosophy and from municipal law into the domain of international law, where the influence of the new ideas was facilitated by the depressing consciousness, strengthened by bitter experience, of the practical inadequacy of positivist international law. Of course, it is not the old law of nature; it is rather the modern 'natural law with changing contents', 'the sense of right', 'the social solidarity', the 'engineering' law in terms of *promoting the ends of the international society.*[68] (emphasis added)

Both Lauterpacht and Brierly rejected the idea that international law's binding force could derive from any metaphysical notions such as the divine rights of states.[69] They shared the kind of progressive internationalism prevalent at this time amongst key inter-war jurists like Georges Scelle,[70]

[66] ibid 73.

[67] See Ch 1 above, at nn 86–87.

[68] Lauterpacht (n 8) 315. Lauterpacht's approach to natural law was essentially more pragmatic than philosophical, seeing it as a means to ensure the law's systemic completeness. For example, in another essay, he describes natural law as the 'lever of progress' in international law. See H Lauterpacht, 'The Grotian Tradition in International Law' (1946) 23 *British Yearbook of International Law* 1, at 24. Interestingly, Morgenthau attacked Lauterpacht's watered-down version of natural law for confounding together 'reality and imagination' in a way which betrayed the older natural law tradition; in contrast, he claimed that scholars such as Suarez and Grotius were 'fully aware of the aprioristic, metaphysical character of their propositions and had good philosophical reasons for adhering to them'. See Morgenthau (n 10) at 264.

[69] See, eg, JL Brierly, *The Law of Nations: An Introduction to the International Law of Peace*, 2nd edn (London, Oxford University Press, 1936) 39–41; JL Brierly, 'The Basis of Obligation in International Law' in Lauterpacht and Waldock (n 64) 3–9 (originally published in French in 1928); Lauterpacht (n 8) 43–50.

[70] On Scelle's internationalism, see A Somek, 'From the Rule of Law to the Constitutionalist Makeover: Changing European Conceptions of Public International Law' (2011) 18 *Constellations* 567, at 568–69; Koskenniemi (n 11) 327–38.

Alejandro Alvarez[71] or Hudson (above),[72] all of whom were attempting to move international law closer to the actual conditions that prevailed between states, whilst at the same time reconciling state practice with the progressive ends of international society as a whole.[73] We see this reconciliation in the preface to Lauterpacht's first major monograph in international law, where he highlights the widespread dissatisfaction with the sovereignty-centred, voluntarist dogma of pre-war international law, yet claims that international lawyers should not merely dismiss its retrogressive nature, but learn lessons from its focus on law as a science, aimed at uncovering juridical realities from the facts of state practice.[74]

In a similar fashion, Brierly explained how the nineteenth-century positivist turn had been beneficial to the study and practice of international law insofar as it recognised the importance of the distinction between the *lex lata* and arguments *de lege ferenda*.[75] As he noted, law could only claim viability and legitimacy if connected concretely to the social bases that it purports to regulate.[76] But it is precisely this kind of sociological enquiry into the prevailing conditions of international relations which led both jurists into a progressive position. For example, in a similar way to Morgenthau, Brierly saw positivism having betrayed its own premises, resulting in an absolutist (and somewhat metaphysical) doctrine of sovereignty, which clearly contradicted the facts of international life:

> [P]ositivism is false to its own professions, for it fails to observe that international practice itself habitually admits recourse to natural law or reason; and it exceeds its function when it regards itself as a system of legal philosophy, teaching that obligation can find its ultimate source in the consenting wills of the subjects of law.[77]

It is here that we see most clearly the middle way between sociological realism and neo-positivism. The doctrine of unrestrained sovereignty and state consent (associated however unfairly with the late nineteenth-century 'professionals') is not only at odds with the facts (ignoring the evident interdependence of states,[78] not to mention the reality that states constantly rely

[71] Alejandro Alvarez's progressive internationalism is well-documented, both on the bench of the PCIJ and in academia: see Koskenniemi (n 1) 209–15.

[72] See, eg, MO Hudson, *Progress in International Organization* (Stanford, CA, Stanford University Press; London, Oxford University Press, 1932).

[73] For reflections on the progressivism of this era, see Skouteris (n 1) 46–47, 98–120.

[74] Lauterpacht (n 8) x. He goes on, in fact, to claim that his critique of positivism is not the same as denying the primacy of custom and treaty in international law, which will always outflank moral concern or principles of natural law (ibid).

[75] Brierly, 'The Basis of Obligation in International Law' (n 69) 18.

[76] For the clearest exposition of Brierly's modernism in this respect, the influence of the sociological approach espoused by, inter alia, Pound, and in particular Brierly's stress on the 'facts' to prove the reality of an obligatory international law as a progressive restraint on inter-state politics, see Landauer (n 12) 884–99.

[77] Brierly, 'The Basis of Obligation in International Law' (n 69) 18.

[78] ibid 7–9.

on principles of justice, equity and 'general principles of law' in arbitration agreements),[79] but also fails in logical and conceptual terms on the basis of its own scientific premises (having, ultimately, to resort to some foundational objectives incapable of explanation on the basis of consent alone).[80]

These background criticisms flow directly into sustaining Lauterpacht's and Brierly's own accounts of the binding force of international law. For Brierly, the foundation of the law's normativity lies in a higher moral duty that ensures the binding force of rules between states.[81] For Lauterpacht, the legal order could only be sustained as an autonomous institution through a juridical hypothesis, but one which was not based on inter-state agreement (eg, *pacta sunt servanda*), but on the idea of a higher community will that would ensure the binding force of the law even in the face of recalcitrant state behaviour.[82] Like Kelsen, legal validity was seen as a matter of a norm's conformity with the foundational rules of the legal order itself, and these foundational rules themselves ultimately had to be grounded outside of the system.[83] Lauterpacht was in fact heavily influenced by Kelsen, his former teacher at the University of Vienna. However, his position—like Brierly's—was also distinctly more sociological. Both were critical of Kelsen's rigid formalism in this respect, which they thought left him unable or unwilling to admit the role of natural law or morality as foundational elements to any legal order, and therefore also unable to justify or explain the nature of the initial hypothesis upon which his theory depended.[84]

Nevertheless, whilst this reconciliation might go some way to resolve the problem of the foundation of legal obligation, they both (again like Kelsen) recognised the apparent weakness of international law theorised in these terms. Brierly, for example, on the one hand acknowledged that all that mattered for the law's conceptual completeness was its *capacity to be* ascertained and determined definitively. Yet, on the other hand, the certainty and efficiency of international law suffered as a result of the lack of centralised law-making and determining institutions of the kind found commonly in domestic legal orders.[85] He was critical of the international legal

[79] Lauterpacht (n 8) 60–67.

[80] ibid 51–59. As Hart rightly claims, such theories necessarily presuppose the existence of superior norms determining the importance of consent within legal sources—such superior norms may be sustained at a general level of societal agreement, but cannot be sustained on the basis of explicit consent. Hart (n 38) 223–25.

[81] Brierly, 'The Basis of Obligation in International Law' (n 69) 66–67.

[82] H Lauterpacht, 'The Nature of International Law and General Jurisprudence' (1932) 37 *Economica* 301, at 316–17.

[83] Brierly, 'The Basis of Obligation in International Law' (n 69) 53; H Lauterpacht, 'The Definition and Nature of International Law and its Place in Jurisprudence' in E Lauterpacht (ed), *International Law, Being the Collected Papers of Hersch Lauterpacht*, vol 1 (Cambridge, Cambridge University Press, 1970) 9, 12–13.

[84] Brierly, 'The Basis of Obligation in International Law' (n 69) 64–65; H Lauterpacht, 'Kelsen's Pure Science of International Law' in Lauterpacht (ed) (n 83) 424–29.

[85] Brierly, 'The Basis of Obligation in International Law' (n 69) 41; Brierly (n 64) 68.

order's continuing attachment to state sovereignty and its deferential respect to states' domestic jurisdiction,[86] which in turn constantly undermined the development of compulsory courts and adequate legislative machinery.[87] One can see here how Brierly's position reverses that of Kelsen to some degree. He did not see the problem of international order as following from the imposition of law, but rather the imposition of order as a necessary condition for a state of legality to flourish. In other words, it was impossible to separate completely the conceptual autonomy of the law from its institutional context. Rather than relying on and systematising the sovereign autonomy of states, Brierly saw it as necessary to annex what was in states' reserved domain, and in particular their ability to use force unilaterally, in order to secure a more coercive legal order capable of restraining state interests.[88]

Lauterpacht was even more vocal in relation to the law's institutional defects. Having accounted for the foundation of legal order at the international and domestic levels on the same basis, he argued strongly that one should not accept the evident deficiencies of international law as permanent or necessary characteristics, as Oppenheim appeared to suggest (as outlined in the previous chapter).[89] He was adamant that such defects must be regarded as temporary or transient. If the basis of obligation lay in the command of the community in both national and international legal orders, then there was nothing in theory stopping the evolution of institutions more capable of determining, expressing and enforcing this community will at the international level. Accepting international law's decentralised institutional structure as a permanent characteristic would therefore undermine law's binding nature:

> International law can form part of jurisprudence only when its present imperfections are regarded as transient. These imperfections are fundamental, and it is only because they are deemed to be provisional that it is possible to treat international law as part of jurisprudence. Once they are regarded as permanent, international law vanishes completely from the horizon of jurisprudence.[90]

This reconciliation is crucial. By equating the international and national legal orders in this way, Lauterpacht has to relativise the legality of the

[86] A point also made later in his *The Outlook for International Law* (Oxford, Clarendon Press, 1944) 10–12.

[87] Brierly, *Law of Nations* (n 69) 62–65.

[88] Brierly, 'International Law: Some Conditions for its Progress' in Lauterpacht and Waldock (n 64) 327–37.

[89] Lauterpacht (n 82) 304.

[90] H Lauterpacht, 'The Place of International Law in Jurisprudence' in Lauterpacht (ed) (n 83) 193, at 208 (paper originally published in French in (1937-IV) 62 *Recueil des Cours* 99–419). Lauterpacht was making reference here to Holland's assertion that international law was the 'vanishing point of jurisprudence'. See TE Holland, *Elements of Jurisprudence*, 9th edn (Oxford, Oxford University Press, 1900) 369.

former by reference to the latter: this not only suggests the possibility of, but also insists on the need for the international legal order to develop more centralised institutions akin to a more federal organisation found within many state-based legal orders.[91]

It is here where we see most critically the result of the compromise position or 'middle way' between the formalism of Kelsen and the functionalism of Morgenthau. Unlike Kelsen, Lauterpacht was not merely concerned with accounting for the formal (or abstract) unity of the international legal order, but attempts to explain its material effectiveness as a restraint upon available political choices.[92] As we saw, Kelsen's pure theory left him unable to account for an objectively valid reason why the idea of the just war should be read as international law's principle sanction. Whilst Lauterpacht engaged in similar doctrinal construction to support a systemic view of international law, particularly with his rejection of the non-liquet argument in the international judicial function,[93] he was able to buttress his argument philosophically by reference to natural law, as well as empirically by referring back to institutional fact. The most fundamental development in this respect was the creation of the League of Nations and the PCIJ shortly after the end of the war. Kelsen's formalism stopped him from seeing in the creation of the League or the Court a fundamental change in the nature of the international legal order: these institutions were grounded in treaties, enjoying only limited, consensual membership.[94] Lauterpacht, moving with more ease between the sociological and the normative, pictured the League Covenant as the first step in a constitutional ordering of the international legal order.[95] What mattered to him was the substance of what the Covenant purported to do: its function, not its formal grounding in the law of treaties.[96] This disconnect between form and function is also particularly evident in Brierly's textbook, which is structured around a constitutionalist reading of the international legal order, including an analysis of international legislative, executive and judicial functions. Whilst Brierly saw international law

[91] Lauterpacht (n 82) 318. On Lauterpacht's often explicit federalism, see Koskenniemi (n 11) 398 and passim.

[92] See, eg, Koskenniemi (n 1) 53.

[93] See principally H Lauterpacht, *The Function of Law in the International Community* (Oxford, Clarendon Press, 1933).

[94] See Kelsen (n 51) 39: 'Since ... the Covenant of the League of Nations and the Kellogg Pact are only instances of particular international law, these statements dealing with the "illegality" of war must be considered merely indications of the actual existence of a commonly accepted international legal conviction.'

[95] See H Lauterpacht, 'The Covenant as the Higher Law' (1936) 17 *British Yearbook of International Law* 54.

[96] Lauterpacht drew heavily on the approach of his former teacher, Arnold McNair, in making this distinction: see, eg, A McNair, 'The Functions and Differing Legal Character of Treaties' (1930) 11 *British Yearbook of International Law* 100; and further discussion below in Ch 8.

as essentially a customary legal order, he saw its future as being shaped through 'legislative' development with the creation of new multilateral conventions, annexing what was then seen as the reserved domain of states' domestic legal orders.[97]

Crucial to this institutional approach, though, is the way in which Brierly, Lauterpacht and others of this era drew on Article 38 of the PCIJ Statute to put an end to pre-war wrangling over the accepted sources of international law. Whilst Article 38 was originally conceived solely in jurisdictional terms to outline the sources of law to be taken into consideration by the Court in the cases before it, with some creative doctrinal imagination, it was seized upon by jurists of this era as concrete confirmation of the completeness of international law as a systemic, autonomous order. As Thomas Skouteris notes, 'within a few years [of the drafting of the Statute] the idea of a "doctrine of sources", in the contemporary sense of a finite list of abstract forms that determine law-creation and law-ascertainment, became introduced and consolidated as the standard approach to normativity'.[98] For instance, Lauterpacht pointed to the fact that Article 38 confirmed the availability of judicial recourse to supplementary sources, such as general principles of law, supporting his reading of the material completeness of the international legal order.[99] As he claimed, Article 38 had 'definitively removed the last vestige of the possibility of gaps conceived as a deadlock in the way of the settlement of a dispute'.[100] For Brierly, similarly, Article 38 represented 'a rich storehouse of materials for the general theory of international law'.[101]

The importance of Article 38, however, is not just that it offered a concrete anchor for the *conceptual* completeness of international law as a system. By linking the sources of international law to a general court—albeit one with limited jurisdiction—it underlines the *possibility of* international law's *material* completeness too: it can be seen to be developing towards a more mature institutional structure, similar to the domestic state, wherein

[97] Brierly, *Law of Nations* (n 69) 59–62. He stressed in particular the limitations of the law in terms of its material scope, the lack of certainty in its determination and its slow pace of development.

[98] Skouteris (n 1) 95.

[99] Lauterpacht (n 8) 68–71; Lauterpacht (n 93) 65–69; Brierly, 'The Basis of Obligation in International Law' (n 69) 17–18; Brierly, *Law of Nations* (n 69) 46–57.

[100] Lauterpacht (n 93) 67.

[101] Brierly, 'The Basis of Obligation in International Law' (n 69) 17. They were certainly not alone in expressing such views. For example, Fischer-Williams wrote at the end of the interbellum period how art 38 'stands as the text of capital importance, the solid basis of rock on which the fabric of international law has now to be built. *Securus judicat orbis terrarium.* The world through the organizations in which for international purposes it is now grouped [*sic*], has given its verdict'. JF Williams, *Aspects of Modern International Law: An Essay* (London, Oxford University Press, 1939) 38–39. See further Skouteris (n 1) 95–98.

the binding force of norms is reinforced through the determinations of authorised officials. As Carty argues:

> [Article 38] has to be seen in the wider context of a broad attempt, following the First World War, to 'institutionalise' relations among States. The reason for the absence of any in-depth consideration of the nature of the sources of international law is that, in this context, the latter was considered as an already existing and definite corpus of rules which quasi-supranational institutions had to develop and to apply effectively, against the arbitrary sovereignty of States.[102] (footnotes omitted)

Whilst this perhaps goes too far, risking a caricature of the complexities of this theoretical reconciliation, it is easy to see how Brierly's and Lauterpacht's work exemplified the kind of 'institutionalist' approach which Carty describes as pervasive amongst prominent post-war international jurists.[103] This approach essentially accepts the formal limitations of international law as a decentralised legal order. As a result of developments occurring within the international legal order, however, it is able to read the law progressively *and functionally* in order to suggest its eventual transformation into a legal order more akin to a well-functioning 'rule of law' state. What started as a theoretical problem is thus turned into an institutional problem—the perceived deficiency lying not at the level of the theory, but at the structural level of an international legal order that remains perpetually incomplete as a legal system.

As before, of course, the coherence and plausibility of such an account of international law appears to rest on the extent to which such institutional developments are indeed changing the structural condition of international law. I take up this question specifically in Part III, where I suggest a number of theoretical and practical problems in this respect. In the next, and final, chapter of Part I, my more immediate aim is to better understand this pervasive sense of structural deficiency as reflected in international legal argument. Specifically, I will show how the attempt to explain international law as an autonomous legal order always remains hampered by such perceived deficiencies, which—as I will thereafter explain—cannot be overcome or compensated for simply through progressive institutional innovation. Instead, I will argue that this problem requires us to revisit and re-imagine the coherence of the paradigms of legality against which international law is traditionally compared and found wanting.

[102] A Carty, *The Decay of International Law: A Reappraisal of the Limits of Legal Imagination in International Affairs* (Manchester, Manchester University Press, 1986) 14.

[103] Brierly's 'institutional' approach is most evident in section VII of his 'Basis of Obligation' essay (n 69) 46–56. See also Carty (n 25) 80; Landauer (n 12) 898–99. On the institutional approach of Lauterpacht, see Koskenniemi (n 11) 396–99.

IV. CONCLUSION

This chapter has outlined three alternative ways in which *inter-bellum* jurists sought to counteract the perceived deficiencies of pre-war international law. Each attempted to give an account of how law operates to control or regulate the conduct of international affairs, but each ends up only really confirming a sense of constitutional weakness or underlying deficiency. All the jurists here begin from the same problem, insofar as they see the need to demonstrate the autonomy of international legal rules in structuring the conduct of international politics. However, they are unable to sustain their particular diagnoses of this problem without at the same time admitting the inadequacies of international law thus conceived. Morgenthau's functionalism saw him take social practice seriously, but left him unable to explain the binding normativity of law. Kelsen's concern for conceptual purity left him unable to account for the coherence of his view of international law as a coercive legal order without also admitting creative political choices that seem at odds with the concrete realities of international politics. Meanwhile, whilst Lauterpacht's and Brierly's methods moved more easily between sociological realism and counter-factual idealism, their effort to reveal the objectivity of international law in the practices of states essentially depended on denying the completeness of international law as a legal system. The emerging institutionalisation of international law suggested its apparent move towards a more centralised, more autonomous, legal form, but such developments also revealed its current structural weaknesses.

Inter-bellum jurists thus developed a range of responses to the apparent weaknesses of pre-war international law, but this was only by further highlighting an apparent structural deficiency in the law which, I will now go on to argue, remains an acute problem for international legal theory. In fact, into the latter half of the twentieth century, after the further disasters of the Second World War and the creation of more ambitious international institutions in its wake, this perception of structural deficiency seems only to have been further reinforced. Contemporary doctrine and theoretical reflection seem constantly plagued by disappointment over the potential for international law to effectively constrain the passions of international politics. International law appears still to be institutionally under-developed, still failing to live up to a paradigm of legality drawn from domestic experience.

3

The Institutional Problem in Modern International Law

The clumsiness of custom-formation as a method of generating authoritative solutions to co-ordination problems is obvious enough … The need for somebody, *or some body*, to settle co-ordination problems with greater speed or certainty is apparent in any community where people are energetic and inventive in pursuit of their own or of common goods, not to mention any community threatened with military, economic, or ecological disaster. (emphasis added)

John Finnis, *Natural Law and Natural Rights*[1]

THE PREVIOUS TWO chapters have charted the difficulties faced by two successive generations of international lawyers in giving a coherent account of international law as an autonomous system of positive legal rules. The scepticism they encountered in attempting to do so would return to haunt the discipline again in the wake of the Second World War. With the growing influence of political realism, there resurfaced an image of international law as, at best, only a marginal or contingent influence in actually shaping the conduct of international politics.[2] As such, another generation of jurists would continue to have to defend both the reality and efficacy of international law for some years more.[3] In the course of doing so, however, the modern discipline has grown an increasingly thick skin, not only by drawing on the empirical reality of widespread state compliance with

[1] J Finnis, *Natural Law and Natural Rights*, 2nd edn (Oxford, Oxford University Press, 2011) 245–46.

[2] See, eg, M Koskenniemi, 'Carl Schmitt, Morgenthau, and the Image of Law in International Relations' in M Byers (ed), *The Role of Law in International Politics: Essays in International Relations and International Law* (Oxford, Oxford University Press, 2000) 17–34.

[3] See, for instance, W Friedmann, 'National Sovereignty, International Cooperation, and the Reality of International Law' (1962–63) 10 *UCLA Law Review* 739; R Falk, 'The Reality of International Law' (1962) 14 *World Politics* 353; W Friedmann, 'The Reality of International Law—A Reappraisal' (1971) 10 *Columbia Journal of International Law* 46; I Brownlie, 'The Reality and Efficacy of International Law' (1981) 52 *British Yearbook of International Law* 1; A d'Amato, 'Is International Law Really "Law"?' (1985) 79 *Northwestern University Law Review* 1293; and see the discussion in M Prost, *The Concept of Unity in Public International Law* (Oxford, Hart Publishing, 2012) 2.

international legal norms,[4] but also by relying on arguably more sophisticated theoretical models in doing so.[5] With the evident expansion of international law in the second half of the twentieth century, including a growing number of increasingly interventionist regimes and institutions, it has come to seem somewhat absurd to deny the evident reality of international law in practice. By the mid-1990s, in fact, Tom Franck could confidently assert the arrival of international law's 'post-ontological' era.[6]

Nevertheless, it is quite revealing that international lawyers have to make such defences at all. Indeed, what is most interesting about Franck's bold claim is that he immediately followed it up with a call-to-arms to international lawyers to face up to what he saw as more pressing challenges related to the effectiveness, enforceability, intelligibility and overall fairness of international law.[7] These kinds of 'rule of law' concerns remain pervasive in the modern discipline, which, despite its ontological self-assurance, seems perpetually troubled by the failure to realise a more autonomous international legal order capable of effectively controlling the conduct of international politics.[8] We might be able to draw a line between the legal and the political at the international level, but it is clearly a blurry, contestable and ultimately more malleable line, leaving the operation of the law very difficult to disentangle from the interplay of underlying political forces.[9]

How are we to understand this recurrent sense of frustration or disappointment? The argument that I have advanced so far in Part I is that, in the main, international lawyers have seen the decentralised institutional architecture of the international legal order as a kind of structural weakness or—as Alexander Somek has recently put this—a 'constitutional deficiency', explaining in part why international law largely fails to live up to the kind of public order values one might associate with the rule of law.[10] As he explains:

> The international legal system is constitutionally deficient in precisely the sense of the term which reflects what we have come to expect a constitutional system to accomplish. Under conditions of constitutional deficiency—in decisive matters, at

[4] L Henkin, *How Nations Behave: Law and Foreign Policy*, 2nd edn (Columbia University Press, 1979) 47.

[5] The most influential account in recent years being HLA Hart, *The Concept of Law*, 3rd edn (Oxford, Clarendon Press, 2012).

[6] T Franck, *Fairness in International Law and Institutions* (Oxford, Oxford University Press, 1995) 6.

[7] ibid 6–7.

[8] See, eg, S Beaulac, 'The Rule of Law in International Law Today' in G Palombella and N Walker (eds), *Relocating the Rule of Law* (Oxford, Hart Publishing, 2009) 197, at 212–20 in particular. I return to this point again in Ch 7, below, but I reflect more on these concerns in R Collins, 'The Rule of Law and the Quest for Constitutional Substitutes in International Law' (2014) 83 *Nordic Journal of International Law* 87, at 93–96.

[9] C Warbrick, 'Brownlie's Principles of Public International Law: An Assessment' (2000) 11 *European Journal of International Law* 621, at 626–27.

[10] See, eg, A Somek, 'From the Rule of Law to the Constitutionalist Makeover: Changing European Conceptions of Public International Law' (2011) 18 *Constellations* 567, at 576; A Somek, 'Kelsen Lives!' (2007) 18 *European Journal of International Law* 409, at 432–33.

> any rate—obligations are not clear … Generally, where obligations are unclear, the powerful have an easy time of kicking the powerless around … A constitution constrains the powerful, not merely by submitting their conduct to the discipline of rules but also by setting a limit to the resourceful renditions of what they would like to present as legal and constitutional.[11]

The problem, in other words, is that in a decentralised legal order there is an inherent lack of clarity—or what Martti Koskenniemi has, more accurately, described as a condition of *indeterminacy*—that is brought about by the structure of the system itself.[12] In the absence of the kind of official or constitutional organs found at the state level, the creation, determination, application and enforcement of international legal norms are left largely in the hands of the same actors—primarily, though not exclusively, states—that the system also purports to bind. It is precisely in this sense, in fact, that HLA Hart denied that international law could be considered as a legal system.[13] Whilst many international lawyers have, quite rightly, taken issue with Hart's claim in this respect, they have been far less successful in rebutting the perception of constitutional deficiency which informed his conclusion.

In what follows, however, I will argue that it makes little sense to treat the structural indeterminacy of international law as a deficiency in this sense. Indeterminacy is intrinsic to a decentralised legal order; it cannot be otherwise without undermining a core aspect of its legitimacy. As such, the recurring perception of deficiency arises only as a result of the long-standing—and widely shared—assumption that international law should function ideally so as to regulate or govern the conduct of international politics. Whilst not agreeing with Hart's conclusion, I will use his theory to illustrate this problem—insofar as it perpetuates this functional understanding as inherent to law—and, in doing so, I will demonstrate why one cannot simply work around, compensate for or explain away structural indeterminacy. Ultimately, I believe that the problem—so far as it is a problem—lies primarily in the theoretical presumptions perpetuated by the analytical method in legal theory, of which Hart's theory remains the leading example. I will say more about this in Part II. My immediate aim is simply to show the pervasiveness of the functional presumptions about law (and international law in particular), which have remained until now largely unchallenged and which result in a thoroughly unconvincing push for continuous institutional reform at the international level. This, in short, is international law's 'institutional problem'.

To explain this problem, I first (in section I) set out the parameters of a pervasive discourse in modern international law, which necessarily presumes that international legal rules should function as autonomous solutions—that

[11] Somek, 'Kelsen Lives!' (n 10) 433.

[12] M Koskenniemi, *From Apology to Utopia: The Structure of International Legal Argument* (Cambridge, Cambridge University Press, 2005).

[13] See Ch X of Hart (n 5).

is, provide determinate outcomes—to specific normative problems. Next, in section II, I show how this view is inherently problematic due to the apparent indeterminacy of the international legal order, thus perpetuating the sense of structural or constitutional deficiency outlined above. In section III, I illustrate this perceived problem through the example of Hart's attempt to reconcile international law as a legal system. As noted above, I do so less to prove Hart's theory correct and more to demonstrate how if one presumes, as Hart does, that legal systems should help secure determinate normative standards, international law cannot but appear deficient at a core, constitutional level. Insofar as international lawyers have therefore tended to set Hart up as a kind of 'bogey man' figure who misunderstood the character of international law, I show how the attempt to qualify or correct his theory is unconvincing: it fails to challenge the kind of functional presumption that underpins and gives meaning to his theory. In section IV, I will use the example of the ascertainment of customary legal norms under international law's sources doctrine—a doctrine that is commonly understood to function as a kind of proto-rule of recognition on Hart's account—in order to further illustrate the effect of structural indeterminacy in undermining the kind of autonomy discourse mentioned above.

Before I begin, a caveat (or perhaps explanation) is necessary in relation to my use of Hart's work in what follows, particularly as I return to critique Hart's account at length in Part II. My focusing on Hart here is certainly not to suggest that his is the only relevant or plausible understanding of legal systems in general, or the international legal system in particular. However, whilst not endorsed by all international lawyers,[14] it still matters that most works defending a systemic construction of international law make reference to Hart's account (even if disagreeing with his substantive conclusions about international law),[15] not to mention that Hartian terminology is widely used in practice, particularly in influential bodies of jurists like the International Law Commission (ILC).[16] More broadly, despite subsequent

[14] For criticism of Hart's approach and method, see, eg, A d'Amato, 'The Neo-positivist Concept of International Law' (1965) 59 *American Journal of International Law* 321; WL Morison, 'The Schools Revisited' in R St J Macdonald and DM Johnston (eds), *The Structure and Process of International Law: Essays in Legal Philosophy, Doctrine, and Theory* (The Hague, Martinus Nijhoff, 1983) 131, at 144–55; and I Brownlie, *The Rule of Law in International Affairs: International Law at the 50th Anniversary of the United Nations* (The Hague, Martinus Nijhoff, 1998) 3–6.

[15] See, eg, d'Amato (n 14) 322–24; GJH van Hoof, *Rethinking the Sources of International Law* (Deventer, Kluwer, 1983) 44–56; T Franck, *The Power of Legitimacy among Nations* (New York, Oxford University Press, 1990) 183–94. See the discussion in D Lefkowitz, '(Dis)solving the Chronological Paradox in Customary International Law: A Hartian Approach' (2008) 21 *Canadian Journal of Law and Jurisprudence* 129, at 137–44 in particular.

[16] See, eg, ILC, *Draft Articles on Responsibility of States for Internationally Wrongful Acts, with Commentaries* (2001), particularly 31–32, at paras 1–5; available at: http://legal.un.org/ilc/texts/instruments/english/commentaries/9_6_2001.pdf; however, see the discussion below at nn 77–79.

refinement, criticism and rejection from many quarters, Hart's account arguably endures as the most influential positivist legal theory in the modern era (at the very least, in the Anglo-American world).[17] At the same time, of course, none of the above actually demonstrates the coherence and cogency of Hart's account, and there arguably still remains the risk that by relying on Hart to begin with, one automatically limits the relevant questions posed in thinking about the nature of law in general or international law in particular.[18] This is a real danger, but it is also exactly the point that I wish to make. In Part II, I will argue that the pervasive influence of Hart, and the analytical method he adopted, has tended to restrict the questions we ask about the nature of law in the global context. In this respect, Hart and his followers can be criticised for straying into evaluative judgements based on certain functional presumptions about law which remain theoretically under-elaborated, as well as normatively undefended. The point is not necessarily that these presumptions are wrong—though, in fact, I believe that they are—but only that they require the sort of independent normative justification that is precluded by the tenets of analytical method. Nevertheless, my more immediate concern—and the reason why I think it remains useful to use Hart's theory here—is that international lawyers themselves do, in the main, largely share this view of law's function. As such, the current chapter is intended more as an 'imminent critique', demonstrating that this view of law's necessary function cannot but result in a perception of a deficiency or weakness of exactly the sort that caused Hart's scepticism in the first place. In other words, it aims to show why the simple factual response to Hart necessarily fails.

I. EXPLAINING THE AUTONOMY OF INTERNATIONAL LAW

So far in Part I, I have tried to illustrate a recurring disciplinary anxiety to defend the autonomy of international law as a persuasive restraint upon the conduct of international politics. This 'discourse of institutional autonomy', as one recent commentator has described it, is arguably pathological in modern international law.[19] We saw it in the approach of jurists like James Brierly or Hersch Lauterpacht outlined in the previous chapter, both of whom sought to rely on natural law arguments as a way of explaining the

[17] See generally MH Kramer, C Grant, B Colburn and A Hatzistavrou (eds), *The Legacy of H.L.A. Hart: Legal, Political, and Moral Philosophy* (Oxford, Oxford University Press, 2008).

[18] I owe this observation to conversations with Margaret Martin, though to some degree the same concern also runs through Jason Beckett's 'The Hartian Tradition in International Law' (2008) 1 *Journal of Jurisprudence* 51.

[19] C Reus-Smit, 'The Politics of International Law' in C Reus-Smit (ed), *The Politics of International Law,* (Cambridge, Cambridge University Press, 2004) 14, at 36–37.

completeness of international law as a system binding over states.[20] We can see a similar concern in the more pervasive form of 'modern positivism' that tends to dominate 'mainstream' understanding of international law today.[21] On this account, international law is understood as:

> [A] *set or system* of rules emanating from a narrow variety of accepted sources, but recognises that the rules themselves require identification (or proof), interpretation, and application; processes which leave scope for the legal imagination but which are, nonetheless, *sufficiently confined to leave the international legal process distinct from politics or morality.*[22] (emphasis added)

Towards the end of the previous chapter, in my discussion of Brierly and Lauterpacht's approach, I suggested that this autonomy discourse is committed to showing what Koskenniemi describes as 'objectivity' in international law. Objectivity on these terms essentially means reconciling, on the one hand, international law's 'concreteness', its grounding in social practices, and, on the other, its 'normativity', that is, its counter-factual binding force.[23] Of course, as Koskenniemi also acknowledges, it does not really amount to much, nowadays, to say that law must be grounded at some level in social facts—that, broadly speaking, international law can therefore be considered as an 'institutional' rather than philosophical practice. As we have seen, the more demanding challenge has been in accounting for international law's objectivity in this counter-factual sense, or, as Koskenniemi puts this, 'how to extract "international law" from other aspects of social life among States, i.e. how to distinguish between political and legal obligation, convenience and custom, violence and enforcement'.[24] As he further explains:

> Law, we learn, arises from human will and interest but can be known regardless of any such will or interest. As a matter of legislation, law is subjective, as a matter of adjudication, objective. If there is anything on which international lawyers—or maybe jurists generally—agree, it is the importance of the distinction between

[20] What distinguished such approaches from an older philosophical tradition in international law was precisely this commitment to the systemic integrity of the law conceived as an autonomous whole. Natural law provided an anchor for this systemic construction, but also a means by which jurists could 'fill in the gaps', outlining the completeness of international law as a normative solution to any given international problem. On this point, see above in Ch 2, section III; and see also M Koskenniemi, 'Lauterpacht: The Victorian Tradition in International Law' (1997) 8 *European Journal of International Law* 215, at 221, 225.

[21] See R Collins, 'Modernist-Positivism and the Problem of Institutional Autonomy in International Law' in R Collins and ND White (eds), *International Organizations and the Idea of Autonomy: Institutional Independence in the International Legal Order* (Abingdon, Routledge, 2011) 22–47.

[22] See C Warbrick, 'The Theory of International Law: Is There an English Contribution?' in P Allott et al, *Theory and International Law: An Introduction* (London, British Institute of International and Comparative Law, 1991) 47, at 61. See also A Paulus and B Simma, 'Responsibility of Individuals for Human Rights Abuses in Internal Conflicts: A Positivist View' (1999) 93 *American Journal of International Law* 302, at 307 in particular.

[23] Koskenniemi (n 12) 17–23 and passim.

[24] M Koskenniemi, 'Theory: Implications for the Practitioner' in Allott et al (n 22) 1, at 7.

> law-creation and law-ascertainment, political opinion and the legal norm. Something of the very identity of law may be contained in that distinction.[25]

Certainly, Koskenniemi may be guilty of over-playing the distinction between law creation and adjudication here. It is unlikely that many jurists—international or otherwise, including many of those surveyed in Part I so far—would see such a clear distinction between the legal and the political realms, or indeed such a bright light between law's enactment and its ascertainment in practice. However, it would be misleading to accuse Koskenniemi of any naivety in this respect. He acknowledges widespread acceptance of what Hart might call 'the relative indeterminacy' or 'open texture' of law in this regard.[26] His point is rather more subtle (and thus also easily misunderstood). To explain further, consider the following remarks from Oscar Schachter:

> A legal system must, in my view, have a relative degree of autonomy. It cannot be nothing but 'power politics' nor can it be only a specialized or symbolic language to describe behaviour. It lacks the character of law if it is not in some degree 'binding', that is, it must be a means of independent control that effectively limits the acts of the entities subject to it. To that degree, law must be independent of politics ... But acknowledging the necessity of that degree of autonomy still allows us to recognize that factors of a non-legal character determine or influence the creation, application and modification of the norms and procedures that constitute the legal system.[27]

Schachter's reference to the 'relative autonomy' of law is no appeal to a 'discredited' or overly naïve form of legal objectivity.[28] He does not claim that law—domestic or international—would be objectively ascertainable or applicable without recourse to sociological, ethical, political or other external factors, only that it cannot simply be *assimilated to* any one or other of these factors if it is to serve any useful social purpose.[29] As the International Court of Justice (ICJ) also claimed in the *South West Africa* advisory opinion, even if international law is deemed to serve certain important moral ends, in order for it to do so, it must be possible to objectively validate the existence of binding legal rules in a way which does not directly implicate this underlying reason or purpose to begin with.[30] It is for this

[25] ibid 4; and see more comprehensively Koskenniemi (n 12) 22–23 and passim.

[26] Hart (n 5), 128–32, 138–39; Koskenniemi (n 12) 36–41.

[27] O Schachter, 'The Nature and Process of Legal Development in International Society' in Macdonald and Johnston (n 14) 745, at 747.

[28] Koskenniemi (n 12) 25.

[29] See also O Schachter, *International Law in Theory and Practice* (Dordrecht, Martinus Nijhoff, 1991) 34–46.

[30] The ICJ was asked to give effect to certain humanitarian objectives and retorted that '[i]n order to generate legal rights and obligations', any such moral objectives had to be 'given juridical expression and clothed in legal form'. The ICJ recognised that international law was there to serve a social need, but 'precisely for that reason it can do so only through and within the limits of its own discipline. *Otherwise, it is not a legal service that would be rendered*'. (emphasis added) *South West Africa, Second Phase*, Judgment, ICJ Reports 1966, 6, at 34, paras 51 and 49.

reason, in fact, that many of the more 'instrumentalist' theories developed in the late twentieth century—for example, rational choice,[31] policy science[32] or interdisciplinary (international law and international relations) perspectives[33]—have often proved so controversial, insofar as they appear to deny, or at least are unable to account for, the autonomy of international legal norms in this normative, counter-factual sense.[34] To account for the autonomy of law on these terms, as Koskenniemi acknowledges, is simply to acknowledge something arguably intrinsic to law and particularly important to the acceptability or persuasiveness of international legal argument:

> Legal concepts and categories do have a degree of autonomy which cannot be explained simply by reducing them to apologies for class interests or ideologies. To understand the law we need to count for this autonomy, the persisting intuition that legal argument somehow follows a logic which is external to lawyers' preferences or those of their social group.[35]

To say that law is autonomous on these terms, therefore, is simply to recognise that it possesses the qualities of a legal system. Despite scepticism from some quarters—most notably from Hart—it is surely beyond doubt that international law now exists, and is widely understood, as an autonomous system in this sense.[36] Indeed, following this logic, we could simply claim that this kind of systemic understanding is 'axiomatic' or intrinsic to the very idea of legal reasoning.[37] Whether or not this is the case, it remains true that international law's existence as a legal system is confirmed regularly in state practice and judicial opinion, as well as in the studies of eminent bodies of jurists like the ILC.[38] In fact, in his role as ILC Rapporteur on the topic of fragmentation in international law, Koskenniemi is quite explicit in confirming this systemic understanding:

> International law is a legal system. Its rules and principles (i.e. its norms) act in relation to and should be interpreted against the background of other rules and

[31] For an example of this kind of approach, see, eg, JL Goldsmith and EA Posner, *The Limits of International Law* (Oxford, Oxford University Press, 2005).

[32] For critical discussion, see I Scobbie, 'A View of Delft: Some Thoughts about Thinking about International Law' in M Evans (ed), *International* Law, 4th edn (Oxford, Oxford University Press, 2014) 53, at 68–71 and 74–76.

[33] See generally M Koskenniemi, 'Miserable Comforters: International Relations as New Natural Law' (2009) 15 *European Journal of International Relations* 395; J Klabbers, 'The Relative Autonomy of International Law or The Forgotten Politics of Interdisciplinarity' (2005) 1 *Journal of International Law & International Relations* 35.

[34] Klabbers (n 33) 42.

[35] Koskenniemi (n 12) 67.

[36] See, eg, E Benvenisti, 'The Conception of International Law as a Legal System' (2008) 50 *German Yearbook of International Law* 393; O Casanovas, *Unity and Pluralism in Public International Law* (The Hague, Martinus Nijhoff, 2001) 14–18.

[37] A Gourgourinis, 'General/Particular International Law and Primary/Secondary Rules: Unitary Terminology of a Fragmented System' (2011) 22 *European Journal of International Law* 993, at 996; Casanovas (n 36) 15.

[38] Gourgourinis (n 37) 998–1003.

> principles. As a legal system, international law is not a random collection of such norms. There are meaningful relationships between them. Norms may thus exist at higher and lower hierarchical levels, their formulation may involve greater or lesser generality and specificity and their validity may date back to earlier or later moments in time.[39]

It is easy to see how this systemic explanation might appear sufficient as an answer to Schachter's challenge. In fact, it might also seem to collapse the apparent dichotomy between law's concreteness and normativity, at least insofar as the system itself can be understood to regulate the social processes by which law is created and, thereafter, the conditions for determining its objective validity in practice.[40] To speak of objectivity on these terms would not be to suggest that international law can be isolated from political opinion and practice, but would simply be to imply its 'distinctness' from political or moral forms of argumentation.[41] Returning again to Schachter's point, we can in fact see exactly this kind of reconciliation. In order to give an account of the relative autonomy of international law, he outlines the role played by the doctrine of sources, which acts as a kind of Hartian 'rule of recognition' for ascertaining the validity of international law.[42] As he claims:

> The principal intellectual instrument in the last century for *providing objective standards of legal validation* has been the doctrine of sources. That doctrine which became dominant in the nineteenth century and continues to prevail today lays down *verifiable conditions for ascertaining and validating legal presumptions.* The conditions are the observable manifestations of the 'wills' of states as revealed in the *processes* by which norms are formed.[43] (emphasis added)

On this explanation, sources doctrine (as set down in Article 38 of the ICJ Statute)[44] acts as a bridge between law's concreteness ('the observable manifestations of the "wills" of states') and its normativity in practice

[39] ILC, 'Fragmentation of International Law: Difficulties Arising from the Diversification and Expansion of International Law', in *Report of the International Law Commission*, 58th Session (2006), UN Doc A/61/10 (2006), Ch XII, p 407, para 251(1), available at: http://legal.un.org/docs/?path=../ilc/reports/2006/english/chp12.pdf&lang=EFSRAC.

[40] D Georgiev, 'Politics or Rule of Law: Deconstruction and Legitimacy in International Law' (1993) 4 *European Journal of International Law* 1, at 3.

[41] ibid 4.

[42] I will explain Hart's use of this concept at length in section III below.

[43] Schachter (n 27) 762. See also S Besson and J Tasioulas, 'Introduction' in S Besson and J Tasioulas (eds), *The Philosophy of International Law* (Oxford, Oxford University Press, 2010) 1, at 10–11, who make a similar point.

[44] Article 38 includes as the sources to be applied by the International Court of Justice: 'international conventions, whether general or particular, establishing rules expressly recognized by the contesting states ... international custom, as evidence of a general practice accepted as law ... the general principles of law recognized by civilized nations ... [and] judicial decisions and the teachings of the most highly qualified publicists of the various nations, as subsidiary means for the determination of rules of law'. For a discussion of the broader significance of art 38, see above (Ch 2, section III) and further below (section III).

('as revealed in the *processes* by which norms are formed'). Employed in this way, the doctrine of sources, alongside other systemic criteria, or 'secondary rules' (for example, the *lex posterior* or *lex specialis* rules, rules of treaty interpretation etc), provide the ICJ judge with a seemingly objective basis for ascertaining and applying the law to concrete situations.[45] Undoubtedly, there will be considerable theoretical disagreement as to how the system is understood and therefore how judges should go about fulfilling their functions within the Court:[46] for instance, as to how far moral or equitable principles or other considerations should enter into judicial reasoning (as to some extent Article 38 seems to permit);[47] whether legal standards can be said to be 'lacking' in a legal system in the absence of an agreed-upon legal rule (ie, whether 'gaps' are theoretically possible within a legal system);[48] or even at the foundational level of legal obligation itself (that is, what validates the ordering principles, sources or other secondary rules to begin with).[49] Still, the fact that this disagreement tends to concern the *nature of* the system, rather than its existence per se, and that we are able to talk about a judicial function at all,[50] seems only to confirm or presuppose the existence of a relatively autonomous normative practice about which we can have such legitimate disagreement.

Nevertheless, the problem here is precisely that different participants in these processes *do* tend to disagree, not only as to what the law is and how it might apply in the particular situation before them (and therefore what the likely outcome of any problem is), but also in their understanding of how the system functions overall. The decentralised institutional architecture of international law *facilitates* such competing understandings, therefore undermining its ability to function—on Schachter's terms—as 'a means of independent control that effectively limits the acts of the entities subject to it'. The fundamental problem, in other words, is that this kind of pre-emptive determinacy appears to be necessarily precluded by the structural condition of a decentralised legal order. In the absence of the kind of centralised

[45] JE Alvarez, *International Organizations as Law-Makers* (Oxford, Oxford University Press, 2005) 47.

[46] Indeed, such differences are often voiced internally through the separate and dissenting opinions given in particular cases. See, eg, RP Anand, 'The Role of Individual and Dissenting Opinions in International Adjudication' (1965) 14 *International and Comparative Law Quarterly* 788, particularly at 800–01.

[47] Koskenniemi (n 12) 34. And as he notes, later jurisprudence of the court is decidedly less conservative in this respect.

[48] On the argument that such a view would be incompatible with the idea of an autonomous international legal order, see H Lauterpacht, *The Function of Law in the International Community* (Oxford, Clarendon Press, 1933).

[49] For instance, contrast Kelsen's hypothetical *grundnorm* with the more social-conventional approach of Hart: see discussion in Hart (n 5) 234–36.

[50] For a good, recent overview, see G Hernandez, *The International Court of Justice and the Judicial Function* (Oxford, Oxford University Press, 2014).

institutions one normally finds at the state level, the 'processes' by which international law is validated, ascertained—or, indeed, interpreted, applied and enforced—are simply left in the hands of international legal participants themselves (states, essentially), who will inevitably attempt to justify unilateral political conduct by bringing law to their side. This indeterminacy is implicated within the doctrine of sources itself, insofar as questions as to the existence and binding effect of legal norms tend only to revert to the practices and opinions of states. Schachter himself admits this, conceding that the absence of a centralised legislative body and, thereafter, independent courts possessing compulsory jurisdiction invokes problems of national bias that undermine the law's objectivity in actually determining conduct and resolving political disputes.[51] It is doubtful, therefore, that this systemic explanation actually gets Schachter all of the way he wants to go. As I show in the next section, indeterminacy is not something that can be read out of international law or somehow worked around: the system itself is perpetually, inherently or—more precisely—*structurally* indeterminate.

II. INTERNATIONAL LAW AS A LEGAL SYSTEM: THE PROBLEM OF STRUCTURAL INDETERMINACY

To say that international law is structurally indeterminate is not to undermine the claim that international law can be understood as an autonomous legal system, though it does qualify what is implied by this claim to autonomy. From one perspective, to defend the autonomy of international law would just be to account for the 'formal' qualities of law as implied in a systemic construction, that is, to recognise that legal argumentation must have a basis of validity which is independent of any subjective moral or political reasons that we may or may not have for abiding by any given norm.[52] In other words, notwithstanding the very good reasons we might have to follow or refrain from any given course of conduct, legal argumentation is meant to introduce new, 'content-independent' reasons, which will necessarily claim to displace the other reasons we might have for acting.[53] On this view, then, the autonomy of legal reasoning is confirmed simply by 'validating' legal norms by reference to criteria entirely endogenous to the system itself.

From another perspective, however, it is doubtful that this abstract systematicity is sufficient to show the autonomy of international law, if this autonomy is understood in a stronger, more pre-emptive sense. To put this

[51] Schachter (n 27) 765–67.

[52] On this point, see R Collins and A Bohm, 'International Law as Professional Practice: The Bounds of Legal Autonomy' in A Nollkaemper, J d'Aspremont, W Werner and T Gazzini (eds), *International Law as a Profession* (Cambridge, Cambridge University Press, 2016, forthcoming).

[53] See, eg, N Gur, 'Are Legal Rules Content-Independent Reasons?' (2011) 5 *Problema* 175.

point the other way, simply confirming that international law follows its own systemic logic might just as much prove the *instrumentality* of law for whoever takes up the task of legal argumentation. In particular, states will inevitably use the autonomous logic of the system to justify their conduct (or to condemn the actions of others), thereby bringing the justification of legality to their side. This instrumentality need not be seen as a problem as such, but it will necessarily appear problematic if we presume that international law should pre-empt or compel the political choices of states. As such, insofar as we see international law as a normative solution to any particular problem or dispute, or as a means to resolve disagreement, such functionality would seem to require that we not only show the distinctness of law as a system of reasoning, but that this reasoning is capable of actually constraining or restricting political choice. As Koskenniemi further explains:

> In as much as law has the function of guiding problem-solution (that is, in as much as it has a controlling social function) it must be envisaged as a set of directives, standards, rules etc. which have "binding force" in that they claim to determine a preference between competing solutions (rival meanings).[54]

The problem, then, as the analyses of the previous chapters have shown, is that international law *does* tend to be judged by its capacity to secure determinate resolution to specific problems in this sense. Despite disagreement about the ends and values of international law, or at least what such purposes and principles actually mean in concrete terms—peace, global justice, human rights etc—it is rarely contested that international law should function, ideally, so as to better secure such goals in the face of recalcitrant state behaviour. On these terms, it becomes difficult to resist the conclusion that international law is deficient or defective at a structural, constitutional level.

This point is easily misunderstood. In highlighting structural indeterminacy, Koskenniemi is certainly not suggesting that domestic legal norms are any more determinate, either on their face value, or as a result of the clarity of their drafting or exposition. The point is rather that at this level, there is ordinarily some agreed-upon process by which legal norms can be authoritatively determined in specific cases and an institutionalised hierarchy according to which divergences in interpretation or application of the law between authorised decision-makers can be definitely resolved. At the international level, in contrast, the lack of any such centralised architecture means that questions as to the existence, meaning and specific applicability of legal norms must be, in the main, determined by the very same participants that the law purports to bind. As Jochen von Bernstoff explains in reflecting upon Koskenniemi's argument:

> For a legal system that … primarily relies on 'auto-interpretation', the consequences of [indeterminacy] … might indeed be more dramatic than for a legal

[54] Koskenniemi (n 12) 27.

> system that disposes of an encompassing system of compulsory jurisdiction. In the absence of binding judicial settlements, legal arguments advanced by states or other actors can easily be countered by an equally valid opposing argumentation. *Without authoritative decisions, the problem of 'indeterminacy' becomes more acute.*[55] (emphasis added)

In other words, the international legal system is purposefully structured so as to *facilitate* competing determinations of legal rules: the validity, scope and applicability of any legal norm always remains subject to the free interplay of political forces characteristic of a decentralised legal order. Any political position can be masked as a legally justified course of conduct, and each legal justification can just as easily be denounced as political manoeuvre. A systemic reading of international law will of course allow legal participants to argue that *there is* a correct, specifically legal answer to any given problem or dispute, but the system itself is incapable of—indeed, *precluded from*—determining absolutely what that correct answer is. In other words, the system serves to perpetuate as much as prevent the pursuit of discrete political agendas; it provides a means of legitimising as much as limiting particular viewpoints.[56] As a result, the unilateral behaviour of any actor can nearly always be conceptualised as permissible legal conduct by prioritising one rule over another or by choosing one interpretation of a particular rule over another. In short, international law seems almost infinitely malleable, incapable of providing a value-free, apolitical or non-arbitrary solution to any dispute, and therefore 'singularly useless as a means for justifying or criticizing international behaviour'.[57]

These are damning words, but Koskenniemi's intention in pointing to this indeterminacy is not necessarily to suggest any fault or deficiency at the international level. Rather, he seeks to show that such indeterminacy is inherent within—indeed, intrinsic to—a customary, decentralised legal order such as international law. In other words, the legitimacy (or, at least acceptability) of international law is conditioned by this indeterminacy. Even where there is agreement to regulate collective action problems or specific normative disputes through the creation of specific rules or legal regimes, this legalisation only transfers the political and moral questions to the legal realm, as each relevant actor seeks to secure their own goals through the imprimatur of the legal form. Rules can be defined very precisely where strategic interests dictate (for instance, the rule defining the twelve nautical mile limit of territorial waters under the law of the sea),[58] but the opposite

[55] J von Bernstorff, 'Sisyphus was an International Lawyer. On Martti Koskenniemi's "From Apology to Utopia" and the Place of Law in International Politics' (2006) 7 *German Law Journal* 1015, at 1022–23.

[56] See, eg, Benvenisti (n 36) 397–99.

[57] Koskenniemi (n 12) 67. For broader considerations of similar themes, see also C Tomlins, 'How Autonomous is Law?' (2007) 3 *Annual Review of Law and Social Science* 45, at 58–59.

[58] See art 3 of the United Nations Convention on the Law of the Sea 1982.

is also true, where interests require leaving rules open to context and future discretion (for instance, in defining key terms such as 'aggression' or 'armed attack' in the context of the *jus ad bellum*).[59] The very rationale for securing a rule in an area of fundamental importance, such as the prohibition of the use of force, will at other times require setting aside, seeking exception from or otherwise arguing some necessary defence to the breach of that same rule:

> And because no rule is more important than the reason for which it is enacted, even the most unambiguous rule is infected by the disagreements that concern how that reason should be understood and how it ranks with competing ones ... It follows that it is possible to defend *any* course of action—including deviation from a clear rule—by professionally impeccable legal arguments that look from rules to their underlying reasons, make choices between several rules as well as rules and exceptions, and interpret rules in the context of evaluative standards.[60]

I shall return to this point again in concluding, below, and then again in Part III. For now, the fact remains that the search for objectivity in international law, to show its autonomy in this stronger, pre-emptive sense, seems impossible to realise due to the apparent institutional problem of modern international law.[61]

III. HLA HART AND THE 'CONSTITUTIONAL DEFICIENCY' OF INTERNATIONAL LAW

Thus far, I have sought to show how a recurring effort to explain international law as an autonomous legal order capable of securing determinate solutions to defined normative problems will be inevitably undermined by the decentralised institutional architecture of the international legal order. In particular, in the preceding section, I outlined how the explanation of international law as a legal system cannot serve to satisfy this kind of autonomy discourse; a systemic construction implies the relative autonomy of international law as a form of normative practice in one sense, but the particular structural form of the international legal system itself only highlights the openness, malleability and contestability of legal rules in the conduct of international politics. As such, if we think that the function of law generally, and international law specifically, is to restrain political choice in this way—international law as a form of 'problem-solution'—its decentralised institutional architecture will inevitably and necessarily appear problematic. In other words, we will confirm exactly the kind of 'constitutional deficiency' that was a recurrent cause for concern in the preceding chapters.

59 Koskenniemi (n 12) 591–95.
60 ibid 591.
61 ibid 26.

This constitutional deficiency is revealed in Hart's consideration of the legal nature of international law—though, as Somek notes, Hart himself does not use the term explicitly.[62] Rather, he saw the absence of certain centralised institutional structures as undermining the idea that international law was a functioning legal system—it was, instead, simply a 'set' of primary norms,[63] more characteristic of the law of a 'primitive' society:[64]

> The absence of these institutions means that the rules for states resemble that simple form of social structure, consisting only of primary rules of obligation, which, when we find it amongst societies of individuals, we are accustomed to contrast with a developed legal system.[65]

Given the preceding analysis and the widespread recognition of international law's status as a legal system—amongst states as much as international lawyers—this claim appears somewhat problematic. Indeed, on the basis of Hart's own methodological approach, that is, the need to conceptualise law by reference to how it is practiced and understood by legal participants themselves, this conclusion does, on the surface at least, seem deeply counter-intuitive.[66] In fact, I think there are very good reasons why Hart is wrong, not only in the rather bogus implication that international law is somehow primitive,[67] but also at a deeper, methodological level. I will say more about this in Part II, where I point out deep inconsistencies in Hart's account and begin to question the functional presumptions which propelled this conclusion. My more immediate concern, however, is that I believe much of the effort to disprove Hart's claim has seen its weakness simply as a kind of factual misunderstanding as to how international law functions in practice. In what follows, I will show why I believe this response fails and, in doing so, why it also only serves to reinforce this perception of constitutional deficiency.

A. The Rule of Recognition and the Practices of Officials

On one level, it is easy to see the broad appeal of Hart's approach in giving an account of international law as an autonomous legal system. In

[62] Somek, 'From the Rule of Law' (n 10) 576.

[63] Hart (n 5) 223.

[64] ibid 227. As Payandeh notes, although Hart does not explicitly state that international law was a primitive system, the overall structure of his analysis throughout *The Concept of Law* makes this comparison inevitable. See M Payandeh, 'The Concept of International Law in the Jurisprudence of H. L. A. Hart' (2011) 21 *European Journal of International Law* 967, at 978.

[65] Hart (n 5) 214.

[66] See, eg, Benvenisti (n 36).

[67] In fact, international law is far more complex as a system than Hart's account suggests. See, eg, Payandeh (n 64) at 982–88 in particular; T Nardin, *Law, Morality, and the Relations of States* (Princeton, NJ, Princeton University Press, 1983) 161–68.

particular, given the parameters set out at the start of this chapter, Hart's account offers an explanation of the reality and functionality of a legal system based simply on shared conventional understandings of legality derived from social practices.[68] This understanding, what Hart termed the 'internal point of view', was revealed simply by the use of legal rules 'as the basis of criticism, and as the justification of demands for conformity, social pressure, and punishment'.[69] In fact, Hart mounted an explicit defence of international law's reality on this very basis.[70] By referring to the self-understanding of international legal participants in this way, he was able, on the one hand, to avoid the overly reductive approach of, eg, Austin or the legal realists, which, as we have seen, tended to equate legal normativity simply with a form of behavioural compliance, and was therefore incapable of distinguishing legal norms from threats backed by physical force.[71] On the other hand, his social-factual explanation meant that he was able to reject the kind of abstract systemic construction adopted by those like Kelsen, which he thought risked distorting understanding of how international legal rules were actually used and understood in practice.[72]

It is precisely for this reason, however, that Hart also rejected the idea that international law should be thought of as a legal system on the same terms as domestic legal orders. Yet his reasons for this rejection are easily, and indeed often have been, misunderstood. To explain, Hart's view of law's systematicity (as opposed to its normativity) was premised on a critical distinction between 'primary' norms of obligation and more procedural, 'secondary' rules—rules of recognition, change and adjudication—the reality of which was revealed through the practices of a distinct class of legal officials. At the heart of this understanding is the 'rule of recognition', a kind of meta-norm for the system as a whole, which validates the existence of all the other rules and, in the hands of the system's officials, is capable of offering a level of certainty or determinacy in ascertaining the law in practice.[73] Whilst Hart's rule of recognition might have the appearance of a kind of Kelsenian *grundnorm*, the two are very distinct concepts. Kelsen's *grundnorm* was simply a conceptual construction, or juristic hypothesis, necessary to explain the formal unity and systemic autonomy of law. In contrast, Hart's claim was

[68] See, eg, J d'Aspremont, *Formalism and the Sources of International Law: A Theory of the Ascertainment of Legal Norms* (Oxford, Oxford University Press, 2011) 16; Payandeh (n 64); S Besson, 'Theorizing the Sources of International Law' in Besson and Tasioulas (n 43) 180; H Thirlway, *The Sources of International Law* (Oxford, Oxford University Press, 2014) 15.

[69] Hart (n 5), 98.

[70] ibid 227, 231, 235.

[71] ibid 88–91 and specifically in relation to international law at 217–20.

[72] ibid 213–16, 232–34.

[73] Hart explains the reason for moving from a primitive towards a mature, systemic order in terms of the added advantage of certainty (through the rule (or rules) of recognition), flexibility (through rules of change) and efficiency (through rules of adjudication). ibid 94–97.

that secondary rules, including the rule of recognition, were observable in practice; they were descriptions of institutionalised processes within which legal officials fulfilled discrete functions and which collectively sustained the coherence of the system as a whole.[74] Whilst Hart sought to resist the simple comparison of international law with an ideal type of law drawn from domestic experience—that is, a legal system possessing centralised institutions of adjudication, legislation and executive enforcement—and its outright dismissal as law per se, its limited institutional structure did still impact international law's coherence as a legal system on the above terms.[75]

For the most part, international lawyers have sought not only to resist this conclusion in defending international law's systemic character—pointing to the 'internal', self-understanding of international law's participants themselves—but also to explain how such understanding is often structured around the Hartian distinction between 'primary' and 'secondary' norms:[76] for example, in areas like the law of treaties[77] or the 'secondary' rules of international responsibility.[78] Whilst they might concede that the international legal order lacks secondary rules of change and adjudication (at least to the extent that these rules are equated with a centralised legislature and system of courts enjoying compulsory jurisdiction), there appears to be broad agreement on the obvious reality of an international rule of recognition—the absence of which being the central premise of Hart's claim

[74] See on this point generally N MacCormick, '*The Concept of Law* and the Concept of Law' in RP George (ed), *The Autonomy of Law: Essays on Legal Positivism* (Oxford, Oxford University Press, 1996) 181–94.

[75] In fact, he went further to outline how the search for these elements on the assumption that they were essential to a condition of legality at the international level would inevitably lead to distortions in understanding rather than a clearer conceptual picture of the nature of law in general and of international law in particular. Hart (n 5), 213–16 and 232–33.

[76] G Abi-Saab, 'Cours général de droit international public' (1987-VII) 207 *Recueil des Cours* 9, at 122–26; Franck (n 15) 184–85. However, one has to be careful not to exaggerate the influence of Hart on the adoption of this terminology by bodies such as the ILC. As noted by Gourgourinis, Hart was not the first to adopt this distinction and—as is argued further below—Hart's own account of primary and secondary rules arguably purports much more than the systemic distinction often employed in international legal doctrine. See Gourgourinis (n 37) 1016–17. For a discussion on some of the ambiguities involved in the use of the distinction, see also H Thirlway, *International Customary Law and Codification: An Examination of the Continuing Role of Custom in the Present Period of Codification of International Law* (Leiden, AW Sijthoff, 1972) 39–42. And on the technical and somewhat artificial nature of this distinction in international law, see E David, 'Primary and Secondary Rules' in J Crawford, A Pellet and S Olleson (eds), *The Law of International Responsibility* (Oxford, Oxford University Press, 2010) 27–33.

[77] *Case Concerning the Gabcikovo-Nagymaros Project* (Hungary/Slovakia), Judgment, ICJ Reports 1997, p 7 at para 47, pp 38–39. J d'Aspremont, 'Formalism versus Flexibility in the Law of Treaties' in CJ Tams, A Tzanakopoulos, A Zimmerman and AE Richford (eds), *Research Handbook on the Law of Treaties* (Cheltenham, Edward Elgar, 2014) 257, at 283–84.

[78] See ILC (n 16). The ILC also adopted the terminology in its work on fragmentation: 'Fragmentation of International Law: Difficulties Arising from the Diversification and Expansion of International Law: Report of the Study Group of the International Law Commission, Finalized by M. Koskenniemi', UN Doc A/CN.4/L.682, 13 April 2006, Section B3, paras 27–36, available at: http://legal.un.org/ilc/documentation/english/a_cn4_l682.pdf.

that international law could not be considered a legal system. In fact, one regularly sees reference to international law's sources doctrine, particularly by reference to Article 38 of the ICJ Statute, as fulfilling exactly this kind of 'secondary' function in international law.[79] For instance, in his defence of the relative autonomy of international law given above, Schachter explicitly rebukes Hart for missing the obvious 'secondary' nature of sources doctrine.[80]

Nevertheless, the problem with this explanation, that is, the claim that Article 38 (or any other principle) functions as a rule of recognition on Hart's terms, is that it tends to misunderstand the function of this rule in his account of a legal system. Such an explanation fails to adequately engage with the broader institutional context underpinning Hart's concept of law, particularly the role played by a discrete class of legal officials and their relationship to the system's secondary rules.[81] In this regard, Hart was not concerned to simply account for the possibility of abstract conceptual relationships between norms. He tried to provide a rationalisation of the institutionalised normative hierarchies that actually pertain in functioning domestic legal systems. His account is certainly open to a number of criticisms, particularly in terms of how he constructs and understands the systemic interaction between officials and secondary rules—criticisms to which I will return at length in Part II—but the point remains that it is difficult to simply divorce the operation of the secondary rules from the hierarchical institutional structures in which they take on specific meaning.[82] As I show below, this official role and recognition is therefore *crucial to and constitutive of the system*, and cannot just be read out of his theory without undermining the underlying functional rationale which gives meaning to his overall account of a legal system.

B. The Functional Presumptions of Hart's Concept of Law

The role of officials in Hart's account is absolutely critical in revealing the functional presumptions that propel his concept of law and in particular the rule of recognition within it. Legal officials not only derive their authority from the secondary rules, but their practices create, conform to and

[79] For instance, P-M Dupuy, 'L'unité de l'ordre juridique international: cours général de droit international public' (2002) 297 *Recueil des Cours* 9, at 39; or more recently Besson and Tasioulas, 'Introduction' (n 43) 10–11; and also in the same volume (and more extensively), Besson (n 68) 180–85. See also Payandeh (n 64) 981–93; H Thirlway, 'The Sources of International Law' in Evans (n 32) 91, at 91–93 and 115–20; Van Hoof (n 15) 53–54 and 60. And for discussion, see Prost (n 3) 84.

[80] Schachter (n 27) 763.

[81] See Prost (n 3) 82–83 and passim.

[82] See N MacCormick, *H. L. A. Hart*, 2nd edn (Stanford, CA, Stanford University Press, 2008) 31–34.

maintain in existence the necessary divide between secondary and primary rules to begin with. In other words, Hart's account is not only premised upon the social fact of subjects obeying the law (or even their recognition of its systemic nature), but a critical dichotomy between the general observance of norms in practice and their promulgation, application and enforcement in the hands of such officials.[83] Hart is quite explicit on this point:

> There are ... two minimum conditions necessary and sufficient for the existence of a legal system. On the one hand, those rules of behaviour which are valid according to the system's ultimate criteria of validity must be generally obeyed, and, on the other hand, its rules of recognition specifying the criteria of legal validity and its rules of change and adjudication must be effectively accepted as common public standards of official behaviour by its officials.[84]

Consequently, his scepticism as to the systemic character of international law was not a denial of the social-factual acceptance of systemic relationships between legal norms, but a recognition of the consequences of constructing those kinds of relationships in the abstract: in the absence of legal officials, such systemic reasoning would only reveal the openness, inefficiency and contestability of international legal rules in comparison to their domestic counterparts.[85] To put this point another way, Hart was not just concerned with the possibility of the formal unity of a legal order, but also sought to explain *what was functionally necessary* to maintain in existence a certain kind of hierarchical normative order. Secondary rules are not ends in themselves, but rather 'starting points' for a broader account of a concept of law which Hart saw as fundamentally structured towards guiding human conduct.[86] Indeed, whilst Hart is at least ambiguous on the question of whether law in general shares a point or purpose, this basic presumption—that 'law's function is to guide and control the behaviour of its subjects'[87]—undergirds his account, and it is against this function that we have to understand the conceptual apparatus of secondary rules within his concept of the legal system. On this account, the rule of recognition thus has a specific functional role in the hands of officials in contributing to the *determinacy of norms*—a quality that is seen as absent at the international level. Mario Prost explains this point well in a passage worth quoting at length:

> Secondary rules are ... the means by which to *dispel doubts* about the existence, scope and operation of primary rules. They specify the way in which the primary

[83] See his more explicit admission in this respect in the *Postscript* to the second edition: Hart (n 5) 254–59. See also the discussion of A Marmor, 'Legal Conventionalism' in J Coleman (ed), *Hart's Postscript: Essays on the Postscript to the Concept of Law* (Oxford, Oxford University Press, 2001) 195–217.

[84] Hart (n 5) 116.

[85] ibid 91–96.

[86] Prost (n 3) 84–85 ff.

[87] ibid 85.

> rules may be conclusively and decisively ascertained and instances of their violation conclusively identified. If a certain degree of uncertainty or indeterminacy is bound to exist in any legal system, this element of uncertainty must thus stop with secondary rules. These rules are, in a sense, 'ultimate rules' or rules of 'last resort'. *They constitute the systemic response to law's open texture and, if they are to fulfil their function, they must therefore be determinate.* This, for Hart, is a 'necessary' and 'crucial' condition of law's unity and integrity as a system.[88] (emphasis added, footnotes omitted)

Whilst Prost might over-simplify the complex interplay between and discrete functions of each of Hart's secondary norms, it is clear that the officially operated rule of recognition plays exactly this type of role in bringing greater determinacy in ascertaining law in practice. As Hart claims, 'if doubts arise as to what the rules are or as to the precise scope of some given rule, there will be no procedure for settling this doubt, either by reference to an authoritative text or to an official whose declarations on this point are authoritative'.[89]

It is for this reason, then, that Hart is so critical of attempts by Kelsen, as well as international lawyers themselves, to find a basic norm or other point of foundational validity for the international legal order.[90] His dismissal of candidate international rules of recognition—the principle *pacta sunt servanda*, the notion that states ought to behave as they customarily have behaved etc—stems from the fact that such principles, to the extent that they can be seen to underpin the sources of international law, cannot fulfil this function that he attributes to the rule of recognition. These claimed foundational rules are either incomplete, indeterminate or else merely refer one back to the need for broad social acceptance. In other words, they merely confirm the customary character of the international legal order; their postulation as 'secondary' serves no functional utility other than in accounting for systemic relationships between norms—relationships which can already be said to exist simply by being accepted as such. To read into international law a rule of recognition therefore seems entirely superfluous, making no difference to the functioning of the international legal order (whether or not we call it a system), as the validity of international legal norms rests solely on the basis of collectively agreed processes enjoying broad social acceptance at any given period of time.

Of course, in line with the concerns raised above, one might legitimately question why these points matter if Hart was simply wrong in his conclusions *as well as the presumptions he makes about law's function.* As noted above, I do believe that Hart is wrong in this respect. Indeed, bearing in

[88] ibid 87.
[89] Hart (n 5) 90.
[90] ibid 232–34. Finnis pursues a similar line of argument in demonstrating the structural limitations of a customary legal order: Finnis (n 1) 244.

mind his uneasy elision of functionalism and conventionalism in his explanation of a legal system, there are at least prima facie reasons to doubt the necessity of certain institutional roles outside of the specific state context. I will return to this point in Part II, where I aim to disprove the view that law must necessarily act to pre-empt and foreclose political choice through the provision of determinate normative standards. Such a function may well seem uncontroversial, but I do not think we can simply presume it a priori. However, my more immediate concern, and the reason why I think Hart's views matter in the current context, is that the discourse of institutional autonomy recounted so far shares in this functional presumption, *indeed, it is premised upon it.* As I have argued here, insofar as many international lawyers have been critical of Hart's conclusions, their argument has tended to be factual (that there are indeed secondary norms within the international legal order) rather than theoretical (for instance, that a legal system need not necessarily function in the way Hart presumes). In leaving this functional presumption untouched, this factual response cannot but prove inadequate as a means of rebutting Hart's scepticism. In the current context, then, whether Hart was correct or not in his conclusion about international law and, indeed, whether this functional presumption is justified are both beside the point. If we share this starting point, our disagreement lies only at the semantic level and thus remains vulnerable to the kinds of concern which propelled Hart's scepticism. If we think that the international legal system should secure determinate solutions to normative problems, the deficiency that Hart identifies does indeed sting.

To illustrate this point, in the next and final section—of this chapter and of Part I overall—I will draw upon the example of the ascertainment of customary international law under the oft-claimed 'international rule of recognition', Article 38 of the ICJ Statute.

IV. AN INTERNATIONAL 'RULE OF RECOGNITION'? INDETERMINACY IN THE SOURCES OF INTERNATIONAL LAW

In the previous chapter, it was noted how Article 38 of the PCIJ (now ICJ) Statute was almost immediately accepted as a summation of international law's sources, standardising and proceduralising the law in this area and, in so doing, buttressing the claim that it could be considered as an autonomous legal system.[91] Nowadays, although often decried as inadequate or incomplete[92]—a point to which I will return below—Article 38 is widely

[91] See above Ch 2, section III.
[92] See, eg, Besson (n 68) 164–65; Alvarez (n 45) 258–59.

accepted as the necessary starting point for an explanation of the sources of international law (and thereafter of international law's status as a legal system).[93] To be sure, there is a sense of pragmatic doctrinal creativity here, glossing over the fact that the recognition of a specific treaty norm as providing a *foundational* point of legal validity in this sense presupposes the existence of a prior foundational norm.[94] At the same time, however, one can still treat Article 38 as a description of an underlying presupposition, meta-norm or—more pertinently for current purposes—a simple social-factual explanation of a set of practices actually pertaining within the international community, which thereafter facilitates a systemic understanding of international law.[95]

As I have suggested above, however, this kind of functional reliance on Article 38 may provide ontological certainty in one sense, but it raises the more troubling question of the efficacy of this understanding in securing the determinacy of international law in practice.[96] In fact, theoretical uncertainties about the operation of the doctrine of sources have come to act as a kind of microcosmic proxy for broader conceptual uncertainty about the legal nature of international law more broadly.[97] Whilst treaties and customary international law are undoubtedly recognised as the principal and most important sources included in Article 38 (even if, at the same time, there is continuing uncertainty about the relationship between them),[98] a huge range of unresolved questions remain, not only about the nature of these two sources, but also pertaining to the status of the other sources either listed or otherwise excluded from the list in Article 38. For instance, what status belongs to 'general principles of law'? Can such general principles form the normative basis to the settlement of disputes between states or do they act only as interpretative guides when giving effect to other legal norms? How many and which legal systems have to support the existence of such principles before their generality can be established? What status

[93] See d'Aspremont (n 68) 149, who observes how art 38 of the ICJ Statute has provided 'the basis on which several generations of international lawyers have been trained'.

[94] In that sense, it could be said that the idea that art 38 is foundational or basal to the rest of the international legal system suffers from the problem of so-called 'foundational regress', on which see P Capps, 'The Rejection of the Universal State' in N Tsagourias (ed), *Transnational Constitutionalism* (Cambridge, Cambridge University Press, 2007) 17, at 19–20.

[95] See also J d'Aspremont, 'Herbert Hart in Today's International Legal Scholarship' in J d'Aspremont and J Kammerhofer (eds), *International Legal Positivism in a Postmodern World* (Cambridge, Cambridge University Press, 2014) 114, at 122.

[96] See, eg, J Kammerhofer, 'Uncertainty in the Formal Sources of International Law: Customary International Law and Some of its Problems' (2004) 15 *European Journal of International Law* 523.

[97] See, in particular, P Weil, 'Le droit international en quête de son identité (Cours général de droit international public)' (1992) 237 *Recueil des cours* 9, at 133, also cited in Prost (n 3) 91, fn 101.

[98] See, eg, recently JJ Bia, 'The Relations between Treaties and Custom' (2010) 9 *Chinese Journal of International Law* 81, particularly at 84–86.

do judicial decisions or case law have as an independent source of the law, if at all? What about other potential sources of international law not listed in Article 38, such as equity, unilateral declarations, resolutions of international organisations, or other forms of so-called 'soft law'?[99]

It is not my intention to suggest answers to these questions, but merely to illustrate that as a whole, there is a significant *penumbra of uncertainty* surrounding international law's sources. Still, to suggest indeterminacy at the margins—even if those margins are somewhat extensive—does not necessarily preclude a degree of certainty at the core. Even if these questions surrounding sources doctrine remain unsettled, it might still be possible to describe with certainty the processes for ascertaining and applying customary international law and treaty obligations. The problem, however, is that the very nature or point of international law's sources thesis is to defer back to states, international law's key participants, on questions of the existence and meaning of legal norms. In other words, there is a kind of structural indeterminacy built into the very fabric of sources doctrine and, indeed, therefore the international legal system as a whole.

To illustrate this problem further, I will focus on the specific problem of indeterminacy in the ascertainment of customary international law. Before doing so, however, I should note that my focusing on custom is not at all to suggest that the law of treaties is free from theoretical difficulties or uncertainty in practice. Indeed, in the ascertainment of treaty obligations, not only are the processes and principles of treaty interpretation themselves open-textured and opaque,[100] but there remain uncertainties as to whether certain agreements actually constitute treaties in the first place and what this might mean in affecting legal obligations.[101] More fundamentally, from a systemic point of view, there is a lingering question over the extent to which, conceptually speaking, treaties represent sources *of law* at all (as opposed to being merely repositories of more specific legal obligations pertaining between the parties in question).[102] In fact, recognising that the binding

[99] Prost (n 3) 91–97.

[100] See, eg, U Linderfalk, 'Is the Hierarchical Structure of Articles 31 and 32 of the Vienna Convention Real or Not? Interpreting the Rules of Interpretation' (2007) 65 *Netherlands International Law Review* 133. For broader reflections on the various factors influencing approaches to interpretation, see the collection of essays in A Bianchi, A Peat and M Windsor (eds), *Interpretation in International Law* (Oxford, Oxford University Press, 2015).

[101] See, generally, J Klabbers, *The Concept of Treaty in International Law* (The Hague, Kluwer International, 1996).

[102] This question might now seem somewhat formalistic and obsolete, particularly bearing in mind the importance of treaties to the functioning of contemporary international law. However, from a conceptual point of view, the question remains pertinent. *cf* G Fitzmaurice, 'Some Problems Regarding the Formal Sources of International Law' in *Symbolae Verzijl* (The Hague, Martinus Nijhoff, 1958) 153, at 157–58; and M Mendelson, 'Are Treaties Merely a Source of Obligation?' in WE Butler (ed), *Perestroika and International Law* (Dordrecht, Martinus Nijhoff, 1990) 81–88.

force of treaty rules can only really be derivative from pre-existing rules of general international law is precisely the point of my focusing on customary international law. Custom not only remains of critical theoretical importance to the overall systemic construction of international law, but for that reason it must also be logically prior to, and constitutive of, the rules of treaty law. Also, from a more practical perspective, to focus on treaties as a general source of law (rather than merely specific legal obligations for consenting parties) would only really highlight the perceived constitutional deficiency outlined above; it would, in other words, only serve to highlight the lack of any efficient means of creating general legal rules *binding all* states. The very fact that some states may or may not be a party to a treaty, and thereafter conflicts between state-parties and non-state-parties have to revert to the level of custom, only highlights the continued importance of customary rules to the overall system of international law.[103] As Ian Brownlie states, 'custom is not a special department or area of public international law: it *is* international law'.[104] Of course, the flipside of this point, as Jörg Kammerhofer also notes, is that: 'The theoretical problems of customary international are [also] the theoretical problems of international law as a whole.'[105]

A. Customary International Law and the *Opinio Juris* Paradox

According to Article 38, the ICJ shall apply custom as 'evidence of a general practice accepted as law'. Customary international law is in this sense sociological—drawn from social practices—but the Statute recognises that practice alone would not account for the binding force of law (ie, the reference to 'practice *accepted as* law'). Being a decentralised order, this reconciliation acknowledges that the binding force of a customary rule in international law can only really be determined from a general recognition of a norm's obligatory force by those subjected to it.[106] In other words, the *opinio juris sive necessitatis* element of international custom accords with Hart's internal point of view, as formulated above, in requiring an acceptance of the normativity of law rather than seeking to make a more

[103] Koskenniemi (n 12) 389–90: 'The generality of custom seems like an incident of its normativity. All States should be bound by the same law, regardless of their subjective will or power. This does not rule out specific conventional arrangements. But just as municipal law requires that the acts of legal subjects are evaluated from the perspective of a unitary normative structure, it must be assumed that there exists a general, uniformly applicable law between States, however abstract or rudimentary, by virtue of which States have the power to create specific obligations and from which these obligations can be evaluated and interpreted.'

[104] Brownlie (n 14) 18.

[105] Kammerhofer (n 96) 536.

[106] See, inter alia, the *North Sea Continental Shelf*, Judgment, ICJ Reports 1969, 3, at 42–43.

'external' judgement with regard to the regularities of state practice, which may equally be influenced by extra-legal factors.

Accordingly, it seems impossible to do away with either element without undermining a key point of legitimacy in the modern discipline: to find the reason for the binding authority of custom merely by reference to the conforming practices of states would make it indistinguishable from political prudence, habit or other social convention;[107] to locate it in the subjective belief of states alone—*opinio juris*—would risk the law becoming an irrelevance insofar as practice does not concur with these subjective beliefs.[108] However, to apply these twin requirements in any coherent way is a notoriously confusing and cumbersome exercise, raising a number of problems which are by now well-rehearsed in the academic literature:[109] for instance, questions over what exactly constitutes state practice (just material acts, or statements and opinions also?);[110] the generality of practice required (if not full unanimity, how many states must actually conform to any given practice? What duration of practice (or number of instances) is required? Do some states' practices have more weight than others?); as well as more deep-rooted anxieties and uncertainties about exactly what is implied in the notion of *opinio juris* in the first place.[111] It is this latter problem, in particular, which has not only proven troubling, theoretically speaking, but also goes to the heart of the practicability of these source criteria as a means of ascertaining customary international law.

Traditionally, the problems associated with the *opinio juris* requirement are subsumed within, or at least illustrated by, what has been referred to as the 'chronological paradox'.[112] Although this is by now a somewhat laboured discussion, it is worth briefly illustrating this apparent problem insofar as it helps shed light on the practical difficulties of actually ascertaining the existence of a purportedly legal rule in practice. To explain, traditionally the notion of the *opinio juris* has been distinguished from a requirement of actual consent (whether explicit or simply tacit) as any such consensual basis for customary norms would seem to dissolve their

[107] See, eg, M Akehurst, 'Custom as a Source of International Law' (1974–75) 47 *British Yearbook of International Law* 1, at 33; CL Lim and OA Elias, *The Paradox of Consensualism in International Law* (The Hague, Martinus Nijhoff, 1998).

[108] Koskenniemi (n 12) 410–11.

[109] For a good overview, see, eg, Ch 8 of M Byers, *Custom, Power and the Power of Rules: International Relations and Customary International Law* (Cambridge, Cambridge University Press, 1999) 129–46.

[110] ibid 133–36. See also A d'Amato, *The Concept of Custom in International Law* (Ithaca, NY, Cornell University Press, 1971) 88 ff; and Kammerhofer (n 96) 525–27.

[111] An extensive discussion of the problems associated with the *opinio juris* element, and suggested solutions to the problem, is included in O Elias, 'The Nature of the Subjective Element in Customary International Law' (1995) 44 *International and Comparative Law Quarterly* 501, at 502–11.

[112] Byers (n 109) 130–33; Lefkowitz (n 15) 130–33 and passim.

normativity altogether, leaving customary international law seemingly useless as a counter-factual normative constraint on state behaviour. However, the problem then becomes how subjective belief in the binding quality of custom can emerge in the formation of a new rule of international law, as it would seem that any such belief would simply be erroneous.[113] Accordingly, when the existence of a rule of customary international law is in question (as is often the case when questions of international legality are under discussion), the paradox would seem to arise. As Kammerhofer explains:

> If it is the belief that something is already law that counts, then it can only be used to identify existent customary international law. The belief cannot be true with respect to conduct that had either hitherto not been covered by a norm or by a different norm, believing something to be law which is only becoming law. Therefore, the belief is necessarily, not just ordinarily, a mistaken belief.[114]

To get around this problem, we might distinguish a belief that something *should be* law as a *constitutive* element of the law-making process (rather than being *declaratory* of prior existing law),[115] but the problem then becomes how binding law can be ascertained if one of the criteria for its ascertainment rests on subjective intent—that is, a claim *de lege ferenda* rather than *lex lata*. This leads to uncertainty due to the fact that one cannot look to the source requirements to determine or validate law because the very act of validation is implicated within the law-creation process (and vice versa). In other words, the criteria for the ascertainment of custom are inseparable from the processes of its formation—there is no defining line between the epistemological question of law's emergence and the ontological question of how to ascertain binding legal obligations.[116]

It might also be the case that this theoretical paradox can be reconciled in conceptual terms to the extent that one imposes a logical separation between these two processes. For instance, a state may exert the belief or will that something *ought to be the law* and this claim is, through consistent usage and acceptance by other states (whether tacitly, through acquiescence etc), subsequently determined to be law. There may be a smudging of the theoretical problem in such a scenario, but imposing this kind of conceptual distinction, we could nonetheless say that ascertainment becomes the search for evidence of concordant practice, intent and acceptance. However, this does nothing to bring determinacy or certainty to the process of ascertaining

[113] Kammerhofer (n 96) 534 ff; d'Amato (n 110) 47 ff; Byers (n 109) 131. However, see also Lefkowitz (n 15) 130–31, who claims that this paradox conflates the processes of law ascertainment and law creation. I reflect more on this below.

[114] Kammerhofer (n 96) 534.

[115] On this distinction between declaratory and constitutive views, and the scholars who propound each view, see Koskenniemi (n 12) 418–24.

[116] ibid 306; and T Skouteris, *The Notion of Progress in International Law Discourse* (The Hague, TMC Asser Press, 2010) 147.

customary norms; it merely begs further questions about how to determine the existence of a norm for those states whose belief or intent is said to be foundational to the rules themselves.[117] This uncertainty thus makes it impossible for legal participants (states) to simply apply the given criteria in order to make a determination of what the law actually is in any given situation.[118]

We might deem it practically more feasible to consider custom ascertainment from the perspective of the seemingly objective, external adjudicator, judge or international jurist. However, whilst such institutionalised processes might provide a short-cut through these difficulties, they are rarely able to escape controversy in their efforts to do so. For instance, to get around the difficulties of having to determine clear intent or belief from seemingly disputed practices, the judge or jurist might simply infer *opinio juris* from a sufficient generality of practice (even if we are not able to give a precise threshold of generality)—such an inference being a kind of tacit consent or acquiescence.[119] However, the problem here is that it is impossible to merely infer motivations in any legitimate way without enquiring further into subjective states of mind, for example, by looking for particular types of practice which go beyond physical acts (ie, statements, claims or assertions).[120] Not only would this raise another area of uncertainty as to what actually constitutes practice in the first place, but as soon as we look for intent or other subjective psychological factors within state practice, we dissolve the necessary distinction between the two source elements.[121] Furthermore, and more practically, the question of the existence of a customary norm more often than not seems to arise in cases where there is a paucity of practice, or a conflict between practices, as well as clear differences in subjective beliefs, leaving the decision-maker in the impossible position of trying to choose between genuine as opposed to erroneous intent or belief of the parties concerned.

It is surely the case therefore that the chronological paradox is not simply a theoretical or conceptual quandary which dissolves as soon as the source requirements are applied in practice. The practical difficulties (if not

[117] Kammerhofer (n 96) 535. See further in J Kammerhofer, *Uncertainty in International Law: A Kelsenian perspective* (Abingdon, Routledge, 2011) 83–84; and Koskenniemi (n 12) 422–24.

[118] Kammerhofer (n 96) 535.

[119] Indeed, this seems to be the conclusion of the International Law Association in its study on the topic of the formation of customary international law. See International Law Association, *Final Report of the Committee on Formation of Customary (General) International Law* (2000), at 31–32, available at: www.ila-hq.org/download.cfm/docid/A709CDEB-92D6-4CFA-A61C4CA30217F376.

[120] Koskenniemi (n 12) 430–31; Kammerhofer (n 96) 529–30.

[121] Thirlway (n 68) 73–74.

impossibility) of looking for the subjective reasons for norm-compliance from this external, sociological perspective most often give rise to a more fluid (and by no means less controversial) form of judicial reasoning in practice: this, for instance, might just smudge the two elements together to some degree[122] or might prioritise one over the other.[123] In practice, very few judgments of the ICJ, for example, are able to convincingly demonstrate proof of both elements.[124] If the existence of custom is not simply just stated, ie, without presenting any corresponding evidence to this effect, more frequently we see intent merely inferred from practice or, vice versa, inconsistent practice sidelined altogether (such as in the controversial *Nicaragua* judgment)[125] in favour of relying on public statements, resolutions of international organisations or treaty practice as sufficient evidence for the existence of a custom.[126] This 'modern' approach to customary international law ascertainment will look for a much looser form of social consensus, perhaps derived from the 'soft' normative output of international institutional fora such as the UN General Assembly (UNGA) or the prior existence of a multilateral treaty, which, though not seen as binding in lieu of consent, is clearly seen as relevant practice and/or *opinio*.[127]

Nevertheless, in its eliding of the two elements of custom in this way, this approach really only goes to show the lack of determinacy within the criteria themselves[128]—the binding force of any given custom merely awaits its recognition as such by any authorised decision-maker. Of course, relying on existing treaty practice, resolutions and statements of international organisations, and codification exercises of bodies such as the ILC, may help to 'streamline' the law-creation process to some degree, but it cannot bring determinacy to the processes of customary law's *ascertainment*. Some controversial choice has to be made, either leading to a cautious,

[122] As Koskenniemi notes, 'standard doctrinal argument makes use of both senses of the *opinio* in a happy mixture, resorting to one when argument would otherwise seem too apologist, to the other when too utopian'. Koskenniemi (n 12) 418.

[123] See, eg, AE Roberts. 'Traditional and Modern Approaches to Customary International Law: A Reconciliation' (2001) 95 *American Journal of International Law* 757; see also FL Kirgis Jr , 'Custom on a Sliding Scale' (1987) 81 *American Journal of International Law* 146, who suggests that a great deal of *opinio juris* can count against the fact of a lack of practice, and vice versa.

[124] Koskenniemi (n 12) 428–29.

[125] *Military and Paramilitary Activities in and against Nicaragua (Nicaragua v United States)*, Merits, ICJ Reports 1986, p 14, at, inter alia, pp 99–100.

[126] Roberts (n 123) 758–59. On the problem of international criminal tribunals applying custom without sufficient consideration of practice, see recently N Arajärvi, *The Changing Nature of Customary International Law: Methods of Interpreting the Concept of Custom in International Criminal Tribunals* (Abingdon, Routledge, 2014).

[127] A Boyle and C Chinkin, *The Making of International Law* (Oxford, Oxford University Press, 2007) 225–29.

[128] RY Jennings, 'What is International Law and How Do We Tell it When We See it?' (1981) 37 *Schweitzerisches Jahrbuch für Internationales Recht* 59, at 67–70.

conservative approach or else leaving the decision-maker always susceptible to the criticism of having misapplied the source determinants in the identification of any given rule.[129] For instance, to the extent that legal codification exercises have a more general, galvanising effect on the process of custom formation, these tend only to smooth over disagreement by leaving draft codes or texts ambiguous or, more commonly, by producing a set of 'rules' which combines the *lex lata* and proposals *de lege ferenda*.[130] In such cases, certainty seems to come (if indeed it does at all) in the *authorised* decision of a court or body charged with resolving disputes or determining specific questions of international law. Yet this is precisely the problem as, notwithstanding the theoretical uncertainties outlined above, the more immediate concern is the continued absence of any hierarchical system of courts with a general, compulsory jurisdiction. Whilst there are a number—a growing number—of regimes created *within* the international legal order, many of which provide for limited forms of compulsory dispute settlement in specific contexts,[131] the lack of any systemic hierarchy, combined with the ability to 'forum shop' between them, leaves states still very much in control in the determination of their specific legal obligations.[132]

[129] A good example is the methodological criticism directed at the International Committee of the Red Cross (ICRC) over its study of customary international humanitarian law: see, perhaps most vociferously, Y Dinstein, 'The ICRC Customary International Humanitarian Law Study' (2006) 36 *Israel Yearbook of Human Rights* 1. See also criticisms of the ICJ's methodology in ascertaining customary international law rules in the *Nicaragua* case (n 125) in TM Franck, 'Some Observations on the ICJ's Procedural and Substantive Innovations (in Appraisals of the ICJ's Decision in Nicaragua vs. United States (Merits))' (1987) 81 *American Journal of International Law* 116, at 118–20.

[130] For example, consider the uncertain status of countermeasures taken in the 'collective interest', on which art 54 of the ILC's Articles on State Responsibility takes no position. James Crawford, the ILC Rapporteur on the topic, claimed, in the commentaries to the Articles, that practice in this area was 'limited and rather embryonic'. See ILC (n 16) 137.

[131] For instance, within the context of the World Trade Organization or under the UN Convention on the Law of the Sea 1982. For an overview of developments in dispute resolution and international adjudication, see RP Anand, 'Enhancing the Acceptability of Compulsory Procedures of International Dispute Settlement' (2001) 5 *Max Planck Yearbook of United Nations Law* 1; C Romano, 'International Organizations and the International Judicial Process: An Overview' in L Boisson de Chazournes, C Romano and R MacKenzie (eds), *International Organizations and International Dispute Settlement: Trends and Prospects* (Ardsley on Hudson, Transnational Publishers, 2002) 3–36; and, more recently, the various contributions to D French, M Saul and ND White (eds), *International Law and Dispute Settlement: New Problems and Techniques* (Oxford, Hart Publishing, 2010).

[132] See JG Merrills, *Anatomy of International Law*, 2nd edn (London, Sweet & Maxwell, 1981) 18–30. This problem also seems to impact upon the formative rules of treaty law, particularly with regard to treaty interpretation—to the extent that we can explain these as secondary rules—as the apparent openness of the law again stresses the importance of institutional *determination* rather than normative determinability: see the discussion in J Klabbers, 'Reluctant *Grundnormen*: Articles 31(3)(c) and 41 of the Vienna Convention on the Law of Treaties and the Fragmentation of International Law' in M Craven, M Fitzmaurice and M Vogiatzi (eds), *Time, History and International Law* (Leiden: Martinus Nijhoff, 2007) 141–61.

B. The Institutional Problem in Customary Law Ascertainment

What these concerns highlight, in other words, is that the chronological paradox is not the result of some badly worded, misconceived or misdirected test for ascertaining customary international law. The problem is intrinsic to the institutional structure of international law itself—a problem which equally affects the claimed scope of norms as much as their prior ontological existence. Consider, for instance, the conflicting conceptions of the rules relating to attribution in the context of the law of state responsibility deployed by the ICJ in the *Nicaragua* case[133] on the one hand, and by the Appeals Chamber of the International Criminal Tribunal for the former Yugoslavia (ICTY) in the *Tadic* case[134] on the other. The rules in question touched on the question of attribution of legal responsibility to states for the conduct of armed belligerent groups and other non-state entities.[135] In the latter case, the ICTY critiqued the 'effective control' test deployed by the ICJ in this regard as too exacting a standard and decreed that the (distinctly less onerous) test of 'overall control' should be applied instead. Unsurprisingly, the ICJ later reconfirmed its earlier formulation, defending the customary status of the effective control test in spite of the criticism of the ICTY.[136] As Koskenniemi comments in the ILC's Study Report on fragmentation, such interpretative disputes are not normally perceived to be a problem in domestic legal orders, where a hierarchy of courts can resolve such conflicts, but they appear problematic if we expect the same degree of normative certainty at the international level:

> The point is not to take a stand in favour of either Tadic or Nicaragua, only to illustrate the type of normative conflict where two institutions faced with analogous facts interpret the law in differing ways. *This is a common occurrence in any legal system. But its consequences for the international legal system which lacks a proper institutional hierarchy might seem particularly problematic.* Imagine, for

[133] See the *Nicaragua* case (n 125) 64–65, at para 115.

[134] See *Prosecutor v Dusko Tadic*, Judgment of 15 July 1999 (1999) 38 *ILM* 1540, at paras 115, 116–45.

[135] The test relates to the application of the rule contained in art 8 of the ILC's Articles on State Responsibility, which provides that: 'The conduct of a person or group of persons shall be considered an act of a State under international law if the person or group of persons is in fact acting on the instructions of, or under the direction or control of, that State in carrying out the conduct.' For discussion of the application of the test in the two cases mentioned, see ILC (n 16) 47–48, at paras 4–5.

[136] See *Case Concerning the Application of the Convention on the Prevention and Punishment of the Crime of Genocide (Bosnia and Herzegovina v Serbia and Montenegro)*, Judgment, ICJ Reports 2007, at para 404, where the Court describes the applicability of the 'overall control' test to the law on state responsibility as 'unpersuasive'. For criticism of the Court's reasoning in light of the earlier cases, see A Cassese, 'The *Nicaragua* and *Tadic* Tests Revisited in Light of the ICJ Judgment on Genocide in Bosnia' (2007) 18 *European Journal of International Law* 649, at 651 ff.

> example, a case where two institutions interpret the general (and largely uncodified) law concerning title to territory differently. For one institution, State A has validly acquired title to a piece of territory that another institution regards as part of State B. In the absence of a superior institution that could decide such conflict, States A and B could not undertake official acts with regard to the territory in question with confidence that those acts would be given legal effect by outside powers or institutions. *Similar problems would emerge in regard to any conflicting interpretations concerning a general law providing legal status.*[137] (emphasis added)

Such normative conflict may be capable of resolution in the abstract, but the rather fragmented institutional structure of international law means that possibilities for dispute settlement depend often upon a choice between diverse regimes and contexts, which may well be affected by certain institutional biases, and between which there is not necessarily any defined hierarchy.[138] In many cases, the underlying conflict can be resolved *within* the international legal order only if both states are in agreement to resolve the conflict in the same tribunal, and even then the decision has no necessary precedential value beyond the dispute in question. What would ultimately seem to bring certainty in the specific case, as well as determinacy over the longer term, would be the existence of an overarching system of centralised adjudication enjoying a priori authority over states. As John Merrills acknowledges: 'With the creation of international law such a decentralised process, so liable ... to give rise to doubt or controversy, much clearly depends on the possibility of obtaining authoritative interpretations of the law.'[139] In the absence of such centralised judicial institutions, the decisions of any institutional body, the ICJ included, will likely remain controversial and contestable, even after a legal determination has been made. International judges, as much as states themselves, remain vulnerable to the criticism of having misapplied the source criteria or having over-stepped the bounds of their authority, thus leaving open the possibility that in any future instance, another tribunal, decision-maker or other body will seemingly ascertain, interpret or apply the law in a different way.

In other words, and as the analysis of the previous section suggested, the problem of indeterminacy in the ascertainment of customary

[137] ILC (n 39) 32, para 51.

[138] See CPR Romano, 'The Shift from the Consensual to the Compulsory Paradigm in International Adjudication: Elements for a Theory of Consent' (2007) 39 *New York University Journal of International Law and Politics* 791, at 854, who comments on the kind of 'unofficial' hierarchies which seem to have been created between an increasing number of courts with forms of compulsory jurisdiction: 'while hierarchies might be inevitable, they have emerged in a system that should by definition have no hierarchies. If hierarchies must exist in such a system, the system itself should be able to control them or should allow states to design them in their role as the ultimate source of legitimacy in the international legal order'.

[139] Merrills (n 132) 15.

international law derives entirely from the structure of international law as a legal system. It not only acts to illustrate Koskenniemi's critical intervention, but it also serves to show the reason why it is difficult to simply reconcile international law's systematicity on Hart's terms. If we accept that secondary norms should bring certain functional benefits, and chief among them is the determinacy brought about by the officially operated rule of recognition, then international law's proto-rule of recognition, whatever it might turn out to be, will inevitably fail to deliver in this role.

One possible response to this conclusion, of course, might be to argue that I have simply over-played the formal, structural distinctions between international and national legal orders, thereby ignoring the way in which this kind of indeterminacy may be compensated for at the international level. On this basis, we might argue that Hart simply misunderstood the way in which a decentralised legal order such as international law fulfils the kinds of functions implicated in his account of secondary rules. Indeed, this point is raised by Mehrdad Payandeh in a recent effort to show how international law can be reconciled with Hart's theory:

> If the main distinction between the social rules of a primitive society and a more sophisticated legal system lies in the ability of the latter to address the problems of uncertainty, of the static character of the social rules, and of the inefficiency of the system in enforcing the rules, then there is no compelling reason why an international legal order needs to resemble the domestic legal order in *form*—the lack of which is the main reason for Hart to qualify international law not as a system but only as a set of rules. It seems more convincing to evaluate the nature of the international legal system on the basis of whether it contains rules and mechanisms which perform the three *functions* which Hart deems necessary for the existence of a legal system.[140]

This kind of approach seems intuitively plausible in one sense. Over the years, in fact, generations of international legal scholars have sought to explain how states themselves fulfil certain 'constitutional functions' which are seen as necessary to the conceptual completeness of international law. To recall from Chapter 2, Kelsen relied on the idea of states' 'self-help', essentially institutionalising a 'just war' theory, in order to explain what he saw as a necessary enforcement function in international law.[141] In Chapter 1, similarly, we saw how Oppenheim relied on essentially the same form of argument in outlining the necessity of international law's enforcement through decentralised processes, specifically as determined by the so-called 'family of nations'.[142] A somewhat more sophisticated, though arguably also more idealistic, variant of this kind of argument might be Georges Scelle's

[140] Payandeh (n 64) 981; and see his attempt to account for these functions in detail, at 982–83.

[141] See above in Ch 1, section II.

[142] See above in Ch 2, section II.

theory of *dédoublement fonctionnel*, or 'role-splitting'. Scelle's approach suggested the importance of the combined functions of legislation, adjudication and enforcement to the conceptual coherence of international law, but explained how state officials can be understood as exercising such functions at an international level when authorised to do so under the constitutive (or 'secondary') rules of the international legal system.[143] Conceived in this way, in fact, Scelle was able to account for most international activity as part of a larger constitutional ordering of the international system.[144]

Nevertheless, the problem in all of these readings is that they do little to alleviate the apparent institutional problem as set out above and as perceived by Hart in particular. Indeed, Hart himself considered and rejected this kind of analogical reasoning, which often seems to rely on controversial external interpretations of state behaviour rather than any internal element of self-understanding.[145] For example, from the point of view of law creation, in deciding whether a certain course of action adopted by states, collectively or in isolation, is breaching the law or establishing new law, we either have to defer to the views of the state(s) concerned—which are inevitably attempting to justify their behaviour as legal—or we have to rely upon controversial readings of subjective intent, or more purposive interpretations or judgements of the surrounding context. In fact, by characterising these subjective interpretations as official functions, we potentially risk legitimising what might actually be more 'deviant' conduct.[146] A similar problem also arises in thinking of inter-state conduct in terms of legal 'enforcement'. Any such reading tends towards over-inclusiveness or over-generalisation in the suggestion that, for example, reprisals, acts of 'self-help' or the resort to war are necessarily concerned with upholding the law, or the enforcement of a state's legal rights, as opposed to simply the pursuit of more individualistic, political ends.[147]

[143] See, inter alia, G Scelle, *Précis de droit des gens: principes et systématique. Pt.2, Droit constitutionnel international* (Paris, Sirey, 1934) 10–12 and passim.

[144] See G Scelle, 'Essai de systématique de droit international (Plan d'un cours de droit international public)' (1923) 30 *Revue Générale de Droit International Public* 116, at 124–41 in particular. Patrick Capps has given a more recent spin to this same idea in P Capps, *Human Dignity and the Foundations of International Law* (Oxford, Hart Publishing, 2009) 244 and passim.

[145] Hart (n 5), 232–33; and see the discussion in Koskenniemi (n 12) 174–77.

[146] Koskenniemi (n 12) 175–76.

[147] Hart (n 5) 232–33. This argument was already well-made by Wolfgang Friedmann, in fact, who criticised Kelsen's systemic account for this reason. See WG Friedmann, 'General Course in Public International Law' (1969-II) 127 *Recueil des Cours* 39, at 74: 'Where states use force at the behest of, and within the legal framework of international authority, they act as executants of the international legal order. Where they act in self-defence, they may still be considered as organs of international law (Art. 51, United Nations Charter). But where the states—as they normally do—allege self-defence as the justification for the use of force, they do so in the absence or in defiance of an international fact-finding or adjudicatory authority and cover up national policy decisions or even naked acts of aggression through allegations of "provocation", "aggression" and similar formulas.'

A recent, and perhaps more relevant, example of this kind of *dédoublement fonctionnel* argument has been developed by David Lefkowitz in an explicit attempt not only to explain away the *opinio juris* paradox, as described above, but also to reconcile customary law ascertainment by reference to a rule of recognition on Hart's terms.[148] Lefkowitz accepts that the essential problem, that is, the idea of predicating at least part of international law's candidate rule of recognition on a persistent misnomer or mistaken belief (that is, states' belief that a customary norm is already binding upon them), would make sources doctrine somewhat useless as a means of ascertaining the law in any given situation. However, he points out that such a belief fails to distinguish two discrete processes at work: first, the need for a given number of states to believe in the binding force of certain customary norms (crucial to the formation of the customary norm); and, second, the general recognition (of states) that a certain norm exists by virtue of sufficient practice and such widespread belief. To be sure, in practice there is a blurry line between the formation of the rule and its acceptance in practice, but conceptually speaking, not only can we think of the processes as separate, but so too can we think of the actors (states) involved as fulfilling discrete roles. Specifically, in the formation of rules, states can be seen as merely participants in a constitutive process which may or may not give rise to the recognition of a legal norm. In the ascertainment of rules, however, states can be understood as international legal officials whose acceptance and operation of the international rule of recognition is what translates state practice and *opinio juris* into a binding rule of international law. Accordingly, the states involved in the formation of a customary rule of international law need not, as a matter of conceptual necessity, be the same as those that recognise the norm as binding law. There will likely be some considerable overlap in practice, of course, but conceptually speaking, one can still identify two processes at work, with states fulfilling discrete functions when involved in each process.[149] As Lefkowitz explains:

> Why ... have so many international legal theorists thought that the creation of new norms of customary international law suffers from the chronological paradox? A likely answer is that they have been misled by the fact that, in the international legal system, states comprise both the primary actors whose conduct and beliefs give rise to the existence of a customary rule, and the vast majority of the officials in the international legal system whose adherence to the rule of recognition leads them to deem that rule legally valid.[150]

[148] See Lefkowitz (n 15); and see also the commentary on Lefkowitz's ideas in K Culver and M Giudice, *Legality's Borders: An Essay in General Jurisprudence* (Oxford, Oxford University Press, 2010) 34–37.

[149] Lefkowitz (n 15) 132–34.

[150] ibid 135.

Following this distinction, therefore, Lefkowitz argues that the chronological paradox exists only by means of a certain conceptual confusion and actually dissolves at the practical level.[151] As ingenious as this form of conceptual reconciliation is, however, the fundamental problem here is that this argument still fails as a solution to the problem of uncertainty as perceived above. In making the distinction he does, Lefkowitz offers a conceptual solution to a problem which, as we have seen, has—both for Hart and for international lawyers—a more functional or practical purport.[152] The fact that states are at one and the same time both officials and subjects—if indeed they are—is precisely the problem, as in practice this structural peculiarity of international law means that the (conceptually distinct) processes of law creation and law ascertainment dissolve into each other.

To read into international law these kinds of functional analogies seems only to confirm the kind of constitutional deficiency outlined above.[153] Indeed, it is telling that authors who have in the past adopted these types of *dédoublement fonctionnel* argument tend to be quite open about the limitations of reading states as fulfilling any important, constitutional functions in this regard,[154] with many also often calling for the development of more autonomous forms of international organisation to overcome the perceived constitutional deficiencies of international law.[155] Intuitively, this latter form of response appears more appealing and, indeed, has become a more widespread and explicit means of countering Hart's scepticism. Essentially, this argument would accept that the institutional problem identified here is

[151] ibid 136.

[152] Culver and Giudice (n 148) 37.

[153] See on this argument Friedmann (n 147) 75, quoting from JL Brierly, *The Outlook for International Law* (Oxford, Clarendon Press, 1944) 4–5, and also drawing on Ch V of (the original 1961 edition of) Hart's *The Concept of Law* (n 5). See also W Friedmann, *The Changing Structure of International Law* (London, Stevens & Sons, 1964) 82–86. Hersch Lauterpacht was perhaps the most vociferous critic in this respect, seeing such models as ultimately undermining the coherence of international law as a legal system. H Lauterpacht, 'The Nature of International Law and General Jurisprudence' (1932) 37 *Economica* 301, at 318–20.

[154] I have noted many of these dissatisfactions and hopes for institutional renewal in the previous two chapters. However, Scelle also saw from the outset that the international legal order was fundamentally flawed in its constitutional architecture and claimed that his scheme of *dédoublement fonctionnel* acted as a 'dangerous substitute' for a more perfect form of international organisation based on a hierarchical structure. See G Scelle, *Manuel de droit international public* (Paris, Domat-Montchrestien, 1948) 22. In commenting on Scelle's scheme, Cassese notes the particular problem of legal certainty revealed in this approach: A Cassese, 'Remarks on Scelle's Theory of "Role Splitting" (*dédoublement fonctionnel*) in International Law' (1990) 1 *European Journal of International Law* 210, at 215.

[155] See, eg, Oppenheim's views in this respect in L Oppenheim, *The League of Nations and its Problems: Three Lectures* (London, Longmans, Green & Co, 1919) 21–22. Scelle also welcomed the development of the League of Nations and, later, the UN, as tentative steps in a more federal ordering of the international system. G Scelle, 'Le phénomène juridique du dédoublement fonctionnel' in W Schatzel and H-J Schlochauer (eds), *Rechtsfragen der Internationalen Organisation—Festschrift für H. Wehberg* (Frankfurt am Main, Klostermann, 1956) 324, at 341; and see Cassese (n 154) 214.

indeed a deficiency or weakness, but would counter that there had been a significant maturation of international law in the years since Hart wrote *The Concept of Law*. It would suggest, in other words, that international law is beginning to look a lot more like the kind of well-functioning legal system with which we are familiar from the state context, including mechanisms for legal change and adjudication, such as to call into question the badge of 'primitiveness' which Hart bestowed upon the modern discipline.[156]

This seems, on the surface at least, a more plausible form of response overall. However, it is also one which is not free from theoretical controversy, nor indeed does it negate the very practical concern that many of these institutional developments seem to be invoking further rule of law concerns in recent years. I will say more about this form of response in Part III; suffice to say that I remain unconvinced that such institutional developments can compensate for, or fix, the apparent deficiency identified above. In fact, I believe the only plausible form of response to this problem is to engage with the cogency of the domestic legal paradigm against which international law is most often compared and found wanting. I will now take up this challenge in Part II in an effort to *re-orient the focus* of this institutional problem—that is, I will suggest that this problem does not at all relate to any structural, constitutional or institutional fault or deficiency at the international level. Rather, I will claim that the problem relates more to a pervasive mode of theorising law, which tends to simply presume—based solely on experience of the domestic law-state—that a governance function inheres in law in general.

V. CONCLUSION

This chapter has described how our intuition to make sense of international law as an autonomous legal order—understood in terms of an objective system of rules capable of pre-empting political or moral decision-making—is undermined considerably by the law's institutional structure. I have used Hart's concept of law to illustrate how, if we conceive of international law's autonomy in this manner, the decentralised international legal order cannot but appear constitutionally deficient as a result. I have drawn upon Hart's account not because I wish to necessarily endorse his method or his substantive conclusion about international law's apparent 'primitiveness'. Rather, I do so because his theory more than any other has been influential in shaping disciplinary understanding of the nature of international law as a legal system that is capable of providing determinate (or at least determinable) answers to questions about the existence, scope and applicability of

[156] Payandeh (n 64) 982 ff.

any purportedly legal norm. The above analysis of sources doctrine, and the core example of customary international law, shows that Hart's concerns about the ability of international law to function at this level are, *to this extent at least*, well-founded. Looked at from the perspective of an ideal type of a centralised system of domestic law (and holding the system to account on this basis), international law's structural weaknesses become all too apparent: its *institutional problem* is confirmed.

Of course, as I have already begun to suggest above, it need not *necessarily* follow that because of its openness to competing uses and ends—its structural indeterminacy—international law should be considered as deficient or defective. Koskenniemi makes this point most clearly in answering his critics in the Epilogue to *From Apology to Utopia*:

> The important point I wish to make … is not that [international law's structural indeterminacy] should be thought of as a scandal or (even less) a structural 'deficiency' but that indeterminacy is *an absolutely central aspect of international law's acceptability*. It does not emerge out of the carelessness or bad faith of legal actors (States, diplomats, lawyers) but from their *deliberate and justified wish* to ensure that legal rules will fulfil the purposes for which they were adopted.[157] (emphasis added, footnotes omitted)

Indeterminacy thus only appears as a problem as such from outside of the system looking in, particularly on the assumption that some form of centralised legislative will or intent could emerge in order to cut through the competing perspectives of international legal participants themselves. However, from the perspective of any actor within the system, it seems difficult, if not impossible, to imagine such a legitimate reference point, that is, one having the a priori authority to give any clearer meaning to the law than that contained within the norm itself.

I will return to this point again in Part III, where I not only present a specific normative defence of the structural openness of international law as a system grounded in an inherently pluralist conception of international society, but also show the inherent difficulties, if not impossibility, of attempting to overcome or compensate for this condition. As I will claim, this structural indeterminacy cannot be 'read out' of international law: *it is intrinsic to a decentralised legal order.* The important point, for current purposes, is that the recurrent scepticism and disciplinary anxiety about the institutional condition of international law only arises because of the presumptions we have made as to the core tasks and features of a well-functioning legal order. In fact (as I have already suggested to some degree), I have some doubts about the cogency of the functional orientation of law presumed on this account, but to challenge this mode of thinking, I need to revert to a

[157] Koskenniemi (n 12) 591–92.

broader, theoretical analysis. In Part II, therefore, I seek to challenge head-on the cogency of the domestic paradigm of a well-functioning legal order which has arguably been perpetuated through the analytical method that is dominant within contemporary legal theory. In doing so, I hope to re-orient our understanding of the institutional problem, which I believe inheres at the level of legal theory and conceptual enquiry, rather than being a fault or failing of the international legal order.

Part II

Cause

4

Presuming Hierarchy: The Problematic Concept of the Legal Official

THE FIRST PART of the book has shown how efforts to give a coherent account of international law as an autonomous system of determinate legal rules are undermined constantly by the decentralised institutional structure of the international legal order. Specifically, as we saw in Chapter 3, this structure appears problematic due to the lack of any ostensible distinction between legal subjects and legal officials, leaving the law seemingly indeterminate in its ability to guarantee objective standards capable of pre-empting or foreclosing available political choices. Whilst this structural indeterminacy has not necessarily undermined international law's ontological reality, there remain lingering and widespread doubts over the normative authority, importance and influence of international law in the conduct of international affairs.

This, in short, is what I have called the 'institutional problem' in modern international law. As I have gone to some lengths to demonstrate throughout Part I, this problem has been widely perceived—amongst legal theorists and international lawyers alike—as a kind of structural weaknesses or constitutional deficiency at the heart of the international legal order. In Part II, however, my aim is to question, re-orient and ultimately subvert this view of the problem. I aim to demonstrate instead how the problem arises out of the limitations and short-sightedness of much conceptual thinking about law, which has, in turn, coloured our perception of the specific institutional characteristics of international law.

Insofar as many international lawyers have perpetuated this sense of structural or constitutional deficiency, the solution that has most often appeared imminent or essential in international legal literature has been the need to move towards a more centralised, more autonomous institutional architecture, that is, an institutional structure more able to effectively guide or regulate the conduct of international affairs. In Part III, I will return to consider some of the conceptual and practical problems related to this form of 'constitutional compensation', particularly where intergovernmental institutional structures are seen to be implicated in forms of 'governance' at the global level. Before doing so, however, my immediate ambition is to demonstrate how this sense of structural deficiency is perpetuated by more widespread, yet contestable, presumptions about the necessary institutional features of law, themselves premised upon a view of law as inherently bound together with the task of governance.

In this opening chapter of Part II, I will focus on what has arguably been the most influential legal-theoretical approach in recent times: the analytical tradition of jurisprudence that has dominated theoretical study in the Anglo-American world since the publication of Hart's *The Concept of Law* in 1961 (a work already discussed at length in Chapter 3 due to its distinct influence in conceptual thinking about international law). Specifically, I examine closely the under-conceptualised, yet absolutely critical explanatory role of the concept of the 'legal official', particularly the reliance on officials' use and acceptance of the Hartian rule of recognition—the structural source criterion grounding and giving effect to the system of law as a whole. Despite the essentiality of officialdom in this respect, I will argue that analytical legal philosophy has failed to provide a convincing explanation capable of conclusively identifying officials or justifying their necessarily constitutive role within legal systems. I will instead suggest that the reliance on officialdom acts merely as an analytical boot-strapping device which does away with the need to justify pre-legal hierarchy and the kinds of political authority found at the state level.

My ultimate ambition in the chapter is to demonstrate that this reliance on the notion of the legal official can only really be explained in more functional terms by thinking about the particular role of domestic law in the maintenance of political authority or social order. To the extent that the concept of law has been premised upon this view of law's function, we should thus exercise caution in invoking it in the case of non-state legal orders, specifically international law, which appears to be widely accepted, even deliberately constructed, as a non-hierarchical form of legal system. This is not to suggest that this view of law's function is necessarily wrong (and, if correct, it may well confirm that there is indeed a structural deficiency at the core of the international legal order), but only that the methodological commitments of many analytical theorists seem unable to substantiate any such claim (and thus any apparently negative conclusions about international law). In fact, I will argue that we can only reach such a conclusion on the basis of a coherent normative or 'focal' justification for the *necessarily* coercive, hierarchical character of law: an explanation that would seem to require a more directly evaluative jurisprudential method. I will return to consider such an alternative approach in Chapter 5. For the moment, my attention is focused specifically on the kind of descriptive-explanatory approach that dominates analytical jurisprudence.

I. OFFICIALDOM AND THE IDENTITY OF LEGAL ORDERS

In Chapter 3, I introduced the distinction between legal subjects and legal officials as critical to Hart's negative conclusion as to international law's status as a legal system. Ever since the publication of *The Concept of Law*, in fact, the 'legal official' has been one of the most under-theorised yet critical explanatory elements of modern analytical jurisprudence.[1] In particular, Hart's 'resurrection' of analytical legal theory established what was to become a central lynchpin of legal-conceptual analysis: the 'practice theory of rules', which aims to give an account of a legal system in terms of a critical dichotomy between the general deference of the population at large and the more committed, systemic viewpoint of legal officials.[2] More specifically—and, again, to recall from Chapter 3—Hart claimed that there were two minimum conditions for the existence of a legal system: that the primary rules are generally obeyed by the populace at large; and that the 'rules of recognition specifying the criteria of legal validity and its rules of change and adjudication must be effectively accepted as common public standards of official behaviour by its officials'.[3]

Even if analytical legal theory since *The Concept of Law* has sought to expand and explicate a more nuanced account of the necessity of different secondary rules,[4] of the likely existence of multiple rules of recognition,[5] or has even challenged the adequacy of the rule of recognition as an explanatory device,[6] what has rarely been questioned is the importance of certain official roles, in particular judicial offices, in maintaining in existence the foundational rules of the legal system.[7] In fact, whilst in the *Postscript* to

[1] See, however, KM Ehrenberg, 'The Anarchist Official: A Problem for Legal Positivism' (2011) 36 *Australian Journal of Legal Philosophy* 89, at 89; and for general discussion, see Ch 1 of K Culver and M Giudice, *Legality's Borders: An Essay in General Jurisprudence* (Oxford, Oxford University Press, 2010).

[2] HLA Hart, *The Concept of Law*, 3rd edn (Oxford, Clarendon Press, 2012) 254; Culver and Giudice (n 1) 1.

[3] Hart (n 2) 115–16. Though as Kramer points out, at other times (eg, at 107) Hart seems at least ambiguous on who must accept the rule of recognition. See M Kramer, 'The Rule of Misrecognition in the Hart of Jurisprudence' (1988) 8 *Oxford Journal of Legal Studies* 401, at 406. A fairer reading might suggest that whilst Hart did not rule out the broader community acceptance of a rule of recognition as enough to sustain its validity, the fuller realisation of a legal system appears to require official acceptance and application of the rule.

[4] See, eg, N MacCormick, 'The Concept of Law and "*The Concept of Law*"' (1994) 14 *Oxford Journal of Legal Studies* 1, at 9–12; L Green, 'The Concept of Law Revisited' (1996) 94 *Journal of Legal Studies* 1687, at 1699.

[5] J Raz, *Practical Reason and Norms* (Oxford, Oxford University Press, 1999) 129–31; J Finnis, 'Revolutions and Continuity of Law' in AWB Simpson (ed), *Oxford Essays in Jurisprudence: Second Series* (Oxford, Clarendon Press, 1971) 44, 67–70; S Shapiro, 'What is the Rule of Recognition (and Does it Exist)?' in M Alder and K Himma (eds), *The Rule of Recognition and the U.S. Constitution* (Oxford, Oxford University Press, 2009) 235, at 246–47.

[6] See, eg, Kramer (n 3).

[7] N MacCormick, *Legal Reasoning and Legal Theory* (Oxford, Clarendon Press, 1978) 55.

the second edition of *The Concept of Law*, Hart accepted certain criticisms of the coherence of his picture of the rule of recognition,[8] he nonetheless continued to defend the core of this idea as resting still upon 'a conventional form of judicial consensus'.[9]

I will return to consider aspects of this critical debate shortly, particularly insofar as it reveals certain ambiguities about the role and purpose of officials in their use or acceptance of the rule of recognition, but my immediate point is to stress the centrality of the concept of officialdom as a constitutive element of descriptive-explanatory accounts of legal order. Consider, for example, Joseph Raz's analysis of the rudiments of a legal system, which he predicates upon the practices of certain 'norm-applying institutions', which are seen not merely as important, but critical and constitutive of the systemic character of law:

> Many, if not all, legal philosophers have been agreed that one of the defining features of law is that *it is an institutionalized normative system*. Two types of institutions were singled out for special attention: norm-applying institutions such as courts, tribunals, the police, etc., and nom-creating institutions such as constitutional assemblies, parliaments, etc. I have argued elsewhere that the existence of norm-creating institutions though characteristic of modern legal systems is not a necessary feature of all legal systems, but that *the existence of certain types of norm-applying institutions is.*[10] (emphasis added)

Similarly, Jules Coleman explains the conceptual necessity of officials to sustaining the rule of recognition, in particular pointing out how legal subjects or citizens need not necessarily accept or be aware of the rule in the same way. As he puts it:

> Law exists (is actual) when there is a rule of recognition and rules valid under it that are generally followed by the majority of the population. *Acceptance from the internal point of view by officials is a conceptual requirement of the possibility of law*; acceptance from the internal point of view by a substantial proportion of the populace is neither a conceptual nor an efficacy requirement. Even if they characteristically do, these individuals, *as a conceptual matter*, need not accept the bulk of the other rules or the rule of recognition in a legal system from the internal point of view.[11] (emphasis added)

Coleman builds on Hart's claim in the *Postscript*, noted above, that the rule of recognition rests on a conventional form of judicial consensus, though at

[8] For a good account, see A Marmor, 'Legal Conventionalism' in J Coleman (ed), *Hart's Postscript: Essays on the Postscript to the* Concept of Law (Oxford, Oxford University Press, 2001) 193, 194–97.

[9] Hart (n 2) in the *Postscript* at 267.

[10] J Raz, 'The Institutional Nature of Law' (1975) 38 *Modern Law Review* 489, at 491.

[11] J Coleman, 'Incorporationism, Conventionality, and the Practical Difference Thesis' in Coleman (n 8) 99, at 115. The same remarks are also included in J Coleman, *The Practice of Principle: In Defence of a Pragmatist Approach to Legal Theory* (Oxford, Oxford University Press, 2001) 76.

the same time he goes further in suggesting—at least initially[12]—that the rule of recognition was essentially a form of 'coordination convention', premised upon a kind of game-theoretic account of shared expectations amongst officials sufficient to create the basis for a stable legal order.[13]

In a sense, Coleman's account of officialdom attempts to locate a normative reason for why officials accept and use the rule of recognition, arguing that: 'Whatever ends it serves ... the distinctive feature of law ... is that it serves these ends through rules that purport to guide conduct.'[14] Thus, for Coleman, the officially operated rule of recognition, as a form of coordination convention, provides a normative foundation for legal order, that is, a purposive justification for law's particular institutional structure (even if, once constituted this way, law is understood thereafter to serve a number of discrete purposes). A similar ambition underlies Scott Shapiro's recent explanation of law as a 'planning institution', which attempts to offer a sociological (and in that sense positivist) account of law which is grounded in an instrumental rationale (the necessity of planning to collective action):

> Legal institutions are structured by shared plans that are developed for officials so as to enable them to work together in order to plan for the community. These norms set out the vertical and horizontal divisions of social labor, specifying who is authorized to formulate, adopt, repudiate, affect, apply, and enforce the plans and instructing them about how to engage in these various stages of social planning.[15]

In fact, for Shapiro, the very point of law can be understood and explained in terms of guiding and organising 'the behavior of legal officials through the specification of roles that each is to play in the collective activity of legal regulation'.[16]

It is thus important to note how, for all concerned here, the existence of a certain class of official is seen as a *necessary* and not merely contingent or important condition for the realisation of a system of law. If they are right, this appears to have significant consequences for international law, where difficulties in accounting for a separate category of legal official suggest, on Hart's account, that international law lacks the status of a legal system,[17] or

[12] Later, he appears to have moved away from this position somewhat. See the remarks in Coleman, *The Practice of Principle* (n 11) 93 ff; and see generally the discussion in J Dickson, 'Is the Rule of Recognition Really a Conventional Rule?' (2007) 27 *Oxford Journal of Legal Studies* 373.

[13] Coleman, *The Practice of Principle* (n 11) 93–94.

[14] ibid 101.

[15] S Shapiro, *Legality* (Cambridge, MA, Harvard University Press, 2011) 176.

[16] Shapiro (n 5) 249–50 and passim.

[17] See Ch 3 above. Although interpretations of Hart's views in this respect do vary, this is a common understanding of his position on international law in Ch 10 of Hart (n 2) 213–37. For a recent affirmation of this view, see J Waldron, 'International Law: "A Relatively Small and Unimportant" Part of Jurisprudence?' in L Duarte d'Almeida, J Edwards and A Dolcetti (eds), *Reading HLA Hart's 'The Concept of Law'* (Oxford, Hart Publishing, 2013) 209–26.

more pervasively—as we have seen—that the international legal order is at best a defective or deficient form of legal system. Before reaching any such conclusion, however, it is necessary to enquire further into the concept of officialdom, in particular to try to define who exactly counts as a legal official and exactly what role they are said to fulfil vis-a-vis the rule of recognition. Indeed, given the centrality of the concept of officialdom to descriptive-explanatory accounts of legal system, one would surely expect to see some settled meaning or clear explanation of the concept. Nevertheless, as I will now go on to demonstrate, there is at the very least a critical ambiguity within such accounts as to the parameters of the concept of officialdom, as well as to exactly what function officials are seen to fulfil vis-a-vis the rule of recognition. In particular, drawing on a recent and important work by Keith Culver and Michael Giudice,[18] I will argue that such accounts fail to move beyond mere supposition based upon collective experience of the domestic law-state.

II. THE PROBLEMATIC CONCEPT OF THE LEGAL OFFICIAL

In suggesting the centrality of officials to post-Hartian descriptive-explanatory accounts of law and legal systems, I do not wish to over-elevate Hart's theory (or other accounts which have followed in Hart's footsteps) as the only applicable or relevant approach to understanding international law. However, as we have already seen in Chapter 3, to the extent that the discipline's own attempts to offer a coherent account of the systemic nature of international law are often premised upon something like Hart's concept of law, it is necessary to understand, and to critically engage with, the widespread reliance on officialdom, without which any such approach makes little sense. Furthermore, it seems that even in the most influential alternative theoretical models developed, for instance, those of modern natural lawyers like John Finnis and Lon Fuller, there is an even greater conceptual interrelation between ideas of legality and law's institutionalisation.[19] In fact, in the most vehemently 'anti-positivist' approaches to legal theory, such as the legal realism of jurists like Alf Ross[20] or, more obviously perhaps, the interpretevist approach of Ronald Dworkin,[21] the law's material application in the hands of judicial bodies and other authorised decision-makers becomes even more critical to its normativity in practice. In fact, one recent

[18] Culver and Giudice (n 1).

[19] J Finnis, *Natural Law and Natural Rights*, 2nd edn (Oxford, Oxford University Press, 2011) 8–9, citing L Fuller, *The Morality of Law* (New Haven, Yale University Press, 1964) 210 and passim.

[20] See, eg, A Ross, *On Law and Justice* (Berkeley, University of California Press, 1959), 34–38 and passim; and see the criticisms of HLA Hart in this respect in 'Scandinavian Realism' (1959) 17 *Cambridge Law Journal* 233, at 237–40.

[21] See generally Ch 2 of R Dworkin, *Law's Empire* (Oxford, Hart Publishing, 2004, first published in 1986).

commentator, writing within an avowedly Dworkinian frame, has gone so far as to claim 'that it is doubtful that there can ever be a legal system without officials running it' and, even if theoretically possible to imagine a system without such officials, 'their importance where they are to be found is undeniable'.[22]

The important point here is that in challenging descriptive-explanatory accounts of legal order, none of these approaches at the same time challenges the over-reliance on specific institutions or structures of authority within those accounts; if anything, the criticism is that such theories fail to adequately explain an important institutional element of law. As such, I will consider further the extent that we can specifically justify officialdom by looking beyond the frames of the descriptive-explanatory method in the following two chapters. Here, I wish to critically examine the claim that we can ground an adequate general concept of law from a description of the necessary features which it is deemed law must possess. Accordingly, the question that arises is as follows: is it possible to give a coherent explanation of officialdom, presuming that legal officials are a necessary, constitutive feature of law in general?

It is in response to this question, however, that certain problems of identification arise. For instance, to say that officials are merely those who *by necessity* accept, use or otherwise rely on the rule of recognition does not in any way mark out anything unique about the office and what it brings to the conceptual coherence of a legal system. After all, it could well be the case that in domestic legal systems, citizens themselves choose to understand legal rules in this way, assessing the validity of substantive legal principles by reference to a rule of recognition. In particular, Hart's account did not preclude this; he (like Coleman also) merely claimed that such acceptance was not a necessary element of a legal system, whilst acceptance by officials was.[23] Are citizens, subjects or other legal persons also deemed to be legal officials merely on the basis of their use or acceptance of the rule of recognition? If so, the problem for international law would surely be resolved, but this clearly was not the case for Hart. Such an identifying criterion is not only implausible, but also seems conceptually unnecessary to the existence of a given legal order: if the only purpose of designating certain individuals or bodies as officials is that they do as a matter of course accept, or reason according to, the rule of recognition, their designation as such makes little

[22] D Kyritsis, 'The Normativity of the Practice of Officials: A Philosophical Programme' in S Bertea and G Pavlakos (eds), *New Essays on the Normativity of Law* (Oxford, Hart Publishing, 2011) 177, at 177.

[23] Hart (n 2) 114–17; and see Coleman, 'Incorporationism' (n 11). However, see the criticisms of Stephen Perry in this respect, who argues that this optionality of wider acceptance is an 'embarrassment' on the part of Hart's account, potentially propping up authoritarianism. S Perry, 'Hart on Social Rules and the Foundations of Law: Liberating the Internal Point of View' (2006) 75 *Fordham Law Review* 1171, at 1203.

conceptual sense in terms of our ability to identify the existence of a legal system. As Culver and Giudice claim, we need to know more about what is distinctive in 'occupy[ing] a special position within the legal system by virtue of the rules of office'.[24]

In attempting to give an answer to this conundrum, however, they note two immediate problems. The first and most obvious is the problem of circularity, as the concept of the legal official seems to depend for its designation on the prior existence of a legal system, yet the official is seen as critical to the constitution of that system—a classic 'chicken and egg' situation.[25] This problem has in fact been a common criticism of the conditions for legal order given by Hart[26] and, perhaps unsurprisingly, a number of jurists have suggested means by which it is possible to escape or otherwise show the falsity of this criticism.[27] In order to defeat this problem, we need some boot-strapping device[28] or social-factual explanation of officialdom which does not simply rely on the pre-existence of a certain type of legal order.[29] For instance, Coleman claims that officials can be identified by reference to those institutions or offices accepted by a population as exercising authority, but whose designation as officials within the context of a particular legal system only arises once the system is constituted as such.[30] MacCormick sees an intrinsic connection and inter-referentiality between rules of change, adjudication and recognition, beyond that conceived by Hart, which provides a sociological explanation for maintaining in existence a legal system.[31] Brian Tamanaha offers a similar, social-factual explanation of officialdom, which essentially sees the emergence of the secondary rules of a legal system and the acceptance of the official status of certain institutions as 'contemporaneous events'.[32] Shapiro also describes the authority enjoyed by courts (and possibly other officials) as a matter of social facts, rather than being determined by the same rule of recognition that their practice helps to constitute. As he puts it:

> [Particular] bodies are courts of a certain legal system because they generate and sustain that system's rule of recognition ... Once we have determined that certain

[24] Culver and Giudice (n 1) 10.

[25] See, eg, IW Duncanson, 'The Strange World of English Jurisprudence' (1979) 30 *Northern Ireland Legal Quarterly* 207, 220.

[26] See, eg, Kramer (n 3), 407–08; B Tamanaha, *A General Jurisprudence of Law and Society* (Oxford, Oxford University Press, 2001) 140–42; MacCormick (n 7) 54–56; and, more extensively, N MacCormick, *H. L. A. Hart*, 2nd edn (Stanford, CA, Stanford University Press, 2008) 136–41; and see further references in Culver and Giudice (n 1) 6, fn 11.

[27] Culver and Giudice (n 1) 10–14.

[28] See, eg, MacCormick (n 7) 55–56; and see the criticism of Kramer (n 3) 413.

[29] MacCormick, *H. L. A. Hart* (n 26) 142–44; plus the further criticism of Kramer (n 3) 414–16.

[30] Coleman, *The Practice of Principle* (n 11) 100–01.

[31] MacCormick, *H. L. A. Hart* (n 26) 139–40.

[32] Tamanaha (n 26) 141.

> bodies have created and sustained the secondary rules of a legal system, we can claim that those bodies *are* the courts of that system, for courts belong to a certain legal system when they have been successful in creating and sustaining its normative infrastructure.[33]

The problem with these claimed solutions, however, is that they only really justify that which is already in place: Shapiro's argument, for instance, cannot be used critically to determine the existence of officials in normative orders where their presence is disputed. Whilst such pragmatic, social-factual explanations, as intuitive as they might seem, seem to solve the problem of circularity, they do so only by relying upon, presuming or passively accepting the prior existence of a certain hierarchy, which tends to escape any independent justification. More critically, however, on their own, they do not solve the second issue identified by Culver and Giudice: the problem of indeterminacy. This problem is particularly troublesome bearing in mind the discussion in Chapter 3, where I explained how in domestic legal orders the problem of *normative* indeterminacy can be mitigated, prima facie at least, by the presence of legal officials in domestic legal systems. If, however, the very concept of officialdom is itself also beset by indeterminacy, the initial problem is merely transferred to another level.

The indeterminacy surrounding the concept of officialdom arises precisely from the social-factual, intuitive nature of the above response to the charge of circularity. This response seems to ground the concept of officialdom in well-known and widely accepted examples of legal officials familiar from domestic legal contexts (courts, legislatures etc). However, this form of intuition—or, less charitably, 'speculative anthropology', as Leslie Green once put this in criticising Hart[34]—raises two particular difficulties. First, whilst obvious examples of domestic legal institutions are easy to identify, such observations do not allow us to determine uncertainty at the margins of the concept: beyond judges, legislatures, the police etc, who exactly counts as a legal official and who does not? Furthermore, such observations tell us nothing about the discrete functions fulfilled by different officials and whether (and, if so, *why*) some official roles might (as Raz suggests) be more important than others in constituting the systemic character of law. Second, if we accept that there is at least a penumbra of uncertainty surrounding the outer margins of the concept of officialdom, then on what basis are we to determine whether officials exist at all in normative orders such as international law that claim the status of a legal system and, indeed, whether such normative orders are therefore forms of law at all?

[33] S Shapiro, 'On Hart's Way Out' in Coleman (n 8) 149, at 156.

[34] L Green, 'Legal Positivism' in EN Zalta (ed), *The Stanford Encyclopedia of Philosophy* (Fall 2009 Edition); available at: http://plato.stanford.edu/archives/fall2009/entries/legal-positivism, as also cited in Culver and Giudice (n 1) 12.

To overcome this uncertainty at the margins, accounts of officialdom tend to leave it to the system itself, and particularly the existence of an identifiable institutional hierarchy, to be able to determine who occupies an official position. In so doing, however, this form of reconciliation just seems to create another kind of circularity: an official being whoever is officially accepted as such. For instance, whilst Andrei Marmor's account of the rule of recognition as a constitutive convention is less categorical than many—ie, he does not portend a rigid distinction between officials and subjects, but instead suggests a kind of 'division of labour' or gradated idea of officialdom—his answer still depends on the existence of a certain kind of hierarchy. Specifically, he suggests that the closer one is to the centre of the practice of law, the more one will be familiar with the constitutive conventions necessary to keep the practice in place. On this (deliberately vague) account, officialdom clearly encompasses more than just judges, but judicial offices again emerge as the most important position in maintaining in existence the coherence of the legal order.[35]

Whilst such deference to judicial hierarchies may be tolerable in the case of domestic law, it is obviously unsatisfactory in making sense of decentralised legal orders such as international law.[36] As Culver and Giudice argue, 'if we can presume a core of officials, such as judges, who sit at the top or center in a hierarchical structure of a legal system, worries about borders become less worrisome, since there is in practice a means of resolving such indeterminacy'.[37] This is certainly a problem to our immediate enquiry, as to rely on a hierarchical structure in this way is clearly at the same time to diminish the utility of such conceptual models in making sense of systems of law beyond the state. The more fundamental problem, though, is that even at the state level, this explanation is inadequate, as its inherent pragmatism seems to end up merely as unquestioning deference to authority. If questions as to the characteristics of officialdom are merely settled by officials themselves, a new form of circularity emerges which seemingly does away with the constitutive nature of the rule of recognition itself. More precisely, if questions about the identification of law depend upon official practice and if questions about the identification of officials are resolved by officials themselves, it seems that the rule of recognition need say no more than that the law is whatever officials say it is. In fact, thinking about the role of judges in particular, it is far from clear that the judiciary in many legal orders have a shared, singular understanding of the system's claimed rule (or rules) of recognition, or indeed whether certain sources of law are merely just accepted

[35] Marmor (n 8) 209–10.
[36] Culver and Giudice (n 1) 14–15, 21.
[37] ibid 16.

regardless of what is commonly taken to be the rule(s) of recognition of that system.[38] What matters from this perspective seems to be only the act of acceptance, not the content of the rule itself.

Such social-factual explanations are tainted by the problem that, whilst subordinating the ascertainment of law vis-a-vis the rule of recognition to official practice, they fail to offer up any countervailing argument that might explain how law determines the normative situation of officials themselves. If evidence of the rule of recognition stems merely from official recognition of the rule and little more is said about *why* officials might find it important or necessary to maintain in existence a *particular kind of* rule of recognition, then it seems that the foundations of legal order can be explained simply in terms of official decree: a justification for institutional hierarchy without any mediating form of accountability.

An alternative explanation, of course, is that officialdom is, after all, simply not necessary for the constitution of a legal system absent a defence of law's specific function or purpose and, thereafter, how such a function structures, guides and, ultimately, restrains officials in their position of authority over other legal participants. However, it is precisely this kind of functional, purposive justification that tends to be avoided, or explicitly rejected, by those adopting a descriptive-explanatory methodology, who purport to offer only an uncommitted explanation of the constitutive features of law (or legal systems) in general terms. Nevertheless, as I will argue in the next section, it is only on the basis of such a justification that legal theory can offer up a convincing and coherent explanation for the necessity of officialdom as a constitutive element of legal order.

III. FUNCTIONAL OFFICIALDOM AND THE PROBLEM OF TRANSLATION

To recap on the previous analysis, the problem of indeterminacy as to the concept of the legal official seems to be incapable of resolution other than by relying on certain clear-cut examples of officialdom, including but not limited to judges and other law-applying institutions, who are able themselves to determine where the distinction between official and citizen might lie in any given situation. In other words, the concept of officialdom only seems to operate effectively if we presume some kind of pre-existing hierarchy in the legal system. However, relying on official acceptance in this way begs the question of why officials are required at all as a distinct legal

[38] This is of course a criticism levelled at Hart most famously by Dworkin: see principally Ch III ('The Model of Rules II') of R Dworkin, *Taking Rights Seriously* (Cambridge, MA, Harvard University Press, 1978).

category; why *their* acceptance might matter over any other form of broader social acceptance. In other words, from a purely *constitutive* perspective, it is not at all clear what the concept of the legal official does in order to prove essential to the concept of law. Why not, in other words, just rely on accepted sources of law in a looser, less essentialist enquiry into law as a social-factual phenomenon?

The answer to this conundrum appears to be that whilst officials may fulfil many useful functions within the legal order—as acknowledged by Hart as much as by others[39]—it is really the authoritative resolution function of law-applying institutions which seems to matter most, bringing determinacy to otherwise indeterminate legal standards. In this way, it can be said that officials contribute to the material, and not merely abstract, autonomy of a legal system. Indeed, as we saw in Chapter 3, only if we presume that authoritative resolution is critical to law's role in society does the structural indeterminacy of international law seem problematic, thus undermining its overall coherence as a legal system. However, to admit this is to equate the regulatory purpose of the domestic law-state with the function of law in general—a purpose for which a measure of determinacy in identifying and applying the law would seem necessary.[40] This point is well made by Margaret Martin, who considers the critical role that judges play within Raz's account:

> Judges are not simply important players in a political game of power and principle. Instead, they are charged with the responsibility of maintaining a stable body of norms that the citizens can turn to for guidance … the judicial duty to apply the law does not simply secure the exclusionary nature of legal norms. This duty also gives shape to the legal system more generally.[41]

This view of law as securing a form of order and control creates a kind of 'creation myth', giving a justification for specific institutional features, the essentiality of which only makes sense if we presume the correctness of the underlying functional commitment: that is, a view of law as 'an autonomous set of legal norms that can serve as reasons for action of the populace enabling order to triumph over chaos'.[42] There is much in this explanation which is problematic if we apply this view to international law—a point to which I return below and in the following two chapters—but the immediate problem is that this functional explanation is explicitly resisted by many analytical legal theorists, Raz included, who purport only to offer an uncommitted descriptive explanation of the necessary features of a legal order, and not an account (or, better, defence) of why a certain kind of

[39] See discussion below at n 56.

[40] Indeed, this is precisely the claim made by those espousing a more openly evaluative, 'normative' or 'ethical' form of positivism. See principally J Waldron, 'Normative (or Ethical) Positivism' in Coleman (n 8) 411; as well as, more comprehensively, T Campbell, *The Legal Theory of Ethical Positivism* (Aldershot, Dartmouth, 1996).

[41] M Martin, *Judging Positivism* (Oxford, Hart Publishing, 2014) 18–19.

[42] ibid 19.

order is important, useful or otherwise preferable to others.[43] In particular, Raz suggests that a functional explanation of officialdom is inappropriate. He admits that if merely looked at in terms of systemic function, the 'law-applying institution' could be understood merely by reference to the acts of *any* authorised body, person or institution accepted as fulfilling this specific function, and he also recognises that a formal account of officialdom is made problematic by the divergences between, and particularities of, distinct legal systems. However, he argues that it can only be the particular nature of the office that matters, that is, the specific *way in which* courts or law-applying institutions fulfil their function.[44] In this respect, Raz offers a definition of officialdom based on the peculiarities of the office itself, with 'law-applying institutions' identified as those bodies 'with power to determine the normative situation of specified individuals, which are required to exercise these powers by applying existing norms, but whose decisions are binding even when wrong'.[45]

On one level, this definition seems to be a very obvious description of a domestic judicial function. This is clearly not very helpful in conceptualising the distinctiveness of the role of the legal official if we disagree with him in his conclusion that, or that only, law-applying institutions are necessary to legal order. However, he does not just leave his concept of a legal system as dependent upon official recognition; he goes further than Hart in setting out certain attributes that a legal system must possess in making a necessary claim to authority (thus making his definition of officialdom more comprehensible): these are what he terms *supremacy*, *comprehensiveness* and *openness*.[46] As, inter alia, Marmor,[47] Tamanaha,[48] as well as more recently (and more extensively) Culver and Giudice[49] have all claimed, aside from arguably being controversial on their own terms, when put to the test, these criteria fail to distinguish adequately the institutions of a legal system from other forms of normative order: they are both over- and under-inclusive in important ways, making the puzzle of the distinctive institutional structure of a legal system only more problematic. Whilst I think there are good reasons why they are correct in making these criticisms, I do not wish to push this point further here. There is, I believe, a more profound problem with

[43] For example, Leslie Green argues that: 'Law is a *modal* kind and not a *functional* kind at all; it is distinguished by its means and not its end. The moral value of law depends primarily on the ends to which its means are put, and that is a contingent matter.' Green (n 4) 1711.

[44] Raz (n 10) 492.

[45] ibid 494.

[46] J Raz, *The Authority of Law: Essays on Law and Morality*, 2nd edn (Oxford, Oxford University Press, 2009) 116 ff.

[47] A Marmor, *Positive Law and Objective Values* (Oxford, Oxford University Press, 2001) 39–42.

[48] Tamanaha (n 26) 139–40.

[49] Culver and Giudice (n 1) 47–62.

Raz's account of law as authority, and more particularly his reliance upon law-applying institutions, in that it really tells us little about why judges themselves are important to the constitution of the system of law beyond their ability to authoritatively bind others (that is, to reach determinate solutions). In other words, read together with the authority claims he sees as intrinsic to law, Raz's approach suggests that judicial institutions are valuable to the extent that they are able to bring determinacy in the application of the law; it suggests that Raz sees a functional benefit to the presence of law-applying institutions that allows the law to better determine the situation of legal subjects, enhancing its ability to offer guidance on conduct, preempt political choice and close off disagreement.[50] However, rather than attempt to defend this view of law's role in society as a necessary good, his account is built on the presumption that such functions are intrinsic to law—they are 'commonplace', he claims.[51] But if we can legitimately question this presumption or indeed challenge its pretention to universality, his refusal to justify and defend this functional orientation begins to seem far more problematic.[52]

This point is picked up by Tamanaha, who argues that Raz is not alone in presuming a certain functional purpose to law, upon which a seemingly more neutral descriptive-explanatory account of law's necessary institutional structure can be erected. He notes how there is an implicit—though, at times, often also explicit—premise at work in the concept of law and legal system developed by analytical theorists, particularly in the accounts given by both Hart and Raz: namely that the function of law is to 'maintain social order'.[53] Though dismissing the possibility of a functional explanation of the necessary institutional features of a legal system, Raz seems to have premised his entire theory on the view that law must guide conduct, pre-empting or foreclosing other political and moral choices.[54] Similarly,

[50] Raz denies that his account of law commits him to a view that law serves any particular role of social coordination, let alone a form of coercive authority. See J Raz, 'Postema on Law's Autonomy and Public Practical Reasons: A Critical Comment' (1998) 4 *Legal Theory* 1, at 2–4. However, see critical comments to the contrary in Tamanaha (n 26) 143–44, pointing out how Raz imposes an efficacy requirement on law as a form of coercive realisation of social order. Furthermore, the idea of authority underpinning Raz's concept of law clearly seems to rely on an unstated view of the role of municipal legal systems which is dangerously close to authoritarianism. See in this respect the criticism in D Dyzenhaus, 'Why Positivism is Authoritarian' (1992) 37 *American Journal of Jurisprudence* 83, at 101 ff. On Raz's clear reliance on the hierarchical structure of the domestic law-state, see generally Ch 2 of Culver and Giudice (n 1). And see also the more general criticisms of Raz's inconsistency in M Martin, 'Raz's The Morality of Freedom: Two Models of Authority' (2010) 1 *Jurisprudence* 63 and developed at length in Martin (n 41).

[51] Raz (n 46) 50–51.

[52] See discussion in Martin (n 41) 97–98.

[53] Tamanaha (n 26) 135.

[54] For an example of this kind of claim, see, inter alia, Raz (n 5) 144. For discussion, see Martin (n 41) 117–23 and passim.

in Hart's work, we see numerous references to the idea of law as a means of 'social control',[55] yet no attempt to justify this purpose beyond intuition from the domestic context.[56]

There is a certain ambiguity in Hart's account in this respect, which is addressed by Lefkowitz in his attempt, noted in Chapter 3, to apply a Hartian approach to the identification of customary international law. Lefkowitz shows how Hart seems to move between two versions of the rule of recognition, which at times is seen to serve an identification function and at other times a more unifying, systematising function, requiring the authoritative resolution of disputes about the meaning and application of any given rule in concrete situations.[57] As he notes:

> Hart elides an important distinction between … the ontological function and the authoritative resolution function of such a rule. The former makes possible the kind of justification and criticism constitutive of a rule-governed practice for identifying norms as legally valid. The latter makes possible the settling of disputes over what the law is, as well as over the scope of particular legal norms.[58]

On the basis of the points raised in Part I, it seems obvious that international law would fail this latter, more ambitious functional test, due particularly to the fact that it lacks the institutional structure necessary to ensure authoritative resolution in the sense described. In order to reconcile Hart's approach with a systemic account of the international legal order, Lefkowitz attempts to decouple these two functions; he argues that if we think in terms of a constitutive, ontological function alone, it would be possible to read states themselves into an official role at the international level.[59] However, as we saw in Chapter 3, whilst such an account could provide conceptual

[55] Hart (n 2) 40, 9–91, 165, 188, 208; and see the discussion in Tamanaha (n 26) 136. On the many meanings which we might attach to the notion of social order/control in this context, see also discussion in W Twining, 'A Post-Westphalian Conception of Law' (2003) 37 *Law & Society Review* 199, 215–17.

[56] As we saw in Ch 3 above, Hart is quite open about the benefits (and risks) of a society moving from the pre-legal and primitive form of legal order to one which is structured according to officially operated rules of recognition, change and adjudication. These benefits include 'adaptability to change, certainty, and efficiency'; however, Hart says that such benefits accruing from the centralisation of authority within the state will have to be weighed against the cost in terms of the 'risk that the centrally organized power may well be used for the oppression of numbers with whose support it can dispense, in a way that the simpler regime of primary rules could not'. See Hart (n 2) 202. These risks are discussed at length in relation to the challenge of the rule sceptics, who for Hart would essentially have the law determined entirely by judicial fiat. In response, Hart outlines how judges' authority will always exist in a precarious balance, having to recognise its limits in the context of the overall coherence of the legal system (ibid 141–45). See further the discussion above in Ch 3, section III.

[57] D Lefkowitz, '(Dis)solving the Chronological Paradox in Customary International Law: A Hartian Approach' (2008) 21 *Canadian Journal of Law and Jurisprudence* 129, at 145–46. For somewhat similar concerns on the ambiguities around the construction and use of the rule of recognition, see also Twining (n 55) 230–31.

[58] Lefkowitz (n 57) 146.

[59] ibid 146–47.

completion to international law as a system in a way that would allow a reconciliation with Hart's concept of law (at least on one reading), it also seems to leave the concept of the legal official logically redundant: one could simply speak of states and other participants or actors as recognising certain sources of law and give a systemic account on those terms alone. In other words, it seems difficult to read Hart in this way, that is, to find a reason for the distinction between subject and official, as well as any justification for the practices of officials, solely in terms of their using, deferring to and reasoning according to the rule of recognition.

As such, to give this kind of descriptive explanation—relying on recognised hierarchies and the prior existence of certain norm-applying institutions as necessary institutional features of all forms of law or legal system—is surely problematic without going further in offering and, *importantly*, normatively defending a specific justification for law as a method of social ordering, facilitated through centralised institutions capable of giving an authoritative resolution to normative problems.[60] It would seem that the accuracy of what, for example, Hart entails to be essential institutional features of a legal system, and therefore seemingly absent or deficient at the international level, depends upon the correctness of the assumptions he makes about the point, purpose or function of law in general, including within the domestic context. As Tamanaha notes, there is an awkward elision of functionalist and essentialist logic in Hart's account, which, in turn, sits uneasily with the social-factual (or conventional) methodology underpinning analytical jurisprudence. This movement between conventionalism, functionalism and essentialism allows Hart to eliminate as not subscribing to certain forms those legal orders which might be constituted differently from domestic law (his essentialism), yet which can be understood, perhaps, to fulfil the same purpose (his functionalism). However, the particular constitutive features of law thus taken to be essential seem to be highly contingent upon a fuller normative justification for the specific functional orientation of law—a justification which is largely absent apart from certain scattered remarks which, as noted above, seem to suggest (but not substantiate or defend) the function of law as a means of social control.[61] To put this same point another way, if the union of primary and secondary rules in Hart's account was seen purely in terms of conventional usage, then it would surely apply to any system which demonstrated systematicity, yet did not necessarily function to maintain social order. At the same time, if functionality was key, it would equally would that a legal order which fulfilled a social-coordination function (or whatever function

[60] See the discussion and criticisms of, inter alia, Martin (n 41) 97–98 and passim; Finnis (n 19) Ch 1; Waldron (n 40) 429–31; and R Cotterrell, *The Politics of Jurisprudence: A Critical Introduction to Legal Philosophy*, 2nd edn (Oxford, Oxford University Press, 2003) 107–11.

[61] Tamanaha (n 26) 138.

we presume is intrinsic to law) yet was constituted differently (for instance, was decentralised in structure) could still qualify as law. However, nowhere is this functional account put to the test due to the essentialist claims Hart makes about the necessary institutional structure of law in general.[62] Ultimately, despite underlying assumptions based on functional utility, it seems that it is essentialism which prevails over functionalism in Hart's account, as well as in much of the analytical tradition that has followed.[63]

IV. MOVING BEYOND THE STATE: A WAY FORWARD FOR CONCEPTUAL ENQUIRY?

This disavowal of functionalism in thinking about necessary features of law thus seems problematic if we have no other convincing justification for the essentiality of legal officials within legal theory. Whilst there have been attempts to plug this apparent gap, aimed at giving a more coherent account of the functional role played by the officially operated rule of recognition, these efforts have proved controversial precisely because they tend to embrace commitments to which a descriptive-explanatory methodology seems opposed. For instance, we saw above that Coleman had developed (though apparently later moved away from) an account of the rule of recognition as a coordination convention. However, this kind of explanation seems controversial precisely because it presumes an essential function at the basal level of the system, without offering up an a priori justification or normative commitment to this view. Many if not most analytical legal philosophers (including, inter alia, Hart, Raz, Dickson and Green) have been explicit that law does not necessarily serve one particular function; that it can be described modally by reference to *how* it functions rather than what function it serves.[64] In the *Postscript* to *The Concept of Law*, Hart makes this point in response to Dworkin, in particular arguing that it is 'quite vain to seek any more specific purpose which law as such serves beyond providing guides to human conduct and standards of criticism of

[62] ibid 142–45.

[63] Similar criticisms have been levelled at those like Postema or Coleman who have presented a 'conventionalist' account of the rule of recognition, but defined this conventional account in terms of social coordination—the presumption being that law has as its function the task of providing a meta-solution to collective action problems. See, eg, G Postema, 'Coordination and Convention at the Foundations of Law' (1982) 11 *Journal of Legal Studies* 165; and the criticisms contained in A Marmor, 'The Conventional Foundations of Law' in Bertea and Pavlakos (n 22) 144, at 150–51.

[64] See, eg, Hart (n 2) 24–50. Raz devotes Ch 9 of *The Authority of Law* (n 46) to law's many functions, but has been clear that law cannot be defined by reference to any one of them: Raz (n 50) 2–4; Green (n 4) 1709–11; and see J Dickson, *Evaluation and Legal Theory* (Oxford, Hart Publishing, 2007) 112.

such conduct'.[65] Nevertheless, it is clear that at other points, this seemingly uncontroversial 'conduct-guidance' function seems to easily morph into a fuller, more regulatory ideal, which, in turn, tends only to reinforce the particular institutional character of the modern state form, particularly the presence of coercive, authoritative dispute settlers.

Following this line of reasoning, and in attempting to rescue the conventionalist explanation as a justification for the institutional and systemic structure of law, Marmor has argued that the rule of recognition cannot be understood as primarily related to a function of social coordination or control. Rather, by necessity, he argues that it can only be held to play a constitutive role in the validation of legal rules and thus the constitution of a legal system (even if the way in which it is used and operated by legal officials may also have benefits in terms of social coordination, that is, by bringing greater determinacy through authoritative resolution). To the extent that the rule of recognition might *also* bring such contingent benefits, however, Marmor points out that, logically speaking, it must be possible to ascertain the law, to define *what it is*, before we seek greater determinacy in identifying the law, that is, in giving it specific meaning in particular instances:

> [I]f there are reasons to have rules of recognition, those reasons must be very intimately linked to the reasons for having law in the first place. Certainty about what the law is cannot be the main reason for having law. There must be some reasons for having law first, and then it might also be important to have a certain level of certainty about it. It cannot be the other way around.[66]

This is an important observation underpinning Marmor's claim that law has to be understood as a relatively autonomous social practice and, as such, that the rule of recognition provides the criteria necessary for achieving that degree of autonomy. To see the rule of recognition as purposefully driven towards a certain aim, ie, social co-ordination, would seem to undermine this claimed autonomy (as there may well be more than one way to achieve this end, thus risking the abstract form of the law becoming subjugated to its function). Rather than thinking in terms of functions or functionalism, however, Marmor describes his defence of law's autonomy as 'historicist':[67]an attempt to explain the form of law as a matter of social contingency that does not prioritise any one particular function.

There is much in this particular observation that is potentially important (and much that is potentially controversial),[68] but it suffices to recognise

[65] Hart (n 2) 249.
[66] Marmor (n 63) 150.
[67] Marmor (n 8) 216–17.
[68] For instance, both Dickson and Green deny that such an account would be a 'conventionalist' account at all; that Marmor is merely describing a practice theory of rules which does not require the concept of the social convention—which, in fact, suggests a functionality which Marmor is not purporting to explain. See Dickson (n 12); L Green, 'Positivism and Conventionalism' (1999) 12 *Canadian Journal of Law and Jurisprudence* 35, at 41–43 and passim.

two particular difficulties for the moment. First, if the rule of recognition is merely an historically contingent social convention (telling us what the law is, who has which powers etc), then why would the existence of this convention necessarily presuppose the kind of division of labour (between subjects and officials) which Marmor also describes as important or necessary to the existence of legal order? Although Marmor suggests a means to resolve the question of who is an official—one which, as we saw above, is hardly satisfactory—it is not at all clear why he needs a concept of officialdom at all. His reliance on legal officials seems persuasive only to the extent that Marmor sees the apparently secondary benefit of greater determinacy brought about through authoritative resolution as a still important, even if perhaps not *constitutively* necessary, component of a mature system of law.[69] At the root of this concern, however, lies a second, deeper problem with Marmor's account, in that he seeks to make essentialist claims about the institutional character of law that are premised merely upon historical contingency rather than specific normative justification. In his effort to prioritise the rule of recognition's constitutive rather than authoritative resolution function, there still seems to be a value judgement which recognises the importance of law's autonomy, a value that might be threatened by any more instrumentalist logic. However, it is questionable whether Marmor can really defend this value coherently due to the conventionalist (or historicist) methodology that underpins his theory. This theory offers no critical ammunition by which to disprove or disregard the views of, on the one hand, those legal participants who would see law's ambitions or ends as more important than its means or methods, or, on the other, those who would defend the ontological reality of putatively legal orders like international law, which appear to function systemically but lack any meaningful distinction between legal officials and other legal actors or participants.

One way out of this apparent conundrum, of course, would be to embrace empiricism at the expense of any such essentialist claims, that is, to give a social-factual, or conventional, explanation of law *all the way down*. This potential—and potentially quite radical—way forward is advocated by Tamanaha, for instance, whose commitment to legal pluralism has caused him to abandon almost all essentialist claims about the necessary institutional characteristics of law. Instead, he seeks to explain the operative validity of any given legal order in purely social-factual terms, based on its societal acceptance alone.[70] Tamanaha's approach does not seek to jettison

[69] I owe this observation to Mike Giudice, who points out how we might be able to specify the existence and content of some social rule to a certain degree of certainty without necessarily depending on legal officials to identify and reason according to this rule. Hence, even if we see certainty as a necessary condition for the existence of a system, it might still not require officialdom per se.

[70] Tamanaha (n 26) 166–70 ff.

criteria for legal validity entirely, but it does mean that 'any members of a given group can identify what law is, as long as it constitutes a conventional practice' and therefore also recognises that '*a given manifestation of law … might completely lack legal officials*'.[71] He recognises the vagaries of this test, in particular that it does not provide a criterion level of acceptance: for instance, it does not tell us how many members of a group need to recognise the binding nature of law for it to be operative over them, nor does it deal with the potential problem of linguistic aberrations. Nevertheless, he contends that these uncertainties do not hinder the acknowledgement and ascertainment of juridical law in operation in a given community, which can be established simply on the basis of both '[c]ontext and usage'.[72]

There is great potential in this approach to move jurisprudential enquiry forward to embrace a more genuinely universal (less parochial) empiricism, aimed at understanding the constituent features of law in its many diverse global contexts.[73] In particular, Tamanaha's effort to show the social and historical contingency of supposedly essential features of legal order—indeed, to demonstrate the back-to-front view that law is somehow constitutive of social order (rather than, for instance, seeing the contingent institutional features of law themselves as a product of the instigation of a certain form of social order)—is a particularly welcome disciplinary move.[74] At the same time, however, in his thorough review of Tamanaha's work, William Twining is surely correct that this attempt to give up on all essentialist claims about law is counter-intuitive and unworkable if jurisprudence is to play any critical role in offering practical truths or useful observations about law, particularly in cases where the law-like quality of a particular normative order is in dispute.[75] Tamanaha's use of 'folk concepts' to draw out conclusions about how law is used and understood is important and critical if jurisprudence is to develop conceptualisations of law which are meaningful to those who use them, but any such enquiry can only be a first step.[76] In particular, to rely on participant perspective alone would seem to run into trouble when there is internal disagreement within communities or a blurring of the boundaries between legal and purportedly legal normative orders, seemingly requiring a conceptual framework that aids

[71] ibid 166.

[72] ibid 168.

[73] The criticism of jurisprudential parochialism has been gaining in force in recent years. See, eg, W Twining, *General Jurisprudence: Understanding Law from a Global Perspective* (Cambridge, Cambridge University Press, 2009) 10–11 ff. And see my commentary on this disciplinary transition in R Collins, 'No Longer at the Vanishing Point? International Law and the Analytical Tradition in Jurisprudence' (2014) 5 *Jurisprudence* 265, at 273–75.

[74] Tamanaha (n 26) 223–24.

[75] Twining (n 55) 229–30.

[76] ibid. On this particular point in relation to international law, see also P Capps, *Human Dignity and the Foundations of International Law* (Oxford, Hart Publishing, 2009) 23.

in distinguishing, or deciding upon relative importance, in coming up with useful generalisations or comparative frameworks. This is a point picked up by Culver and Giudice, who, whilst being sympathetic to Tamanaha's ambitions, as well as many of his observations, argue that his ultimate conclusion 'disarms legality of its special explanatory task and role',[77] with his account therefore ceasing to be useful as a way of resolving disputes about the legality of putatively legal orders.[78]

If Culver and Giudice are right, how are we to move forward to account adequately for what might or might not be necessary institutional features of law or legal systems? One option might be to follow what Twining refers to as a 'thin functionalist' approach, seeking to re-integrate law's institutional and normative aspects to understand the role that it plays in ordering societal relations. As he explains:

> If 'ordering' is interpreted to be wider than social control and social order to include constitutive, facilitative, facultative, symbolic, benefit-conferring, and educative functions, this allows for the possibility that a given example of law is not necessarily concerned with any particular function, such as dispute processing or authoritative regulation, but still invites attention as 'law'.[79]

Pared down to a certain level of abstraction, this view of law's function—itself premised on Karl Llewelyn's famous 'law jobs' theory[80]—seems largely uncontroversial, easily mapping on to international as much as domestic legal practice. At the same time, however, it does seem to come up short in two ways. First, even if less demanding, and in that sense more universal, in its apparent reach, simply positing or presuming certain functional truisms doesn't seem any less controversial a methodological approach if we accept that there may also be a view of law's function which extends beyond simply ordering human affairs in the way suggested. By positing this function—suggesting essentially the empty formal autonomy of law as an end in itself—Twining's argument seems to accord with the approach of those, like Marmor, who are anxious that any more instrumental task may undermine the distinctive identity of law. However, precisely for this reason, this approach suggests something valuable and important in law's formal autonomy, therefore requiring evaluative judgement on the part of

[77] Culver and Giudice (n 1) 145.

[78] ibid 146.

[79] Twining (n 55) 241. This approach also has some affinity with the kind of systemic inter-referentiality inherent in the notion of *autopoiesis* advocated by Luhmann. This would re-orient Hart's rule of recognition to demonstrate how the legal system can assign roles and specify relationships between norms, without at the same time needing to defend a specifically hierarchical concept of officialdom. See N Luhmann, 'Operational Closure and Structural Coupling: The Differentiation of the Legal System' (1992) 13 *Cardozo Law Review* 1419, at 1426–29.

[80] See, eg, KN Llewellyn, 'The Normative, the Legal, and the Law-Jobs: The Problem of Juristic Method' (1940) 49 *Yale Law Journal* 1355.

the theorist to not merely record but also defend this view against those who may take a different position on law's ultimate purpose.

Recognising this point, however, raises a second issue. Without endorsing and justifying some account of human goods in this respect, how are we to non-arbitrarily prioritise this view over the more demanding 'regulatory governance' model of law outlined above? Just because certain hierarchical institutional forms are defended intuitively or presumptively based on shared experiences of the domestic law-state does not, in itself, demonstrate the falsity of their importance to a successful account of law viewed in functional or 'focal' terms. Might it not be the case, for example, that some form of compulsory form of adjudication would improve upon the existing international legal order if it were so instigated? Unless we are able to reflect upon, critically consider and test the normative assumptions which underpin these views as to law's limited functions, we surely do not have the methodological tools necessary to give an answer to such questions.

As it happens, I believe the answer to this question is in the negative, but my reason for thinking this depends upon a distinctly non-instrumental account of legality, an account which requires a specific normative defence of the autonomy of international law in order to explain its critical importance to the conduct of international politics. I will say more about this briefly in Chapter 6 and then further throughout Part III, but to get to this point, it is necessary to re-orient the methodological approach which we might employ in engaging in such conceptual analysis. This is the task I take up in the next chapter.

V. CONCLUSION: PRESUMING THE LAW-STATE?

There is a danger that the above critique may come across as a hair-splitting exercise, looking for some justification for certain presumptions or intuitions about law which are widespread, ingrained and largely uncontroversial. However, the critique is necessary in making a more fundamental point that is particularly germane to our current enquiry: if legal orders such as international law are widely understood, practised *and practicable* as legal systems, and if the only basis upon which this system might appear defective or deficient is the lack of a hierarchical, centralised institutional structure, then it must be the case, I would submit, that we have a strong underpinning rationale for why those features are seen as essential or important. Such features cannot simply be presupposed in order to thereafter build our legal theories upon them; indeed, to do so would seem to undermine any pretension to generality or universality in our conceptual enquiry.

As such, to the extent that a widespread reliance on the concept of officialdom reveals certain hidden, under-theorised or simply unjustified views about the functional orientation of law, there seems to be enough room to doubt the coherence of the conceptual models against which international law is so often held up and found deficient. It appears that without an attempt to move beyond description and intuition, to set out to defend an account of law's essential purpose or aim by reconnecting legal theory and political philosophy to a significant extent, it will be hard to sustain any such presumptions. Nevertheless, such a disciplinary move appears to be excluded by the descriptive-explanatory methodology prominent in analytical jurisprudence, and indeed is explicitly resisted by many theorists working within this tradition. Recognising these methodological limitations is not enough, of course, to suggest that these theorists' intuitions and presumptions about law's function or purpose are necessarily wrong, but it does suggest that we need to consider whether we are able to vindicate this view of law's task and whether thereafter this justification offers a plausible conceptual model by which to critically engage with international law. The next chapter begins the task of taking up this challenge.

5

A Functional Jurisprudence? Methodological Controversies in Contemporary Legal Theory

TO WHAT EXTENT are we able to conceptualise law, to define it, by reference to an inherent point, purpose or function? This was the question left open at the end of the previous chapter, and to which I now turn my attention. An increasing number of analytical theorists have sought to defend a more explicitly functional account of law in this respect, accepting that an explanation or analysis of law's structural or institutional aspects can only really follow once we have a plausible account of law's overarching purpose. For instance, in developing his 'institutional theory of law', Neil MacCormick argues that:

> [H]uman artefacts and contrivances, including any rules by which people try to live, or get others to live, have to be understood functionally. What is their point, what is the final cause to which they are oriented? They perform well or ill, are in good shape or bad, to the extent that they can be seen to work towards these essential ends with a minimum of regrettable side-effects.[1]

Scott Shapiro develops a similar argument in defending his view of law as a 'planning institution', which, as we have seen, specifically premises questions of law's institutional design upon a proper appreciation of its function in society:

> [L]egal systems exist, and exist in the form that they do, because they serve certain functions. By having available institutions that create, modify, and apply rules, the law is able to secure benefits that it would not be able to secure, or secure as well, without them. The functionalist view does not imply that the functions served by the law are worthy ones ... [it] does, however, require that the proper way to evaluate the law is to assess whether legal institutions are serving worthwhile functions and whether they are serving them well.[2]

[1] N MacCormick, *Institutions of Law: An Essay in Legal Theory* (Oxford, Oxford University Press, 2007) 305; and see further on this point N MacCormick, 'Norms, Institutions, and Institutional Facts' (1998) 17 *Law and Philosophy* 301, at 335–36.

[2] S Shapiro, 'On Hart's Way Out' in J Coleman (ed), *Hart's Postscript: Essays on the Postscript to the* Concept of Law (Oxford, Oxford University Press, 2001) 149, at 187.

In methodological terms, this argument seems to offer an interesting move forward for analytical legal theory. Rather than defining legal orders by reference to whether or not they possess certain structural features or institutional characteristics, those features become parasitic upon a proper appreciation of law's point or, to borrow MacCormick's terminology, its 'final cause'.

At the same time, there lies a critical point of controversy at the core of Shapiro's remarks above: he claims that the legal theorist is required to identify 'worthwhile', but not necessarily 'worthy', functions, suggesting still a critical distance that divests the theorist from any responsibility in having to *endorse and morally defend* a particular view of the function or purpose of the law. The question which this necessarily provokes, however, is how one is to understand law functionally in anything other than an arbitrary way? If officials, citizens and other legal 'participants' disagree over what the necessary function of law is, *within as well as between different legal orders*, how are we to choose between these views to decide upon law's necessary functions and institutional characteristics other than through intuition, arbitrary selection or a kind of lowest-common-denominator aggregation of common and uncontroversial claims about law's role in society?

This is what Patrick Capps has recently termed the 'methodological problem in legal science', that is, the difficult question of how 'objective knowledge can be had of law as a practical phenomenon'.[3] It is this question that I take up in this chapter. Specifically, I will consider whether it is possible and plausible to normatively defend a functional account of law which is not in some sense arbitrary or specific to a particular social and political context. To do so, I draw on the approach of John Finnis and in particular his methodological critique of HLA Hart (and, by implication, many others developing Hart's 'practice theory' of rules, as outlined in the previous chapter), and his own efforts to re-orient legal theory towards a more 'focal' method. In doing so, I will agree with Finnis as to the need to reconnect legal and political philosophy, that law must be understood on the basis of its functional purpose in human communities, and that it behoves the legal theorist to advance a rationally defensible ideal account of this purpose. Nevertheless, whilst I will accept and adopt Finnis' methodological critique in this respect, I will cast doubt on his substantive conclusions as to law's purpose, and more specifically how this translates at the institutional level: his account ultimately vindicating the kind of hierarchical institutional structure which one might more readily associate with the task of domestic governance. In fact, in Chapter 6, I will return to explain in more detail why this view fails as a theory of law in the domestic as much as the international context.

[3] P Capps, *Human Dignity and the Foundations of International Law* (Oxford, Hart Publishing, 2009) 23.

I. METHODOLOGICAL CONTROVERSY IN LEGAL THEORY

How might we begin to forge a response to the methodological problem just outlined? Intuitively, in line with the kind of analysis and approach to international law advocated in Chapter 3, it surely behoves the legal theorist to take account of how law is understood or valued amongst those individuals, institutions or officials who are immersed within, or subject to, law as a form of social practice.[4] Indeed, recognition of the importance of this 'internal point of view' has arguably been one of the most important legacies of Hart's contribution to jurisprudence, reflected not only in the 'social thesis' shared amongst most contemporary forms of legal positivism,[5] but also of much wider significance as a starting point for many, if not most, forms of contemporary jurisprudential enquiry.[6] As Julie Dickson argues, 'legal theorists making judgments of importance and significance about their subject matter must be guided by what is considered important and significant by those who create, administer, and are subject to the law and whose views and activities constitute the subject matter of jurisprudential inquiry'.[7] For instance, at the international level, relevant participants might include states and international lawyers, but also a much broader array of non-state actors, individuals and institutions. As Capps explains:

> [I]nternational law is a practice which is meaningful to those involved in it. For the sake of convenience, those involved in this practice can be called international lawyers, but it can obviously involve a much wider array of individuals and groups. The job of the legal scientist is to articulate general concepts about this practice which take into account its meaning for those involved in it. This is a well-known starting point which unifies a wide range of positions in legal and social science.[8]

[4] As Postema explains, the analysis of law 'requires that legal theorists frame their accounts of the nature of law in terms that take … participant beliefs into account and make them intelligible'. G Postema, *Bentham and the Common Law Tradition* (Oxford, Clarendon Press, 1986) 335.

[5] For instance, J Raz, *The Authority of Law: Essays on Law and Morality*, 2nd edn (Oxford, Oxford University Press, 2009) 41–45.

[6] On this point generally, see J Dickson, *Evaluation and Legal Theory* (Oxford, Hart Publishing, 2001) 39–40; M Martin, *Judging Positivism* (Oxford, Hart Publishing, 2014) 96–97. On the relationship between participant perspective and the construction of hermeneutic concepts, see also the thoughtful analysis of I Farrell, 'H.L.A. Hart and the Methodology of Jurisprudence' (2006) 84 *Texas Law Review* 983, at 1002–03.

[7] J Dickson, 'Methodology in Jurisprudence: A Critical Survey' (2004) 10 *Legal Theory* 117, at 124. Frederick Schauer makes a similar point when he notes that in order 'to understand the phenomenon of law and the behaviour of its inhabitants, we need an accurate empirical understanding of the legal enterprise, without which we cannot hope to analyse even its normative and philosophical aspect'. F Schauer, 'The Limited Domain of the Law' (2004) 90 *Virginia Law Review* 1909, at 1414.

[8] Capps (n 3) 23. I engage with Capps' work, and many of its methodological claims, at length in R Collins, 'No Longer at the Vanishing Point? International Law and the Analytical Tradition in Jurisprudence' (2014) 5 *Jurisprudence* 265. Some of the remarks which follow in this and the next chapter are informed by or follow on from the claims defended in that work.

Whilst this might be a relatively straightforward and uncontroversial starting point, Capps is surely correct in his assertion that the more pertinent problem facing the legal theorist is that such participant perspective is far from concordant or homogeneous: individual participants tend to disagree not only about what *the* law is, but also about what law is and, importantly, *what it is for*.[9] To merely record, collate or aggregate widespread perspectives about the nature of law is likely itself only to reproduce conceptual uncertainty. If the nature of law or legal practice is understood differently from one participant to another (and, in fact, from one legal order to another), then it will be impossible to arrive at any coherent understanding of law in general (or international law in particular) simply by referring to this 'raw data' alone—or, indeed, *and more acutely*, the interpretations placed upon such data by the participants themselves. The more difficult question therefore concerns how we are to *choose between* such competing accounts in order to evaluate and select what is important and significant about law in a non-arbitrary way.

In many ways, the question of how to go about making sense of this 'raw data' has been one of the most central, controversial and divisive issues in modern legal theory, particularly since Ronald Dworkin's engagement with Hart's work,[10] and Hart's own attempt in the *Postscript* to *The Concept of Law* to reflect on his method and defend a value-neutral, descriptive form of conceptual analysis.[11] Whilst I do not intend to revisit and re-open that specific debate, it is Hart's reassertion of the descriptive methodological commitment underpinning his (and others') approach which has arguably given rise to the most amount of methodological controversy.[12] As we saw in the previous chapter, theorists following in the Hartian tradition tend to argue that whilst law plays an important function in society—perhaps even many important functions—it cannot be *defined by* reference to any one or more of those functions. Rather, any plausible conceptualisation of law, it is argued, must purport to identify the law by *how if fulfils* its functions: its specific institutional features and defining characteristics. We have already considered certain versions of this argument in the previous chapter (particularly from Raz), but, for convenience, Dickson summarises this distinctly 'institutional approach' well:

> On such an approach, the primary focus of jurisprudential inquiry lies with those distinctive legal institutions and processes which reveal the structure and mode of law's operation, and which help us to place and understand legal institutions in

[9] Capps (n 3) 70–71. Ronald Dworkin makes a similar point in *Law's Empire* (Oxford, Hart Publishing, 2004, first published in 1986) 4–5.

[10] See, eg, Ch II ('The Model of Rules I') of R Dworkin, *Taking Rights Seriously* (Cambridge, MA, Harvard University Press, 1978) 14–45.

[11] HLA Hart, *The Concept of Law*, 3rd edn (Oxford, Clarendon Press, 2012) 239–44.

[12] See, eg, SR Perry, 'Hart's Methodological Positivism' in Coleman (n 2) 311–54.

> relation to other social and political institutions. Many theorists in this tradition do not even accept that law has one overall point or function, let alone that a whole tradition of jurisprudential thought converges upon one view of law's function such as to render it uncontroversial.[13]

Towards the end of the previous chapter, I began to sketch out one particular problem with this view of the task of legal theory. Specifically, the 'distinctive legal institutions and processes' vindicated by those following a descriptive-explanatory methodology seem still to be highly contingent upon the presumptions and intuitions of legal theorists as to law's underlying regulatory purpose. Insofar as those same theorists claim not to premise the essentiality of these institutional features on any one function, then, there seems to be a certain level of methodological 'blindness' in such 'institutional' approaches. Any such function cannot just be incorporated (or overlooked) as simply obvious or uncontroversial. The critical question thus becomes whether theorists like Hart are able to maintain or justify the concept of law that they ultimately vindicate absent a morally evaluative judgement aimed at defending such functionality.[14] Surely it is only on the basis of such moral judgement that Hart was able to select and choose between the significant and insignificant in order to construct the necessary institutional features of legal order?

Bearing in mind Hart's methodological claims, and indeed those of many others following his approach to conceptual analysis, it would seem that the selection of the relevant from the irrelevant is premised only upon certain (by no means uncontroversial) abstraction strategies[15] or else rests upon a necessary distinction between substantive and (meta-)theoretical value judgements.[16] As Dickson has pointed out, however, it is a rather banal point to note that Hart had to engage in evaluation at this meta-theoretical level—that is, to make 'judgments about which data to focus on and how to order and arrange materials for explanation in order for one's theory to exhibit such general theoretical virtues as simplicity, clarity, consistency, and comprehensiveness'.[17] Arguably, such theoretical values can only really help to 'streamline' conceptual distinctions about the nature of law and do not help us to choose between competing accounts of law's essential features.[18] In other words, these strategies cannot, at least on their

[13] Dickson (n 6) 112.

[14] For a summary of these debates, see principally Dickson (n 7) 22 ff; and see further Ch 2 of Dickson (n 6) 29–49. See also Capps (n 3) 65–75.

[15] Capps (n 3) 70–75.

[16] See, eg, HLA Hart, 'Comment' in R Gavison (ed), *Issues in Contemporary Legal Philosophy: The Influence of HLA Hart* (Oxford, Clarendon Press, 1987) 39; see also the discussion in Dickson (n 6) 30–38.

[17] Dickson (n 7) 125–27. See also on this point Pt 3 of Jules Coleman, *The Practice of Principle: In Defence of a Pragmatist Approach to Legal Theory* (Oxford, Oxford University Press, 2001).

[18] Capps (n 3) 70.

own, offer an account of *why* certain phenomena are important to those who are engaged in the practice of law as a social institution.

The more pertinent issue, therefore, is whether such conceptual analysis can legitimately be seen as purely neutral and descriptive; to what extent, in other words, the legal theorist must choose, select and defend what they believe are the most important features of law. In this regard, Dickson is right to point out the misleading nature of the claim that Hart's approach is merely 'descriptive', in the sense that it suggests that the theorist does not evaluate, analyse or critically engage with the object of their study.[19] At the same time, however, she admits that much of the recent methodological controversy in analytical jurisprudence has related to a stronger claim: that in order to offer up an account of law's specific characteristics, one must necessarily engage in moral evaluation or political justification. This controversy is perhaps best illustrated through John Finnis' engagement with Hart's work.[20] Although directed specifically at *The Concept of Law*, Finnis' criticisms will have obvious methodological consequences for the coherence of many of the perspectives outlined in the previous chapter, particularly his argument that law's specific institutional characteristics are not simply self-evident, but must be defended as essential to meeting law's underlying purpose—a defence that requires committed moral engagement from the legal theorist.[21] Nevertheless, despite this methodological difference, I will go on to show how, substantively, Finnis' ideal theory vindicates an institutional model of law very similar to that which was defended by Hart and his followers, as outlined in the previous chapter. I will say more about this shortly, but first I need to consider in more detail his critical engagement with claimed lacuna in Hart's theory.

II. THE PROBLEM OF VALUE NEUTRALITY IN CONCEPTUAL ANALYSIS

Finnis' argument, essentially, is that if we engage with Hart's theory (and, by implication, others like it) on the basis of its own premises—that is, as a social-factual methodology prioritising the 'internal point of view' over other viewpoints—then we realise that the process of selection involved, between the relevant and irrelevant social facts, is difficult to understand in value-free terms. The internal point of view is chosen over others as it is the viewpoint most likely to sustain the coherence of the law as a system with all the benefits that this is meant to entail—benefits (along with risks)

[19] Dickson (n 6) 33–37. See also Perry (n 12) 321–22.

[20] J Finnis, *Natural Law and Natural Rights*, 2nd edn (Oxford, Oxford University Press, 2011) 11–15.

[21] ibid 231–33.

about which Hart is quite open in his work.[22] In differentiating the internal from the external viewpoint, Finnis argues that Hart could not, on his own premises, engage with the former in an evaluative way. Whilst he recognised that those sharing the internal point of view may do so for a variety of reasons—eg, 'calculations of long-term interest; disinterested interest in others; an unreflecting inherited or traditional attitude; or the mere wish to do as others do'[23]—there is no way of choosing between these reasons for their practical significance to the concept of law he develops (which, as we saw in the previous chapter, seems to be drawn more from what is already pre-existing). This is particularly problematic as the accumulated reasons Hart gives seem contradictory, or at least sit uneasily with each other, but nonetheless happen to achieve the result of sustaining the coherence of the legal order as he saw it. It is difficult to see how Hart, or indeed any other theorist adopting a descriptive-explanatory method, can offer any substantive justification for choosing between the views of one participant over the other, even the majority over the minority; they surely cannot explain *why* participants conceptualise the law in this way and therefore whether they are right or wrong in doing so. As a result, Hart's passive acceptance of the internal point of view leaves us unable to determine why these collective reasons necessarily result in something like the kind of well-functioning domestic legal order which his theory ultimately vindicates.

This form of conceptual enquiry therefore appears of limited value when employed in any critical way. We cannot abstract from what is supposed to be important in law absent an explanation of why it is valued outside of the historically and socially contingent contexts in which law functions at any given time and place. And when presented with social practices which do not conform to Hart's concept of law (eg, international law), these can only be seen as deviant aberrations, or dismissed simply as non-legal.[24] In fact, this issue becomes particularly problematic when we consider the 'pre-legal' form of 'primitive' normative orders,[25] such as how Hart described international law, as it reveals little about the *necessary* motivating factors that would bring about a transition towards Hart's more ambitious concept of law. The fact that there are a number of already-committed individuals holding out a particular kind of 'internal point of view'—a view which happens to support or sustain the particular characteristics of developed domestic legal systems—will itself tell us nothing about why those individuals feel it important to do so. Moreover, their attitudes towards, as well as use of, the rule of recognition cannot

[22] See primarily Ch 5 of Hart (n 11); and see the previous discussion in Ch 3, section III and Ch 4, section III, at n 56.

[23] Hart (n 11) 203, also cited in Finnis (n 20) 13.

[24] Hart (n 11) 92 and passim.

[25] ibid 117.

be specifically prioritised without being able to determine in advance on what basis they are seemingly justified in their views. Finnis puts this point particularly well:

> [Such] attitudes … will, up to a point, tend to maintain in existence a legal system (as distinct from, say, a system of despotic discretion) if one already exists. But they will not bring about the transition from the pre-legal … order of custom or discretion to a legal order, for they do not share the concern, which Hart himself recognizes as the explanatory source of legal order, to remedy the defects of pre-legal social orders. Similarly, Hart's persons who are moved by 'calculations of long-term interest' (sc. self-interest) water down any concern they may have for the function of law as an answer to real social problems … they dilute their allegiance to law and their pursuit of legal methods of thought with doses of self-interest which it is an elementary function of law … to subordinate to social needs.[26]

It is perhaps obvious to see the significance of this criticism for our consideration of international law, the institutional structure of which, as we saw in Chapter 3, makes it arguably more difficult to disentangle self-interest from a more systemic concern to maintain the coherence of the international legal order. Moreover, we can see that if, for example, there is a distinctly widespread view that international law *should* function as a system capable of normatively pre-empting the self-interest of states, then the form of descriptive 'conceptual analysis' undertaken by Hart seems incomplete or even self-defeating in undermining this most obvious aspect of the internal point of view.

Similar criticisms have been developed by others, such as Stephen Perry and Jeremy Waldron, both of whom question the value neutrality of Hart's claims in *The Concept of Law*.[27] For instance, Perry argues that Hart's approach betrays its own methodological commitments by straying into normative evaluation of social practices, which cannot just be explained in terms of the kind of meta-theoretical values—for example, simplicity, clarity etc—outlined above. Specifically, he notes how if one adopts a view of law as normatively oriented towards securing social coordination or order, as Hart indeed appears to, then one cannot escape necessary evaluative judgement:

> The statement that a regime of primary rules has defects, like the statement that these defects are remedied by the introduction of a rule of recognition and other secondary rules, is an evaluative claim. *The values in question relate … to the guidance of conduct, which means that they have a normative dimension.*

[26] Finnis (n 20) 14.
[27] J Waldron, 'Normative (or Ethical) Positivism' in Coleman (n 2) 429.

> The descriptive-explanatory method assesses theories by means of criteria that are properly called evaluative, such as predictive power and simplicity, but the values in question are applicable to all scientific theories, and they are not normative in character ... *Hart is making evaluative claims not about theories but about the very social practices he is studying.*[28] (emphasis added)

Similarly, Waldron notes how Hart deliberately outlines the choice of moving towards a constituted legal order, of correcting the defects of a regime of primary rules, as a choice involving both costs and benefits,[29] and indeed therefore suggests that the costs outweigh the benefits—at least for most societies.[30] However, he refuses to endorse these reasons as germane to understanding the concept of law that his theory ultimately vindicates. Consequently, if in the international legal order, for example, there are good reasons for sustaining law as a decentralised legal order, Hart's theory cannot explicitly illuminate these reasons; conversely, if there are good reasons why international law should be reformed towards a more centralised institutional structure, his theory is incapable of grounding the evaluative judgement necessary to justify such a reform. Instead, international law is simply dismissed as defective according to the 'central case' of legality drawn from domestic experience.

As we saw in the previous chapter, many of those taking forward and refining the form of conceptual analysis deployed by Hart have attempted to provide a more open normative justification to explain *why* the specific institutional configuration of law is important or necessary—for example, by casting the rule of recognition as a form of coordination convention, by explaining law by reference to the task of governance (as a 'planning institution') etc—but such theories seem still to have hedged this functional explanation simply on intuitions drawn from shared experience of the law-state. Without going further in order to philosophically defend such understandings as important and necessary to law's purpose in more universal terms, they emerge as question-begging as soon as they are applied to a legal order not already constructed around this model (particularly, and most pertinently, when they are applied to international law). For instance, in one of his earlier works, MacCormick attempted to provide a more lucid historical and sociological explanation of law's defining nature as an institutionalised normative order in a form similar to the concept of law

28 Perry (n 12) 323.

29 I set out these gains in brief in Ch 3—ie, 'adaptability to change, certainty, and efficiency'. However, Hart says that such benefits accruing from the centralisation of authority within the state will have to be weighed against the cost in terms of the 'risk that the centrally organized power may well be used for the oppression of numbers with whose support it can dispense, in a way that the simpler regime of primary rules could not'. Hart (n 11) 202.

30 Waldron (n 27) 429–31.

developed by Hart.[31] However, as Matthew Kramer notes, his explanation relies essentially on a (presumed, even fictional) historical narrative, where the present is simply reconstructed through a selective viewpoint and presumed endpoint that has already vindicated certain institutional features as essential to the concept of law:

> His historical narratives take on significance, for MacCormick's purposes, only in the light of the terminus or telos to which they lead. MacCormick tells his story of the development of the British legal system because the story culminates in the advent and solidification of a full-fledged system; but this entails that he knows what qualifies as a full-fledged system. If he tried to justify his selection of particular narratives, he would confront all the problems that the narratives supposedly had eliminated.[32]

Ultimately, the problem seems to be an idealisation of form without *real* historical contingency: either, as with Hart, historical and socio-political context is read out of theory, thus leaving particular institutional forms removed almost entirely from their specific socio-political setting; or, as with (early) MacCormick, such context is read back in as a non-empirical account of the inevitability of the current form of juristic organisation. This creates a space in which the normative idea, as well as the institutional form, of the state is somehow subordinated to, or at the very least theorised as a product of, the legal order—rather than the legal order's particular institutions being seen as historically and socially contingent features of the state itself, responding to the constitutional demands of legitimate public order and governance.[33]

The same problem arguably hampers Scott Shapiro's explanation of law as a 'planning institution', which, as we saw in the previous chapter, attempts to offer a functional account of officialdom as necessary to law's governance task. On Shapiro's account, constitutional law forms the basis of 'a plan for governance', the purpose of which is to 'guide and organize the shared activity of legal officials', an institutional configuration seen as necessary itself in order 'to overcome the enormous complexity, contentiousness and arbitrariness associated with arranging a system of social regulation'.[34]

[31] See specifically Ch 10 of N MacCormick, *H. L. A. Hart*, 2nd edn (Stanford, CA, Stanford University Press, 2008) 130–52; though note his explicit disavowal of this explanation in his later work: N MacCormick, 'The Concept of Law and *The Concept of Law*' in RP George (ed), *The Autonomy of Law: Essays on Legal Positivism* (Oxford, Oxford University Press, 1996) 163, at 179–80.

[32] M Kramer, 'The Rule of Misrecognition in the Hart of Jurisprudence' (1988) 8 *Oxford Journal of Legal Studies* 401, at 421.

[33] See, eg, IW Duncanson, 'The Strange World of English Jurisprudence' (1979) 30 *Northern Ireland Legal Quarterly* 207.

[34] S Shapiro, 'What is the Rule of Recognition (and Does it Exist)?' in M Alder and K Himma (eds), *The Rule of Recognition and the U.S. Constitution* (Oxford, Oxford University Press, 2009) 235, 252.

From one perspective, of course, this counts as an advance on Hart's concept of law to the extent that Shapiro explicitly adopts a specific normative justification for the importance of officialdom to deliver on the purpose of law as he sees it. However, the problem here is that, despite his own efforts to move past the coordination convention explanation of the rule of recognition,[35] his account of law's functional purpose itself suffers from the very same problem: it works backwards from the existing institutions of the law-state to provide what appears to be an intuitively plausible explanation of law's defining task of social coordination and governance, but which is simply self-reinforcing from a methodological perspective. Indeed, despite the efforts of theorists like Twining and Tamanaha, outlined in the previous chapter, that were aimed at broadening the empirical raw data well beyond state-based legal experience, Shapiro's view seems still rigidly one-dimensional in focus. At no point does he see it as necessary to philosophically defend his starting point by explaining the inherent universality of the kind of liberal governance model that itself then vindicates the importance of certain institutional forms. These features are simply posited as *necessary* or *inevitable* components of his general concept of law.[36]

This criticism is developed further by Sean Coyle, who notes how Shapiro's methodology begins with an honest and open exposition of his intuitive starting point, but then limits the task of legal philosophy to a process of refining this intuition through its accordance, or otherwise, with underlying social facts. The ostensible intellectual honesty of this mode of 'reflexive equilibrium' is therefore undermined by the realisation that the relevant social facts are simply the ones which have already been vindicated from Shapiro's intuitive starting point.[37] This has particular relevance to the account of officialdom outlined in the previous chapter, as Shapiro's theory glosses over any complexities of historical and social context to explain the hierarchical character of domestic legal governance as simply a matter of institutional design. Coyle continues:

> The processes whereby political and legal power in Western societies came to be vested in distinct 'offices', often defined and limited constitutionally, are both complex and not easily detachable from the deeper currents of Western civilisation. The problem ... is not that Shapiro neglects to concern himself with

[35] Indeed, Shapiro's account is justified as an attempt to correct the tension between normativity and social-factuality in Hart. By giving a rational, functional account of law as a planning system, he provides a justification for the normativity of law grounded outside of the system itself. See Ch 5 of S Shapiro, *Legality* (Cambridge, MA, Harvard University Press, 2011) 154–92.

[36] For a good discussion of this problem, see, for example, V Rodriguez-Blanco, 'The Moral Puzzle of Legal Authority: A Commentary on Shapiro's Planning Theory of Law' and K Schaubroeck, 'Legal Normativity and the Instrumental Principle' in S Bertea and G Pavlakos (eds), *New Essays on the Normativity of Law* (Oxford, Hart Publishing, 2011) 86–106 and 107–40 respectively.

[37] S Coyle, 'Legality and the Liberal Order' (2013) 76 *Modern Law Review* 401, 406–07.

> the historical causes which oversaw the development of political offices out of the 'estates' with which political power was traditionally associated, but that his arguments are informed almost entirely by the terminology and assumptions of 'institutional design'. The existence of offices of power can be the result of only one thing: creation.[38]

By framing an account of law's functional purpose by what is familiar and seemingly uncontroversial in this way, it is difficult, if not impossible, to distinguish the contingent from the essential: the historical, political or social contingency of the 'deep conventions'[39] of society that give rise to its specific institutional structures are read out of the concept of law as moral or political justifications that are seemingly beyond the purview of legal theory.[40] As a result, such a functional view of law ends up providing only an incomplete and not particularly satisfying justification for the kinds of institutions that already exist in many domestic societies.

Unless these intuitively vindicated institutional features are defended, not merely by empirical reflection, but direct evaluative judgement—that is, endorsed as a moral or political good to which any legal order *ought to* subscribe—legal theory loses its critical potential altogether. It ends up almost rigidly one-dimensional, excluding other intuitively plausible explanations of the functional importance of law: for example, rights-based approaches which suggest the importance of non-instrumental rationality, or approaches informed by the kind of reflexive 'ideality' often associated with the common law tradition.[41] More importantly and immediately—bearing in mind the argument developed up to this point—the problem with this jurisprudential 'narrowing' is that when faced with putatively legal orders that differ in structure from state-based law, such accounts both overreach, by holding what may well be wholly contingent features as essential or necessary conditions for a legal system, and under-explain, by ignoring the social, political and moral contexts in which law takes its meaning, and against which particular instantiations of law can only really be understood.

III. FROM THE *CONCEPT* TO THE *RULE* OF LAW? IN SEARCH OF LAW'S 'FOCAL MEANING'

Ultimately, if we are to understand law as it is used *and valued* as a social practice through the eyes of legal participants, it seems difficult to avoid the conclusion that the theorist must embrace the necessarily value-laden nature of the task of conceptual enquiry. To admit this, of course, still leaves

[38] ibid 411.

[39] I borrow this phrase from Andrei Marmor in his defence of the necessary autonomy of law; see, inter alia, A Marmor, 'The Conventional Foundations of Law' in Bertea and Pavlakos (n 36) 143, at 154–56.

[40] Coyle (n 37) 408–09.

[41] See S Coyle, 'The Ideality of Law' (2009) 6 *Journal of Moral Philosophy* 521.

open the question of how we are to go about this task; how we are to non-arbitrarily choose between the competing and not necessarily commensurable valued-based judgements unearthed from our socially reflective starting point. In this respect, Finnis argues that we should embrace an approach which—with a nod to Max Weber[42]—he describes in terms of the search for law's 'focal meaning'.[43] Specifically, he outlines the distinctly practical-philosophical nature of the task of conceptual analysis, which implies:

> [T]hat the evaluations of the theorist himself are an indispensable and decisive component in the selection or formation of any concepts for use in description of such aspects of human affairs as law or legal order ... the most important things for the theorist to know and describe are the things which, in the judgement of the theorist, make it important from a *practical* viewpoint to have law—the things which it is, therefore, important in practice to 'see to' when ordering human affairs. And when these 'important things' are (in some or even in many societies) in fact missing, or debased, or exploited or otherwise deficient, then the most important things for the theorist to describe are those aspects of the situation that manifest this absence, debasement, exploitation, or deficiency.[44]

There is much in this passage which deserves further consideration, not least of which is exactly what Finnis means when speaking of the 'practical viewpoint'. I will return to this specific question in the last section (below). My immediate concern is the methodological implications of adopting Finnis' approach, particularly in terms of how this might impact on our critical engagement with international law. The first thing to note in this respect is that whilst this kind of focal method will point in the direction of certain institutional features deemed *important and useful* to the fulfilment of law's purpose (that is, in meeting the central case of legality), it will not necessarily hinge the question of the ontological reality of law upon the existence or otherwise of certain institutional features. Law's existence would be discernible simply on the basis of social usage. As such, the question of law's reality can be distinguished from the broader and more ambitious *ideal* of 'legality', understood in a more evaluative sense, which is encapsulated in the 'central case' or 'ideal-type' of a well-functioning legal order. This central case can be summarised briefly—though I will return to consider this again shortly—as a legal system complying with the kind of procedural values implied by the rule of law.[45] As Finnis states:

> If there is a viewpoint in which the institution of the Rule of Law ... and compliance with rules and principles of law according to their tenor, are regarded as at least presumptive requirements of practical reasonableness itself, such a viewpoint

[42] See generally M Weber, *Economy and Society* (New York, Free Press, 1964).

[43] Finnis (n 20) 9 ff.

[44] ibid 16.

[45] This is in many respects a disputed and multifaceted concept, though Finnis himself defines it as similar to Fuller's desiderata for a state of legality, including values such as prospectivity, clarity, coherence etc. See ibid 270–71 and, more specifically, Fuller's definition below, at n 71.

> is the viewpoint which should be used as the standard of reference by the theorist describing the features of legal order.[46]

Applying this form of focal analysis, therefore, the central case of a well-functioning rule of law system provides a necessary benchmark against which paradigm cases of law can be assessed, appearing more or less legal depending upon the extent to which they are institutionally structured towards fulfilment of this ideal.[47] Consequently, deploying a form of focal analysis, we might agree with Finnis (and probably Lon Fuller too)[48] that legal systems (as well as the rule of law itself) might exist 'as a matter of degree'.[49]

Applying this methodological approach to international law, therefore, would allow one to see how paradigm cases of international legality (ie, those principles, rules and practices that are commonly referred to as forming part of international law) can be judged to be *more or less legal* to the extent that they satisfactorily fulfil what are seen to be the functions of (international) law. In this respect, the focal method will place emphasis on certain institutional features (for example, courts with compulsory jurisdiction) that may be *more or less present* and which are deemed important to the fulfilment of law's focal purpose, whilst not necessarily being essential to proving international law's ontological reality as such. Applying focal analysis in this way might thus provide a way of reconciling international law's reality as a legal order whilst also suggesting a direction for its institutional reform and improvement. In other words, from the central case, we can form a *concept of* international law, which, as Capps notes, can be used as a mediatory device, functioning 'between our conception of international relations and questions of institutional design'.[50] This concept of international law will suggest ideally how international law should be organised (the 'central case' of international legality) to achieve its focal purpose. That international law might fail to meet this ideal will not therefore disqualify it as law, at least not necessarily, but will rather suggest how the existing international legal order (as a more 'peripheral case' of legality) might be better improved to meet this purpose. We might therefore agree with Tom Franck's assertion (noted in Chapter 3) as to international law's clear ontological reality, whilst at the same time recognising certain imperfections or deficiencies, which help to explain more long-standing disciplinary anxieties, as well as the international legal order's susceptibility to being relegated to a kind of 'defective' or 'peripheral' case of legality.[51] This approach would thus leave space to critically engage with the law's institutional structure and suggest

[46] ibid 15.

[47] Capps (n 3) 35.

[48] See L Fuller, *The Morality of Law*, revised edn (New Haven, CT, Yale University Press, 1969) 41 and passim.

[49] Finnis (n 20) 279.

[50] ibid 245.

[51] For a thorough discussion of the distinction between 'central' and 'peripheral' cases of legality, see Capps (n 3) 35–39.

ways in which international law may be positively reformed to make it *more* law-like.

As such, this methodological approach would seem to provide a promising way forward in critically engaging with the institutional condition of modern international law. In fact, I believe that Capps is probably correct that many international lawyers, including, inter alia, Hersch Lauterpacht (as outlined in Chapter 2) already employ this kind of focal approach[52]—albeit often in a distinctly unreflective way. However, to endorse such a methodology as a potentially more useful and intellectually coherent approach in this respect is not—at least not yet—to necessarily endorse the focal concept of law as Finnis (and others) see this. Indeed, if we accept that there are differences of opinion over the function or purpose of law—law's 'focal meaning' being still inherently controversial in that respect—there remains the troubling question of how we are to judge if Finnis' (or others') central case of legality is coherent and defensible, both in general and when applied to make sense of international law specifically.

In response, the first point to note, as by now might be clear, is that the theorist cannot escape necessary value choices in their defence of the functional orientation of law.[53] The task is not simply selecting the participant viewpoint that best reflects the meaning of law, for one would need to be able to make this judgement, determining what is important about law, before any such selection is made. Nor can the task of conceptualisation really just be a distillation of shared factors which are deemed to be important about law from one participant to another—and, indeed, from one legal order to another. Rather, to conceptualise law in its ideal, focal sense requires a distinctly rational or 'practical' form of philosophical reflection.[54] How we go about this task, as well as what this might mean in terms of the focal concept of law, are the issues I take up in the following and final section.

IV. THE PRACTICAL VIEWPOINT AND THE NECESSARY AUTONOMY OF LAW

To recap on the claims of this chapter up to this point, I have argued that the task of legal theory is necessarily value-laden—that the role of the theorist cannot just be to passively choose the most descriptively accurate concept of law. Rather, they must present and defend an account of law's necessary

[52] ibid 77 and passim.

[53] Both Finnis and, more recently, MacCormick make this point in one form or another. See Finnis (n 20) 17; MacCormick (n 1) 305. On the ambiguities surrounding an apparent shift in MacCormick's position in this regard, see V Villa, 'Neil MacCormick's Legal Positivism' in M del Mar and Z Bankowski (eds), *Law as Institutional Normative Order* (Farnham, Ashgate, 2009) 45–64.

[54] See, eg, Capps (n 3) 102.

point by reflection on its central importance in society. Whilst this account should be informed by empirical reflection in order to understand law as it is valued amongst those who use or are bound by it, such enquiry can only ever be a first step in determining what is valuable about law. The theorist must thereafter provide some rational defence of law's unique and valuable contribution to the ordering of human affairs—a perspective that is distinctly practical-philosophical rather than empirical in nature.

It might appear somewhat counter-intuitive to speak of the need to adopt such a practical viewpoint, insofar as this view does not necessarily have to reflect any particular participant perspective. Bearing in mind that I began this chapter by outlining and endorsing the widespread view that the task of legal theory is to develop concepts of law which are meaningful to those who use them, it might seem odd to claim that our focal concept of law is not intended to simply reflect, or map onto, actual viewpoints in practice. However, such a misgiving perhaps misunderstands what is at stake in this methodological debate. To explain, let us consider again Hart's position of indifference as to the reasons why officials might accept, use and reason according to the rule of recognition. Putting aside for the moment the troubling questions over the concept of officialdom outlined in the previous chapter, and in particular why we might wish to prioritise such official perspectives over other committed viewpoints, this indifference seems to lead Hart down a conceptual blind alley. He explicitly rejects the view that judges have any specifically moral duty to accept the rule of recognition, or indeed to sustain the fundamental values and ordering principles of the legal system as it is commonly understood.[55] In so doing, he offers the empirical (and plausible) claim that as a matter of fact, officials, characteristically judges, clearly do not (and need not) always fulfil their role out of the altruistic motivation to protect the integrity of the legal system (nor indeed pursue the sorts of values often encompassed within ideals like the rule of law). As Gerald Postema points out, however, whilst Hart may well be correct in this claim, the factual, empirical nature of his explanation misses the point of conceptual enquiry. The point is not to understand the *actual* motivating factors that propel those officials in positions of legal authority, but rather to work out what kind of view they must legitimately—indeed, publicly—subscribe to in order to justify the authority which they wield according to the law. It is therefore irrelevant that some—indeed, many—legal officials might fail to take up this attitude as a matter of fact.[56] Postema continues:

> The practical perspective is not the point of view of someone who internalizes, commits herself to, social or legal norms; nor is it the point of view of one who is puzzled or curious about those norms. Nor again is it the point of view of one who

[55] Hart (n 11) 197–98, 203.

[56] See both GJ Postema, 'Norms, Reasons, and Law' (1998) 51 *Current Legal Problems* 149 and GJ Postema, 'Jurisprudence as Practical Philosophy' (1998) 4 *Legal Theory* 329.

> rejects, or seeks to evade, or seeks to undermine them. It is not the point of view of any of these because it is not the point of view *of anyone*. It is a *logical*, hence constructed or hypothetical, point of view, not a *personal* one. This perspective defines a framework for inquiry of a certain kind, inquiry into reasons for acting. Whether there are any norms or rules or reasons in the context that generates the inquiry is not settled by taking up this perspective. Rather, the perspective provides the framework of inquiry within which such issues are considered, deliberated, and disputed.[57]

This 'practical' perspective cannot therefore be an 'internal point of view' in the factual sense described by Hart, but it is internal to legal practice in the sense that it is developed through reflection on law *as a distinctive social practice*. In other words, adopting the practical perspective does not challenge the importance of participant viewpoint as a foundation for constructing a conceptual account of law, for the relevance of participant perspective stems precisely from the fact that the concept one is describing is itself a social construct or form of social practice.[58] This point is perhaps better described by reference to Nigel Simmonds' 'reflexive' view of the task of conceptual construction in legal theory. As he explains:

> Understanding the nature of law is not ultimately a matter of achieving a careful description of social practices but a matter of grasping the idea towards which those practices must be understood as oriented. The idea of law is the focal point that enables us to make coherent sense of the otherwise diverse features of practice, but it is not itself a matter of observable practice.[59]

In his later work, MacCormick appears to have come to a similar view:

> [T]he character of the whole enterprise [of law] determines that its intrinsic ends, or 'final causes', are the realisation of justice and the common good, *according to some reasonable conception of these*. Hence you cannot sincerely participate in this enterprise without a serious orientation to these values, and you cannot intelligibly participate in it without at least pretending to have such an orientation.[60] (emphasis added)

Like Postema and Simmonds, MacCormick's argument here is that the focal point of law—its final cause—is a viewpoint to which one must *logically* be committed, *or at least publicly profess to be committed*, in order to possess any authority within the legal enterprise taken as a whole. MacCormick's focus on the 'reasonable' conception of the common good stresses that the task that confronts the theorist is to construct a distinctly rational perspective: one that is able to cut through the incommensurability of competing perspectives, indeed, that respects this incommensurability

[57] Postema, 'Norms, Reasons, and Law' (n 56) 172–73.
[58] ibid 174.
[59] N Simmonds, 'Reflexivity and the Idea of law' (2010) 1 *Jurisprudence* 1, 18.
[60] MacCormick (n 1) 264.

by reflecting that which is necessary for humans to live together under conditions of moral pluralism.[61] For his part, Finnis describes this as the 'practically reasonable viewpoint', which should be:

> [C]onsistent; attentive to all aspects of human opportunity and flourishing, and aware of their limited commensurability; concerned to remedy deficiencies and breakdowns, and aware of their roots in the various aspects of human personality and in the economic and other material conditions of social interaction.[62]

Whilst Finnis justifies this viewpoint by reference to his distinctly Thomist natural law epistemology,[63] insofar as it translates into a legitimate and coherent account of legal order, the 'limited commensurability' of moral viewpoints in practice justifies a construction of law as an artificial, institutional order very similar to that vindicated in positivist discourses.[64] Indeed, Finnis himself makes connections between Aquinas' thought on law and the more 'Kantian, liberal, positivist' tradition—that is, exactly the kind of tradition from which normative positivists like Waldron or MacCormick end up defending a very similar view of legal order.[65] In fact, there is a remarkable degree of synergy now between the kind of modern natural law perspective, adopted by, inter alia, Finnis and Fuller, and the more explicitly 'normative' form of positivism defended by theorists like Waldron.[66] In fact, an apparent 'entente cordiale' sees many legal positivists now attempting to justify and defend the law's limited domain (its positivity) on distinctly moral grounds, whilst many natural lawyers increasingly accept the need for an artificial, institutional view of law, conceived as 'an autonomous sphere of practical reason established specifically to respond to the co-ordinatory and regulatory problems of moral indeterminacy and societal complexity'.[67]

[61] Capps (n 3) 104–05.

[62] Finnis (n 20) 15, also quoted by Capps (n 3) 101.

[63] Finnis (n 20) passim.

[64] ibid, passim, but 276–77 in particular.

[65] See J Finnis, 'The Truth in Legal Positivism' in George (n 31) 195, at 198.

[66] *cf*, on the one side, Fuller (n 48) passim; J Finnis, 'On Hart's Ways: Law as Reason and as Fact' (2007) 52 *American Journal of Jurisprudence* 25, at 42–44, Finnis (n 65) 204–05; and, on the other, Waldron (n 27); J Waldron, 'Kant's Legal Positivism' (1996) 109 *Harvard Law Review* 1535; N MacCormick, 'A Moralistic Case for A-Moralistic Law?' (1985–86) 20 *Valparaiso University Law Review* 1; Postema (n 4) 328 et seq. See also the discussion in Capps (n 3) 125–26. On the breakdown between positivist and naturalist theories as rival accounts of the concept of law, and instead conceiving them as competing modes of understanding how moral concepts translate into posited law (and how, thereafter, morality re-enters the picture of legal reasoning), see S Coyle, 'Positivism as a Statist Philosophy of Law' (2008) 59 *Northern Ireland Legal Quarterly* 49.

[67] HP Olsen and S Toddington, *Law in its Own Right* (Oxford, Hart Publishing, 1999) 11. See further EJ Weinrib, 'Legal Formalism: On the Imminent Rationality of Law' (1988) 97 *Yale Law Journal* 949, especially 996–99; A Ripstein, *Force and Freedom: Kant's Legal and Political Philosophy* (Cambridge, MA, Harvard University Press, 2009), briefly at 9 and passim.

My point here is that, despite their philosophical differences, these perspectives are united, not only in their convincing disavowal of descriptive-explanatory methodology, or their insistence on the need to reconnect legal theory and political philosophy, but also, ultimately, in seeking to morally defend and justify an account of law's function and institutional aspects very similar to that which was set out in the previous chapter and which was, as we saw, either simply presumed or else defended by intuition by those theorists working in the analytical tradition. For Finnis, Waldron and others following suit, however, it is the very condition of incommensurability in participant perspective which not only highlights the fallacy of the value neutrality of descriptive-explanatory approaches, but which also, at the same time, provides the specific normative justification for a form of legal order that is able to mediate this disagreement due to its structural autonomy and institutional character. As Postema puts it, whilst 'law's ultimate aspiration may be justice, its proximate aim and defining task is to supply a framework of practical reasoning designed to unify public political judgment and coordinate social interaction'.[68] In other words, whatever account of human goods, or rational or moral purpose we begin from, it is the pluralistic conditions of human societies which are widely accepted as justifying the more immediate or proximate purpose of law: 'to establish the conditions by which each person can safely predict how others will act, as well as to facilitate co-operation and to resolve social conflict'.[69]

When not simply presumed but instead philosophically vindicated on these terms, this view of law's function seems intuitively plausible. Furthermore, where Fuller asserts that law's function ultimately resides in 'subjecting human conduct to the governance of rules', and therefore that the concept of law should be understood ideally as best structured to fulfil this function, his argument seems in many respects so obvious as to be largely unobjectionable.[70] Accepting this premise, therefore, we might have cause to agree that our central case of legality ought to be a form of legal order that meets the requirements of the rule of law, perhaps by reference to the kind of desiderata supplied by Fuller's notion of 'legality', requiring the kind of systematicity that ensures that legal rules are, for instance, general, non-retroactive, consistent, coherent etc.[71] Of course, the ideal of

[68] GJ Postema, 'Law's Autonomy and Public Practical Reasoning' in George (n 31) 79, at 80.
[69] Capps (n 3) 83.
[70] Fuller (n 48) 106.
[71] Fuller's eight desiderata for the existence of a state of 'legality' include the law's generality, public promulgation, non-retroactivity, clarity, non-contradiction, capacity to be obeyed, constancy, and a reasonable level of congruence between law in the books and law as it is practised by authorised officials. ibid 39 and passim.

the rule of law is a deeply contested notion—a point to which I will return in Chapter 7—but it would seem plausible to suggest that, whatever its best interpretation, the *rule* and the concept of law cannot be easily separated.[72] On its own terms, therefore, this approach seems internally coherent and convincing.

At the same time, however, there remains a fundamental ambiguity in this account insofar as the concept of the rule of law is merely co-opted to suggest a certain ideal, hierarchical institutional structure. As Gianluigi Palombella has shown, if the rule of law has an inherent meaning at all, discernible from the historical, social and political contexts in which it has been applied, it is in stressing the need for an institutional structure which resists the law's instrumentality towards any pre-defined ends. In other words, the rule of law suggests the necessary autonomy of law as an end in its own right.[73] In that sense, the concept should not be seen simply as a justification for a certain kind of institutional structure, rather than that institutional structure being reflective of this idealisation of law worked out in some specific historical, social and political context—that is, in the context of the modern state.[74] I will say more about the rule of law specifically, as well as the difficulties of its translation in the international context, in Part III. My concern here, however, is less with the broad idea that law should be best understood by reference to such an ideal, but more with the way in which the specific character of the state itself seems still to be presumed or, rather, explicitly justified by those adopting this more focal approach to legal-conceptual analysis. Applied to international law, therefore, the risk is that rather than attempting to work out what kind of institutional model might best secure law's autonomy—as opposed to instrumentality—in the specific political context of international relations, the rule of law is applied in a less reflective, indeed, more instrumental,

[72] See chiefly in this respect J Waldron, 'The Concept and the Rule of Law' (2008–09) 43 *Georgia Law Review* 1. Although the rule of law is a contested concept, Palombella and Walker note how, at the very least, the concept 'seeks to inform us of the ways in which and the characteristics through which it is plausible to think of law as something that rules over things—as an institution which regulates the other forces that shape our common life. It also seeks to provide *a justification for such a claim to ascendency*'. See G Palombella and N Walker, 'Introduction' in G Palombella and N Walker (eds), *Relocating the Rule of Law* (Oxford, Hart Publishing, 2009) xi, at xi (emphasis added).

[73] See, in this respect, G Palombella, 'The Rule of Law as an Institutional Ideal' in L Morlino and G Palombella (eds), *Rule of Law and Democracy: Internal and External Issues* (Leiden, Brill, 2010) 3–40; and see further this point applied in relation to international relations in T Nardin, *Law, Morality, and the Relations of States* (Princeton, NJ, Princeton University Press, 1983) passim.

[74] I reflect more on this at length in R Collins, 'The Rule of Law and the Quest for Constitutional Substitutes in International Law' (2014) 83 *Nordic Journal of International Law* 87.

way as a justification for a certain kind of governmental or regulatory institutional form. In the following, final chapter of Part II, therefore, I will agree that law should be conceived ideally as an autonomous institutional practice, but I will also show why this ideal is often mischaracterised, being instead understood less as an end in its own right and more as a means to a more effective regulatory ideal.

V. CONCLUSION

I began this chapter by suggesting that an important first step in understanding the nature of law is to attempt to give an account of how it features in the social practices of legal participants themselves (however broadly we define this group). At the same time, I have also noted how these practices are inevitably conflicted or controversial, with legal participants themselves often disagreeing over the nature of what is important about law: its necessary features, ultimate point or function. This realisation calls into question the ability of descriptive-explanatory approaches to adequately determine what is important about law without being open about the value choices involved in such a determination. In developing this argument, I have endorsed the claim, propounded most explicitly by Finnis, that law's necessary institutional characteristics depend not only on an explanation, but also on an explicit normative defence of law's point or overall function in society. The theorist must attempt to understand the importance of law as it is practised and understood by those who use the law, and amongst whom law's distinctive features take on practical meaning. In reflecting upon and evaluating these practices, however, it is necessary to determine, judge and ultimately vindicate a central case or ideal view of law, against which one can engage critically and coherently with putative legal forms in order to assess prospects for institutional or structural reform, that is, what is required to make such practices more 'law-like'.

To the extent that a range of otherwise quite diverse legal theorists and philosophers have adopted this view of the task of legal theory, however, they have also, in the main, sought to justify a view of law's function as inherently bound up with ordering human affairs under conditions of moral pluralism. On this basis, we seem to have a more plausible justification for a concept of law which we might simply understand as mirroring a well-functioning rule of law state, thereby underlining the importance of the kind of institutions and offices that are often simply presumed as necessary under more descriptive-explanatory forms of conceptual analysis. Accordingly, this approach would seem to give us a more plausible methodological approach by which one can explain the reality of international law, whilst at the same time critiquing perceived institutional defects or deficiencies at the international level. In other words, this view might help us to explain, understand and judge the cogency of the apparent institutional problem unearthed in Part I. However, before making any such judgement, it is necessary to consider whether this view of law's function, as well as the institutional implications taken as following from this function, are coherent and plausible on their own terms, as well as more specifically when they are applied to make sense of international law and in order to pass critical judgement upon its institutional architecture. This is the task I now take up in Chapter 6.

6

Law's 'Creation Myth': Instrumental Reasoning and the Necessary Autonomy of Law

IT MAY SEEM a trite point, self-evident even, that law plays an essential purpose in guiding conduct, thereby securing social order in human societies.[1] So far in Part II, we have seen how such a functional view is implicit within, or simply presumed by, many of the most prominent theorists in the analytical tradition in jurisprudence. Despite convincing methodological criticisms of these approaches by more idealist theorists like John Finnis, this view of law's immediate or proximate function remains widely shared (including by Finnis himself). As I noted towards the end of the last chapter, despite significant philosophical and methodological differences, there seems to be a considerable degree of convergence in contemporary legal theory, justifying a view of law as an 'institutional framework for unifying our community's judgements and stabilising and structuring our social relations'.[2] Margaret Martin explains this as a kind of 'creation myth', setting out a normative justification for law's autonomous institutional form. As she explains more fully:

> Law, on this view, is conceived of as a set of public norms that serve to unite a populace that would otherwise descend into chaos. Law is able to unify judgment because it offers a set of rules that enjoy autonomy—that is to say, the citizenry can identify the content of any given legal norm without relying on moral arguments. This is important as moral issues are the source of disagreement and law's ability to unify judgment is therefore ... dependent on the ability of legal norms to offer practical guidance without recreating the very disagreements that legal norms are introduced to solve.[3]

[1] See on this point M Martin, *Judging Positivism* (Oxford, Hart Publishing, 2014) 1–3.

[2] P Capps, *Human Dignity and the Foundations of International Law* (Oxford, Hart Publishing, 2009) 127.

[3] Martin (n 1) 2.

This creation myth appears in many respects 'familiar and uncontroversial'.[4] It underpins, in one form or another, many of the most influential works in legal and political philosophy over the past few centuries,[5] uniting figures as diverse as Thomas Hobbes[6] and Immanuel Kant[7] with more contemporary legal theorists, including, in addition to Finnis,[8] legal positivists such as Joseph Raz.[9] Furthermore, as I sought to demonstrate throughout Part I—a point to which I will return again in Chapter 7—international legal discourse seems itself to contain a version of this myth, with international lawyers having to explain how the practices and will of states translate into an autonomous institutional framework capable of binding those same states (and other actors) independently of their free will.

Bearing in mind the ubiquity of this view, and the value accorded to the autonomy of law more broadly, it is necessary to delve a little deeper in order to understand the core tenets and institutional implications of this account of law's function. Considering, in particular, the difficulties that international lawyers have faced in explaining the autonomy of international legal rules in this respect—which, as we have seen, has been the primary cause of international law's perceived constitutional deficiency—I want to test the coherence of this view of law's function, both on its own terms and as a way of engaging with the international legal order. In order to do so, I will draw upon a paradigmatic version of this creation myth, as set out by Gerald Postema: the *Autonomy Thesis*.[10] Postema not only aims to demonstrate the institutional implications of this view of law's function, but also, importantly, how these institutional demands seem to end up undermining the very ideal of autonomy at the heart of the thesis. In following this critique, I will show why I agree with Postema that the thesis fails in fulfilling its core premise of offering an institutional framework capable of mediating and

[4] Capps (n 2) 127.

[5] ibid 127–28 ff; and see further GJ Postema, 'Law's Autonomy and Public Practical Reasoning' in RP George (ed), *The Autonomy of Law: Essays on Legal Positivism* (Oxford, Clarendon Press, 1996) 79, at 80.

[6] This is perhaps best expressed, albeit at a very abstract level, in the following passage from Hobbes' *Leviathan* (CB Macpherson (ed), London, Penguin, 1968, first published in 1651) 263–64 [108–09]: 'as men, for the atteyning of peace, and conservation of themselves thereby, have made an Artificiall Man, which we call a Common-wealth; so also have they made Aritficiall Chains, called *Civill Lawes*, which they themselves, by mutuall covenants, have fastned at one end, to the lips of that Man, or Assembly, to whom they have given the Soveraigne Power; and at the other end to their own Ears. These Bonds in their own nature but weak; may neverthelesse be made to hold, by the danger, though not by the difficulty of breaking them'.

[7] For a thorough view of Kant's views in this respect, see Capps (n 2) 134–39.

[8] See, eg, J Finnis, *Natural Law and Natural Rights*, 2nd edn (Oxford, Oxford University Press, 2011) 266–70.

[9] See, eg, J Raz, *The Authority of Law: Essays on Law and Morality*, 2nd edn (Oxford, Oxford University Press, 2009); though see further below (at n 13) for Raz's refutation of this view.

[10] Postema (n 5).

pre-empting the kind of moral disagreements which characterise modern political communities. Nevertheless, whilst Postema (and others) see this failure as potentially negating the ideal of law's autonomy—in fact, arguing instead for the re-introduction of moral reasoning as key to fulfilling law's functional premise—I will rather claim that the failure of the thesis stems from the nature of this functional premise itself, that is, the instrumental rationale that justifies law's autonomy as necessary to secure a particular kind of social order.

In order to make this argument, the chapter is structured as follows. First, I set out the contours of the *Autonomy Thesis*, pointing out in particular how the pre-emptive strategy underpinning it acts as an obvious justification for the introduction of officialdom into our concept of law—as originally suggested in Chapter 4. However, in section II, I will follow Postema's critique in order to show how this re-introduction of human agency causes problems for the claimed autonomy of law. Specifically, I note how widespread reliance on judicial determinations to enhance the certainty and effectiveness of the law actually ends up only demonstrating its inherent indeterminacy. The re-introduction of human agency in this context might not necessarily undermine completely the broad claim to law's autonomy, but if this autonomy is justified as a means to mediate moral and political disagreement, then it still raises problematic questions about the authority of legal officials to give determinative content to the law. In particular, it seems necessary to admit that officials have a degree of freedom to introduce into the law considerations from outside of the legal domain, seemingly requiring a rather different justificatory model that explains how such authorised decision-makers are either legally or morally constrained in making any such determination. As such, I will agree with Postema's diagnosis that this is a fatal flaw for this theory. Accordingly, in the third section, I consider two plausible ways forward. One option—hinted at by Postema, but argued for more forcibly by others—would essentially entail abandoning the idea of law's 'limited domain', re-integrating an account of moral determinacy in our concept of law to enhance its presumed guidance function. The other option would be to instead abandon the idea that law must necessarily pre-empt moral choice and guide conduct in this way, therefore rejecting the instrumental rationale of the thesis in order to defend law's autonomy as a valuable normative good in and of itself. In demonstrating the implausibility of the former option, I hope to ultimately vindicate the latter view. I will argue that the kind of creation myth underpinning the *Autonomy Thesis* makes sense only as a theory of the state, akin to the ideal of the social contract, and therefore ends up justifying a much more ambitious political and institutional architecture than that furnished by law (and legal institutions) alone.

Before I begin, however, a couple of caveats are necessary in relation to my choice to focus on the *Autonomy Thesis* as necessarily representative of a broad range of views as to the nature and function of law. The first point to note is that insofar as it may well be true that a wide array of theories converge around a justification for law's necessary autonomy, this very notion—the autonomy of law—is something of a nebulous concept.[11] For instance, Roberto Unger has identified at least four different senses in which law may be viewed as autonomous: *substantively*, insofar as law's validity does not depend on the substantive merits of candidate norms; *institutionally*, in the sense that the field of law is maintained through specialised institutions, particularly adjudicative or law-applying institutions; *methodologically*, where those specialised institutions construct, develop or perpetuate a particular kind of justification based on the substantive autonomy of legal rules; and *occupationally*, insofar as a 'special group, the legal profession, defined by its activities, prerogatives, and training, manipulates the rules, staffs the legal institutions, and engages in the practice of legal argument'.[12] As Unger's typology suggests, however, these forms of autonomy are not necessarily mutually exclusive. In fact, part of the point of this chapter—and, indeed, of Postema's working through of the thesis—is that when justified on the basis of law's ability to pre-empt moral choice, one form of autonomy (*substantive* autonomy) naturally leads into other forms (particularly *institutional* or *occupational* autonomy).

Second, in line with the argument of the previous chapter, I will accept—as with Postema—that the *Autonomy Thesis* applies as much to analytical positivists like Hart and Raz as it does to more idealist theorists such as Fuller or Finnis. For the reasons given in the previous two chapters, I agree with Postema that this view of law's necessary autonomy is presumed within descriptive-explanatory approaches, even if not justified explicitly. In making this claim, however, there remains a certain risk of over-generalisation, potentially setting up 'strawmen' by ignoring the important differences between discrete, and not necessarily commensurate, theoretical perspectives. In fact, Raz has responded critically to Postema's thesis for this very reason, denying that he is committed to an account of law's autonomy on Postema's terms.[13] Whilst he makes a valid point in recognising this danger of theoretical distortion, I also believe that Raz is wrong both to think that his own approach is not compatible with the tenets of the *Autonomy Thesis*—indeed, much of the analysis of Chapter 4 has attempted to show that he is indeed committed to such a view[14]—

[11] For a discussion, see BH Bix, 'Law as an Autonomous Discipline' in P Cane and M Tushnet (eds), *The Oxford Handbook of Legal Studies* (Oxford, Oxford University Press, 2003) 975–87; R Unger, *Law in Modern Society* (New York, Free Press, 1976) 52–54.

[12] Unger (n 11) 52–53.

[13] See J Raz, 'Postema on Law's Autonomy and Public Practical Reasons: A Critical Comment' (1998) 4 *Legal Theory* 1.

[14] I am not alone in holding this view. Margaret Martin has gone to some lengths to demonstrate exactly why Raz's refutation of Postema's argument is misguided. See Martin (n 1) 155–56 ff.

and in missing the fact that Postema's thesis is not intended as a full and accurate account of the specificities of any particular theoretical approach. Rather, it aims to draw out what are the *necessary* implications of either explicitly adopting, or implicitly accepting, a view of law's function related to social ordering, which therefore draws upon the artificial or institutional nature of law as important to the fulfilment of this purpose. For this reason, I believe Postema is justified in attributing this view to Raz (as well as to Hart also).

I. LAW'S 'CREATION MYTH': THE *AUTONOMY THESIS*

The justification for law's autonomy given above and towards the end of the previous chapter is premised on the view that law's function resides in its ability to guide conduct under conditions of political plurality. The capacity of law to unite otherwise divergent viewpoints therefore depends on its ability to supplant the other reasons we might have for action, instead offering up the purely artificial, source-based normativity of the legal domain. This view is set out by Postema as the core rationale of the *Autonomy Thesis*:

> According to the Autonomy Thesis, legal reasoning is a viable and vital form of public practical reasoning that is able to serve the task assigned to it because of its autonomy from moral and political reasoning. This autonomy consists, roughly, in the fact that the existence, content, and practical force of norms from which legal reasoning proceeds are determined by criteria that make no essential reference to considerations of political morality, and so legal reasoning can proceed entirely without engaging in arguments of political morality.[15]

In making this claim, a few points of clarification are necessary. First of all, this claim to law's autonomy is not necessarily central to the conceptual definition of law per se: one could in principle accept law's ontological validity on the basis of a much more limited set of criteria, without necessarily requiring its autonomy in the form described by the *Autonomy Thesis*. Second, and following on from the previous point, this commitment to law's autonomy is not simply a different formulation of the 'separation thesis', common to certain methodological claims espoused principally by legal positivists, which insist on a complete conceptual distinction between law and morality. Rather, as noted above, if not assumed as a basic feature of legality, the *Autonomy Thesis* acts as a shorthand justification for the moral, prudential or political imperatives compelling the subjugation of individual moral judgement to the public, promulgated standards of legality. Third and finally, and again relatedly, in claiming that legal reasoning 'can proceed entirely without engaging in arguments of political morality',

[15] Postema (n 5) 80.

Postema is not suggesting that legal reasoning necessarily *does* so proceed, but merely that even if moral or political considerations figure considerably in legal reasoning, they *necessarily must not* play the decisive part in determining law's normative force. Legal validity (rather than overall systemic legitimacy) is in this sense determined 'entirely' by criteria endogenous to the legal order itself.

Accordingly, whilst there may be a moral or political justification that propels the need to isolate law's limited domain, and whilst this limited domain will undoubtedly open up again to moral and political concerns when interpreting, applying or otherwise engaging the law, a legal order may still be described as autonomous to the extent that legal norms enjoy content-independent validity derived purely from their conformity with certain social sources. As Postema further explains:

> The status of any norm as a *law* in a given jurisdiction is strictly a function of its roots in sources (conventionally) recognized in the jurisdiction. While the norm will have gained entry into the law's domain in virtue of its extra-legal merits, its status and force as a practical norm change. This status is rooted in its source-base, and the practical meaning or interpretation it is given in application is determined by reference to that source (and perhaps its relationship to other sourced-based norms in the domain). Its application—that is, its practical meaning or interpretation and its practical force—are now *opaque* to the merits which first recommended it ... It follows that, where there no doubt will be important moral reasons for identifying a separate legal domain, these reasons will not be available to the practical reasoning of participants in legal practice.[16]

Following this reasoning, we can say that the normative reasons underpinning the thesis—whether moral, practical, prudential etc—*become opaque* to the extent that they justify the construction of a certain kind of legal system which, once established, allows those engaged in legal practice to justify their specific normative commitments by reference to an entirely artificial form of practical reasoning grounded in certain sources (and constructed by reference to certain other secondary ordering principles) that are entirely endogenous to the system itself. To buttress the 'limited domain' of the law in this sense is to recognise and acknowledge the importance of the formality of legal sources as a necessary factor in mediating social discord and pre-empting individual moral judgement.[17]

Insofar as we can accept this instrumental rationale, Postema is probably also right in recognising that the *Autonomy Thesis* can actually be broken down further into three underpinning and necessarily interconnected theses: these being what he terms the *Limited Domain*, *Pre-emption*

[16] ibid 87.

[17] See, eg, F Schauer, 'Formalism' (1988) 97 *Yale Law Journal* 509; F Schauer, 'The Limited Domain of the Law' (2004) 90 *Virginia Law Review* 1909.

and *Sources* theses. Henrik Palmer Olsen and Stuart Toddington provide a useful summary of what Postema intends here:

> These, respectively, express the demands of the [*Autonomy Thesis*] in that 'law' (autonomous normativity) operates in a limited domain of practical reason common to officials and citizens alike; that these norms constitute exclusionary reasons for action in that they preclude acting for reasons outside the domain, and these, therefore pre-emptive, norms be identifiable at source without recourse to moral argument or political evaluations outside the limited domain.[18]

There thus seems to be a crucial interrelation between these three theses: the *Limited Domain Thesis* is intelligible only because of the way in which the other two theses necessarily act on each other. More specifically, the *Pre-emption Thesis* suggests that law's usefulness as a means of social mediation depends on its ability to provide reasons for action which exclude, or, better, trump, other moral or political reasons for action.[19] The *Sources Thesis* suggests that in order for legal reasons to be accepted as exclusionary in this respect, the law's validity must be verifiable on the basis of source-based criteria—social facts—which themselves are distinct from moral or political reasons for action.[20] As Postema goes on to note:

> [T]he Pre-emption Thesis and the Sources Thesis are [therefore] mutually dependent. It would be pointless to isolate law's limited domain from the normal reach of practical reasoning, and especially from the balance of moral considerations lying behind the rules, unless membership in law's domain could be determined by citizens and officials alike without recourse to moral argument … Similarly, it would be pointless to displace practical reasoning onto a limited domain of source-based rules, if citizens and officials alike could not count on compliance with those rules.[21]

This position seems convincing and logically coherent within the terms of its rationale—accepting, still, the instrumentalist justification which undergirds this view, that is, the idea of law as a means of mediating social discord and pre-empting moral judgement. But, as soon as we work through each of these requirements, it seems difficult to fulfil these demands without further supplementing the thesis. Law's ability to secure compliance surely depends on one's capacity to determine the law's content, which is likely not to be clear-cut simply on the basis of there being certain social sources validating legal normativity or an abstract, systemic logic defining the contours of

[18] HP Olsen and S Toddington, 'Legal Idealism and the Autonomy of Law' (1999) 12 *Ratio Juris* 286, 296.

[19] A norm's acceptability must therefore depend on second-order procedural rules which are distinct from evaluative considerations. As Raz puts it, legal norms must exclude other reasons for acting on the basis of their being accepted at a second-order level, as independent and distinct from all other reasons for acting: see J Raz, *Practical Reason and Norms* (Oxford, Oxford University Press, 1975) 79–80.

[20] Postema (n 5) 82 and passim.

[21] ibid 92.

legal reasoning. This indeterminacy suggests—as was noted in Chapter 3 in particular—the probability of reasonable disagreement, in turn leading to a certain degree of flexibility and malleability in the law. If left uncoordinated, the law thus potentially offers a variety of possible justifications for particular, not necessarily commensurable political positions.

To explain further, consider again Raz's critical engagement with Postema, wherein he denies that his theory is committed to anything other than the *Sources Thesis*—a form of autonomy which he takes to be a defining element of all forms of legal positivism.[22] The problem, however, is that it is difficult to understand how the *Sources Thesis* can exist independently of the broader commitment to pre-emptive normativity that appears so critical to Raz's overall theory.[23] Indeed, despite his refutation of the argument that law has any overarching and *necessary* function, the idea that law aims necessarily to pre-empt moral choice and claims authority for itself must necessarily presuppose the function of guiding conduct or social ordering. Indeed, we saw in Chapter 4 how Raz's reliance on law-applying authorities can only really be explained by presuming such a function—as unremarkable as such a function may seem. If we presume this view of law's function to be correct, it therefore seems doubtful that one could simply refer to a defined list of sources in order to reach determinate solutions capable of normatively pre-empting political or moral choice without the introduction of an institutionalised hierarchy, as suggested above. The unrealistic assumption that law has any inherent, discernible and determinate meaning is undermined by a number of recurrent and basic truths about legal practice: for example, that normative disputes are often structured in terms of divergent interpretations of existing legal rules; that different, sometimes potentially conflicting, legal rules, entitlements or rights will exist independently of each other without any obvious relation between them; and that, prior to law's ascertainment in certain adjudicatory contexts, it may be questionable whether particular candidate norms actually 'exist' in the first place—this being particularly the case at the international level, where adjudicators are left to fill in the gaps caused by international law's uncoordinated and decentralised law-creating processes.

This might be a somewhat trite illustration of the open texture of legal rules, but it is precisely for this reason that most who defend an account of law akin to the *Autonomy Thesis*—Raz included—will tend to ground this autonomy within a broader institutional theory,[24] outlining the necessary

[22] Raz (n 13) 3–4.

[23] Martin (n 1) 158–60.

[24] This is not necessarily the same as *The Institutional Theory of Law* developed by MacCormick, though this approach accords significantly with what Postema hereby intends. See most recently N MacCormick, *Institutions of Law: An Essay in Legal Theory* (Oxford, Oxford University Press, 2007).

intermediary role of a class of legal officials—particularly, though by no means exclusively, judicial offices[25]—the purpose of which can only really be to enhance the determinacy (and perhaps also the efficiency and effectiveness) of legal norms. In other words, the abstract notion of legal autonomy is supplemented through the introduction of a specific institutional context that is understood as securing the overall systemic integrity of the legal order in question. Insofar as we do not simply presume, but instead seek to justify and defend this institutional structure—thus avoiding the methodological controversy outlined in Chapters 4 and 5—we can follow Postema in referring to this model as the *Institutionalised Autonomy Thesis*. As he explains:

> [T]he law's solution to the pervasive problems of social co-operation essentially includes, but is not limited to, defining a set of norms that meet the conditions of the Autonomy Thesis; for these norms are authoritatively interpreted and applied, and the system of norms is maintained by adjudicative institutions. Moreover, adjudicative institutions are authorized to settle issues left unsettled by the set of source-based legal norms available at any point in time.[26]

This reliance on certain authoritative institutional structures should come as no surprise bearing in mind the perspectives covered in the previous two chapters. The pre-emptive capacity of the law seems to depend upon incorporating, centralising and streamlining law-determining processes or institutions: *substantive* autonomy eventually implies—indeed, necessitates—*institutional* autonomy. In this respect, a legal system's 'secondary rules' would need to offer guidance that goes beyond identifying legal norms (and, perhaps, clarifying the relationships between them), having to outline procedures and processes, not only for determining the validity and meaning of these norms, but also for clarifying which official or authorised body has the ultimate say in any continuing conflict—that is, *whose view is ultimately to be determinative*.[27] In other words, rather than simply presume the presence of legal officials, a more explicitly normative theory akin to the *Institutionalised Autonomy Thesis* provides a specific justification for their presence—or, at the very least, provides a justification for independent courts of compulsory jurisdiction capable of authoritatively determining the law and enforcing their judgment on disputing parties.[28]

This movement from abstract to institutionalised autonomy seems, again, familiar and uncontroversial. Insofar as these institutional processes are

[25] See, eg, J Raz, *The Concept of a Legal System*, 2nd edn (Oxford, Clarendon Press, 1980) 215–16; Postema (n 5) 92.

[26] Postema (n 5) 93.

[27] Though not always clearly expressed as such, it is possible to see this kind of interrelation in Hart's discussion of secondary norms: HLA Hart, *The Concept of Law*, 3rd edn (Oxford, Clarendon Press, 2012) 91–99.

[28] See, eg, J Raz, *Ethics in the Public Domain: Essays in the Morality of Law and Politics*, revised edn (Oxford, Clarendon Press, 1994) 330–35.

seen as authorised by the system itself, that is, so long as there is acceptance of the structural and institutional rules capable of sustaining the finality of legal decisions (and probably also law-creating and enforcement processes),[29] a legal order can be defended still as a coherent and (relatively) autonomous system of public practical reasoning.[30] Indeed, insofar as those institutions are themselves staffed or serviced by relatively homogeneous legal professions, this view further reinforces the inter-related and mutually reinforcing forms of legal autonomy outlined at the beginning of the chapter. At the same time, however, there is a certain tension revealed in institutionalising our legal theory in this way: once we re-introduce human agency into the picture by justifying—indeed, necessitating—some form of institutionalised authority or 'final say', we surely need to supplement our theory to account for the authority of the thus-authorised decision-maker, particularly insofar as such authorities are understood as possessing adjudicative discretion. In other words—and as I will explain more clearly in the following section—it would appear that law itself is no longer acting as the pre-emptive normative restraint, but instead the particular determinations of legal decision-makers (officials). On this view, legal norms themselves do not necessarily have any pre-emptive authority until bestowed with determinate content by officials. The problem, however, is that this content must necessarily come from *outside of law's limited domain* and therefore further begs the question of how to constrain or pre-empt the discretion of our thus-authorised officials. In fact, as I now go on to demonstrate, if we retain the instrumental justification for the *Autonomy Thesis*, we seem pushed into having to embellish the thesis to such an extent that it threatens the very idea of the autonomy of law at its heart.

II. THE FAILURE OF THE *AUTONOMY THESIS*

The problem just outlined can perhaps best be illustrated by further considering the task being asked of legal institutions (specifically, what has been termed law- or norm-applying institutions in Chapter 4). The kind of justification for adjudicative institutions contained in the *Institutionalised Autonomy Thesis* does not suggest that judges (or any other official) are tasked with authoritatively determining law's *inherent* meaning in cases of conflict—such truth claims being precluded by the very same moral agnosticism and political pluralism that are taken together to justify the necessary autonomy of law in the first place. Rather, adjudicative institutions are

[29] Postema (n 5) 92–94; and for examples of this kind of justification, see, eg, Raz (n 25) 215–16; N MacCormick, 'The Concept of Law and *The Concept of Law*' in George (n 5) 180–81.

[30] Postema (n 5) 92–93.

seen as *giving* meaning to legal standards, gap-filling and often creatively interpreting norms in novel situations. As Postema explains:

> [Adjudicative institutions] are authorised to *add to or alter* the norms of law. Since, in such cases by hypothesis, the existing legal considerations are silent, indeterminate, or in conflict, the courts' settling of them is determined not by appeal to the law, but by appeals to considerations outside its limited domain.[31] (emphasis added, footnotes omitted)

To admit this is, again, perhaps a trite point, but recognising this basic truth surely points to the fact that legal *reasoning* is not in itself an autonomous process.[32] What would appear to be most important in authorised adjudicative processes are the non-legal factors which are introduced into judicial reasoning to give meaning to otherwise indeterminate legal standards.[33] This might not necessarily be perceived as a problem insofar as the claim to the autonomy of law goes only to the nature of law and not to its application as such, but such a limitation would suggest the incompleteness of the *Autonomy Thesis* (and thus any theory of law premised upon it), particularly bearing in mind that the initial justification for the thesis was to secure social coordination under conditions of political plurality. Whilst one might therefore get around this problem at a surface level by distinguishing a theory of adjudication from a conceptual analysis of law,[34] this distinction would be somewhat disingenuous to the extent that our concept of law is justified by a functional purpose that can only really be fulfilled by integrating adjudicative processes in this way. At the same time, to instead follow through on the idea that law only instantiates itself through adjudication would seem to admit the plausibility of the critique of those such as Ronald Dworkin, whose interpretivist approach essentially entails the denial of the law's autonomy through a necessary re-integration of moral reasoning into the legal domain vis-a-vis authorised institutions.[35]

As Postema ultimately concludes, it seems difficult to institutionalise the *Autonomy Thesis* in this way without undermining its core rationale, which, as we have seen, relies on the artificiality of the legal framework to overcome the moral indeterminacy created by the plural political conditions of human communities. In fact, the irony of this realisation is that the apparent discord between functional ambition and institutional implication

[31] ibid 93; also cited in Olsen and Toddington (n 18) 297.

[32] Raz perhaps makes this point most forcibly in his repudiation of Postema's argument: see Raz (n 13) 4.

[33] Capps (n 2) 143–44.

[34] See also the discussion in Schauer (n 17) 1949–50.

[35] See R Dworkin, *Law's Empire* (Oxford, Hart Publishing, 2004, first published in 1986). See also section 5 of N Stavropoulos, 'Legal Interpretivism' in EN Zalta (ed), *The Stanford Encyclopedia of Philosophy* (Summer 2014 edn); available at: http://plato.stanford.edu/archives/sum2014/entries/law-interpretivist.

is only amplified when applied to societies that are particularly marked by moral and political disagreement—most obviously at the international level—for it would seem that in these societies there would be the greatest need for autonomous law, so that legal participants can determine their action in accordance with 'deliberations about matters that are common to them all, rather than considerations which most divide them'.[36] In such cases, though, the fact that legal institutions are guided by factors outside of law's limited domain surely creates a problem for the law's task of social coordination. By drawing on such extra-legal justifications in order to complete the task of instantiating the law in specific contexts, it is difficult to see official determinations as in any sense *pre-empted by* law—it being those non-legal factors (moral or political considerations) that are ultimately decisive in ascertaining the law and applying it to concrete situations. Why would legal participants have a reason to follow the judgments of courts if they do not feel that judges themselves are somehow constrained by the law?

We therefore seem to need a reason to sustain the authority of legal officials that would go beyond, for example, a claim to expertise or neutrality—claims that are surely controversial, if not indeed precluded, in societies marked by deep moral and political disagreement. If the authority of law-applying institutions cannot be sustained a priori then legal participants are arguably forced to somehow track and evaluate judicial reasoning by some theory of legitimacy, thus once again undermining the social coordination justification for autonomous law.[37] As Postema recognises, 'in the absence of a plausible claim of expertise on contested matters of political morality, law can hope to maintain its legitimacy in a society in which serious issues of political morality remain unsettled, only if it provides institutional devices by which the conditions of its own legitimacy can be assessed'.[38]

One can see this tension at work, once again, in the approach of Raz, as Martin has recently demonstrated. In his later work in particular, specifically *Ethics in the Public Domain*, Raz looks at the moral duties incumbent on adjudicators when giving judgment in legal disputes.[39] Bearing in mind, as we have already seen, that Raz's argument is that law necessarily claims authority, and this theory is, in turn, premised upon the practice of law-applying institutions (whose acceptance of the rule of recognition is seen as constitutive of legal order), one can legitimately question how Raz can maintain this position without also incorporating an account of how morality acts upon and guides our thus-authorised decision-makers. In this

36 Postema (n 5) 106–07.
37 ibid 100–01.
38 ibid 108–09.
39 Raz (n 28); and see also Martin (n 1) 49–54.

respect, as Martin recognises, it seems impossible to divorce Raz's account of adjudication from his overarching legal theory:

> Citizens have a reason to defer to legal norms when deciding how to act *because* they can depend on judges to enforce the rules. The exclusionary status of norms is itself dependent on the duty of judges to apply pre-existing positive law ... [But o]nce judges are thought of as moral reasoners, we can wonder whether citizens have the requisite incentive to treat legal norms as pre-emptive (or exclusionary) reasons for action.[40]

This kind of embellishment of the theory thus seems to corrupt its core tenets; it seems impossible to complete the *Autonomy Thesis* without also undermining it, for we need to look outside of law's limited domain—either to some theory of inherent moral restraint, or political mechanism by which we might account for, and ultimately restrain, judicial discretion—in order to find the operative factors at play in actually facilitating social coordination.[41] In fact, as Capps also acknowledges, this problem only appears to get worse when we relocate our analysis to the international level, which, in addition to being a characteristically pluralistic society of the sort described by Postema, clearly lacks both institutions for authoritatively determining the law, as well as any means by which the legitimacy of any such determination could be checked—at least other than through the free interplay of political forces that arguably characterises international society. In short, the ad hoc nature of international adjudication and the lack of any systemic hierarchy between courts and other institutionalised decision-makers mean that international legal participants are themselves left to track the legitimacy and cogency of each legal determination given by any particular court or other authorised decision-maker.[42] This institutional structure thus seems to contain within itself the very same social tensions which, it is claimed, law has the purpose of mediating.

III. RESCUING THE *AUTONOMY THESIS*?

With this problem in mind, we seem left with two plausible ways forward. The first would be to give up entirely on the apparent fiction of legal autonomy, to recognise the necessarily moral character of law, conceding the critiques of those such as Dworkin, who sees law as only really instantiating itself when adjudicators attempt to synthesise law's content with the underlying social values at play in any given community.[43] Bearing in mind the

40 Martin (n 1) 53.
41 Postema (n 5) 110.
42 Capps (n 2) 146–47.
43 Dworkin (n 35) 52–53 and passim.

direction of the argument of Part II so far, it might seem somewhat strange to reach the conclusion that law might not, after all, be autonomous (at least not in the sense described). The problem, though, is that if we follow through the logic of the *Autonomy Thesis* as formulated above, seeing law as an instrumental solution to the problem of social order in pluralist societies, we appear to be drawn towards this conclusion. Indeed, this is echoed by Postema himself, who claims that the *Autonomy Thesis* will be unlikely to survive its necessary 'completion' unless we abandon the very claim to law's autonomy at its heart. To carry through the functional ambition at the heart of the thesis—an ambition which, in fact, seems to underpin the vast majority of contemporary theories of law—we seem to need some theory of institutional rationality, or interpretative practice, re-introducing moral argumentation as crucial to the task of legal reasoning and thus, ultimately, the fulfilment of law's function.[44]

That this conclusion seems somewhat paradoxical, perverse even, particularly bearing in mind the value that has been attributed to the idea of law's autonomy thus far, causes me to veer towards a second option, however. This option would be to maintain the value of law's abstract, systemic autonomy as a virtuous end in itself and, instead, to reject almost entirely the instrumentalist logic of the kind of 'creation myth' that propels the *Autonomy Thesis* in the first place. This option would be to recognise the abstract rationality of law as an important end in itself; that law's function is to structure, channel and facilitate a way of managing disagreement in plural political communities. To be sure, this is still to recognise that law is best defined *and rationally defended* by reference to its point or purpose, but, importantly, this point or 'final cause' can be seen as inherently *non-instrumental* insofar as it subsists in law being its own end. I will say more about this claim shortly, but to support my position in this respect, I must first say why I think the alternative view—the attempt to re-introduce moral reasoning, indeed, to equate moral and legal validity, in order to fulfil the instrumentalist logic at the heart of the *Autonomy Thesis*—inevitably fails.

A. On the Reflexivity of Legal Reasoning

Postema's concerns are picked up by Capps, who notes how in seeking to rescue the *Autonomy Thesis*, we would need to show how law acts upon and guides authorised decision-makers (officials essentially), who cannot merely have free rein to interpret the law as they see fit. If they have to interpret the law at all, officials must engage in a form of justification that

[44] Postema (n 5) 111; Olsen and Toddington (n 18) 298. See also J Finnis, 'The Truth in Legal Positivism' in George (n 5) 204–05.

cannot simply refer back to the internal logic of an autonomous legal order, the indeterminacy of which being precisely the reason why, in the domestic context at least, adjudicatory institutions are called upon to finally settle the legal disputes that arise between other legal participants.[45] For Capps, legal adjudicators are thus compelled to carry through the initial moral imperative for autonomous law into the adjudicative setting, essentially binding them to reason according to moral imperative (ie, by giving effect to human dignity, respecting moral autonomy or some other similar ends or values).[46]

In making this point, Capps follows Postema, who seeks to show how adjudication has to be a 'reflectively self-critical' practice—by which he aims to underscore the sense in which this task is, ultimately, a *justificatory* activity. In other words, it places an onus on decision-makers to refer back and reason according to the moral imperatives which grant their authority in the first place.[47] This would seem to accord considerably with the views of those like Finnis, who highlight how legal decision-making must be informed by the prevailing social mores in the community in which law is operative.[48] Specifically, Finnis claims that a host of non-posited norms will inevitably act upon legal subjects in terms of how they conform (or not) to legal rules, just as a considerable number of different non-posited (often procedural) norms will be at play in the deliberations and decision-making of legal officials when giving effect to the law in specific contexts.[49] In this way, he draws a contrast between the artificial, institutional nature of positive law and the broader social-moral context of its instantiation in practice:

> Though human law is artefact and artifice, and not a conclusion from moral premises, both its positing and the recognition of its positivity (by judges, professionals, citizens, and thence by descriptive and critical scholars) cannot be understood without reference to the moral principles that ground and confirm its authority or challenge its pretention.[50]

This argument seems intuitively plausible in many respects. It is surely not unreasonable to suggest that legal participants (including authorised

[45] Capps (n 2) 152–54.

[46] Postema (n 5) 111–12.

[47] ibid 111.

[48] This is a point well made by Finnis, with a useful, though he claims also 'hackneyed', example of the 'rule of the road'. See Finnis (n 8) 285: 'There is a sense in which … the rule of the road gets "all its force" from the authoritative custom, enactment, or other determination which laid it down. Until the stipulation "dive on the left, and at less than 70 miles per hour" was posited by one of these means, there was no legal rule of the road; moreover there was no need for the legislator to have a reason for choosing "left" rather than "right" or "70" rather than "65". But there is also a sense in which … the rule of the road gets "all its normative force" ultimately from the permanent principles of practical reason (which require us to respect our own and others' physical safety) in combination with non-posited facts such as that traffic is dangerous and can be made safety by orderly traffic flows and limitation of speed, that braking distances and human reaction times are such-and-such, etc.'

[49] ibid 286–87.

[50] Finnis (n 44) 204–05.

adjudicative bodies) operate in a political and social context in which they must look beyond law and legal texts to reason, make determinations and adapt the law to new circumstances in accordance with prevailing moral principles or political realities. Insofar as law can therefore only really be implemented by legal decision-makers by making reference to this broader context, clearly the *Autonomy Thesis* requires some form of qualification.

At the same time, however, this reflexivity of adjudicative practice does not necessarily undermine the recognition of law's limited domain—as Postema, Capps and others seem to suggest—but, I would argue, really only demonstrates the futility of the pre-emption strategy underpinning the thesis. In other words, it suggests that law only takes on normative meaning by reference to standards already prevailing within a given society; that one cannot simply trace a causative path from legal norm to behavioural adjustment.[51] I will say more about why this might be shortly, but first let me consider further the way in which legal reasoning may be reflexive in the form that I have just suggested.

This idea is fleshed out in particular in an important work by Nigel Simmonds,[52] who highlights the 'symbiotic relationship' between legal norms and the background social mores and normative understandings held in the community as a whole.[53] Importantly, however, Simmonds argues that the idea that law is used functionally to implement moral standards, that is, to instruct a community, inverts the actual order of things: 'that community is the matrix of interpretation, not its result', by which he means that 'if social life did not already exhibit some stable expectations and shared understandings, law could not provide them'.[54] If Simmonds is correct, then, rather than completing or supplementing the *Autonomy Thesis*, this realisation points directly to the incoherence of the pre-emptive strategy that drives it and which, at least in Postema's model, sits at its heart; it suggests that law plays a part in resolving, but cannot authoritatively determine the outcome of, any given normative problem. In Simmonds' words, it 'embodies an authoritative interpretation of social relationships and in that way enters into our understanding of social life', but it is this understanding which, in turn, also 'makes a vital contribution to the stability and ascertainability of law'.[55]

This realisation would thus seem to cast doubt on the cogency of the creation myth explanation of law's function in society. Rather than seeing law as being bound up with the task of securing order, of governing or

[51] See on this point J Griffith, 'Is Law Important?' (1979) 54 *New York University Law Review* 339.

[52] N Simmonds, 'Between Positivism and Idealism' (1991) 50 *Cambridge Law Journal* 308. Simmonds appears to have moved away from this view to some degree in his later work, particularly in N Simmonds, *Law as a Moral Idea* (Oxford, Oxford University Press, 2007).

[53] See on this point Capps (n 2) 150.

[54] Simmonds, 'Between Positivism and Idealism' (n 52) 326.

[55] ibid 322.

guiding conduct, law might be better understood as an attempt to give an 'authoritative interpretation' of the social and political context in which it is found; it embodies the shared understandings of participants in a particular practice, which will in themselves embody broader notions of political legitimacy as they feature in those relations, giving structure and authority—in the domestic context at least—to governmental institutions.

I believe that Simmonds' views in this respect are insightful and important. They offer a normative account of law's necessary and important function in society (law's instrumentality), whilst at the same time recognising that law holds out its own idea, or end, which is bound up with the idea of justice itself (its autonomy, in one sense at least). As such, this realisation may well offer a way of rescuing the *Autonomy Thesis* not by supplementing it as such, but by radically scaling back that which is demanded of law in instrumental terms. On this view, law's autonomy would not be seen as important as a means to social order, of instructing a community, but as an important end in itself: giving a specific (and important) institutional form to our social conflicts (rather than resolving those conflicts in any definitive sense). This does not mean that law cannot be used for immoral ends, nor does it disconnect it from morality—at least not when conceived as an ideal. What it does mean, however, is that there is specific value in law's institutional nature, its artificiality.

It is not my intention yet to draw out the consequences of this way of thinking about law for our consideration of international law—I take up this task in Part III. For now, I want to remain at the more abstract level of legal theory in order to show why I believe the attempt to rescue the instrumentalist view, specifically by incorporating a more deterministic moral viewpoint, will inevitably fail. In this regard, I must engage with one quite fundamental objection to the kind of 'reflexive approach' I have sketched out briefly above.

B. Morality 'All the Way Down'? The Failure of the Interpretivist Challenge

In following through on Postema's challenge, Capps considers and ultimately rejects the kind of reasoning presented by Simmonds. He argues that such a strategy fails to guard against the attendant risk that a legal order becomes corrupted, sustaining fundamentally unjust practices (for instance, racial apartheid or the subjugation of women) which are often tolerated by certain societies or perhaps even regarded as fair or just by a significant enough section of the community in question.[56] In order to guard against

[56] Capps (n 2) 152–53.

this risk, Capps argues that legal standards must possess some objective moral content that stands above the positive law, aprioristically determining the range of permissible responses available to authorised decision-makers.

Though this conclusion clearly challenges the autonomy of law, Capps follows Postema's lead by referring to this approach as the *Integrated Autonomy Thesis*, which he describes as 'a version of the [*Autonomy Thesis*] that reflects all its features except for the isolation strategy which is at its heart'.[57] Whilst space precludes giving Capps' theory, particularly insofar as it applies to international law, the full consideration it deserves—a challenge I have taken up elsewhere[58]—it suffices for current purposes to note that the *Integrated Autonomy Thesis* is 'predicated on an integration of law with *objective moral interests*', a state of affairs 'achieved by officials exercising their role in legal institutions so as to establish the conditions by which each legal subject has human dignity'.[59] Capps' claims in this regard largely follow those of Olsen and Toddington, who adopt a similar argument in their critical engagement with Postema's account, arguing that the normative justification that was made opaque under the *Autonomy Thesis* should again become 'transparent' in the process of the law's application in adjudicative contexts.[60] Specifically, they claim that in order to fulfil the functional justification that propels the original *Autonomy Thesis*, one must at least defend 'the possibility of a sufficiently determinate system of practical reason which can survive positive complexity'.[61]

To this extent at least, this final move pushes these approaches in the direction of those like Dworkin who argue for a constructive interpretation of practices based on an account of 'law as integrity'.[62] Although philosophically—indeed, epistemologically—distinct in their philosophical commitments, methodologically speaking, there is a considerable degree of convergence here in a collective disavowal of law's limited domain (as conceived under the original *Autonomy Thesis*). In fact, Olsen and Toddington describe Dworkin's account of integrity as following the functional logic of the *Autonomy Thesis*, whilst at the same time denying one of its core, defining features: the wish to clearly distinguish legal from moral validity.

[57] ibid 151.

[58] See R Collins, 'No Longer at the Vanishing Point? International Law and the Analytical Tradition in Jurisprudence' (2014) 5 *Jurisprudence* 265. Some of the points raised here develop themes from this work.

[59] Capps (n 2) 184.

[60] HP Olsen and S Toddington, *Law in its Own Right* (Oxford, Hart Publishing, 1999) 129 ff.

[61] Olsen and Toddington (n 18) 308.

[62] See, eg, R Dworkin, *Freedom's Law: The Moral Reading of the American Constitution* (Cambridge, MA, Harvard University Press, 1996). Capps outlines and endorses an interpretation of Hersch Lauterpacht's method in international law based on a Dworkinian reading. See P Capps, 'Lauterpacht's Method' (2012) 82 *British Yearbook of International Law* 248.

Following this rationale, they argue—as Capps does also—that legal decision-makers should strive for the realisation of the practical reason that propels the thesis in the first place. Whilst this would not solve the problem of indeterminacy or secure a precise infallible outcome, it would limit and guide the decision-maker in the right direction by placing an interpretative obligation upon them.[63]

It is difficult to dispute these collective diagnoses of the failure, or at least incompleteness, of the *Autonomy Thesis* as originally promulgated, but it is far from clear that these efforts to resurrect and re-orient the theory would help resolve the kind of moral discord, or danger of moral subversion, which these theorists wish to expunge from the law. Even if the value which ultimately propels their work, the recognition and necessary protection of human dignity, seems unobjectionable as a broad moral commitment, it surely adds nothing to the quandary of legal decision-making to claim that adjudicators are somehow bound to reason according to this specific end when applying law to a particular set of circumstances in specific social and political contexts. To be sure, values like human dignity or Kantian moral autonomy might suggest certain boundaries to the freedom of decision-makers, but they surely cannot reveal any more definite and determinate solutions to the kinds of complex moral problems that often arise in societies marked by political and moral pluralism—that is, in exactly the kind of situations where the *Autonomy Thesis* seemed to reveal its inherent limitations. More specifically, if it is the non-ideal conditions pertaining in society (and the attendant moral discord such conditions imply) that explain why our moral imperatives translate into the abstract formality of legal form, then to refer back to the underpinning moral rationale will reveal little until such values are interpreted within the specific historical and social contexts in which they are fleshed out and given meaning in practice.

It is very likely, therefore, that whilst legal practice, broadly speaking, cannot be understood when divorced from the moral or political values that the law seeks to promote—as scholars such as Finnis, Simmonds and Dworkin all insightfully suggest—such values cannot offer any concrete determinate outcomes in mediating the kind of moral discord that characterises many areas of human activity. Consider, for example, the issue of abortion in societies deeply divided on the moral and legal issues involved. Suppose that a judge finds herself in the (unlikely) position of ruling on the legality or constitutionality of the practice in general, and in doing so finds herself equally persuaded as to the merits of arguments of both pro-life and pro-choice camps—*particularly when such arguments are considered from the perspective of the moral autonomy and dignity afforded to human*

[63] Olsen and Toddington (n 18) 306.

beings. In this case, to say that the judge must apply the objective demands of practical-reasonableness to decide how to resolve this dispute surely leaves open reasonable arguments either way.[64] In such an instance, Capps would not suggest that judges or other adjudicators would have any kind of special access to knowledge about what, for instance, human dignity might specifically require in particular disputes or controversies, especially areas of such sensitive moral disagreement. Rather, like Dworkin, the claim is more methodological, suggesting that the onus is on the decision-maker to reach the most justifiable outcome—the claim to integrity—in these particular circumstances. However, the problem here is that one is left wondering in what way infusing moral and legal validity would help to secure this end.

In these circumstances, it seems much more convincing—I would maintain—to recognise the institutional nature of legal decision-making, which is, in Neil MacCormick's words, *morally* 'heteronomous' rather than 'autonomous'.[65] In other words, what is required of the decision-maker is a balancing of interests in order to do justice in the specific context of the social and political setting in which they operate. Waldron has made a similar point and is worth quoting at length:

> Neither judges nor legislators are deciding what to do as individuals. When they deliberate and vote in their respective institutions, they are deciding what is to be done in the name of the whole society. On abortion, for example, the judge or the legislator is not like a private citizen wrestling with the question of whether it is right or wrong to procure an abortion for herself. The judge or the legislator is participating in the establishment of a national abortion policy. He has to make a decision that will stand in the name of large numbers of others in the society, including others who he knows reason from premises that differ from his premises to conclusions that differ from his conclusions. He may feel he has a duty to take the views of some of these others into account, and in a way that has no parallel in the case of strictly individual reasoning. One way of putting this is to say that, although it is appropriate, even necessary, for the ordinary citizen's moral reasoning to be autonomous (in the sense of its being incumbent upon her just to think morally for herself), it may not be appropriate for the judge's or the legislator's moral reasoning to be autonomous in that sense.[66]

Following this reasoning, it would seem that objective instantiations of values like human dignity can only really materialise by reference to particular social and historical contexts, and even then may only reveal deep

[64] See generally on this point J Waldron, 'The Irrelevance of Moral Objectivity' in RP George (ed), *Natural Law Theory* (Oxford, Clarendon Press, 1992) 158–87.

[65] MacCormick (n 29) 170–71; MacCormick (n 24) 249–51.

[66] J Waldron, 'Judges as Moral Reasoners' (2009) 7 *International Journal of Constitutional Law* 2, at 5–6.

areas of moral disagreement when applied to concrete circumstances—thus underlining the importance of the kind of symbiosis that Capps sees as inadequate.

C. The Autonomy Thesis as a Social Contract Theory

Whilst history suggests that Capps' fears over the moral subversion of the law by authorised decision-makers are not unfounded, the attempt to fill out or augment the *Autonomy Thesis* as a coherent theory of law misses its most fundamental flaw. If anything, the lesson from the state context is that to the extent that such risks have presented themselves, certain checks and balances will exist (or, at least, can be put in place) through the instigation of complex institutional arrangements, including, but not limited to, a separation of powers, mechanisms of judicial review, as well as necessary democratic inputs into constitutional processes. This may well be a drastic over-simplification of a more thorough, worked-through model of constitutional legitimacy at the state level, but this is only really to highlight the underlying point of contention: the best version of the *Autonomy Thesis* is probably not, or *not just*, a theory of law at all. Rather, taken to its logical extreme, the *Autonomy Thesis* actually morphs into a fuller social contract theory, specifically because what the thesis is attempting to establish is legitimate political authority and not, or *not just*, law alone.

This conclusion is not really surprising. In setting the *Autonomy Thesis* out as a 'creation myth', Postema appears to imply as much, particularly when grounding it in a tradition of thought which dates back to Hobbes and Locke.[67] Capps as well as Olsen and Toddington make explicit reference to the idea of the social contract when working through the implications of Postema's thesis.[68] Of course, law clearly plays an important part in the kind of constitutional theory that seeks to explain legitimate authority in the state context, responding specifically to the fact of domination and hierarchical political rule. However, attempting to explain this legitimacy problem through the lens of legal theory alone will not only distort reality, but will also miss the particular—and important—role that law plays within this broader institutional and political setting. In other words, it completely fails to explain the value of law's autonomy in acting as a non-instrumental check on political action.[69]

The point that I am trying to make here is that the failure of the *Autonomy Thesis* arises from the fact that what law is being asked to do—

[67] Postema (n 5) 79–80.

[68] Capps (n 2) 138–39, 177–78 and passim; Olsen and Toddington (n 18) 303 and 308; and more extensively, see Ch 5 of Olsen and Toddington (n 60) 113–28.

[69] See, eg, Griffith (n 51).

the task of social coordination through coercion—is not a task which law alone can fulfil. In other words, the goal to which the *Autonomy Thesis* is committed aims to solve a particular legitimacy problem faced by those subject to hierarchical authority in a state context. Those propounding such an argument thus seem to commit the basic error 'of confusing certain features of the modern state with the idea of law as such'.[70] The social contract does not act solely as a justification for legal institutions, but provides a broader rationale for, at best, something like a democratic, functioning rule of law state. As such, the *Autonomy Thesis* fails because of what we demand from it, but what is demanded from it in this respect is not only unrealistic, but also hugely problematic in undermining the very thing that makes law valuable to these constitutional processes: its autonomy, in this restricted, non-instrumental sense. Unless we continue to maintain a necessary distinction between legal and moral validity, law will be unable to make any kind of important and valuable contribution to the life of a community. Simmonds is therefore correct that, in its essence, law is a deeply moral idea, but it is surely also one which has its own imminent rationality.

IV. CONCLUSION

In reaching the conclusion that the *Autonomy Thesis* is essentially a version of a social contract theory, it must also be the case that this thesis cannot simply be watered down by missing out the fuller institutional context of the state as a coercive legal order with a specific function, and subject to specific legitimacy pulls, requiring a particular kind of institutional solution. As a theory of (or at least a justification for) law, and as a theory applicable to international law in particular, the *Autonomy Thesis* can thus be accused of over-reaching in its ambition, pointing towards the broader institutional and political context of legitimate rule and authority that one commonly finds at the state level, and which is not only characteristically absent from international law, but is arguably antithetical to such a decentralised legal order.

I do not doubt that Capps is correct in foreseeing that a legal order may well become corrupted and that law's abstract autonomy may be used to do bad as much as good, but this does not take away from the fact that this autonomy on its own may be a valuable (albeit contextually dependent) end in its own right. To the extent that the kinds of risks he foresees present themselves within the context of coercive political communities justified through something like the social contract, our attempts to guard against them necessarily involve a range of constitutional questions of institutional

[70] T Nardin, *Law, Morality*, and the *Relations of States* (Princeton, NJ, Princeton University Press, 1983) 132.

design which stretch beyond the ambit of law's limited domain. Law has to play a role in this context, but its specificity depends upon it retaining its unique artificiality, distinguishing legal and moral validity. In other words, the best version of the *Autonomy Thesis* is not one which is supplemented in order to explain this problem of constitutional authority, but one which is scaled back to recognise this rather more limited but no less important end. To paraphrase yet ultimately disagree with Capps, the best version of the thesis is the one that reflects Postema's model in all aspects, *except for the pre-emption strategy at its core*.

With this conclusion in mind, we should be very cautious in accepting the plausibility of the kind of legal-theoretical models against which international law is commonly reconciled and is so often found wanting. In this chapter, and indeed in this part of the book overall, I have not sought to disprove international law's claimed institutional deficiency—as outlined in Part I—but by drawing on some popular modes of conceptual thinking about law, I hope to have questioned the plausibility of a view of law's function and necessary institutional architecture against which this criticism most often arises. Reaching this conclusion thus prompts further thought on how best to understand the institutional architecture of international law, of the unique role that law plays in the circumstances of international politics, with its own legitimacy pulls and discrete political constraints. This is the task I now take up in Part III.

Part III

Effect

7

Domestic Analogy, the Rule of Law and the Relations Between States

In no field of intellectual endeavour has the domestic experience of liberalism been so overwhelming as in this. The application of domestic legal experience to international law is really the main stock in trade of modern international thought.

Hans Morgenthau, *Scientific Man vs. Power Politics*[1]

THE USE OF domestic analogy has long played a pivotal role in shaping thought about the nature of relations between states, as well as the potential for legal rules to structure or regulate those relations.[2] The analogy is explicit in some of the most famous writings in political theory, for instance, in the works of Rousseau or Kant, though it has also been of more implicit reach in structuring understanding of the nature of and basis of legitimacy within the international legal system.[3] The effort to understand international law as an autonomous system of positive rules, detailed in Part I, presupposes the analogy: 'a legitimate social order [being] one which is objective, one that consists of formally neutral and objectively ascertainable rules, created in a process of popular legislation'.[4] In fact, the resulting (and recurring) perception of a 'constitutional deficiency' in international law only really makes sense by reference to such an idealised

[1] H Morgenthau, *Scientific Man vs. Power Politics* (Chicago, University of Chicago Press, 1946) 113.

[2] As Joseph Weiler suggests: 'Analogies to domestic law are impermissible, though most of us are habitual sinners in this respect.' JHH Weiler, 'The Geology of International Law—Governance, Democracy and Legitimacy' (2004) 64 *Zeitschrift für Ausländisches Öffentliches Recht und Völkerrecht* 547, at 550. See further H Suganami, *The Domestic Analogy and World Order Proposals* (Cambridge, Cambridge University Press, 1989).

[3] P Capps, 'The Rejection of the Universal State' in N Tsagourias (ed), *Transnational Constitutionalism* (Cambridge, Cambridge University Press, 2007) 17, at 19–22 and passim; see also M Koskenniemi, *From Apology to Utopia: The Structure of International Legal Argument* (Cambridge, Cambridge University Press, 2005) 22–23; and, more recently, I Hurd, 'The International Rule of Law and the Domestic Analogy' (2015) 4 *Global Constitutionalism* 365, at 366–67 in particular.

[4] Koskenniemi (n 3) 71; and see further M Koskenniemi, 'The Politics of International Law' (1990) 1 *European Journal of International Law* 4, at 4–7; and FV Kratochwil, 'How Do Norms Matter?' in M Byers (ed), *The Role of Law in International Politics* (Oxford, Oxford University Press, 2000) 35, at 39–40.

paradigm of a well-functioning rule of law state.[5] As Hidemi Suganami has argued, the domestic analogy can be understood to 'form part of the assumptions of any contemporary writer on international affairs who attributes the instability of the international system primarily to its decentralized structure'.[6]

Nevertheless, following the argument developed in Part II, we should at least be cautious in presuming that the discrepancies revealed in applying the analogy are necessarily faults or deficiencies at the international level. Insofar as such discrepancies reveal important structural differences, the analogy can be particularly useful in helping to better understand the discrete nature of and specific basis of legitimacy within the international legal order. Indeed, domestic analogies only become problematic when applied uncritically and unreflexively as an argument for necessary institutional reform. In other words, the analogy risks distortion and misunderstanding when the peculiarities of the object being compared are seen simply as faults or deficiencies that run in one direction only. As Thomas Poole recently remarked:

> What's problematic about analogies is not so much that the act of being compared to something else heightens the risk of misunderstanding or devaluing the object being described. Rather it is that when pressed into the service of normative theory analogies have a propensity to short-cut argument. Such-and-such is like so-and-so; therefore such-and-such should be treated like so-and-so. There's nothing necessarily objectionable about the first step. It's the next step that needs to be treated with real caution. *There may be plenty of very good reasons, even if such-and-such is like so-and-so, not to treat the two in the same way. It depends.*[7] (emphasis added)

This warning is particularly salutary in relation to the normative ideal of the rule of law, which, despite being a rather ambiguous, contested concept that is difficult to disentangle from the peculiar constitutional relationship enjoining citizen and sovereign,[8] has come to function as an important

[5] See, eg, A Somek, 'From the Rule of Law to the Constitutionalist Makeover: Changing European Conceptions of Public International Law' (2011) 18 *Constellations* 567; A Somek, 'Kelsen Lives!' (2007) 18 *European Journal of International Law* 409, at 432–34; and see further discussion above in Ch 3.

[6] Suganami (n 2) 19.

[7] T Poole, 'Sovereign Indignities: International Law as Public Law' (2011) 22 *European Journal of International Law* 351, at 351–52.

[8] As noted in the book's introduction, it is perhaps unhelpful to try to give a precise definition of the rule of law, but it can be assumed to possess a meaningful core in the sense of securing a well-functioning legal system, though this function is usually understood—particularly in the current context—by reference to the restraint of arbitrary political power. See G Palombella and N Walker, 'Introduction' in G Palombella and N Walker (eds), *Relocating the Rule of Law* (Oxford, Hart Publishing, 2009) xi: 'Whatever its best interpretation, the rule of law necessarily involves a claim in principle about the centrality of law to the enterprise of living together—about law's title to rule, so to speak. What is more, such a claim always has both a practical and a normative dimension. It seeks to inform us of the ways in which and the characteristics through which it is plausible to think of law as something that rules over things—*as an institution which regulates the other forces that shape our common life*. It also seeks to provide a justification for such a claim to ascendency.' (emphasis added)

critical benchmark in understanding the point and potential of contemporary international law.[9] This ideal finds expression increasingly not just in the academic literature,[10] but also in the legal and political commitments of states and global institutions.[11] Such is the ubiquity of the rule of law in contemporary international law discourse, in fact, that one might be tempted to conclude that it is 'the *raison d'être* of international law to bring power under law'.[12] As Gabriella Blum claims:

> International lawyers and diplomats characterize the 'rule of law' as the single most important goal of the international system, upon which all other goals—peace, prosperity, and effective international cooperation—depend. In its simplest iteration, 'rule of law' means that international law should guide the conduct of states: it is the final arbiter of the exercise of power and states must comply with its provisions.[13]

Following the argument developed in Part II and bearing in mind the importance of this commitment to the self-understanding of international legal participants, we should therefore take seriously the critical potential of this ideal in developing a rationally defensible, or 'practically reasonable', concept of international law. As Patrick Capps argues, persuasively in my view, this kind of conceptual enquiry is necessary if we are to develop meaningful critical paradigms for engaging with the institutional condition of modern international law.[14]

Nevertheless, I will argue in this chapter that applying a coherent account of the rule of law at the international level is not without its difficulties. In Chapter 3, I have already suggested certain reasons why—on Poole's terms—international and domestic legal orders cannot be considered alike in important ways. I develop this argument further here. Specifically, in the first section (I), I explain how the application of the domestic analogy to

[9] Hurd (n 3).

[10] The literature is voluminous, but see, recently, J Crawford, 'International Law and the Rule of Law' (1993) 24 *Adelaide Law Review* 3; I Brownlie, *The Rule of Law in International Affairs: International Law at the Fiftieth Anniversary of the United Nations* (The Hague, Martinus Nijhoff, 1998); and S Chesterman, 'An International Rule of Law?' (2008) 56 *American Journal of Comparative Law* 331.

[11] At the 2005 World Summit meeting, heads of state and other leading officials expressly recognised 'the need for universal adherence to and implementation of the rule of law at both the national and international levels'. See United Nations, *2005 World Summit Outcome*, UN Doc A/RES/60/1, 24 October 2005, at 29, para 134, available at: www.un.org/en/ga/search/view_doc.asp?symbol=A/RES/60/1. A similar commitment has been reaffirmed each year since in successive United Nations (UN) General Assembly resolutions, each of which has made the connection between the rule of law and the necessary adherence to and respect for core principles of the international legal order. See most recently, for example, UNGA Res 69/123 (10 December 2014).

[12] A Nollkaemper, *National Courts and the International Rule of Law* (Oxford, Oxford University Press, 2011) 1.

[13] G Blum, 'Bilateralism, Multilateralism, and the Architecture of International Law' (2008) 48 *Harvard International Law Journal* 323, at 331–32.

[14] P Capps, *Human Dignity and the Foundations of International Law* (Oxford, Hart Publishing, 2009) 104, 158 and passim.

international law reveals important points of principle and prudence as to why international law cannot be subjected to a centralised institutional structure akin to a constitutional state. In section II, I consider how far this structural difference makes problematic the idea of an international rule of law. In particular, insofar as the concept is seen as primarily or substantially related to the restraint of political power through objective legal rules, and therefore difficult to apply to the decentralised structure of international law, I will argue that this apparent 'lack of fit' cannot be understood simply as a structural or constitutional deficiency at the international level. Rather, I will claim, it only reveals the discrete character of international politics and the particular role that international law plays therein. This should not be taken to completely undermine the rule of law as a normative ideal, but it does, as Terry Nardin argues, make its application to the international legal order somewhat more 'indirect and complex'.[15] As such, in section III, I consider a more meaningful articulation of an international rule of law, which can be understood more in terms of a culture of 'legality', or what Nardin describes as 'the basis of association' in international relations. This culture of legality is secured insofar as international law is utilised as a framework of interaction, where agreement to play by the rules—to conduct international politics through the legal form—is an important end in itself in a system characterised by political pluralism and moral agnosticism. Whilst suggesting the importance of a certain degree of 'formalism' in this regard, I will nonetheless close the chapter by highlighting a rival, necessarily more demanding and purposive conceptualisation of the international rule of law, brought about largely as a result of the impact of international institutions from the early years of the twentieth century onwards. This rival formulation is in many respects 'anti-formal' in character, suggesting the need to limit international law's decentralised legal form to achieve a more effective realisation of certain community values and agreed-upon objectives. This is a real challenge to the account of the concept I develop here and, accordingly, I will consider this view at length in Chapter 8. In doing so, however, I will show how, far from securing the rule of law, this more purposive or instrumental ambition appears to threaten or undermine the concept's central ethos. As the analysis of Part III progresses, however, I will argue that the tension between these rival understandings of the international rule of law—one purposive and instrumental, the other more formal—helps us to better come to terms with the legitimacy dynamic at play in 'post-modern' international law.

[15] T Nardin, *Law, Morality, and the Relations of States* (Princeton, NJ, Princeton University Press, 1983) 183.

I. DOMESTIC ANALOGY AND THE *DISCONTINUITY THESIS*

Intuitively, it seems both plausible and familiar to understand the claim to legitimacy of international law and its necessary institutional architecture by reference to the kind of 'creation myth' explanation set out in the previous chapter. The same kind of reasoning implied in the social contract tradition,[16] which has often been understood (historically at least) as a justification for the authority of the state, can be, and indeed often is, applied in the abstract as a justification for international law.[17] As Patrick Capps suggests, in both traditions, the concepts of 'consent, obligation and institutional form, are mutually supportive and logically parasitic upon each other'.[18] More precisely, the legitimacy of the international legal system is often grounded in a similar respect for the autonomy (consent) of its constituent members (states), where the ever-present risk of societal discord or disagreement necessitates an autonomous legal framework (institutional form) designed to mediate between competing positions and unify judgement (obligation).

Accordingly, as Terry Nardin has also noted, we can say that the domestic analogy holds explanatory purchase here only in a structural and artificial sense, as the inherent inter-subjectivity of relations between states is understood as requiring the imposition of a system of common rules.[19] In other words, the analogy presumes the rule of law as the governing principle of international society, that is, as the 'basis of association' between states (and other actors).[20] Martti Koskenniemi makes a similar point, describing how the domestic analogy is necessarily implicated in international legal discourse, following a similar 'liberal theory of politics' that sees in the rule of law a means of mediating the pluralistic conditions of international relations:

> This is a theory which identifies itself on two assumptions. First, it assumes that legal standards emerge from the legal subjects themselves. There is no natural

[16] There are numerous formulations of the contract idea, including most famously J-J Rousseau, *The Social Contract and Other Later Political Writings*, (V Gourevitch (ed), Cambridge, Cambridge University Press, 1997), as well as T Hobbes, *Leviathan*, (CB Macpherson (ed), London, Penguin, 1968). More recently, social contractarian reasoning has been employed by John Rawls in *A Theory of Justice*, revised edn (Cambridge, MA, Harvard University Press, 1999), particularly at 10–11, where he relates his notion of the original position to something like the Hobbesian state of nature. For a recent overview of the different formulations of the social contract (as well as their critics), see the collection of essays in D Boucher and PJ Kelly (eds), *The Social Contract from Hobbes to Rawls* (Abingdon, Routledge, 2005).

[17] See generally Capps (n 3). For a recent example of a model of international legitimacy worked out on these terms, see J Rawls, *The Law of Peoples* (Cambridge, MA, Harvard University Press, 2001).

[18] Capps (n 3) 18.

[19] See Nardin (n 15) 16.

[20] ibid 9–11, 17 and passim.

> normative order. Such order is artificial and justifiable only if it can be linked to the concrete wills and interests of individuals. Second, it assumes that once created, social order will become binding on these same individuals. They cannot invoke their subjective opinions to escape its constraining force. If they could, then the point and purpose of their initial, order-creating will and interest would be frustrated.[21]

This kind of rationale should be familiar from the analysis of Chapter 3, reflecting—at least in part—the pervasive 'discourse of institutional autonomy', which, as we saw, has tended to see in the rule of law not simply a basis of association, but a means by which to hold political power to account at the global level.[22] The systemic character of international law is thus implicated in this understanding, particularly its doctrine of sources, insofar as it presupposes a foundational commitment on the part of states (and other relevant international actors) to be bound by rules which are 'enacted' in accordance with agreed-upon processes (source criteria).[23] For instance, Philip Allott explains this rationale at work in customary international law with an explicit reference to the social contract tradition:

> Customary law ... shares in the transcendental aspect of constitutionalism ... at least to the extent that it is systematically independent of the will of current society-members, especially current controllers of the public realm. Customary law may also be said to depend on an implicit form of 'social contract' theory, which finds the authority of the law in the hypothetical 'consent' of the subjects of the law, where consent is postulated as a corollary of their participation in the society in question, including its law-making system.[24]

Of course, the analogy is somewhat clumsy[25] and the use of consent (whether explicit or implicit) as a justification for legitimate authority is not without controversy, both in practical-philosophical terms[26] and as a basis for the authority of international law specifically.[27] However, Allott's point—as he

[21] Koskenniemi (n 3) 21–22.

[22] See above in Ch 3, section III in particular.

[23] On the relation between the rule of law and a legal system, and the specific role of international law's sources in this regard, see S Besson, 'Theorizing the Sources of International Law' in S Besson and J Tasioulas (eds), *The Philosophy of International Law* (Oxford, Oxford University Press, 2010) 163, at 172 and passim.

[24] P Allott, 'The Concept of International Law' (1999) 10 *European Journal of International Law* 31, at 39.

[25] See the criticisms of, eg, J Finnis, *Natural Law and Natural Rights*, 2nd edn (Oxford, Oxford University Press, 2011) 247–48; and HLA Hart, *The Concept of Law*, 3rd edn (Oxford, Clarendon Press, 2012) 224.

[26] See, alternately, the discussions in T Christiano, 'Authority' in EN Zalta (ed), *The Stanford Encyclopedia of Philosophy* (spring 2013 edn), available at: http://plato.stanford.edu/archives/spr2013/entries/authority and L Green, 'Legal Obligation and Authority' in EN Zalta (ed), *The Stanford Encyclopedia of Philosophy* (Winter 2012 edn), available at: http://plato.stanford.edu/archives/win2012/entries/legal-obligation.

[27] See, eg, the discussion in OA Elias and CL Lim, *The Paradox of Consensualism in International Law* (The Hague, Kluwer Law International, 1998); and F Kratochwil, 'The Limits of Contract' (1994) 5 *European Journal of International Law* 465.

goes on to clarify—is not to suggest a theory of voluntarism of the sort that was rejected so persuasively by Lauterpacht's generation in the aftermath of the First World War (outlined at length in Chapter 2). Rather, he uses the analogy in more illustrative terms to stress how the institutional form of customary international law embodies within itself a certain kind of justificatory commitment to the objectivity of publically promulgated, binding rules as an answer to the inherent subjectivities of the pluralist international society.[28] Rather than suggesting explicit consent, therefore, we can use the social contract analogy—in line with the analysis of Part II—as illustrative of a 'practical-philosophical' justification for international law's specific institutional form.[29]

Whilst accepting that the exact nature of this justification remains controversial and contested, my more immediate concern is to point to an obvious disjuncture in the chain of reasoning which, in the social contract tradition, leads from consent (however implicit or tacit) to the specific institutional form of the state and, in international legal and political theory, tends instead only to justify the decentralised institutional form of the international legal order.[30] In the main, political theorists and international lawyers alike have tended not to endorse the idea of a universal state as a realisable or desirable form of international organisation.[31] There are a variety of reasons often mooted as to why international relations either cannot or should not be constituted or organised in the same way, including both descriptive, empirical arguments (eg, that states as moral or legal persons in international society cannot be considered as perfect analogues of the individual within the state, or that the nature of international society is fundamentally

[28] Allott (n 24) 39–40.

[29] This is exactly how, for instance, Capps explains Rousseau's notion of the 'general will', or what Kant might call 'omnilateral will', which is not an aggregated form of consensual validation, but a notion of the common good that structures the legitimate institutional form of the legal order in question. See Capps (n 14) 158.

[30] ibid 215–18; and, generally, Capps (n 3).

[31] For instance, Gaetano Arangio-Ruiz claims that it is 'self-evident' for most of the discipline that the analogy cannot go as far as justifying explicitly a world-state. See G Arangio-Ruiz, *The UN Declaration on Friendly Relations and the System of the Sources of International Law* (Alphen aan den Rijn, Sijthoff & Noordhoff, 1979) 199. Insofar as some international lawyers have endorsed this ambition, it is often seen as a more utopian, distant ideal and is very often heavily qualified. For instance, Lauterpacht's views are often interpreted this way, but his ambition was only to bring about the 'realizable and certainly not infinite ideal of the Federation of the World conceived as a commonwealth of *autonomous States exercising full internal independence*'. (emphasis added) See H Lauterpacht, 'The Nature of International Law and General Jurisprudence' in E Lauterpacht (ed), *International Law: Being the Collected Papers of Hersch Lauterpacht—Volume 2: The Law of Peace, Pt 1* (Cambridge, Cambridge University Press, 1975) 1, at 47. On the other hand, Kelsen did seem to endorse something like a universal state as a distant goal to finally overcome the defects of international law's decentralisation. See, eg, H Kelsen, *Law and Peace in International Relations: The Oliver Wendell Holmes Lectures, 1940–41* (Cambridge, MA, Harvard University Press, 1942) 272–79; and see further in Ch 2, section II above.

different from the character of domestic society), as well as more normative arguments (essentially that it would be unjust to impose centralised command over the more pluralistic society of states)—though the two claims are obviously not mutually exclusive.[32]

Capps labels this type of normative disjuncture the *Discontinuity Thesis*.[33] As he puts this most prosaically: 'It is often said that while the [Hobbesian] state of nature hypothetically existed, it *actually does* or did exist in some form in international relations.'[34] Whilst for many theorists (Hobbes included), this discontinuity might be taken to undermine the legal quality of international law,[35] usually the effect is simply to differentiate the nature or quality of legal order thus created. Indeed, whilst the idea of the social contract has—at least since Locke—come to be identified more precisely with a community's submission to the authority of a ruler (and in that sense seems to fit with an idealised view of law as a largely hierarchical system of institutionalised authority), we may well be able to use the same logic as a justification for a society's submission to legal order in a less hierarchical sense. The Lockean contractarian tradition[36]—as opposed to, for example, the Hobbesian approach[37]—presupposed a two-step contract: the first step a coming together of peoples to form a society in terms of a collective pact, with each bound only by their pledge to each other; and the second a more submissive act to form a government above that society.[38] Whilst the second step naturally follows the first in forms of constituted authority within states (though this mandate may, according to Locke, be revocable thereafter),[39] the second step need not necessarily occur as a result of the first in all forms of political association. As Hannah Arendt once claimed in a comment on this tradition:

> The mutual contract by which people bind themselves together in order to form a community is based on reciprocity and presupposes equality; its actual content is a promise, and its result is indeed a 'society' or 'cosociation' in the old Roman

[32] Capps (n 14) 216 ff; Capps (n 3) 28–40. To give just one example of this form of reasoning, in defending the institutional structure of international law as a decentralised legal order, Lassa Oppenheim claimed that the social conditions which apply at the level of the state that give rise to the conditions of its legitimate authority do not pertain at the international level in the more limited relations between states. See L Oppenheim, *International Law: A Treatise, Vol 1*, 3rd edn (London, Longmans, Green & Co, 1920) 6.

[33] Capps (n 3) 17 and 28–40; and see Ch 9 of Capps (n 14) 215–41.

[34] Capps (n 3) 18. On the 'state of nature', see Hobbes (n 16) 183–88 [60–64].

[35] Hobbes (n 16) 187–88 [63].

[36] See, eg, sections 95–99 of Locke's Second Treatise: J Locke, *Two Treatises of Government: A Critical Edition with an Introduction and Apparatus Criticus by Peter Laslett* (Cambridge, Cambridge University Press, 1967) 348–51.

[37] For an overview, see J Hampton, *Hobbes and the Social Contract Tradition* (Cambridge, Cambridge University Press, 1986).

[38] Capps (n 3) 27–28.

[39] See sections 135–42 of Locke's Second Treatise: Locke (n 36) 375–81.

> sense of *societas*, which means alliance ... In the so-called social contract between a given society and its ruler, on the other hand, we deal with a fictitious, aboriginal act on the side of each member, by virtue of which he gives up his isolated strength and power to constitute a government.[40]

As such, without necessarily meaning to endorse the cogency of the social-contractarian explanation, which clearly has conceptual limits,[41] I employ this logic here simply to illustrate the conceptual possibility and, importantly, the *desirability* of a form of political organisation which is inherently non-hierarchical in character.[42] Rather than presupposing submission to any higher authority, this form of political community places importance upon the kind of authority created in acts of mutual agreement or, as Arendt puts it, the act of promising itself (*pacta sunt servanda*).[43] It is this kind of *practical association* that Hedley Bull intended when he spoke of the 'anarchical society', which was not meant as a denial of the possibility of international relations, but a description—and, to some degree, a normative defence—of the idea of the inter-state system, founded on common rules, as the most appropriate form of order in the pluralistic conditions of international society.[44] On these terms, and in a continuation of the analogy, we might follow Allott in describing international legal order as a 'permanent negotiation of a social contract, the forming and re-forming of a legal basis of social co-existence from day to day, with a necessary and inherent deep-structural mutuality of legal relationships'.[45]

Although it is doubtful that this picture gives a complete and (in Allott's view) completely satisfactory characterisation of the nature of contemporary international law, in pointing to the 'deep-structural mutuality' of the legal relationship that is reflected in the specific institutional form of international law, this contractarian logic still proves informative. The question that it is necessary to consider further, therefore, is how far and in what ways this

[40] H Arendt, *On Revolution* (New York, Penguin, 2006) 161.

[41] For (critical) discussion, see Kratochwil (n 27) 477–86.

[42] Nardin (n 15) 40 and passim.

[43] H Arendt, 'What is Freedom?' in *Between Past and Future: Eight Exercises in Political Thought* (New York, Penguin, 1977) 143, at 164; and see the discussion in J Klabbers, 'Possible Islands of Predictability: The Legal Thought of Hannah Arendt' (2007) 20 *Leiden Journal of International Law* 1, at 9.

[44] See, primarily, Chs 3 and 4 of H Bull, *The Anarchical Society: A Study of Order in World Politics*, 4th edn (Basingstoke, Palgrave Macmillan, 2012).

[45] Allott (n 24) 44. For a similar rationale, see Hurd (n 3) 367: 'Interstate relations ... rest on a different model of the relation between agents and law. Some elements which are essential to the domestic rule of law (for instance, a certain kind of control over political authority) do not translate well to the international setting. But others (such as the legitimacy of transferring obligations via consent) are better suited to the international than to the domestic realm—international actors (i.e. states) make very explicit acts of consent to binding legal instruments, while domestic social-contract theory has endless trouble specifying how or when individuals give consent to their state.'

discontinuity and specific justification for international law's decentralised institutional structure might impact our understanding of the rule of law as it applies, insofar as it does, at the international level. As I will now demonstrate, the answer to this question will depend both on what we take the rule of law to necessarily require of law in general and, more particularly, what specific institutional demands this places on international law.

II. AN INTERNATIONAL RULE OF LAW?

What does it mean to say that there should be a rule of law in international affairs? It is by now perhaps trite to recognise that the concept of the rule of law is somewhat ambiguous and amorphous, capable of thinner (more formal) and thicker (more substantive) applications. At the thinner end of the spectrum, it can be said to encompass a commitment to 'legality' in a systemic, procedural sense—encompassing values like legal certainty, equality, non-retroactivity etc—which, as argued by Lon Fuller, go to make up a healthy legal system.[46] At the thicker end, it is also often taken to require more substantive protections of basic rights and liberties of the citizen.[47] For instance, the UN uses the rule of law in this thicker, more ambitious sense in its commitment to domestic legal reforms around the world:

> [T]he rule of law refers to a principle of governance in which all persons, institutions and entities, public and private, including the State itself, are accountable to laws that are publicly promulgated, equally enforced and independently adjudicated, and which are consistent with international human rights norms and standards. It requires, as well, measures to ensure adherence to the principles of supremacy of law, equality before the law, accountability to the law, fairness in the application of the law, separation of powers, participation in decision-making, legal certainty, avoidance of arbitrariness and procedural and legal transparency.[48]

[46] Fuller gives eight desiderata for the existence of a state of 'legality': the law's generality, public promulgation, non-retroactivity, clarity, non-contradiction, capacity to be obeyed, constancy, and a reasonable level of congruence between law in the books and law as it is practised by authorised officials. See L Fuller, *The Morality of Law*, revised edn (New Haven, CT, Yale University Press, 1969) 39 and passim. For an application of Fuller's theory to international law, see J Brunnée and SJ Toope, *Legitimacy and Legality in International Law: An Interactional Account* (Cambridge, Cambridge University Press, 2010).

[47] For discussion, see J Raz, 'The Rule of Law and its Virtue' (1977) 93 *Law Quarterly Review* 195; G Palombella, 'The Rule of Law and its Core' in Palombella and Walker (eds) (n 8) 17–42; P Craig, 'Formal and Substantive Conception of the Rule of Law: An Analytical Framework' (1997) *Public Law* 467; and, perhaps most extensively, BZ Tamanaha, *On the Rule of Law: History, Politics, Theory* (Cambridge, Cambridge University Press, 2004) 91–113.

[48] Report of the Secretary-General, *The Rule of Law and Transitional Justice in Conflict and Post-conflict Societies*, 23 August 2004, UN Doc S/2004/616; available at: http://www.un.org/en/ga/search/view_doc.asp?symbol=S/2004/616.

It is quite apparent that this thicker conception of the rule of law is particularly wedded to the modern state context, being difficult to disentangle from the peculiar constitutional relationship enjoining citizen and sovereign.[49] In fact, it is hard to find such an ambitious conceptualisation of the rule of law used to make sense of the role of law in international politics. Where there have been explicit studies into how the rule of law could, *or should*, be applied in the international context, scholars will usually attempt to 'externalise' a thinner, more formal version of the concept.[50] This understanding would not therefore suggest any commitment to any particular set of global public goods, but instead only the kind of procedural values inherent in a well-functioning legal system.[51]

Nevertheless, even when applied in this less ambitious sense, it is doubtful that this concept is easily reconcilable with international law's decentralised institutional structure. This argument has been taken up recently by Ian Hurd, who adopts a fairly uncontentious characterisation of the rule of law as it might apply in the national context, requiring: (i) that 'society should be governed by stable, public, and certain rules'; (ii) that such rules 'should apply equally to the governed and to the rulers'; and that (iii) they 'should be applied equally and dispassionately across cases and people'.[52] Inevitably, there are considerable obstacles in applying these criteria in a coherent way to the contemporary functioning of international law—notwithstanding (and I will return to this point again in Chapter 9) that we may now recognise forms of 'governance' at the international level (eg, in international institutions like the UN Security Council).[53] At a more basic and foundational level, the problems of certainty and generality in the

[49] For a critique in this respect, see A Somek, 'Administration without Sovereignty' in P Dobner and M Loughlin (eds), *The Twilight of Constitutionalism?* (Oxford, Oxford University Press, 2010) 267, at 272.

[50] See, for instance, S Beaulac, 'The Rule of Law in International Law Today' in Palombella and Walker (eds) (n 8) 197, at 204 ff.

[51] As Samantha Besson has suggested: 'To identify a society as having a system of law, as opposed to some other sort of order, is to identify it as satisfying some or all of the requirements associated with the Rule of Law.' Besson (n 23) 172.

[52] Hurd (n 3) 369. Whilst, as he notes, different scholars give slightly different formulations of these three elements, the 'differences are minor because there is a great deal of overlap in the core propositions'. For instance, perhaps the most influential recent model is that developed by Brian Tamanaha, which includes: (i) the necessity of formal legality (ie, the ability to distinguish valid law in order to be able to coordinate social conduct according to the law); (ii) the idea of sovereign limitation (though we might say limitation of public authority more broadly); and (iii) the notion of non-arbitrariness (that is, the rule of law as opposed to the rule of man). See Tamanaha (n 47) 114–26. A similar formulation is also found in G Palombella, 'The Rule of Law as an Institutional Ideal' in L Morlino and G Palombella (eds), *Rule of Law and Democracy: Internal and External Issues* (Leiden, Brill, 2010) 3, at 9 ff. For discussion, see further in R Collins, 'The Rule of Law and the Quest for Constitutional Substitutes in International Law' (2014) 83 *Nordic Journal of International Law* 87, at 102–07.

[53] See, eg, Hurd (n 3) 376–90.

law caused by the deep inter-subjectivity of international legal relations suggest an inherent 'lack of fit' on these terms:

> [T]he international legal system cannot satisfy the standard expectation in a rule-of-law society that law be clear and stable and known in advance. No matter how clearly it is written, it cannot indicate whether an action is legal or illegal independent of the identity of the actor-state in question. Because states are free to tailor their commitments to suit their needs and interests, the bundle of laws that attach to each state are unique to that state and the legality of an act may not be determinable as a general matter. What it means to 'comply' with international law depends on who is doing it, and what that state has done and said about the rule in the past and what it might do and say in the present case ... The legality of an act is endogenous to the choices of the state in question, rather than independent of it as it is in the domestic setting.[54]

One might, of course, accuse Hurd of sticking too rigidly to an account of the rule of law as it pertains to the hierarchical political relationships within states however, even where these rule of law criteria are formulated in a looser, less literal sense, their application fares little better. For instance, in one of the more balanced assessments of the rule of law applied at the international level, Stephane Beaulac comes up with the following tripartite formulation of the concept, which he believes can be more meaningfully 'externalised' beyond the state. This includes: '(1) the existence of principled normative rules, (2) [that are] adequately created and equally applicable to all legal subjects and (3) enforced by accessible courts of general jurisdiction'.[55] Unsurprisingly, Beaulac still finds significant problems in meeting these requirements, not only, again, in terms of the generality and certainty of the law, but particularly in relation to his call for enforcement of the law through courts of accessible, general jurisdiction. In part, this problem relates to the consensual basis of jurisdiction of the International Court of Justice (ICJ), but also the overwhelming national influence over international judicial decisions more generally.[56] Beaulac is certainly not alone in raising such concerns about the capacity of the international judicial function to live up to rule of law standards.[57] Furthermore, others have expressed doubts about the adequacy of the international law-making process from a rule of law perspective, which, as Arthur Watts observes, is 'not a process calculated to produce precision and clarity'.[58]

[54] ibid 380.

[55] Beaulac (n 50) 203–04. For similar views, see also Chesterman (n 10); Brownlie (n 10) 213–14.

[56] Beaulac (n 50) 197, at 212–20.

[57] See, eg, Y Shany, 'No Longer a Weak Department of Power? Reflections on the Emergence of a New International Judiciary' (2009) 20 *European Journal of International Law* 73, at 74–75; Crawford (n 10) 10–12; A Watts, 'The International Rule of Law' (1993) 36 *German Yearbook of International Law* 15, at 37.

[58] Watts (n 57) 28.

Bearing in mind the argument developed in this volume so far, it is hardly surprising that these sorts of discrepancy are interpreted as fundamental structural weaknesses, deficiencies or defects, undermining the coherence and importance of international law as compared to state-based legal orders. Whatever its best interpretation and however loosely these kinds of criteria are applied, the realisation of an international rule of law seems to be judged, for the most part, in terms of the capacity of international legal rules to actually control the conduct and determine the political choices of states and other powerful international actors.[59] As we saw in Chapter 3, this kind of view is implicated in the pervasive 'discourse of institutional autonomy' that tends to structure debate on the nature and potential of modern international law.[60] As such (and as noted above by Blum in particular), even without precise definition there seems to be a broad consensus that international law should act as 'the final arbiter of the exercise of power and [that] states must comply with its provisions'.[61] Mattias Kumm puts this same idea in much starker terms, arguing that at its most basic level the international rule of law requires 'that nations, in their relationships to one another, are to be ruled by law'.[62]

On these terms, then, it becomes difficult to avoid the conclusion that decentralisation itself is inherently problematic from the point of view of the rule of law. Whilst most of the studies in this area tend to acknowledge the necessary structural differences between domestic and international orders, in attempting to hold the international system to account on the same basis, they seem still to push in the direction of a necessary centralisation of authority. For instance, in a recent, influential book addressing the rule of law in both its domestic and international settings, the late Tom Bingham argued passionately that the differences between national and international legal orders did not negate the fact that the latter should be subjected to similar standards and expectations, such that the international rule of law was merely its domestic counterpart 'writ large'.[63] Bingham was not suggesting an overly simplistic analogy in applying these standards, but was merely claiming that the expectation of strict compliance with the law should be

[59] As Hurd argues, whether applied in a domestic or international setting, it is commonly assumed that 'the rule of law is an alternative to the arbitrary exercise of power; and that the ultimate product of a rule-of-law system is the choice by the law's subjects to *comply* with the rules'. Hurd (n 3) 367.

[60] See C Reus-Smit, 'The Politics of International Law' in C Reus-Smit (ed), *The Politics of International Law,* (Cambridge, Cambridge University Press, 2004) 14, at 36–37; and the discussion above in Ch 3, section I.

[61] Blum (n 13) 332.

[62] M Kumm, 'International Law in National Courts: The International Rule of Law and the Limits of the Internationalist Model' (2003–04) 44 *Virginia Journal of International Law* 19, at 22.

[63] T Bingham, *The Rule of Law* (London, Penguin, 2010) 111.

the same at the international and national levels, and therefore that similar institutional characteristics would be required in order to 'complete' the international legal system.[64] As he puts it:

> If the daunting challenges now facing the world are to be overcome, it must be in important part through the medium of rules, internationally agreed, internationally implemented and, if necessary, internationally enforced. That is what the rule of law requires in the international order.[65]

Amongst international lawyers, James Crawford reaches similar conclusions as to the relativity of the distinction between international and national legal orders, suggesting certain institutional requirements, in particular a strong independent judiciary, as being critical to the realisation of an international rule of law.[66] Whilst there is rarely a suggestion (and I do not think that Bingham nor Crawford are necessarily suggesting) that a full suite of constitutional institutions would be feasible or, indeed, desirable—that is, a centralised legislative body, a global executive or enforcement arm, and compulsory international courts of general jurisdiction—the argument is often simply that the rule of law still requires greater certainty in the promulgation and identification of international legal rules, as well as a more effective means for the law's application and enforcement in the last measure.

On these terms, one might therefore be tempted to agree with Simon Chesterman 'that there is presently no such thing as the international rule of law, or at least that international law has yet to achieve a certain normative or institutional threshold to justify use of the term'.[67] But to conclude in this way appears to leave us in something of a bind, with a choice between two equally unpalatable alternatives. Following the argument set out in Part II, to simply abandon the idea (or ideal) of an international rule of law would seem to suggest that states, diplomats, international lawyers and other international legal participants are deluded in the value they attach to this commitment to legality in international relations. At the same time, to suggest that international law has 'yet to achieve a certain normative or institutional threshold' serves only to confirm an apparent structural or constitutional deficiency, which itself begs the obvious question of how an international rule of law might be more feasibly realised without undermining the pluralistic justification for international law's non-hierarchical institutional structure. This impasse suggests that we need to rethink and, perhaps, radically reformulate our understanding of the rule of law as it might pertain to the context of international relations. I consider this possibility further in the following and final section.

[64] ibid 112–13.
[65] ibid 129.
[66] Crawford (n 10) at 12 in particular.
[67] Chesterman (n 10) 358 (footnote omitted).

III. THE RULE OF LAW AS THE BASIS OF ASSOCIATION IN INTERNATIONAL RELATIONS: ON THE SPECIFIC CHARACTER OF INTERNATIONAL LAW

So far, I have argued that there has been widespread (though most often implicit) reliance on a form of domestic analogy in structuring understanding of international law, which seems to presume the rule of law as the basis of association in international relations. I have developed this argument not necessarily to suggest that the state can be analogised like the individual in some kind of Hobbesian state of nature—though, clearly, this more literal analogy has often been employed over the years—but only that there is a similar basis of legitimacy at play in structuring understanding of interstate relations and the role of law therein.[68] In other words, the analogy holds only in the structural sense, insofar as it identifies a similar liberal theory of politics, whereby the artificial or institutional rationality of law provides a solution to the inevitable clash of subjective wills characteristic of international society. At the same time, I have argued that the analogy is necessarily qualified insofar as we recognise a normative disjuncture (or *discontinuity*) in this contractarian reasoning, which recognises the specific conditions of political legitimacy that pertain in international relations, and which therefore justifies the specific institutional form of international law in comparison to a paradigmatic state-based legal order. In the previous section, I demonstrated how this disjuncture tends to undermine, or at least make problematic, the application of even the most minimal formulation of the rule of law at the international level.

We might well conclude from this problem that international law is still deficient in some form, but if the solution to this deficiency is seen to require a centralisation of international authority—that is, exactly the kind of institutional structure that was rejected under the *Discontinuity Thesis*—any such conclusion would be inherently problematic. International law's institutional form is not an omission or a sign of its immature development, but an important aspect of its overall legitimacy: it is deliberately structured so as to defer back to states on questions of the existence, meaning and application of international legal norms.[69] Whilst this argument does not disprove the claim that international law might be deficient in some other way, my point is that one cannot simply reach such a conclusion based solely on its dissimilarity to domestic law, that is, the simple fact of its decentralisation—or, consequently, its apparent structural indeterminacy. Indeed, to do so would seem to be a logical non sequitur. As Nardin notes:

> [W]e cannot say how the rule of law might be more fully realized in the relations of states until we have a clear conception of what it is, in the circumstances

[68] Koskenniemi (n 3) 22.
[69] Nardin (n 15) 165–67.

> of the society of states. It does not follow from the conclusion that legislation, enforcement, or even authoritative determination by a common judge are neither essential features nor necessary conditions of law that international law might not be strengthened if these institutions were to develop in international society. But neither can one simply assume that the remedy for the deficiencies of international legal order lies in policies intended to model it more closely on the modern state. The society of states is not itself a state, and therefore judgments concerning the existence and prospects of legal order within it must take account of the specific character and circumstances of that society.[70]

Accordingly, if the rule of law has any useful application in the international context, this must be worked out by reference to the kind of legitimacy dynamic at play in international law, specifically, by taking account of its 'deep-structural mutuality'. We cannot therefore fix on some idealised institutional structure that makes sense only because of the very different political conditions or structural dynamic of domestic society. In this respect, as Hurd goes on to argue, many of the accounts of an international rule of law set out above appear 'conceptually inconsistent and empirically unrealistic'.[71] In particular, referring back to his three-pronged definition of the rule of law, he claims that these criteria are 'more than procedural requirements: *they require a substantive commitment to dividing political power in a certain way*'.[72] (emphasis added)

This lack of fit thus sets up the question of whether it is possible to retain the broadest ethos of the rule of law—a commitment to 'legality'—and still make sense of this ideal in a society defined by its diffuse and decentralised political relations and its non-hierarchical institutional form. In taking up this challenge, Hurd suggests that such a reformulation is indeed possible, but it requires that we abandon some of our preconceptions about what a 'well-functioning' legal system would necessarily require:

> The rule of law is central to both the conception of the modern state and to the study of international law and international politics. The two versions of the rule of law, domestic and international, were invented as solutions to very different problems. In domestic society, the rule of law addresses the problem of centralised authority. It is meant to place limits on the exercise of state power and to create a stable set of known rules that apply equally to all citizens. In international affairs, *th*e rule of law is a response to the absence of such centralised authority—and to the externalities, inefficiencies, and other implications of the formally decentralised and atomised arrangement of authority that is characteristic of the sovereign state system.[73]

[70] ibid 147–48.
[71] Hurd (n 3) 366.
[72] ibid 369.
[73] ibid 366–67.

Hurd's account of the rule of law is not simply a justification for watering down the requirements of the concept applied in the international context. Rather, his point is that this form of 'accommodation' makes little sense in a legal order that is very much defined by its openness and indeterminacy. For Hurd, therefore, the international rule of law inheres simply in 'the idea that all state behaviour should conform to whatever international legal obligations relate to it … which in practice means that [states] will use the resources of international law to explain and justify their policies'.[74] Whilst he characterises this as an 'instrumental' understanding of international legality, this description seems to underplay his 'intellectual and political commitment' to international law's decentralised institutional form.[75] This view is in many respects similar to what I referred to in the previous chapter—in explicitly *non-instrumental* terms—as a commitment to international law's 'abstract' or 'systemic' autonomy.[76] Whilst Hurd is clearly correct that international law is an inherently instrumental form of normative practice, the important point is that its utility as such requires that we recognise the non-instrumental value of the deep 'constitutional structure' of the system itself—that is, the structure that allows states' particular commitments to be expressed in legal form.[77] As Nardin also notes, this framework is important in allowing states not only to justify their decisions by reference to international law, but also to hold other decision-makers to account on the same basis. In other words, a commitment to the rule of law on these terms ensures that 'there exist procedures for evaluating these decisions and thus implementing the principle of accountability', as well as that such procedures are 'known, public, alterable only by some regular procedure, and consistently applied'.[78] This account of the international rule of law thus places significant emphasis on the legal form, but recognises the particular character of this form as important to secure some measure of accountability at the international level.

As such, we might refer to this kind of rule of law ideal in terms of what Koskenniemi has called 'a culture of formalism', which recognises the structural indeterminacy of international law as an important aspect of its legitimacy and acceptability in practice.[79] Rather than seeing law as a

[74] ibid 391.
[75] ibid.
[76] See above in Ch 6, section III.
[77] Hurd (n 3) 390.
[78] Nardin (n 15) 183.
[79] See M Koskenniemi, *The Gentle Civilizer of Nations: The Rise and Fall of International Law 1870–1960* (Cambridge, Cambridge University Press, 2001) 494–509; M Koskenniemi, 'What is International Law for?' in M Evans, *International Law*, 4th edn (Oxford, Oxford University Press, 2014) 29, at 47–49 in particular.

means to depoliticise the inherently political practices of international legal relations, this commitment—what, elsewhere, Koskenniemi calls a 'constitutionalist mindset'—aims simply to bring those politics into clear view, helping to level the playing field of substantively unequal political relations through the juridical equality embedded in international law's structural form.[80] As he puts it:

> [I]t is international law's formalism that brings political antagonists together as they invoke contrasting understandings of its rules and institutions. In the absence of agreement over, or knowledge of, the 'true' objectives of political community—that is to say, in an agnostic world—the pure form of international law provides the shared surface—the *only* such surface—on which political adversaries recognize each other as such and pursue their adversity in terms of something shared, instead of seeking to attain full exclusion—'outlawry'—of the other. In this sense, international law's value and its misery lie in its being the fragile surface of political community among social agents—States, other communities, individuals—who disagree about their preferences but do so within a structure that invites them to argue in terms of an assumed universality.[81]

This kind of formalism may well sound like an apologetic description of the status quo, as a justification for the kinds of power play that arguably only perpetuate global injustice, but I believe that any such criticism misses the important point—already outlined to some degree in Chapter 3—that law can only serve more progressive ends insofar as it is able to distinguish its own rationality. The point of committing to the rule of law is precisely to limit one's subjective motivations and political ambitions by agreeing to adhere to a formal legal framework. Such formalism not only secures some degree of accountability in how actors relate to one another, but it also provides a structure upon which we can agree to cooperate further towards any more substantive goals and ambitions.

Nevertheless, as plausible as this view seems, it also seems somewhat inadequate or insufficient in giving a full account of the way in which the rule of law has come to be understood, in many respects, in its opposition to the externalities and inefficiencies of the inter-state legal form. In fact, this kind of formalist logic seems increasingly outdated and anachronistic in the light of the kind of structural shifts and institutional innovations witnessed from the early to mid-twentieth century onwards. With the emergence and proliferation of a growing number of regimes and institutions, the rule of law has come to seem more meaningful as a call to restrain the political interests of powerful actors in order to realise certain agreed-upon ends or ambitions—peace, order, human rights, global justice etc. Indeed, Nardin

[80] M Koskenniemi, 'Constitutionalism as Mindset: Reflections on Kantian Themes about International Law and Globalization' (2007) 8 *Theoretical Inquiries in Law* 9.

[81] Koskenniemi, 'What is International Law for?' (n 79) 48.

himself concedes as much, arguing in particular that since the creation of the UN, the rule of law has come to be thought of less as a pre-existing basis of association (which would allow political actors to engage in such institutionalised cooperation in the first place) and more as a goal to be achieved through enhancing the institutional capacity of international law to secure agreed-upon values or objectives.[82] Koskenniemi makes a similar point, arguing that for a considerable period of time now, there have been 'two types of logic at play in the international rule of law', with a more pragmatic, institutional and functional view competing with, and providing a critical counterpoint to, the more formalist understanding set out above.[83]

There would appear to be an inherent tension and instability between these seemingly opposed perspectives. From the point of view of this alternative, more instrumental account, my previous argument appears vulnerable to both empirical and normative critique: susceptible to the charge of not only ignoring important structural changes in the international legal order, but also of potentially over-fetishising its inter-state institutional form (and thereby undermining the possibility of a more effective international institutional architecture). From this alternative point of view, the hope would be that international institutions are able to move beyond the structural limitations of their inter-state constitutions in order to adequately uphold agreed-upon objectives in opposition to sovereign freedom.[84] This is obviously therefore a serious challenge to the rather less demanding account of an international rule of law that I have just set out, and in the next chapter I will consider this argument at length. However, in doing so, I will show why it is impossible to completely follow through on this kind of instrumentalist logic without also undermining the equally important formalist counterpoint—that is, an account of the rule of law which will aim to minimise or contain the structural impact of such empowered global institutions in order to adhere to an important principle of accountability at the global level.

IV. CONCLUSION

In this chapter, I have considered the plausibility of a widespread understanding of international law built upon a kind of implicit domestic analogy that sees in the rule of law a means to structure international relations. There are obvious limitations and problems in this analogy, in particular the ever-present risk of distorting understanding of the actual functioning of the international legal system. However, I have highlighted the analogy

[82] Nardin (n 15) 105–12.
[83] Koskenniemi, 'What is International Law for?' (n 79) 39 ff.
[84] Nardin (n 15) 71, 77 and 83.

here primarily to bring out certain differences and points of tension in order to stress the distinctive basis of legitimacy inherent in the institutional form of international law as a decentralised legal system. Insofar as the rule of law therefore remains meaningful in this political context, I have argued that it must be understood—*at least in part*—as a commitment to rule-based association, which necessarily implies the importance of formal legal rules as a normative counterpoint to the plural subjectivities inherent in international politics. However, as I have equally noted, this kind of formalism and commitment to international law's decentralised institutional framework is increasingly contested, particularly as a result of some of the normative and structural shifts witnessed in the evolving international legal system. Specifically, with the increasing 'institutionalisation' of international law since the start of the previous century, a more communitarian, functional logic appears to challenge the adequacy and legitimacy of the kind of formalist understanding I have outlined above. I will now turn to consider the cogency of this critique and its implications for understanding the institutional problem as outlined thus far.

8

Form and Function in the Institutionalisation of International Law

> Perhaps international law is at present in a stage of transition towards acceptance of … [certain] forms which would bring it nearer in structure to a municipal legal system. If, and when, this transition is completed the formal analogies, which at present seem thin and even delusive, would acquire substance, and the sceptic's last doubts about the legal 'quality' of international law may then be laid to rest. Till that stage is reached the analogies are surely those of function and content, and not of form.
>
> HLA Hart, *The Concept of Law*[1]

IT IS BY now perhaps a trite point to say that modern international law has been steadily transformed by the emergence and growing normative influence of international organisations from the early twentieth century onwards.[2] Since the creation of the League of Nations and the Permanent Court of International Justice (PCIJ) after the First World War, there have been successive attempts to re-order or re-structure international relations through institutional mechanisms which bear more than a superficial resemblance to parliamentary-style diplomacy, executive enforcement and judicial dispute settlement.[3] With the proliferation of international organisations witnessed since the end of the Second World War, many international lawyers have held out the hope that through the enhanced autonomy of these institutions, there might be realised a more mature, more authoritative international legal order capable of securing the restraint of arbitrary political power.

[1] HLA Hart, *The Concept of Law*, 3rd edn (Oxford, Clarendon Press, 2012) 236–37.

[2] Koskenniemi notes how: 'From the outset, international institutions were conceived less in terms of routine administration than progressive transformation of the international system.' M Koskenniemi, *From Apology to Utopia: The Structure of International Legal Argument* (Cambridge, Cambridge University Press, 2005) 611.

[3] D Kennedy, 'The Move to Institutions' (1987) 8 *Cardozo Law Review* 841, at 857–59.

For some time, it seemed that this desire was beginning to bear fruit. The post-war institutions—the UN family of organisations, Bretton Woods institutions, regional integration organisations and human rights bodies, amongst many others—have in many ways transformed international law at both a substantive and a structural level. The resulting changes have been variously described in terms of, inter alia, a shift from a private, transactional view towards a more 'public' or constitutional understanding of international law,[4] from sovereignty towards community[5] or—as Wolfgang Friedmann most famously described it—from a law of 'co-existence' to one of 'co-operation'.[6] However one characterises it, it may now appear as something of a 'truism to state, or so it seems, that international law is increasingly starting to look like the sort of legal order we are familiar with from our domestic legal systems'.[7]

Nevertheless, the hesitancy in these remarks is particularly telling, for these sorts of progress narrative tend towards over-simplification and are apt to mislead, potentially misconstruing the nature of the transformation that has been witnessed. As I will demonstrate in this chapter, whilst it is difficult to deny a growing depth and complexity to modern international law as a result of its institutionalisation, the peculiar institutional form of intergovernmental organisations, itself parasitic upon the decentralised institutional form of international law, suggests a number of problems in understanding this transition as a simple 'maturation' or 'constitutionalisation' of the international legal system. Such descriptions pay scant attention to the way in which this legal form both shapes the kind of authority exercised by international institutions and at the same time necessarily restricts their normative influence within international law overall. Whilst I think it is

[4] B Simma, 'From Bilateralism to Community Interest in International Law' (1994-VI) 250 *Recueil des Cours* 221; C Tomuschat, 'International Law: Ensuring the Survival of Mankind on the Eve of a New Century, General Course on Public International Law' (1999) 281 *Recueil des Cours* 9.

[5] C Warbrick and S Tierney (eds), *Towards an International Legal Community? Sovereignty of States and the Sovereignty of International Law* (London, British Institute of International and Comparative Law, 2006).

[6] W Friedmann, *The Changing Structure of International Law* (London, Stevens & Sons, 1964). More recently, former ICJ Judge Mohammed Bedjaoui also adopts this idea of transition, though he also talks about a move from an 'oligarchic law to a law of community', from a 'law of states to a law for people' and from a 'law of co-ordination to one of finalities'. See M Bedjaoui, 'General Introduction' in M Bedjaoui (ed), *International Law: Achievements and Prospects* (Dordrecht, Martinus Nijhoff, 1991) 1, at 5–17 in particular. For others, international law may have already moved past cooperation: Wellens asserts a move from cooperation to 'solidarity'; see K Wellens, 'Solidarity as a Constitutional Principle: Its Expanding Role and Inherent Limitations' in R St J Macdonald and DM Johnston (eds), *Towards World Constitutionalism: Issues in the Legal Ordering of the World Community* (Leiden, Martinus Nijhoff, 2005) 775–807; whilst Capaldo asserts, instead, a new 'global law' phenomenon or, as she also terms it, an international 'law of "integration"'; see GZ Capaldo, *The Pillars of Global Law* (Aldershot, Ashgate, 2008) 173.

[7] J Klabbers, 'Setting the Scene' in J Klabbers, A Peters and G Ulfstein, *The Constitutionalization of International Law* (Oxford, Oxford University Press, 2010) 1, at 11.

necessary to look beyond the treaty base of institutions like the League or, more latterly, the UN in order to understand their role and influence in contemporary international law, their functions cannot simply be equated with those of the kind of constitutional 'organs' found at the state level. The point is not simply that *intergovernmental* institutions cannot be considered as 'organs' or 'officials' of the international legal system in any formal sense, nor is it that their actual functions only superficially reflect what we might expect from a functioning rule of law state. Rather, the very fact of their intergovernmental character, their origin and grounding in decentralised international law, makes their functional authority *within* international law overall far more contingent and contestable.

As such, the interplay of the competing formalist and functionalist logic inherent in the international rule of law—as described at the end of the previous chapter—necessarily undermines the explanatory potential of any progress narrative describing an increasing centralisation of authority within, or the maturation of contemporary international law. Insofar as institutionalisation has resulted in certain structural and normative changes to the nature and functioning of the international legal system, in many respects these changes seem to exist in a growing state of tension with international law's decentralised legal form. The structural impact of institutionalisation seems increasingly to have heightened rather than assuaged concerns for a global rule of law. In fact, it is precisely because of the perceived impact of the functional autonomy exhibited by a range of powerful global institutions that many international lawyers have begun to describe an emerging legitimacy crisis, increasingly finding expression through the 'postmodern' leitmotifs of 'fragmentation' and 'deformalisation' in international law. I will say more about these concerns specifically in the following chapter. Here, my ambition is to better understand the structural constraints of the international legal order which help to explain why such concerns might arise in the first place.

The chapter is structured as follows. In the opening section (I), I chart how the emergence and growing influence of international institutions has often been interpreted, at least in part, as an attempt to compensate for the perceived deficiencies of a decentralised legal order. In particular, I describe how international lawyers have tended to stress the plausibility of this kind of 'constitutional compensation' only by dislocating the function of institutions like the League or the UN from their underlying legal form (grounded in an intergovernmental treaty agreement). In section II, I consider the cogency of these claims, assessing the undoubted impact of 'institutionalisation' on the contemporary functioning of international law. In doing so, I show how the influence of international organisations has in many ways re-shaped our understanding of the nature, scope and institutional capacity of the international legal system. In reviewing these changes, however, I argue that the system overall appears to be 'straining' under the weight of institutionalisation, seemingly incapable of effectively accommodating (or constraining) the functional autonomy exhibited by many powerful institutional actors. In section III, I therefore consider how the structural limitations of international institutions, derived from the formal constraints of the international legal order, reveal a much more complicated view of their legal nature, as well as their structural impact on international law overall. International organisations embody within themselves an irresolvable tension between their functionality (their openness to the international legal order) and the legal form in which they fit into international law (as 'closed' legal actors in their own right), which I argue undermines, or at least fundamentally limits, their capacity to act as functional 'organs' of the international legal system as a whole. In recognising this structural condition, I conclude with some thoughts on how the emergence of so-called 'global governance' through international organisations has precipitated growing concern over certain legitimacy and accountability deficits. It is this concern, in particular, which I will address in the following and final chapter.

I. FORM AND FUNCTION IN THE INSTITUTIONALISATION OF INTERNATIONAL LAW

Given the problem outlined in this volume thus far, it is hardly surprising that, in the main, the discipline has tended to interpret international law's 'move to institutions' as a means of correcting, fixing or compensating for the perceived structural weaknesses of the international legal order.[8] Even before the creation of the League of Nations in 1919, many late nineteenth-century jurists had already tied the fate of the international legal system to the development of an integrated international organisation capable of securing some means for the creation, adjudication and enforcement of the law.[9] As the very first rudiments of the modern intergovernmental organisation began to develop throughout the nineteenth century—with experiments in conference diplomacy, great power alliance and forms of international administration[10]—it began to seem feasible to imagine a transition towards

[8] See Kennedy (n 3).

[9] Of the more abstract proposals for international organisation conceived according to a model of domestic governance, see, eg, P Fiore, *International Law Codified and its Legal Sanction; or the Legal Organization of the Society of States*, translated from the 5th Italian edn by Edwin M Borchard (New York, Baker, Voorhis & Company, 1918) 467–70 and passim; and J Lorimer, *The Institutes of the Law of Nations: A Treatise on the Jural Relations of Separate Political Communities, Vol II* (Edinburgh and London, William Blackwood and Sons, 1884) 179–87.

[10] The emergence of the modern intergovernmental organisation is most often traced to three particular nineteenth-century trends: first, the emergence of multilateral conference diplomacy; second, the creation of an administrative bureaucracy through the creation of public international unions (PIUs); and, finally, the organisation of the great powers into a form of hegemonic alliance. See, eg, IL Claude Jr , *Swords into Plowshares: The Problems and Progress of International Organization*, 4th edn (New York, Random House, 1971) 38–39; J Klabbers, 'The Life and Times of International Organizations' (2001) 70 *Nordic Journal of International Law* 287, at 291–92; and C Brölmann, *The Institutional Veil in Public International Law: International Organizations and the Law of Treaties* (Oxford, Hart Publishing, 2007) 14–17.

a more centralised institutional architecture for international law.[11] Of the more modest readings, the emerging international bureaucracies in the Public International Unions (including bodies such as the International Telecommunications Union and the various River Commissions) were described as part of an emerging 'international administrative law'.[12] More ambitiously, others saw in the Hague Conferences of 1899 and 1907 a broader move towards a more centralised, federal structure for international law.[13] Even the avowed legal positivist Lassa Oppenheim read these institutional developments as instigating a transformation in the character of international law-making, with a tentative recognition of the phenomenon of 'international legislation' through the multilateral treaty form.[14]

However, it was not until the creation of the League and, shortly thereafter, the PCIJ in the wake of the First World War that there was more widespread recognition of the impact of 'institutionalisation' on the contemporary functioning of the international legal order. Taken together, these developments seemed to suggest a movement towards the centralisation of international law-making, enforcement and dispute settlement functions. This reading was not just scholarly ambition or the vision of some utopian international federalists. EH Carr, one of the pioneering 'realist' scholars of the twentieth century, noted how much of this ambition was shared by statesmen themselves, who, fuelled by Wilsonian idealism in the wake of the Great War, saw the necessity of subjecting inter-state relations to the demands of the rule of law, with the League being the first tentative step in this direction.[15]

[11] On the trend towards a view of administrative cooperation as contributing to a more 'federal' ordering of the international system, see particularly D Bederman 'The Souls of International Organizations: Legal Personality and the Lighthouse at Cape Spartel' (1996) 36 *Virginia Journal of International Law* 275, at 337–38.

[12] Se, eg, P Kazansky, 'Théorie de l'administration internationale' (1902) IX *Revue Générale de Droit International Public* 366; and particularly PS Reinsch, 'International Administrative Law and National Sovereignty' (1909) 3 *American Journal of International Law* 1, at 18, who described such administrative developments as contributing to a 'the feeling of a common humanity' which through further integration would necessarily lead to more peaceful relations between states.

[13] See, eg, W Schücking, *The International Union of the Hague Conferences*, Charles G Fenwick (trans) (Oxford, Oxford University Press, 1918). The American jurist Frederick Holls even went as far as describing the Hague Conventions as the 'Magna Charta of International Law': see FW Holls, *The Peace Conference at the Hague, and its Bearing on International Law and Policy* (New York, MacMillan, 1900) 354.

[14] L Oppenheim, 'The Science of International Law: Its Task and Method' (1908) 2 *American Journal of International Law* 313, at 320–21 and 348–49. Oppenheim was himself giving effect to Heinrich Triepel's concept of the *Vereinbarung* – on which, see Ch 1, section II above. On the functional nature of the distinction between 'law-making treaties' and other types of treaties, see C Brölmann, 'Law-Making Treaties: Form and Function in International Law' (2005) 74 *Nordic Journal of International Law* 383, at 384–85.

[15] EH Carr, *The Twenty Years' Crisis 1919–1939: An Introduction to the Study of International Relations*, 2nd edn (London, MacMillan, 1946) 27–28; and see the discussion in JE Alvarez, *International Organizations as Law-Makers* (Oxford, Oxford University Press, 2005) 18–19.

In many respects, the League Covenant seemed to offer up significant evidence in support of this reading. For example, provisions on collective security[16] or mechanisms—albeit somewhat tentative and weak—for effecting legal change[17] clearly aimed to reach beyond the institution's treaty base to have a broader effect on the structure of the international legal order overall. Importantly, Article 20 of the Covenant—a precursor to Article 103 of the UN Charter[18]—was seen as attempting to create a de facto hierarchy between the Covenant and other international agreements.[19] For this reason, most contemporary reflections on the League tended to stress the *sui generis* character of its constituent instrument compared to other multilateral treaties,[20] which, in particular, highlighted the difficulties many *inter-bellum* jurists faced in reconciling the somewhat revolutionary ambition of the organisation with the decentralised institutional architecture of international law overall.[21] As we saw already to some degree in Chapter 1, Oppenheim, towards the end of his life, acknowledged the 'unprecedented' nature of the League's ambition and its effect on international law—ultimately giving rise to an attempt 'to organise the hitherto unorganised community of States by a written constitution'.[22]

This apparent dichotomy between the League's perceived 'constitutional' function—or, at least, ambition—and its more limited 'contractual' legal form became a recurring narrative around this time. One can see this also in the cautious assessment of Alfred Zimmern, who, in a famous study on

[16] The collective security provision was included in the ill-fated art 10, which provided that the League's members 'undertake to respect and preserve as against external aggression the territorial integrity and existing political independence of all Members of the League'.

[17] For example, art 19 provided that: 'The Assembly may from time to time advise the reconsideration by Members of the League of treaties which have become inapplicable and the consideration of international conditions whose continuance might endanger the peace of the world.'

[18] See below at n 36.

[19] The text of art 20 reads, inter alia, that the League's members agree 'that this Covenant is accepted as abrogating all obligations or understandings *inter se* which are inconsistent with the terms thereof, and solemnly undertake that they will not hereafter enter into any engagements inconsistent with the terms thereof'.

[20] See, eg, discussion in Claude Jr (n 10) 38–39. A Nussbaum, *A Concise History of the Law of Nations* (New York, Macmillan, 1954) 200; Klabbers (n 10) 291–94; Brölmann (n 10) 56–57; ND White, *The Law of International Organisations*, 2nd edn (Manchester, Manchester University Press, 2006) 14–15.

[21] For an excellent discussion of the difficulties of coming to terms with the independent identity of international organisations from the inter-war years onwards—particularly contrasting more formalist continental readings with the pragmatism of Anglo-American approaches—see Bederman (n 11), particularly at 333–49.

[22] L Oppenheim, *International Law: A Treatise, Vol. 1*, 3rd edn (London, Longmans, Green & Co, 1920) 269. See further L Oppenheim, *Future of International Law* (Oxford, Clarendon Press, 1921) 11–13 and 66–67; see also EA Whittuck, 'Professor Oppenheim' (1920–21) 1 *British Yearbook of International Law* 1, at 8. For a critical assessment in this respect, see M Schmoekel, 'Consent and Caution: Lassa Oppenheim and His Reaction to World War I' in R Lessafer (ed), *Peace Treaties and International Law in European History: From the Late Middle Ages to World War One* (Cambridge, Cambridge University Press, 2004) 270, at 281–82.

the League assessed from a rule of law perspective, described the Covenant as neither entirely contractual nor constitutional.[23] Zimmern drew on the work of Max Huber, who had been an enthusiastic proponent of the institutionalisation of international law since the early experiments with inter-state arbitration at the Hague, the significance of which for him lay 'less in what [these institutions] are, as seen from a formally legal perspective ... than in the moral weight that they lend to the ideas and aspirations which led to their creation and which they embody at least in part'.[24]

As was noted in Chapter 2, this more functional (and aspirational) approach was, at least in part, a reaction against the perceived formalism of late nineteenth-century international law. In their urge to modernise the law, most *inter-bellum* jurists trod an uneasy path between the certainty of legal form and a more purposive functionalism: for example, as we saw, by reading Article 38 of the PCIJ (now ICJ) Statute into a kind of quasi-constitutional position as a kind of *functional* meta-norm—or rule of recognition—with the ambition of concretising the law's *formal* qualities as a legal system.[25] This kind of reading carried over into a new approach to multilateral treaties more broadly, which were increasingly seen to perform a myriad number of contractual, constitutive and 'legislative' functions. This is nowhere clearer than in the leading work on the law of treaties from this era by Arnold McNair, who argued that the treaty was 'the only instrument available for doing many of the things which an individual state would do by means of its legislature'.[26] Accordingly, if the international community wished to 'enact a fundamental, organic, constitutional law, such as the Covenant of the League of Nations was intended to be and in large measure is in fact, it employs the treaty'.[27]

This functional reading of the nature of multilateral treaties was influential amongst his contemporaries and has arguably remained so since, despite

[23] A Zimmern, *The League of Nations and the Rule of Law, 1918–1935* (London, MacMillan and Co, 1936) 284–85. See also White (n 20) 14.

[24] M Huber, 'Die soziologischen Grundlagen des Völkerrechts' ['The Sociological Foundations of International Law'], reprinted in M Huber, *Gesellschaft und Humanität—Gesammelte Aufsätze* (Zürich, Artemis, 1948) 147, and cited in D Thürer, 'Max Huber: A Portrait in Outline' (2007) 18 *European Journal of International Law* 69, at 71. As Thürer further comments (at 72), for Huber, these institutional developments formed '*a symbol of* an international legal system' around which public opinion would coalesce, helping in turn to further enhance the institutionalisation of international law. In line with the analysis in Ch 2, in fact, it was Huber's modern, sociological approach—'his sensitivity to the facts and the history of law'—which enabled him 'to perceive tendencies which would have remained concealed if the situation were viewed from a purely positivist perspective'.

[25] For an analysis of the controversy in this respect, though ultimately endorsing such a functionalist reading, see GM Danilenko, *Law-Making in the International Community* (Dordrecht, Martinus Nijhoff, 1993) 30–43.

[26] A McNair, *The Law of Treaties* (Oxford, Clarendon Press, 1961, first published in 1938) 259.

[27] A McNair, 'The Functions and Differing Legal Character of Treaties' (1930) 11 *British Yearbook of International Law* 100, at 101.

the evident difficulties in explaining legislation as a decentralised process.[28] James Brierly, for instance, made a similarly cautious endorsement of the League Covenant's constitutional ambition and effects:

> The real justification for ascribing a law-making function to these treaties is the practical one … that they do *in fact perform the function* which a legislature performs in a state, *though they do so only imperfectly*; and that they are the only machinery which exists for the purposive adapting of international law to new conditions and in general for strengthening the force of the rule of law between states … *It is right that we should look behind the form of these treaties to their substantial effect.*[29] (emphasis added)

Similarly, Lauterpacht was careful to stress the importance of the formal differences between treaties compared to legislation, but by taking a particular view on the law-creating (rather than obligation-inferring) effects of treaties, he sought to highlight a similar functional interpretation based on a purposive reading of state sovereignty. In other words, if 'freedom of contract' prevailed amongst states, then this had to be interpreted as a freedom to create any law, including one which elevated the League Covenant to a higher status.[30]

Whilst the collapse of the League project with the outbreak of the Second World War may have further highlighted the already-evident gap between substantive ambition and structural legal form, for most this failure did not undermine that ambition, instead merely confirming that the League had not gone far enough in its realisation.[31] The Covenant had been, in other words, 'too formal and inflexible'.[32] By tying a collective security model to a conference structure grounded in unanimity, the League was seen to be paralysed from the outset.[33] Its constitutional architecture reflected an outmoded form of international politics: to paraphrase Martti Koskenniemi,

[28] See, eg, A McNair, 'International Legislation' (1933–34) 19 *Iowa Law Review* 177, at 178–79; and later CW Jenks, 'The Conflict of Law-Making Treaties' (1953) 30 *British Yearbook of International Law* 401. For commentary, see also Brölmann (n 14).

[29] JL Brierly, *The Law of Nations: An Introduction to the International Law of Peace*, 2nd edn (Oxford, Oxford University Press, 1936) 48–49.

[30] H Lauterpacht, 'The Covenant as the Higher Law' (1936) 17 *British Yearbook of International Law* 54, 64–65. On Lauterpacht's commitment to the constitutionalisation of international politics generally, see also M Koskenniemi, *The Gentle Civilizer of Nations: The Rise and Fall of International Law 1870–1960* (Cambridge, Cambridge University Press, 2001) 376–88. Of particular importance in Lauterpacht's reading of the League Covenant's status was the wording of art 20, as set out above at n 19.

[31] See, eg, M Koskenniemi, 'The Politics of International Law' (1990) 1 *European Journal of International Law* 4, 6; F Kratochwil, 'How do Norms Matter?' in M Byers (ed), *The Role of Law in International Politics: Essays in International Relations and International Law* (Oxford, Oxford University Press, 2000) 35, at 39.

[32] M Koskenniemi, 'The Police in the Temple. Order, Justice and the UN: A Dialectical View' (1995) 6 *European Journal of International Law* 325, at 334.

[33] The backbone of the League's approach to collective security was contained in art 10, on which see above at n 16.

the system relied for its effectiveness on the existence of precisely the kind of community which the League had attempted, and failed, to bring about in the first place.[34]

The more realist political climate after the Second World War may have arguably blunted any overt enthusiasm—at least initially—for reading the UN Charter as a constitution for the international system (or indeed the UN itself as a form of proto-world government). In fact, not only was the institution immediately hidebound by Cold War politics and constitutional crises, but the seemingly more 'constitutional' provisions establishing the pre-eminence of the Security Council,[35] combined with Article 103 (the so-called 'supremacy clause'),[36] only suggested, if anything, that the drafters had put political realism before any transformative ambition—with such provisions, in effect, further institutionalising the political hegemony of the 'great powers'.[37] Nevertheless, as the UN grew in size, scale and ambition over the years, it would not take long before similar constitutional analogies would begin to colour reflections on the Charter and the 'UN system' overall. Although few would come to see the Charter as an actual constitution for the international system—with some notable exceptions, of course[38]—at the very least, the UN institutions (often combined with other international institutional organs, courts and regimes) have come to be seen in more compensatory terms, 'gap-filling' for the lack of actual constitutional organs at the international level:[39] for example, the Security Council as fulfilling

[34] Koskenniemi (n 32) 333, summing up the views of Carr (n 15).

[35] The effects of arts 24 and 25 taken together are essentially to transfer primary responsibility for peace and security on the Council and to make the members subordinate to its authority. When combined with the Council's power under Chapter VII (art 42, in particular, giving the Council a monopoly on the use of force in international affairs), the effect of the Charter can be read as effectively legalising a de facto hegemony.

[36] The text of art 103 is somewhat ambiguous in providing that in case of a 'conflict between the obligations of the Members of the United Nations under the present Charter and their obligations under any other international agreement, their obligations under the present Charter shall prevail'. For some, this has been taken to override provisions of customary international law, to secure the almost omnipotent authority of the UN Security Council; for others, it has been construed more narrowly to deal with other agreements between states which may compromise the operation of the Charter collective security system. For discussion, see R Livoja, 'The Scope of the Supremacy Clause of the United Nations Charter' (2008) 58 *International and Comparative Law Quarterly* 583.

[37] Koskenniemi (n 32) 336 and passim; see further in Ch 6 of G Simpson, *Great Powers and Outlaw States: Unequal Sovereigns in the International Legal Order* (Cambridge, Cambridge University Press, 2004) 165–93.

[38] Though such a reading certainly has not been uncommon, particularly (though not exclusively) amongst German academics: see, eg, A Verdross and B Simma, *Universelles Völkerrecht: Theorie und Praxis*, 3rd edn (Berlin, Duncker & Humblot, 1984); B Fassbender, *The United Nations Charter as the Constitution of the International Community* (Leiden, Martinus Nijhoff, 2009), especially the works he surveys at 27–51; and see also R St J Macdonald, 'The International Community as a Legal Community' in Macdonald and Johnston (n 6) 853–909; and, more tentatively perhaps, P-M Dupuy, 'The Constitutional Dimension of the Charter of the United Nations Revisited' (1997) 1 *Max Planck Yearbook of United Nations Law* 1.

[39] See, eg, A Cassese, *International Law in a Divided World* (Oxford, Clarendon Press, 1986) 401–03; A Cassese, *International Law*, 2nd edn (Oxford, Oxford University Press, 2005) 66–67.

executive (as well as *quasi-legislative*) functions; the ICJ as the upper tier of the international judiciary; as well as recognition of the *soft-legislative* normative influence of the General Assembly.[40]

Most of these readings have, once again, stressed the need to look beyond the strict legal form of the UN, which remains grounded in a treaty agreement between its member states, and the underlying effect of the institution on the contemporary functioning of international law. Generations of lawyers, from the late 1950s and 1960s onwards, have embraced this kind of pragmatic, functionalist approach not only in order to understand the nature of the perceived structural change brought about by the post-war institutions, but also, more normatively, as a means of further enhancing the rule of law at the international level.[41] At times, this approach has been subtle in influence—for example, in the post-war direction of Lauterpacht's work[42]—and at other times much more explicit: for instance, in the academic works or judicial reasoning of some of the most prominent names of mid- to late twentieth-century international law, such as Philip Jessup,[43] Wilfred Jenks,[44] Manfred Lachs[45] or Wolfgang Friedmann.[46] The latter half of the twentieth century increasingly saw ambitions for progress in international

[40] See, eg, J Crawford, 'The Charter of the United Nations as a Constitution' in H Fox (ed), *The Changing Constitution of the United Nations* (London, British Institute of International and Comparative Law, 1997) 3–16; ND White, 'The United Nations System: Conference, Contract or Constitutional Order?' (2000) 4 *Singapore Journal of International and Comparative Law* 281; and I Brownlie, 'The United Nations as a Form of Government' in JES Fawcett and R Higgins (eds), *International Organization: Law in Movement (Essays in Honour of John McMahon)* (Oxford, Oxford University Press, 1974) 26–36, in particular at 27, where he claimed that: 'As a matter of description it is much *less* accurate to say that the United Nations is *not* a form of government than to say that it is.'

[41] On this turn generally, see Koskenniemi (n 30) 474–80. For a more comprehensive discussion, see DM Johnston, 'Functionalism in the Theory of International Law' (1988) 26 *Canadian Yearbook of International Law* 3.

[42] Contrast the tone and tenor of Lauterpacht's *The Development of International Law by the International Court* (London, Stevens and Sons, 1958) with his earlier more theoretical works (canvassed above in Ch 2), for example. For discussion, see M Koskenniemi, 'Lauterpacht: The Victorian Tradition in International Law' (1997) 8 *European Journal of International Law* 215, at 255–63.

[43] See PC Jessup, *A Modern Law of Nations: An Introduction* (New York, Macmillan, 1952) 2–3, 8–12 on the defects of a sovereign-centred and decentralised legal order. See also his stress on function over form in his separate opinion in the *South West Africa* case: ICJ Reports 1966, 319, at 411; and see further on this case below, at n 53, and in Ch 3, at n 30.

[44] See, eg, the functional orientation of CW Jenks, 'Craftsmanship in International Law' (1956) 50 *American Journal of International Law* 32, and developed at length in *The Common Law of Mankind* (London, Stevens and Sons, 1958). Whilst in the latter, Jenks claims that international law now possessed formal universality as a result of the creation of the UN (at 77–79), he constantly stresses that a more pragmatic, functionalist method is required of the international lawyer, particularly in perceiving the effects of international organisation on the law (eg, at 173–207).

[45] M Lachs, 'Some Reflections on Substance and Form in International Law' in W Friedmann, L Henkin and O Lissitzyn (eds), *Transnational Law in a Changing Society: Essays in Honour of Philip C Jessup* (New York, Columbia University Press, 1972) 99–112.

[46] See, most famously, Friedmann (n 6).

law—for instance, in regulating the use of force, realisation of human rights, or tackling environmental or other global problems—expressed in institutional rather than substantive terms.[47] As José Alvarez notes, many twentieth-century international lawyers began to see:

> [P]rospects for multilateral cooperation in the promise that IOs [international organisations] have become international legal persons to some extent independent of the states that have established them and that IO processes will encourage the consideration of 'community' interests and not merely the interests of self-interested states.[48]

This functional, institutionalist agenda[49] has arguably been further encouraged by the approach of the ICJ in its progressive readings of the UN Charter during the organisation's formative years, which is particularly evident in the approach taken by judges such as Alejandro Alvarez.[50] This is nowhere clearer than in the Court's recognition of the UN's legal personality,[51] certain 'implied powers',[52] and a presumption against ultra vires in cases where UN organs were deemed to have developed competencies beyond the strict terms of the Charter.[53] In turn, many of these judgments would foster the development of important principles in the emerging field of 'international institutional law', itself further buttressing the apparent

[47] As Abi-Saab notes, 'the law of cooperation approach is deeply institutional, precisely because of the more ambitious tasks it tackles ... norms resulting from the law of cooperation approach ... cannot have a real social hold without adequate institutional arrangements for applying them'. G Abi-Saab, 'Whither the International Community?' (1998) 9 *European Journal of International Law* 248, at 256 (footnotes omitted), quoting from his 'Cours général de droit international public' (1987-VII) 207 *Recueil des Cours* 9, at 93. For a similar perspective, see also A Paulus, 'International Law and International Community' in D Armstrong (ed), *Routledge Handbook of International Law* (Abingdon, Routledge, 2009) 44, at 47–48. For a critical discussion of a similar view of the realisation of progress through the creation of judicial fora, see T Skouteris, *The Notion of Progress in International Law Discourse* (The Hague, TMC Asser Press, 2010) 175–79.

[48] Alvarez (n 15) 585.

[49] This is not necessarily as ambitious as the functionalist movement in political science, which has particularly influenced late twentieth-century international law scholarship in the US. However, there is clearly some synergy between this idea—promoting greater systematicity and rule of law values through institutional integration—and what is suggested here. For a discussion, see in particular Johnston (n 41) 28–29 ff.

[50] See, eg, his Dissenting Opinion in *Competence of the General Assembly for the Admission of a State to the United Nations*, Advisory Opinion, ICJ Reports 1950, 12, at 17–18.

[51] See, eg, *Reparation for Injuries Suffered in the Service of the United Nations*, Advisory Opinion, ICJ Reports 1949, 174, at 179, where the court directly combines intent based arguments with the functional needs of the international community. See further on this case below at nn 101–109.

[52] See particularly the generous reading of implied powers in *Certain Expenses of the United Nations (Article 17, paragraph 2, of the Charter)*, Advisory Opinion, ICJ Reports 1962, 151, at 168; and for commentary, see White (n 20) 86–87.

[53] *South West Africa, Second Phase, Judgment*, ICJ Reports 1966, 6, at 16, para 89; see also J Klabbers, 'The Changing Image of International Organizations' in J-M Coicaud and V Heiskanen (eds), *The Legitimacy of International Organizations* (Tokyo, United Nations University Press, 2001) 221, at 235.

autonomy of international organisations in international law overall.[54] Perhaps freed from some of the practical and ideological limitations of the preceding Cold War years,[55] in 1996, the ICJ would come to give one of its most explicit endorsements of this 'functionalist' reading of the constituent instruments of international organisations:

> From a formal standpoint, the constituent instruments of international organizations are multilateral treaties, to which the well-established rules of treaty interpretation apply ... But the constituent instruments of international organizations are also treaties of a particular type; their object is to create new subjects of law endowed with a certain autonomy, to which the parties entrust the task of realizing common goals.[56]

Nevertheless, in recognising their 'certain autonomy' in this way, the ICJ also acknowledged the impossibility of completely moving out of the inter-state framework which grounds international institutions: both in terms of the formal treaty instrument underlying the organisation and in the rather derivative, or delegated, nature of the functional autonomy they thereafter enjoy. Therefore, whilst their recognition as separate actors—or 'subjects'—clearly has a significant impact on the shape, substance and operation of modern international law, this complex interplay between decentralised legal form and limited functional autonomy means that their impact cannot be interpreted as any kind of centralisation of authority in the international legal system overall. Insofar as this functional autonomy can—and indeed often does—have a normative impact outside of the specific institutional legal order, seen from the outside, their authority is necessarily more contingent and contestable. As I will now go on to explain, in fact, the impact of institutionalisation has been somewhat schizophrenic from the point of view of the international rule of law—an effect which is arguably reflective of the tensions inherent in that ideal itself—seemingly necessary to overcome the perceived inefficiencies and externalities of a decentralised legal system, but also potentially threatening to the overall coherence of the system.

II. THE IMPACT OF INSTITUTIONALISATION: STRAINING THE SYSTEM

Looking back on the impact of international organisations throughout and since the twentieth century, it is difficult to deny that international law has

[54] For a general overview, see R Collins and ND White (eds), *International Organizations and the Idea of Autonomy: Institutional Independence in the International Legal Order* (Abingdon, Routledge, 2011).

[55] Compare, for instance, Jenks, *Common Law* (n 44) 173–74; and GI Tunkin, *Theory of International Law* (Cambridge, MA, Harvard University Press, 1974) 322–64. For comment, see White (n 20) 10–11.

[56] *Legality of the Use by a State of Nuclear Weapons in Armed Conflict*, Advisory Opinion, ICJ Reports 1996, 66, at 74–75, para. 19.

been shaped by their presence and influence in numerous and quite significant ways.[57] The number and scale of intergovernmental organisations, agencies, regimes and specialist dispute settlement bodies has grown to such an extent that such institutions can be said to 'now address virtually every field of human endeavour'.[58] Not only has this growth impacted on the scale of international legal regulation at a substantive level, it also brings with it '[n]ew forms of dispute resolution, executive action, administrative decision-making and enforcement, and legislation', which, together, are taken as transforming the law at a deeper, structural level: the emergence of 'a transnational legal process that influences national conduct, transforms national interests, and helps constitute and reconstitute national identities'.[59]

By the end of the Cold War, with an emerging atmosphere of ideological triumphalism, it became easy to see in such developments the beginnings of a transition in the very nature of international law itself. A quick review of the annual Hague Academy lectures from the late 1980s onwards, given by some of the discipline's most prestigious names, reveals a broadly 'constitutionalist' narrative that describes a movement away from Westphalian 'transactionalism' towards a more communitarian, more authoritative international law, which increasingly penetrates state sovereignty to secure the protection of community interests.[60] In perhaps the most spirited endorsement of this progress narrative, Christian Tomuschat declared a transition between 'the traditional model of sovereign self-sufficient states and a world with a hierarchical structure, topped by a single command structure'.[61] In a

[57] See, inter alia, D Pulkowski, 'Structural Paradigms of International Law' in T Broude and Y Shany (eds), *The Shifting Allocation of Authority in International Law: Considering Sovereignty, Supremacy and Subsidiarity* (Oxford, Hart Publishing, 2008) 51, at 69–72; Alvarez (n 15) 23–24 and passim; D Vignes, 'The Impact of International Organizations on the Development and Application of Public International Law' in R St J Macdonald and DM Johnston (eds), *The Structure and Process of International Law: Essays in Legal Philosophy, Doctrine, and Theory* (The Hague, Martinus Nijhoff, 1983) 809, at 809 ff.

[58] JE Alvarez, 'International Organizations: Then and Now' (2006) 100 *American Journal of International Law* 324, at 325. See also NM Blokker and HG Schermers (eds), *Proliferation of International Organizations: Legal Issues* (The Hague, Kluwer, 2001).

[59] HH Koh, 'Why Do Nations Obey International Law?' (1997) 106 *Yale Law Journal* 2599, at 2631.

[60] See, for instance, Abi-Saab's lecture from 1987 (n 47), as well as T Franck, 'Fairness in the International Legal and Institutional System: General Course on Public International Law' (1993-III) 240 *Recueil des Cours* 9; C Tomuschat, 'Obligations Arising for States Without or against their Will' (1993-IV) 241 *Recueil des Cours* 195; Simma (n 4); Tomuschat (n 4); P-M Dupuy, 'L'unité de l'ordre juridique international: Cours général de droit international public' (2002) 297 *Recueil des Cours* 9; T Meron, 'International Law in the Age of Human Rights: General Course on Public International Law' (2003) 301 *Recueil des Cours* 9, particularly at 228 and passim, criticising the structural and institutional limitations of Westphalian international law for the protection of human rights. On the progressive orientation of the Hague General Course, see M Koskenniemi, 'Repetition as Reform: Repetition as Reform: Georges Abi-Saab Cours Général de droit international public' (1998) 9 *European Journal of International Law* 405, at 406–07.

[61] Tomuschat (n 4) 90.

perhaps more sober reflection, Bruno Simma and Andreas Paulus described a movement in which:

> [T]he world of the famous 'Lotus principle', according to which states are only bound by their express consent, seems to be gradually giving way to a more communitarian, more highly institutionalized international law, in which states 'channel' the pursuit of most of their individual interests through multilateral institutions ... the system as a whole increasingly permeates state boundaries for the sake of protection of individual and group rights.[62]

At one level, one can in fact present a compelling body of evidence in support of these sorts of claim. On the structural side, first of all, international lawyers have noted a fundamental change in the enforcement capacity of international law brought about as a result of the prohibition on the use of force under the UN Charter and the peace and security function bestowed upon the Security Council.[63] Similarly, organisational fora such as the UN General Assembly are deemed to play an increasingly important role in the processes of international law-making and application,[64] with UN-sponsored conferences seen to be 'centralising' the multilateral treaty-making process[65] or even 'democratising' law-making in general by engaging non-state actors such as NGOs.[66] Similarly, whilst limited to more technical fields, organisations such as the World Health Organization (WHO) and the International Labour Organization (ILO) enjoy considerable 'law-making' powers in terms of regulatory standard-setting and other policy initiatives.[67] In other fields, a proliferation of dispute settlement bodies in particular regional and technical organisations has led to claims of an increasing 'legalisation' in the conduct of international politics,[68] which in turn is seen as potentially

[62] B Simma and A Paulus, 'The 'International Community': Facing the Challenge of Globalization' (1998) 9 *European Journal of International Law* 266, at 276.

[63] See, eg, the discussion in GG Fitzmaurice, 'The Foundations of the Authority of International Law and the Problem of Enforcement' (1956) 19 *Modern Law Review* 1, at 3–4; for a more recent view of the UN Security Council as a proto-global 'executive', see JA Frowein and N Krisch, 'Introduction to Chapter VII' in B Simma (ed), *The Charter of the United Nations: A Commentary*, 2nd edn (Oxford, Oxford University Press, 2002) 701, at 702 in particular.

[64] See, perhaps most famously, R Higgins, *The Development of International Law through the Political Organs of the United Nations* (Oxford, Oxford University Press, 1963); see also, more recently, Alvarez (n 15) 259–60; JL Charney, 'Universal International Law' (1993) 87 *American Journal of International Law* 529, at 543–50; and ND White, 'Separate But Connected: Inter-governmental Organizations and International Law' (2008) 5 *International Organizations Law Review* 175, at 181–87.

[65] Brölmann (n 10) 101–12.

[66] S Charnovitz, 'Nongovernmental Organizations and International Law' (2006) 100 *American Journal of International Law* 348, at 359–63.

[67] For an overview, see Alvarez (n 15) 217–44; A Boyle and C Chinkin, *The Making of International Law* (Oxford, Oxford University Press, 2007) 108–41.

[68] J Goldstein et al (eds), *Legalization and World Politics* (Cambridge, MA, MIT Press, 2001).

enhancing the determinacy of law and compensating for the kinds of deficiencies outlined in the previous chapter.[69]

In addition, international organisations have arguably added 'dimensionality' to the systemic nature of international law, particularly in terms of its sources and subjects. For instance, a number of institutional developments are seen to have introduced degrees of normativity—or 'relative normativity'—into international law.[70] Codification exercises undertaken by the UN's International Law Commission (ILC) have resulted in treaty and customary recognition that certain norms possess a peremptory (*jus cogens*) character, thus signalling an emerging normative hierarchy,[71] which in turn has been accepted and tentatively progressed by international courts and tribunals.[72] Alvarez, for example, describes the critical role of institutional *fora* in this development:

> *Jus cogens* and *erga omnes* obligations are products of the age of IOs [international organisations] precisely because they made real (or more real than ever before) the idea of a 'community of states as a whole' on which such hierarchical concepts could be built. The articulation of *jus cogens*—in Article 53 of the Vienna Convention on the Law of Treaties—resulted from the kind of 'package deal' that characterizes treaty making in institutionalized global venues involving UN expert bodies ... and UN-authorized treaty-making conferences.[73]

[69] See, eg, JE Alvarez, 'The New-Dispute Settlers: (Half) Truths and Consequences' (2003) 38 *Texas International Law Journal* 405, at 408.

[70] For an enthusiastic embrace of the blurring of the normativity threshold in international law in this respect, see Charney (n 64); D Shelton, 'International Law and "Relative Normativity"' in M Evans (ed), *International Law*, 4th edn (Oxford, Oxford University Press, 2014) 137–65. For a critical reflection, see P Weil, 'Towards Normative Relativity in International Law?' (1983) 77 *American Journal of International Law* 413.

[71] On the applicability and effect of *jus cogens* norms, see arts 53 and 64 of the Vienna Convention on the Law of Treaties 1969; on the responsibility of states for breaches of peremptory norms of international law and on the possibility of invocation of responsibility by third states for breaches of obligations *erga omnes*, see arts 41–42 and 48, respectively, of the *Draft Articles on Responsibility of States for Internationally Wrongful Acts*, available (with commentary) at: http://legal.un.org/ilc/texts/instruments/english/commentaries/9_6_2001.pdf. However, note that the customary law status of these provisions, particularly with regard to third party enforcement of community interests, remains somewhat controversial.

[72] For example, on the *jus cogens* status of the prohibition of unlawful force in international law, see *Military and Paramilitary Activities in and against Nicaragua (Nicaragua v United States)*, Merits, Judgment of 27 June 1986, ICJ Reports 1986, 14, at 100–101; on the peremptory status of human rights norms as limiting the powers of the UN Security Council, see also the following before the European Court of First Instance: Case T-306/01, *Yusuf and Al Barakaat International Foundation v Council and Commission*, 21 September 2005 [2005] ECR II-3533; Case T-315/01, *Kadi v Council and Commission*, 21 September 2005 [2005] ECR II-3649.

[73] Alvarez (n 58) 327.

As he goes on to note, it is also the UN family of organisations—human rights treaty bodies, the ILC, the ICJ and others—which has been most likely to cite the peremptory status of particular norms, increasing the UN's recognition—amongst many at least—as the ostensible representative of the international community as a whole.[74] Furthermore, to recall from Chapter 3, the 'normative' output of the General Assembly has had a significant impact on traditional sources doctrine, with its resolutions increasingly recognised as important evidence of emerging customary international law,[75] if not also constituting in themselves a new 'soft' form of international obligation, with significant normative force.[76]

Meanwhile, in terms of the subjects of the law, not only have organisations themselves been recognised as legal persons,[77] but institutional developments in the protection of human rights and the prosecution of international criminal law have also strengthened the recognition of the individual as bearer of rights and responsibilities in international law.[78] Overall, as David Bederman notes, since the ICJ's recognition of the personality of the UN in 1949,[79] an increasingly functional view of legal personality has pertained which recognises the legal standing of various non-state actors on the basis of the contemporary needs of the international community.[80]

Taken together, these trends clearly suggest that the impact of international institutions has been significant, radically altering the structural

[74] ibid. See also D Shelton, 'Normative Hierarchy in International Law' (2006) 100 *American Journal of International Law* 291.

[75] AE Roberts, 'Traditional and Modern Approaches to Customary International Law: A Reconciliation' (2001) 95 *American Journal of International Law* 757.

[76] See generally A Boyle, 'Soft Law in International Law-Making' in Evans (n 70) 118–36; KW Abbott and D Snidal, 'Hard and Soft Law in International Governance' (2000) 54 *International Organization* 421; Boyle and Chinkin (n 67) 211–29; and, more particularly, White (n 64) 179–87.

[77] This change is normally attributed to the recognition of the legal personality of the UN in the *Reparations* Advisory Opinion (n 51); see the discussion in Bederman (n 11).

[78] For a general overview of this development, as well as the recognition of individual legal personality through international criminal law and human rights law, see Chs 6 and 7 respectively of R Portmann, *Legal Personality in International Law* (Cambridge, Cambridge University Press, 2008) 80–172.

[79] See *Reparations* (n 51).

[80] Bederman (n 11) 279. This functional approach seems to have won out as the dominant approach to legal personality for non-state actors. This is the approach adopted explicitly by the International Law Association recently: see ILA, First Report of the Committee on Non State Actors in International Law, Hague Conference 2010, 4–5; available at: www.ila-hq.org/en/committees/index.cfm/cid/1023; and see further, M Noortmann, 'The International Law Association and Non-state Actors: Professional Network, Public Interest Group or Epistemic Community?' in J d'Aspremont (ed), *Participants in the International Legal System* (Abingdon, Routledge, 2011) 233–47.

landscape of international law. Many of these institutional innovations are indeed quite difficult to reconcile with the idea of international law as a decentralised legal order existing primarily—even if not entirely—between sovereign states. In fact, already in 1958, when reflecting on the impact of institutionalisation, Jenks had contrasted the increasingly 'public' substance of international law brought about largely through the post-war international organisations with its formal, inter-state nature:

> [I]t does not suffice to attempt to relate these developments to a pre-existing structure and arrangement of the law originally evolved on the assumption that international law is a law between 'States solely and exclusively' and to give an account of them within, or by somewhat haphazard and illogical modifications of or accretions to, a pre-established framework.[81]

This perception seems to have only intensified in recent years. The introduction of institutional innovation and hierarchy, and the increasingly communitarian or humanistic focus of international law seem difficult to explain and legitimise simply on the basis of treaty consent and intergovernmental cooperation.[82] A more 'constitutional' regulatory order seems to have been 'bolted on' to the more traditional 'Westphalian' legal form, resulting in a degree of 'ad-hocism' at the institutional level.[83] As a result, not only does this structure seem incapable of adequately securing many of the more communitarian values and goals brought about through institutional innovation, but it also seems itself to push in the other direction: invoking a growing sense of accountability deficit and legitimacy crisis. On the one hand, the intergovernmental nature of international institutions seems to inhibit their ability to adequately represent community interests in opposition to state concerns.[84] This results in the ironic position where intergovernmental cooperation through international institutions is credited as having brought about the shift in international law's substantive focus, but a continuing reliance on intergovernmental institutional structures to deliver

[81] Jenks, *Common Law* (n 44) 7–8.

[82] See, eg (though far from exclusively), Simma (n 4); Tomuschat (n 4); and J Delbruck, 'Prospects for a "World (Internal) Law?" Legal Developments in a Changing. International System' (2002) 9 *Indiana Journal of Global Legal Studies* 401.

[83] A Bianchi, 'Ad-Hocism and the Rule of Law' (2002) 13 *European Journal of International Law* 263, particularly at 268–89. And see further JHH Weiler, 'The Geology of International Law—Governance, Democracy and Legitimacy' (2004) 64 *Zeitschrift für Ausländisches Öffentliches Recht und Völkerrecht* 547.

[84] See, eg, Simma (n 4) 233 and 373–74; Tomuschat (n 4) 44 and 47. See also B Simma, 'International Crimes: Injury and Countermeasures: Comments on Part 2 of the ILC Work on State Responsibility' in JHH Weiler, A Cassese and M Spinedi (eds), *International Crimes of State: A Critical Analysis of the ILC's Draft Article 19 on State Responsibility* (Berlin, De Gruyter, 1989) 283, at 315. And see also the discussion in T Nardin, *Law, Morality, and the Relations of States* (Princeton, NJ, Princeton University Press, 1983) 161–62.

(or protect) global public goods threatens to potentially undermine those same values, interests and goals.[85] As Cassese laments:

> [T]he momentous advance represented by the emergence of a network of normative standards has not gone hand in hand with commensurate progress in the setting up of international law enforcement machinery ... In this vacuum, the UN has been called upon to play the role of an implementation mechanism.[86]

As we saw in Part I, this kind of reflection is an oft-heard decrial of the inefficiency and inadequacy of relying on the institutional architecture of a decentralised international legal order to secure community goals and protect global public goods.[87] On the other hand, however, and as noted in the previous chapter, it seems difficult to comprehend how further institutionalisation might occur *within* international law without further straining or undermining a core aspect of its coherence as a decentralised legal system: *the very same system which underpins and gives legal force to many of these institutional innovations*. In fact, to the extent that such institutions are seen to possess increasingly significant normative powers, exercising authority in a manner that is difficult to reconcile with traditional, 'Westphalian' international law, there also appears to be a growing anxiety pushing in the opposite direction. Many of these institutional developments seem to be undermining more traditional channels for legitimating the exercise of public power (at the global as well as the national level).[88] Indeed, despite long-standing hopes that further institutionalisation would secure global public goods in the face of national interests, as the post-Cold War years have unfolded, the once benevolent image of international institutions

[85] See, eg, recently S Villalpando, 'The Legal Dimension of the International Community: How Community Interests are Protected in International Law' (2010) 21 *European Journal of International Law* 387, at 409–10. As Shelton claims, 'in most cases the problem is one of ensuring compliance by States that have freely consented to [peremptory norms of international law] and not one of imposing obligations on dissenting states'. Shelton (n 70) 148. On the under-developed nature of international law and the need for further institutional development of the law-making function, see Danilenko (n 25) 11–15 and passim; and similar concerns in Abi-Saab (n 47); M Cherif Bassiouni, 'The Philosophy and Policy of International Criminal Justice' in LC Vorah et al (eds), *Man's Inhumanity to Man: Essays on International Law in Honour of Antonio Cassese* (Leiden, Martinus Nijhoff Publishers, 2003) 65, at 67–68; and A Pellet, 'Brief Remarks on the Unilateral Use of Force' (2000) 11 *European Journal of International Law* 385, at 391, who points to the lack of effective institutional protection of community interests as directly causative of the increasing trend towards unilateral enforcement of those interests.

[86] Cassese, *International Law* (n 39) 66–67.

[87] This is most evident in many of the contributions to Simma (n 63); for a critical review in this respect, see A Orford, 'The Gift of Formalism' (2004) 15 *European Journal of International Law* 179.

[88] For a representative view of concerns from an international law perspective, see Weiler (n 83); and A von Bogdandy, 'Globalization and Europe: How to Square Democracy and Globalization' (2004) 15 *European Journal of International Law* 885.

seems increasingly to be called into question, prompting demands for greater scrutiny and control of institutional activities. I will return to consider these concerns in more detail in the next chapter. To understand better why they arise in the first place, however, it is necessary first to cast a more critical eye over some of the limitations (both conceptual and practical) of thinking of international institutions (or, indeed, any global actor) as fulfilling, or at least compensating for, the kinds of constitutional functions that appear necessary to secure this more purposive rule of law ambition.

III. ON THE COMPLEX CHARACTER OF INTERNATIONAL INSTITUTIONS

The point of the previous analysis was not to suggest that all, or indeed most, international lawyers subscribe to an explicitly 'constitutionalist' reading of international law. However, in line with the concerns of the previous chapter, there does seem to have been a broad assumption at play that through the development of autonomous international institutional mechanisms, we might compensate for the lack of centralised institutions at the international level.[89] As Gaetano Arangio-Ruiz has argued, this kind of reading is not merely the preserve of utopian federalists, but is part of a widespread disciplinary commitment that draws on the idea that certain institutional innovations, introduced through inter-state agreements, are beginning to re-structure international law towards a more hierarchical legal form.[90] As he puts it himself, this approach—what he refers to as the doctrine of the 'organised international community'[91]—can be seen to:

> [D]raw upon the notion that in any society the ultimate sources of law are social facts and structures *not always*—especially at the inception—*translated into*

[89] I have written elsewhere on the way in which 'international constitutionalism' in this context is often merely the continuation of more mainstream international law concerns: see R Collins, 'Constitutionalism as Liberal-Juridical Consciousness: Echoes from International Law's Past' (2009) 22 *Leiden Journal of International Law* 251. Similarly, on the positivist orientation of much of the constitutionalisation literature, see also WG Werner, 'The Never-Ending Closure: Constitutionalism and International Law' in N Tsagourias (ed), *Transnational Constitutionalism: International and European Perspectives* (Cambridge, Cambridge University Press, 2007) 329, at 330.

[90] As he puts it himself, 'this tendency manifests itself in a great variety of degrees. In most cases the analogy is neither deliberately adopted nor organically developed. It is just assumed: and it goes without saying that no one pushes the analogy so far as to assert, for example., that the United Nations is the World State'. G Arangio-Ruiz, *The UN Declaration on Friendly Relations and the System of the Sources of International Law* (Alphen aan den Rijn, Sijthoff & Noordhoff, 1979) 199.

[91] ibid, particularly the 'Appendix' to this volume on 'The Concept of International Law and the Theory of International Organization', at 199–301.

> *formal rules*. This would be particularly true in a society in transition like the international society, moving as it is from a state of so-called 'decentralisation' of the law-making and law-determining (and law-enforcing) functions to a state of progressive 'centralisation'.[92] (emphasis added)

Arangio-Ruiz's analysis is useful in highlighting some of the theoretical difficulties that beset this reading. As he notes, this view of international law seems to be premised upon the (for him, misapprehended) idea that intergovernmental organisations created within the formative rules and structures of the international legal order can, at the same time, radically alter or re-structure international law. Organisations such as the League or the UN may be constituted 'horizontally' *between* their member states, but thereafter are seen to re-structure those relations on a more vertical basis—to some degree placing law *above* them.[93] For Arangio-Ruiz, this seems to misunderstand the nature of such institutions, which within their legal orders can indeed re-structure inter-state relations towards a more hierarchical legal paradigm—the European Union being a prime example in this respect—but, being subordinate and separate legal orders, this internal hierarchy has no bearing on the overarching rules of international law. The nature of the organisation is such that it is constituted *within* international law and in that respect is subordinate to the constitutive rules of this 'higher' law, making it impossible in formal terms for it to alter those constitutive rules to any degree.[94] As he notes:

> [T]he constituent treaty is not a legal instrument of the international community of men designed to alter the system's structure by delegating to other entities some of the functions allegedly exercised by States as 'organs' of a universal community. The inter-State compact involves really ... neither the universal society as a whole nor the peoples of the constituent states ... any organisation set up by inter-State compact bears within itself ... an 'original flaw', inherent in the very nature of the transaction which is at the basis of its existence: the inter-State compact ... [which is] a far less sophisticated phenomenon than the 'constitutionalists' seem to believe it to be.[95]

Accordingly, he sees the creation of an international organisation, however 'constitutional' in nature or function, as fundamentally different from a 'constitutional moment'[96] in the renegotiation of an existing social order. Unlike the foundational authority which the act of constituting a polity brings to all subsequently enacted law, in signing up to membership in

[92] ibid 30–31.
[93] ibid 211–14.
[94] ibid 255–58.
[95] ibid 43–44.
[96] The term 'constitutional moment' is often attributed to Bruce Ackerman; see, eg, BA Ackerman, 'Constitutional Politics/Constitutional Law' (1989) 99 *Yale Law Journal* 453; BA Ackerman, 'Transformative Appointments' (1988) 101 *Harvard Law Review* 1164.

an international organisation, 'States and their peoples seem to remain in their respective places, and in the condition in which they respectively were before the operation'.[97] In other words, the treaty may bring into being a new legal order, one which in certain respects may legitimately be labelled 'constitutional', but this act does not itself serve to reconstitute international law in any structural sense.

On the terms of the previous chapter, the domestic analogy therefore remains incomplete; the *discontinuity* impacts not only on the legal character of international law, but also on the institutions created within its parameters. This point is picked up by Terry Nardin, who makes a similar argument as to the capacity of states, as well as the institutions, courts and other bodies they create, to act as 'organs' of the international community in the sense suggested:

> The term 'organ' implies a body authorized to create and apply rules for the community, one whose decisions can be attributed to the community. But the acts of a state do not in themselves create international law, nor are they authorized by the international community as a whole. These limitations apply to the collective action of states in concluding treaties or establishing international agencies and tribunals, as well as to unilateral state acts. Although the joint action of some number of states may in various ways modify general international law as it applies to themselves, it does not alter the law as it applies to other states.[98]

These arguments are, to this extent at least, logically consistent and compelling. They certainly should not be interpreted as conservatism or outright scepticism: neither author denies the possibility of evolution and transition in the nature of international law, nor indeed the idea of international organisations being more than the sum of their constituent parts (their member states). Their point is merely that insofar as this autonomy translates into any kind of hierarchy, this will have only an internal effect within the confines of the institutional order itself.[99] Insofar as this autonomy finds expression in international law generally, it can only be accommodated in the form of the institution's distinct legal personality, placing it alongside (rather than above) states as a separate legal actor in its own right.[100] In fact, Arangio-Ruiz takes this argument further in a critique of the reasoning of the ICJ in the *Reparations* Advisory Opinion, briefly outlined above,[101] with its reliance on a functional autonomy-based argument to justify the international

[97] Arangio-Ruiz (n 90) 244–45.

[98] Nardin (n 84) 162–63.

[99] On this tension, generally, see principally J Klabbers, *An Introduction to International Institutional Law*, 2nd edn. (Cambridge, Cambridge University Press, 2009) passim.

[100] Arangio-Ruiz (n 90) 245–50. See further T Gazzini, 'The Relationship between International Legal Personality and the Autonomy of International Organizations' in Collins and White (n 54) 196–212.

[101] *Reparations* (n 51).

legal personality of the UN. According to Arangio-Ruiz, though he is by no means alone in this respect,[102] whilst states may have equipped the organisation with the necessary characteristics capable of giving rise to its personality under international law, the criteria for determining personality at this level can only really be settled by a rule of general international law.[103]

From a formal perspective, Arangio-Ruiz is clearly correct to point out the inconsistent reasoning in the advisory opinion. As I have had reason to point out elsewhere,[104] there are a number of troubling aspects in the Court's ruling, particularly in its amalgamation of functional and will-based argument: for instance, its stress on the intent of member states, whilst also noting the opposability of international legal personality to non-member states,[105] or the somewhat troubling contention that there could exist various degrees or 'measures' of legal personality.[106] At the same time, however, it is precisely because the Court has to eschew a completely formalist logic that the case is so significant, highlighting the actual character of the UN and the way in which it overlaps with general international law.[107] The ICJ sums up this functionalist logic in its conclusion that the UN is 'at present the supreme type of international organization, and it could not carry out the intentions of its founders if it was devoid of international personality'.[108]

The case therefore serves, somewhat ironically, as a good example of the limitations of the *overly* formalist approach of Arangio-Ruiz. Faced with a legal problem which had not yet been tested, ie, the existence or otherwise of the personality of a non-state actor (the UN), it is hardly surprising that the ICJ reconciled the will of the creators of the organisation and a more functional argument in the (rather pragmatic) way that it did. However,

[102] See also White (n 20) 44–45; Gazzini (n 100) 197.

[103] See Arangio-Ruiz (n 90) 247, at fn 118, where he elaborates this point further, but essentially reconciles the so-called 'subjective' and 'objective' views of international legal personality in this way.

[104] See R Collins, 'Non-state Actors in International Institutional Law: Non-state, Inter-state or Supra-state? The Peculiar Identity of the Intergovernmental Organization' in J d'Aspremont (ed), *Participants in the International Legal System: Multiple Perspectives on Non-state Actors in International Law* (Abingdon, Routledge, 2011) 311, at 315–20.

[105] See, eg, the discussion of Brölmann (n 10) 78–79; and J Klabbers, 'The Concept of Legal Personality' (2005) 11 *Ius Gentium* 35, at 50–56.

[106] As White claims, international legal personality is either there or it is not, the Court seemingly confounding the organisation's level of autonomy vis-a-vis its member states with its objective personality in international law. ND White, 'Discerning Separate Will' in WP Heere (ed), *From Government to Governance: The Growing Impact of Non-state Actors on the International and European Legal System* (The Hague, TMC Asser Press, 2004) 31–38. See also White (n 20) 30–31, 40; Gazzini (n 100) 199.

[107] Bederman (n 11) 367. For an explicitly pragmatic approach to international legal personality—the idea of 'presumptive personality'—see also Klabbers (n 99) 49–51.

[108] *Reparations* (n 51) 179.

what is most significant about the case is the Court's inability to completely close off the internal order of the institution and the broader constitutive rules of general international law: to do so would have undermined the purpose and function of the organisation, which was clearly intended by its member states to effect a certain level of change in international law overall. As Bederman notes, whilst the functional autonomy of institutions like the UN can find formal expression solely in terms of legal personality, the court recognises the reality that for the states that use these institutions, they exist more as 'communities' of interest.[109] In other words, they function as a means through which states participate in the international legal order, even at times—as I have suggested above—changing the rules or affecting the operation of that same order.

Accordingly, whilst the kind of conceptual distinction outlined by Arangio-Ruiz is logically consistent and theoretically coherent, it might still betray the 'internal point of view', that is, the collective understanding of international legal participants, which, as argued in Part II, remains critical to an effective conceptual understanding of international law in this broadest sense. This is particularly evident in institutions like the UN, where in many areas it is impossible to effect a strict separation between the internal legal order of the institution and the broader rules of international law overall. Whilst Arangio-Ruiz's argument may be more plausible with regard to closed, regional or more technical organisations, one cannot confine or limit the impact of the organs and rules of the UN system in this way. This is not simply because of the near-universal membership of the institution—though that alone makes the distinction somewhat more artificial—but more because many of the constituent rules of the UN Charter—for instance, those relating to the sovereign equality of states or the principle of non-intervention[110]—overlap with and give meaning to many of the 'constitutive' rules of general international law more broadly.[111] This is particularly the case in relation to the rules on the use of force, which prove almost impossible to disentangle from the rules of general international law overall.[112] Furthermore, the effect of the 'supremacy clause' in Article 103 of the

[109] Bederman (n 11) 371.

[110] Article 2 of the UN Charter.

[111] See further R Collins and ND White, 'International Organizations and the Idea of Autonomy: Introduction and Overview' in Collins and White (n 54) 3, at 15. On the external 'ripples' of internal law more generally, see Alvarez (n 15) 122–45.

[112] Indeed, although the Court in *Nicaragua* recognised the separate conceptual co-existence of Charter law and general international law in relation to self-defence, in effect it recognises the influence of Charter law, as well as institutional practice (particularly through UN General Assembly Resolutions), in giving content to the customary rule as it had developed since the signing of the Charter. See *Nicaragua* (n 72) 92–117; and for critical commentary, see A d'Amato, 'Trashing Customary International Law' (1987) 81 *American Journal of International Law* 101.

Charter seems to be to further entrench, and arguably give greater authority to, these rules as part of general international law.[113]

Nevertheless, one can see still how the two identities of international organisations—one formal, grounded in a treaty between the member states and expressed outside the institution as legal personality, and the other functional, suggesting the constitutional character of the treaty and recognising the impact that institutions have upon international law's functioning more broadly—give them a somewhat ambiguous character overall. To understand the nature of international institutions and their impact on contemporary international law, we need to account for these formal and functional aspects together. They result in a legal entity which is 'neither entirely "open", in the sense that it blends with general international law, nor entirely "closed", in the way of states'.[114] This is well described by Catherine Brölmann's conceptualisation of international organisations as 'transparent' entities: 'a systemic condition, resulting from the continuous tension between the organisation's servicing, functional, open aspect, on the one hand, and its independent, centralised, closed aspect, on the other'.[115]

At the same time, we also need to consider the impact of these formal and functional aspects on our understanding of the changes recounted above. Specifically, the increasing autonomy of international organisations does not result in a one-dimensional increase in the authority of the regime vis-a-vis the member states, but 'complex interplays of equal and subordinate relations with states, with other organisations, and within the organs of the entity itself'.[116] On a functional level, organisations are open to the broader international legal order, but remain servants of their member states. States can in this respect use organisations to create complex governance arrangements, hierarchy and centralisation, but these internal institutional characteristics cannot effect any hierarchy more broadly (and formally) due to the 'flat' structural plain of the decentralised international legal system,[117] which can only recognise the organisation (again, in formal terms) by closing it off from general international law as a distinct legal actor in its own right.[118]

One can easily see, therefore, how the tension between these formal and functional aspects colours the operation of universal organisations such as

[113] Though see its rather ambiguous text, and discussion of this ambiguity by, inter alia, Livoja (n 36).

[114] Brölmann (n 10) 30.

[115] ibid 32.

[116] Bederman (n 11) 371. For a more detailed extrapolation of the complex interplay of authority claims between the international, the institutional and the state, see also IF Dekker and RA Wessel, 'Governance by International Organizations: Rethinking the Normative Force of International Decisions' in IF Dekker and WG Werner (eds), *Governance and International Legal Theory* (Leiden, Martinus Nijhoff, 2004) 215–36.

[117] Nardin (n 84) 152, 162–63.

[118] Brölmann (n 10) 28–29.

the UN. It seems somewhat illogical to deny the obvious fact that in creating the UN, states did intend in many ways to re-shape the nature of the international legal order: for example, to introduce elements of hierarchy (the role of the Security Council), to create more efficient means for developing international law (for example, through ILC codification exercises and UN-sponsored conferences), as well as a general system of adjudication for the international legal order as a whole (in the ICJ). But none of this is to see UN organs as having any formal status as constitutional 'organs' of the international community overall or, indeed, to effect any structural change to the underlying formal character of international law as a legal system. The external normative influence of UN organs in shaping general international law depends either upon states' express legal commitments in the Charter itself or remains always contestable and potentially controversial (as is the case, for instance, in relation to the normative influence of General Assembly resolutions, either as evidence of customary international law or as representing a discrete 'source' in its own right).[119]

Accordingly, we can concede that Arangio-Ruiz is right in one sense: recognising that states work through institutions in this functional way does not *necessarily* alter the legal situation of the underpinning legal order. To the extent that underlying many of the purported changes outlined above are foundational legal acts, the validity of which derives from the constitutive rules of international law, the changes are still explicable, however formalistically, within the structural tenets of the decentralised international legal order. Even where institutions have taken on important roles in influencing how international law now works—again, the influence of the General Assembly on the customary law-making process is a good example—these institutional innovations, in isolation or in aggregation, are unable—without going a step further—to impact the *theoretical* ability of states to re-structure, withdraw from or negate all such commitments if the collective will is present. To put this another way, whilst international law may be generally understood as a more complex, more institutionalised form of legal order as a result of the changes and developments recounted above, of itself this realisation does not also negate the acceptance of the traditional sources thesis which underlies and gives authority to this functional situation, and which—on the terms of the previous chapter—remains a still important aspect of international law's legitimacy and acceptability overall.

This argument is not deference to legal form for form's sake, but merely to suggest that international law's underlying decentralised architecture still matters to legal participants; there is no other acceptable alternative. It would be illogical to say that states could not, if they so choose, effect a shift in the constituent rules of international law overall, or even radically

[119] For a fairly comprehensive discussion of these problems, see GJH van Hoof, *Rethinking the Sources of International Law* (Deventer, Kluwer, 1983) 180–87.

re-structure that same legal order, if the underlying will to do so is present. From a theoretical perspective, there is nothing immutable about international law's legal form in this way. My point is rather that there remain strong normative justifications for this legal form. If the rule of law has any meaningful application at the international level then it must at least require a culture of respect for the legal framework agreed between legal participants themselves.

At the same time, we can also see how Arangio-Ruiz's strict formalism causes him to miss the reality of the change that has occurred and its impact on our understanding of international 'legality' in broad terms. The functional and formal understandings of the international rule of law play off against each other, with the instrumental urge towards institutional effectiveness causing a strain from the perspective of the formal rules of the system, and the formal rules of the system seemingly limiting the attainment of communitarian goals. As such, one begins to understand more clearly the fragile balance of authority claimed by treaty-based institutions: their functionality (as opposed to constituted sovereignty) makes their claim to authority always contingent, revisable and challengeable—ultimately dependent upon the continued support of the states underlying the institution. Where organisations are deemed to be fulfilling 'governance' functions at some remove from intergovernmental control, these de facto expressions of 'public authority' cannot rely upon any a priori legitimacy. From a formal point of view, the only mediatory point of legitimacy is the intergovernmental authorisation within the rules of general international law. This creates a certain tension and strain, as the kind of functions fulfilled by many institutions seem to require a different form of legitimisation beyond the intergovernmental treaty that underpins them, thus highlighting significant accountability gaps.

To push the functional too far at the expense of the formal, then, is to potentially undermine something intrinsic to the identity and legitimacy of international organisations, as well as to strain the systemic coherence of international law to the detriment of the international rule of law. As Bianchi notes:

> It may well be true that the ever-increasing expansion and complexity of international law is credited to its maturity ... However, the very same phenomenon is likely to produce deep anxieties among international lawyers and to cause some objective difficulties in ensuring the smooth functioning of the system. Inevitably, in a highly complex normative system without any centralized authority, issues of coordination and conflict among its different components are likely to arise and their solution may not be immanent.[120]

[120] A Bianchi, 'Looking Ahead: International Law's Main Challenges' in D Armstrong (ed), *Routledge Handbook of International Law* (Abingdon, Routledge, 2009) 392, at 404.

This realisation is in fact given added support by the sense of a growing legitimacy crisis in the years following the end of the Cold War, as the increasing recognition of the phenomenon of 'global governance' through autonomous institutional structures seems to have further heightened such rule of law concerns. As I will now show in the next and final chapter, these concerns highlight that institutionalisation cannot be seen, necessarily, as resulting in greater unity, coherence or hierarchy within the international legal order, as the functional autonomy of international institutions in the plural, 'post-national' political space seem to constantly threaten disunity, incoherence and heterarchy.[121]

IV. CONCLUSION

The above reflections reveal deep theoretical and practical problems in a popular narrative that suggests that the institutionalisation of international law is inevitably pushing it towards a more centralised, or at least more authoritative, structural architecture akin to that often found at the state level. In other words, I have suggested certain problems in the idea that international law is equipping itself with institutional mechanisms of legal change, adjudication and enforcement, such as would be required to correct the widespread perception of a structural or constitutional deficiency at the core of the international legal order. This view of the effect of institutionalisation fails to take proper account of the specific legal form of international law, which is itself mirrored in the legal nature of international institutions themselves. Whilst this means that it is perfectly feasible to create demanding, more centralised and authoritative arrangements through the creation of international organisations, and whilst those institutional arrangements may well 'spill-over' to impact on the contemporary functioning of international law overall, this impact does not specifically change the structural character of the international legal system, even if it does necessarily complicate its operation. In fact, the effect of institutionalisation—as I will now go on to demonstrate—has in many ways been to create discrete sites of variegated authority and normative power that sit outside of any formal hierarchy and that, in many instances, have begun to create deep anxieties over the impact of 'global governance' activities on the overall structural coherence of international law.

[121] See, eg, M Koskenniemi, 'Global Governance and Public International Law' (2004) 37 *Kritische Justiz* 241, at 242–43; N Krisch, 'International Law in Times of Hegemony: Unequal Power and the Shaping of the International Legal Order' (2005) 16 *European Journal of International Law* 369, at 390–95.

9

International Law as Governance: An Emerging Legitimacy Crisis?

There is ... governance, but critically there is no government and no governed. It is Governance without government and without the governed.

JHH Weiler, 'The Geology of International Law'[1]

IN THE YEARS that have passed since the end of the Cold War, it is hard not to note a certain disciplinary angst emerging amongst international lawyers in response to the intensification of forms of governance activities through international organisations. After an initial wave of enthusiasm and ideological triumphalism,[2] fuelling hopes for the revitalisation of the authority of intergovernmental organisations such as the UN that were previously seen as hidebound by superpower rivalry and ideological divide,[3] much of this optimism has been increasingly called into question. The image of international organisations has suffered due to perceived ideological biases, coupled with a growing sense of legitimacy deficit, as the pervasive normative influence of global regimes seems to penetrate state sovereignty without any countervailing means of constitutional accountability.[4]

The emergence of global governance has thus resulted in increasing political contestation at both 'horizontal' (from states and between diverse international actors) and 'vertical' levels (with growing popular discontent that

[1] JHH Weiler, 'The Geology of International Law—Governance, Democracy and Legitimacy' (2004) 64 *Zeitschrift für Ausländisches Öffentliches Recht und Völkerrecht* 547, at 560.

[2] This enthusiasm was no better expressed than in Francis Fukuyama's polemical *The End of History and the Last Man* (New York: Avon Books, 1992). For the impact of this kind of rhetoric in international legal scholarship, see in particular S Marks, 'The End of History? Reflections on Some International Legal Theses' (1997) 8 *European Journal of International Law* 449.

[3] See, eg, T Franck, 'United Nations Based Prospects for a New Global Order' (1990) 22 *New York University Journal of International Law and Politics* 601.

[4] See, eg, J Klabbers 'The Changing Image of International Institutions' in J-M Coicaud and V Heiskanen (eds), *The Legitimacy of International Organizations* (Tokyo, United Nations University Press, 2001) 221–55, as well as many of the other contributions in the same volume, noting issues of accountability and perceived institutional bias.

international standard-setting and regulation is undermining fragile constitutional safeguards at the national level).[5] To give just some of the most prominent examples, one could cite the increasing cynicism at the purported universality of the free trade and economic liberalisation agendas of the World Trade Organization (WTO)[6] and International Financial Institutions (IFIs),[7] leading to calls for greater democratic representation and avenues for legal contestation;[8] concerns over the growing activism and the potential illegality of the conduct of the UN Security Council, precipitating calls for legal restraint, whether through institutional reform[9] or judicial review by the ICJ or other international courts;[10] and serious accusations of human rights abuses by UN peacekeepers,[11] and alarming reports of institutional corruption, garnering enthusiasm for enhanced forms of internal political accountability,[12] as well as external forms of legal control.[13]

Whilst my aim in this chapter is not to focus specifically on existing or emerging mechanisms of accountability and responsibility in international law, I do want to consider how the structural impact of the phenomenon of global governance is seen as impacting the structural coherence of modern international law. In particular, this growing concern is illustrative of the fact that institutionalisation is increasingly seen to contribute to, as much as alleviate, certain rule of law deficits at the international level. In particular,

[5] See JE Alvarez, 'International Organizations: Then and Now' (2006) 100 *American Journal of International Law* 324, at 341–2; and further in JE Alvarez, *International Organizations as Law-Makers* (Oxford, Oxford University Press, 2005) 630–40.

[6] This was manifest in particular in widespread popular protest, as famously populated in the so-called 'Battle in Seattle': see, eg, RM Buchanan, 'Protesting the WTO in Seattle: Transnational Citizen Action, International Law, and the Event' in F Johns, R Joyce and S Pahuja (eds), *Events: The Force of International Law* (Abingdon, Routledge, 2011) 221–33. On legitimacy concerns in general, see R Howse, 'The Legitimacy of the World Trade Organization' in Coicaud and Heiskanen (n 4) 355–407.

[7] See, eg, A Anghie, 'International Financial Institutions' in C Reus-Smit (ed), *The Politics of International Law* (Oxford, Oxford University Press, 2004) 217–37.

[8] See, eg, the discussion in E Stein, 'International Integration and Democracy: No Love at First Sight' (2001) 95 *American Journal of International Law* 489.

[9] See the useful summary of reform proposals and the debate surrounding them in B Fassbender, 'Pressure for Security Council Reform' in D Malone (ed), *The UN Security Council: From the Cold War to the 21st Century* (Boulder, CO, Lynne Rienner, 2004) 341–71.

[10] The literature in this area is voluminous, but see particularly on review and limitations to the Security Council's powers: A Orakhelashvili, 'The Impact of Peremptory Norms on Interpretation and Application of the UN Security Council Resolutions' (2005) 16 *European Journal of International Law* 59; E de Wet, *The Chapter VII Powers of the United Nations Security Council* (Oxford, Hart Publishing, 2004).

[11] See, eg, AJ Millar, 'Legal Aspects of Stopping Sexual Exploitation and Abuse in U.N. Peacekeeping Operations' (2006) 39 *Cornell International Law Journal* 71.

[12] J Wouters, N Hachez and P Schmitt, 'Managerial Accountability: What Impact on International Organizations' Autonomy?' in R Collins and ND White (eds), *International Organizations and the Idea of Autonomy: Institutional Independence in the International Legal Order* (Abingdon, Routledge, 2011) 230–56.

[13] See J Klabbers, 'Autonomy, Constitutionalism and Virtue in International Institutional Law' in Collins and White (n 12) 120, at 127–30.

two discrete but related anxieties have begun to preoccupy international lawyers. On the one hand, insofar as these different regimes and institutions are seen to develop a range of normative instruments, standards and forms of policy influence which fall outside of the recognised sources of international law, the rule of law seems compromised by the apparent *deformalisation* of international law. On the other hand, where such regimes and institutions *do* apply, interpret or enforce formal legal rules, the worry is rather that the structural bias of each may well contribute to the apparent *fragmentation* of international law, thereby undermining its overall systemic coherence. Taken together, these more 'postmodern' anxieties reveal a growing ambivalence as to the perceived benefits of institutionalisation: the international rule of law seems to necessitate the development of autonomous institutional structures to overcome or alleviate the perceived inefficiencies and externalities of a decentralised legal order and secure agreed-upon legal objectives, but the more autonomous and effective such regimes and institutions become, the more they appear threatening to that very same ideal.

In this final chapter, I will argue that this tension is not only inevitable, but may even be desirable and important in giving effect to some degree of accountability within the procedural parameters of the international legal order. Specifically, I will claim that far from signalling some kind of aberration or deviation from the norm, fragmentation and deformalisation should be seen as the inevitable result of the push for institutional effectiveness within a decentralised legal order. This is not to suggest that the identified legitimacy and accountability deficits are of no concern, but only that the formal, open, decentralised framework of international law still remains an important legitimacy and accountability restraint in this regard. In particular, the retention of the formal-informal binary opposition ensures that when global governance actors make claims to authority or normative influence, we are left to evaluate these claims on their own terms, without giving them any a priori legitimacy they may well not deserve.

I will return to explain this rationale more clearly towards the end of the chapter. Before I do so, however, the rest of the chapter is structured as follows. I will first of all illustrate the impact of institutionalisation through the twin optics of *fragmentation* and *deformalisation*. I describe each concern in detail in section I, noting how both can be seen as distinct products of the push for institutional autonomy outlined in the previous chapter. Next, in section II, I turn to consider how these distinctive concerns are illustrative of a broader legitimacy crisis in contemporary international law. I frame this apparent crisis by reference to the tension inherent within the ideal of an international rule of law, as outlined in Chapter 7, insofar as it appears to simultaneously pull in opposing formalist and functionalist directions: on the one hand, measuring the legitimacy of international law *substantively* by reference to its ability to reach beyond its inter-state framework to more effectively realise agreed-upon objectives; and, on the other hand, measuring legitimacy *procedurally* by insisting on the need to play by the rules of this same inter-state system. For this reason, in section III, I highlight a number of difficulties in much of the recent disciplinary response to this emerging legitimacy crisis, insofar as it appears to advocate the need to take a distinctly less formal approach to the question of international 'legality' in its broadest sense. Specifically, I show how the crisis has prompted a number of lawyers to argue for a more evaluative legality standard inspired by certain public law principles and practices. In response, however, I argue that by side-stepping the issue of formal source-based legal validity and attempting to introduce a more evaluative legitimacy standard, such perspectives miss the way in which such determinations are merely left to inter-subjective assessment, thus allowing political actors to legitimise potentially illegitimate conduct. In other words, these perspectives ignore the unavoidable structural indeterminacy in international law. By attempting to impose a framework of legality and legitimacy derived from a very different institutional form, such idealisations tend only to distort rather than clarify our understanding of the complex interplay of political forces apparent in the increasingly institutionalised, yet perennially decentralised international legal order. Accordingly, I conclude by stressing the residual importance of this legal form as a necessary foundation for modern international law, leaving open a space for legal accountability by resisting its own instrumentalisation towards any apparently universal purpose or end.

I. POSTMODERN ANXIETIES: THE DEFORMALISATION AND FRAGMENTATION OF INTERNATIONAL LAW

Within a decade or so of the fall of the Berlin Wall, in the infancy of a post-Cold War world, much of the enthusiasm surrounding an increasingly institutionalised international legal order had already begun to seem somewhat naïve and utopian. Whilst an array of autonomous institutions and regimes had come to be increasingly effective 'law-makers' and regulators, often with a significant impact at the state level, this normative influence had come at the price of an apparent gap in any countervailing means of accountability or democratic scrutiny.[14] Whilst concerns were initially voiced more

[14] The literature in this area is vast, encompassing political perspectives on globalisation and global governance, and more legal literature suggesting strains in the theoretical coherence of international law. From the political side, see most explicitly A Buchanan and RO Keohane, 'The Legitimacy of Global Governance Institutions' (2006) 20 *Ethics and International Affairs* 405; for a penetrating legal critique, see Weiler (n 1). For an overview of legitimacy concerns, see also the useful summary of literature included in Alvarez, 'International Organizations: Then and Now' (n 5) 342–47. This concern also appears to have prompted a great number of inter-disciplinary studies: see, eg, the contributions to R Wolfrum and V Röben (eds), *Legitimacy in International Law* (New York, Springer, 2008), as well as Coicaud and Heiskanen (n 4).

in the political than the legal literature—the ideas of 'governance without government'[15] and 'new medievalism'[16] becoming popular leitmotifs in international relations literature from the mid-1990s onwards—by the end of that decade, international legal scholars had begun to take the phenomenon of globalisation and its impact on international law much more seriously.[17] In other words, it had soon become apparent that international law's institutionalisation had failed to secure the rule of law in terms of greater accountability and systemic coherence, and had instead resulted in an increasingly fragmented and kaleidoscopic 'disorder of normative orders'.[18]

As such, the kind of functional authority exercised by global institutions is increasingly seen in a more qualified light. Rather than enhancing the systemic coherence and effectiveness of international law in holding powerful actors to account, there has instead emerged a rather complex, fragmented regulatory landscape, the normative impact of which is very difficult to square with the formal doctrines of international law.[19] As Paulus claims,

> Today, this institutionalist reading of international law has fallen prey, in a certain regard, to its own success. While an increasing institutionalization and organisation of [international law] ... can hardly be doubted, the general impression is one of fragmentation rather than constitutionalization of the international legal system. In other words, the diverse and divergent institutions fail to come under a single scheme; rather, the systemic character of international law seems threatened by a multiplicity of international régimes without obvious coherence.[20]

[15] See, eg, JN Rosenau, 'Governance, Order, and Change in World Politics' in JN Rosenau and E-O Czempiel (eds), *Governance without Government: Order and Change in World Politics* (Cambridge, Cambridge University Press, 1992) 1–29, as well as the individual contributions that follow. On the globalisation debate generally, see P Hirst and G Thompson, *Globalization in Question*, 2nd edn (Cambridge, Polity Press, 2000); and D Held and A McGrew (eds), *The Global Transformation Reader: An Introduction to the Globalization Debate*, 2nd edn (Cambridge, Polity Press, 2003).

[16] For an overview, see J Friedrichs, 'The Meaning of New Medievalism' (2001) 4 *European Journal of International Relations* 475.

[17] For an early and critical response, see P Alston, 'The Myopia of the Handmaidens: International Lawyers and Globalization' (1997) 8 *European Journal of International Law* 435; followed by A von Bogdandy, 'Globalization and Europe: How to Square Democracy, Globalization, and International Law' (2004) 15 *European Journal of International Law* 885; and Weiler (n 1).

[18] N Walker, 'Beyond Boundary Disputes and Basic Grids: Mapping the Global Disorder of Normative Orders' (2008) 3 *International Journal of Constitutional Law* 373.

[19] I comment on this more directly in R Collins, 'Mapping the Terrain of Institutional "Lawmaking": Form and Function in International Law' in E Fahey (ed), *The Actors of Postnational Rule-Making: Contemporary Challenges of European and International Law* (Abingdon, Routledge, 2015) 27–46. See also M Koskenniemi, 'Constitutionalism as Mindset: Reflections on Kantian Themes about International Law and Globalization' (2007) 8 *Theoretical Inquiries in Law* 9, at 12–13; and M Koskenniemi and P Leino, 'Fragmentation of International Law? Postmodern Anxieties' (2002) 15 *Leiden Journal of International Law* 553, at 558–60.

[20] A Paulus, 'The International Legal System as a Constitution' in JL Dunoff and JP Trachtman (eds), *Ruling the World? Constitutionalism, International Law, and Global Governance* (Cambridge, Cambridge University Press, 2009) 69, at 69–70.

Bearing in mind the structural condition of international organisations explained in the previous chapter, however, it is perhaps unsurprising that such anxieties should arise. The push for effectiveness has precipitated the development of a number of institutional fora for the management of contemporary global problems, which in their institutional structure can be seen to overcome many of the perceived limitations and inefficiencies of the decentralised and customary international legal order. However, insofar as the normative effects—or 'ripples'[21]—of these regimes are not entirely self-contained, the impact of institutionalisation on international law overall is a complicating one: the normative influence of autonomous institutional actors does not so much restructure international law as sit in an acute tension with its underlying legal form. As noted towards the end of the last chapter, in particular, where institutional autonomy manifests itself, it does so internally in terms of a dynamic of competing authority claims between the member states and the institution, but in international law overall, this autonomy cannot translate into any kind of formal hierarchy or relationship of constitutional subordination.[22] Rather, organisations exist as separate legal actors, on the same flat 'Westphalian' plain as states—a situation of structural heterarchy as opposed to hierarchy.[23]

This realisation, then, gives rise to two specific anxieties. First, insofar as the normative influence of international institutions seems increasingly difficult to square with the formal doctrines of international law, particularly the doctrine of sources, one sees increasing anxiety as to the apparent *deformalisation* of contemporary international law.[24] Second, and relatedly, these discrete sites of uncoordinated normative authority precipitate concern over the apparent *fragmentation* of international law, undermining its overall systemic coherence.[25] In many respects, these 'postmodern anxieties' are inter-related and overlap, but it is worth dealing with each in turn to give a clearer picture of how they seem threatening to the kind of rule of law idealism that propels contemporary international legal discourse.

Deformalisation can be understood as an inevitable reaction to the perceived institutional problem outlined so far. The rule of law ambition to

[21] Alvarez, *International Organizations as Law-Makers* (n 5) 122–45.

[22] See Ch 8, section III above; and on this point in particular, see G Arangio-Ruiz, *The UN Declaration on Friendly Relations and the System of the Sources of International Law* (Alphen aan den Rijn, Sijthoff & Noordhoff, 1979) 249–52.

[23] See, eg, D Pulkowski, 'Structural Paradigms of International Law' in T Broude and Y Shany (eds), *The Shifting Allocation of Authority in International Law: Considering Sovereignty, Supremacy and Subsidiarity* (Oxford, Hart Publishing, 2008) 51, at 72–76.

[24] J d'Aspremont, *Formalism and the Sources of International Law: A Theory of the Ascertainment of Legal Rules* (Oxford, Oxford University Press, 2011) 2–3 and passim.

[25] Koskenniemi and Leino (n 19); and see further Koskenniemi (n 19) 13. See also M Koskenniemi, 'Global Governance and Public International Law' (2004) 37 *Kritische Justiz* 241, at 242–43; and M Prost, *The Concept of Unity in Public International Law* (Oxford, Hart Publishing, 2012) 4–8 and passim.

secure order through the normative restraint of formal legal rules is seen to be frustrated by the decentralised institutional structure of the international legal order—its *structural indeterminacy*. Accordingly, the desire to find institutional solutions to complex normative problems has increasingly led to the creation of innovative institutional solutions rather than concrete legal obligations; that is, by seeking solutions in more informal, management arrangements or compliance mechanisms, or delegating authority to institutional decision-makers.[26] In short, deformalisation can be understood as a move towards 'procedures or broadly formulated directives to experts and decision-makers for the purpose of administering international problems by means of functionally effective solutions and "balancing interests"'.[27]

The phenomenon of deformalisation is therefore closely related to the recognition of so-called 'soft law',[28] which in its broadest sense implies a situation where 'legal arrangements are weakened along one or more of the dimensions of obligation, precision, and delegation'.[29] In situations of protracted conflict, the choice may be between a binding, but nonetheless vague and indeterminate, legal norm (a form of 'soft *negotium*') or a non-binding form of instrument which is, however, more definitively prescriptive or proscriptive as the need arises (a form of 'soft *instrumentum*').[30] The two forms of soft normativity tend to lead into one another: in order to garner agreement, legal standards are often watered down to a framework commitment—what Tom Franck might have called 'sophist' as opposed to 'idiot' rules[31]—which then allows solutions to common problems to be managed or negotiated further through regimes and agency relationships in the context of intergovernmental organisations.[32] As Franck himself puts it: 'While an idiot rule more-or-less applies itself, sophist rules usually require an effective, credible, institutionalized, and legitimate interpreter of the rule's meaning in various instances.'[33] However, owing to the structural condition of international law, the normative output of the particular

[26] M Koskenniemi, 'The Fate of Public International Law: Between Technique and Politics' (2007) 70 *Modern Law Review* 1, at 9–10.

[27] Koskenniemi (n 19) 13.

[28] See generally d'Aspremont (n 24) 1–8, 118–36.

[29] KW Abbott and D Snidal, 'Hard and Soft Law in International Governance' (2000) 54 *International Organization* 421, at 422. For a critique of this idea, see both J Klabbers, 'The Redundancy of Soft Law' (1996) 65 *Nordic Journal of International Law* 167 and J d'Aspremont, 'Softness in International Law: A Self-Serving Quest for New Legal Materials' (2008) 19 *European Journal of International Law* 1075.

[30] D'Aspremont (n 29) 1081–87.

[31] TM Franck, *The Power of Legitimacy among Nations* (Oxford, Oxford University Press, 1990) 67–90.

[32] Abbott and Snidal (n 29) 430–31.

[33] Franck (n 31) 81.

regime or institution—whether in the form of decisions, standards or other instruments—will inevitably fall outside of the formal sources of international law, even though it often exerts a strong normative compliance pull.[34] As Christine Chinkin puts it:

> The complexity of international legal affairs has outpaced traditional methods of law-making, necessitating management through international organizations, specialized agencies, programmes, and private bodies that do not fit the paradigm of Article 38(1) of the Statute of the ICJ. Consequently the concept of soft law facilitates international co-operation by acting as a bridge between the formalities of law-making and the needs of international life by legitimating behaviour and creating stability.[35]

To recognise this institutional problem-solving as a concern is not necessarily to ignore certain benefits of institutionalisation, a phenomenon which has in many ways secured new means of socialisation and common action in situations where simple treaty targets and obligations might otherwise be divisive.[36] However, when combined with the kind of push for effectiveness which emerged in the post-Cold War era, institutionalisation has a tendency to result in a kind of Weberian bureaucratisation:[37] an urge to depoliticise otherwise contentious issues, whilst at the same time masking over the particular politics and pathologies of institutions themselves.[38] This—what Martti Koskenniemi refers to as a 'managerial mindset'[39] and Joseph Weiler as a 'practice management' approach[40]—provides a rationalisation for the exercise of quite significant power at some remove from traditional intergovernmental decision-making and has a particularly coercive effect

[34] The most comprehensive study in this respect is Alvarez (n 5), though see also IF Dekker and RA Wessel, 'Governance by International Organisations: Rethinking the Source and Normative Force of International Decisions' in IF Dekker and WG Werner (eds), *Governance and International Legal Theory* (Leiden, Martinus Nijhoff, 2004) 215–36. This form of soft governance is particularly evident in the field of environmental law: see, eg, R Churchill and G Ulfstein, 'Autonomous Institutional Arrangements in Multilateral Environmental Agreements: A Little-Noticed Phenomenon in International Law' (2000) 94 *American Journal of International Law* 623; D French, 'Autonomy in International Environmental Law and Governance: A Case Study of the Actual (Somewhere between the Fable and the Threat)' in Collins and White (n 12) 366–79.

[35] C Chinkin, 'Normative Development in the International Legal System' in D Shelton (ed), *Commitment and Compliance: The Role of Non-binding Norms in the International Legal System* (Oxford, Oxford University Press, 2003) 21, at 42.

[36] M Koskenniemi, 'International Legislation Today: Limits and Possibilities' (2005) 23 *Wisconsin International Law Journal* 61, at 80.

[37] See, eg, M Weber, *Theory of Social and Economic Organization* (New York, Oxford University Press, 1947).

[38] M Barnett and M Finnemore, 'The Politics, Power, and Pathologies of International Organizations' (1999) 53 *International Organization* 699.

[39] Koskenniemi (n 19) 13–14; Koskenniemi (n 26) 14.

[40] Weiler (n 1) 550 and 557.

within many states, often those whose economic and political independence depends on continued engagement with such institutions.[41] As Koskenniemi describes it:

> [T]he new developments in the law did not point to unity. The more powerfully [particular regimes or institutions] dealt with international problems ... the more they began to challenge old principles and institutions. Specializations such as 'trade law', 'human rights law' ... 'security law' ... and so on started to reverse established legal hierarchies in favour of the structural bias in the relevant functional expertise. Even though this process was often organised through intergovernmental organisations, the governmental delegations were composed of technical (economic, environmental, legal) experts in a way that transposed the functional differentiation at the national level onto the international plane. Moreover, the resulting regimes have often been formulated in an open-ended manner, leaving power to decide ... to the legal and technical experts appointed to the supervisory organs.[42]

This concern is most obvious where international authority claims direct superiority over national constitutional structures: for instance, in recent anti-terror measures approved by the UN Security Council[43] or the UN's broader involvement in post-conflict territorial administration, where international standards effectively replace local ones, yet international actors remain largely unaccountable at this level.[44] Nevertheless, the concern also relates to more indirect standard-setting and regulatory authority, particularly in bodies such as the WTO,[45] to the economic development policies of the IFIs,[46] the effects of 'soft' governance, through the determinations of bodies such as the World Health Organization (WHO),[47] more informal processes[48] or, indeed, the phenomenon of transnational

[41] ibid 557–58.

[42] Koskenniemi (n 26) 4.

[43] A Bianchi, 'Assessing the Effectiveness of the UN Security Council's Anti-terrorism Measures: The Quest for Legitimacy and Cohesion' (2007) 17 *European Journal of International Law* 881.

[44] See, eg, Ch 8 of B Knoll, *The Legal Status of Territories Subject to Administration by International Organizations* (Cambridge, Cambridge University Press, 2008) 326–403.

[45] For one of the most studied assessments of the legitimacy deficit in WTO rule-making, see A von Bogdandy, 'Law and Politics in the WTO: Strategies to Cope with a Deficient Relationship' (2001) 5 *Max Planck Yearbook of United Nations Law* 609.

[46] For a particularly pointed critique in this respect, see A Orford, 'Locating the International: Military and Monetary Interventions after the Cold War' (1997) 38 *Harvard International Law Journal* 443.

[47] See, eg, B Reinalda and B Verbeek, 'Policy Autonomy of Intergovernmental Organizations' in Collins and White (n 12) 87, at 87–88.

[48] For a good example, see A von Bogdandy and M Goldmann, 'The Exercise of International Public Authority through National Policy Assessments: The OECD's PISA Policy as a Paradigm for a New Standard Instrument' (2008) 5 *International Organizations Law Review* 241.

'government networks',[49] all of which impact at the domestic level in a way which often pre-determines, re-orients or otherwise influences national policy-making.

As such, the second concern, *fragmentation*, can be perceived in many ways as the structural effect of deformalisation: 'the splitting of law into functionally defined "regimes" ... each geared to further particular types of interests and managed by narrowly defined expert competence'.[50] In other words, the push for effectiveness means that problems tend to be defined narrowly in order to secure the possibility of greater autonomy of decision-making, for example, in the areas of trade, human rights, the environment etc.[51] Accordingly, in order to move beyond the limiting constraints of a decentralised legal order, specific regimes or institutions incorporate structures and management solutions that may depart substantially from the formal rules of international law. This has the effect of potentially bringing a particular institution or regime into conflict with others due to the specialised nature of its focus or, indeed, the particular structural means of realising this interest.[52]

This concern has arisen in particular in terms of a particular preoccupation with the phenomenon of 'forum shopping', which is perceived as a particular risk to the overall systemic coherence of international law.[53] It was this particular threat to international law's unity that caused the International Law Commission (ILC) to appoint a recent study group to address the systemic impact of regime fragmentation.[54] Forum shopping arises as a distinct concern primarily because international problems do not present themselves as isolated specialisations which can be managed by the most appropriate body; more often, the same problem can be looked at from a

[49] See, eg, A-M Slaughter, *A New World Order* (Princeton, NJ, Princeton University Press, 2004) 12–15 and passim.

[50] Koskenniemi (n 19) 13.

[51] As Abbott and Snidal (n 29) 443 put it: 'Effective institutions ... require a certain autonomy that states may be reluctant to grant over truly important issues.' See further A Paulus, 'From Territoriality to Functionality? Towards a Legal Methodology of Globalization' in Dekker and Werner (n 34) 59, at 75.

[52] Koskenniemi and Leino (n 19) 559.

[53] ibid, passim; and for a useful critical overview of the debates, see M Prost and PK Clark, 'Unity, Diversity and the Fragmentation of International Law' (2004) 5 *Chinese Journal of International Law* 341. Much of the concern has related to the potential for normative clashes, though others have stressed the potential for institutional overlap and other jurisdictional issues: see, eg, NM Blokker and HG Schermers, 'Proliferation of International Organizations: An Exploratory Introduction' in NM Blokker and HG Schermers (eds), *Proliferation of International Organizations: Legal Issues* (The Hague, Kluwer Law International, 2001) 1–50. For a consideration of the relationship between the two elements of fragmentation, see T Broude, 'Fragmentation(s) of International Law: On Normative Integration as Authority Allocation' in Broude and Shany (n 23) 99–120.

[54] G Hafner, *Risks Ensuing from the Fragmentation of International Law*, in International Law Commission, 'Report of the Working Group on Long-term Programme of Work', ILC (LII)/WG/LT/L.1/Add. 1 (25 July 2000).

number of different perspectives, resulting in different conclusions being reached accordingly.[55] For instance, when the Security Council considers issues of security, these inevitably involve matters which affect, inter alia, human rights;[56] when WTO dispute settlement panels decide upon the validity of specific exceptions to free trade rules, they inevitably must consider conflicts between WTO law and other international rules and principles, such as environmental law or standards of public health.[57]

Of course, there are systemic rules—for instance, conflicts of norms principles such as *lex superior*, *lex posterior* or indeed substantive normative hierarchies with the development of peremptory norms of international law[58]—which allow for the resolution of disputes in the abstract.[59] However, the problem—as we saw in Chapter 3—is not the absence of any possible solution in the abstract; as always, it is more structural. For instance, to the extent that the WTO Dispute Settlement Body is empowered to consider general international law in giving answers to trade disputes, it has to give its own interpretation of that law—that is, whether it has effect, whether it applies to the dispute in question and so on. This is particularly evident in cases like the *Beef Hormones* dispute between the EU and the US, where the Appellate Body of the WTO considered that the precautionary principle developing in international environmental law had no direct legal effect in the dispute at hand.[60] In such cases, the problem is not merely applying the *lex specialis*, but the way in which the dispute is characterised in line with the structural bias of the institution itself.[61]

This structural bias thus has a distorting effect which inevitably sees organisations, regimes or other institutional actors prioritise the immediate

[55] As Dunoff and Trachtman express it: 'specialized law making, institution building, and dispute resolution in any particular field tend to be relatively insulated from developments in adjoining fields, risking inconsistent judgments, conflicting jurisprudence, and outcomes that fail to take sufficient account of the full range of relevant values'. JL Dunoff and JP Trachtman, 'A Functional Approach to International Constitutionalization' in Dunoff and Trachtman (n 20) 3, at 6.

[56] See further below in section III.

[57] Koskenniemi and Leino (n 19) 571–74.

[58] See generally International Law Commission, 'Fragmentation Of International Law: Difficulties Arising from the Diversification and Expansion of International Law: Report of the Study Group of the International Law Commission, Finalized by M Koskenniemi', UN Doc A/CN.4/L.682, 13 April 2006, available at: http://legal.un.org/ilc/documentation/english/a_cn4_l682.pdf.

[59] Though even in the abstract, key issues remain uncertain: for instance, the lack of a clear hierarchy between customary international law and the law of treaties. See, eg, recently JJ Bia, 'The Relations between Treaties and Custom' (2010) 9 *Chinese Journal of International Law* 81, particularly at 84–86.

[60] *European Communities—Measures Concerning Meat and Meat Products (Hormones)*, 13 February 1998, WT/DS26/AB/R (13 February 1998), at paras 123–25.

[61] This is particularly evident in the three institutions which heard the *MOX Plant* dispute: the OSPAR Arbitral Tribunal, the International Tribunal for the Law of the Sea, and the European Court of Justice. For discussion, see N Lavranos, 'The *MOX Plant* and *IJzeren Rijn* Disputes: Which Court is the Supreme Arbiter?' (2006) 19 *Leiden Journal of International Law* 223; PJ Cardwell and D French, 'Who Decides? The ECJ's Judgment on Jurisdiction in the MOX Plant Dispute' (2007) 19 *Journal of Environmental Law* 121.

institutional context over the coherence of international law overall.[62] As Paulus claims:

> By dealing with a clearly limited issue area, these institutions may develop a highly sophisticated jurisprudence. However, specialized judicial bodies have difficulty in balancing the values embodied in their statute with the values embodied in other institutions. This creates the danger of overreaching and of a biased approach to questions of clashes between different values and issue areas. Ultimately, the unity of international law seems to be at stake.[63]

The issue of structural bias is not necessarily a problem per se; indeed, we might just see it as a natural consequence of institutionalisation in a decentralised legal order. However, it appears as a particular concern insofar as the bias is seen to reflect already dominant political interests:[64] for instance, the ascendency of the permanent five members of the Security Council or the de facto veto enjoyed by the US in the international financial institutions.[65] The example of the development of the International Criminal Court gives stark focus to this perception: the US remains outside the institution, yet can use its privileged position in the Council to avoid the Court's authority,[66] whilst at the same time using the Court as a tool through which to tackle international security concerns.[67] In the absence of any truly independent and international authority, therefore, the threat of neo-imperial domination and instrumentalisation of global institutions looms large. Furthermore, the effect of this structural bias tends to be particularly marked insofar as the

[62] Koskenniemi (n 26) 5–8; Koskenniemi and Leino (n 19) 574–79. On the idea of structural bias as inherent in the idea of governance in a decentralised legal order, see M Koskenniemi, *From Apology to Utopia: The Structure of International Legal Argument* (Cambridge, Cambridge University Press, 2005) 600–15.

[63] Paulus (n 51) 75.

[64] For critical reflections on the pathologies of administrative bureaucracy delivered through international institutions, see, inter alia, from a political science perspective M Barnett and M Finnemore, *Rules for the World: International Organizations in Global Politics* (Ithaca, Cornell University Press, 2004); and from a more legal perspective Anghie (n 7). For a more left-leaning, critical concern for ideological bias, see, eg, BS Chimni, 'International Institutions Today: An Imperial Global State in the Making' (2004) 15 *European Journal of International Law* 1.

[65] On this point, see in particular N Krisch, 'International Law in Times of Hegemony: Unequal Power and the Shaping of the International Legal Order' (2005) 16 *European Journal of International Law* 369, at 398–99.

[66] SC Res 1422 of 12 July 2002. For discussion, see also R Cryer and ND White, 'The International Criminal Court and the Security Council: An Uncomfortable Relationship' in J Doria, H-P Gasser and M-C Bassiouni (eds), *The Legal Regime of the International Criminal Court: Essays in Memory of Igor Blishchenko* (Leiden, Martinus Nijhoff, 2009) 455–84; M Weller, 'Undoing the Global Constitution: UN Security Council Action on the International Criminal Court' (2002) 78 *International Affairs* 693; N Jain, 'A Separate Law for Peacekeepers: The Clash between the Security Council and the International Criminal Court' (2005) 16 *European Journal of International Law* 239.

[67] Although the power of referral has been open to the Council for some time (under art 13(b) of the Rome Statute), the first such referral occurred relatively recently in relation to the situation in Libya under SC Res 1970 of 26 February 2011.

normative influence of powerful global institutions tends to impact more upon those states in a de facto position of dependence upon the institution.[68]

Unsurprisingly, the accumulation of these kinds of anxieties has only further exacerbated existing concerns over institutional accountability and responsibility.[69] To the extent that such concerns have led to welcome institutional reforms and the introduction of oversight mechanisms within particular organisations,[70] and to a growing concern over issues of legal responsibility in international law overall,[71] they are to be particularly welcomed. Nevertheless, trying to conceive of accountability and responsibility at the broadest level is problematic precisely because it is far from clear, first of all, that much of this post-national, or post-Westphalian, normative influence fits neatly into a formal legality-illegality binary and, second, whether there is any available institutional means to hold many of these actors to account in more practical terms. Nevertheless, pursuing these specific questions here goes beyond the immediate scope of my enquiry. Rather, what I am concerned with is how this phenomenon impacts on our understanding of the international legal system. It is to this question that I now turn my attention.

II. INTERNATIONAL LAW AS 'GOVERNANCE'?

The perceived threat of deformalisation and fragmentation seems to confirm the rather fractured, or even schizophrenic, understanding of an international rule of law outlined towards the end of Chapter 7 in particular.[72]

[68] See, eg, Chimni (n 64).

[69] It is hardly a coincidence that at the turn of the new millennium, the International Law Association established a study group on the accountability of international organisations (see, eg, International Law Association, 'Accountability of International Organisations' (Final Report of Committee on Accountability of International Organizations, Berlin Conference, 2004), available at: www.ila-hq.org/download.cfm/docid/6B708C25–4D6D–42E2–8385DADA752815E8) or that the International Law Commission began to address the topic of the responsibility of international organizations in 2001 (see most recently 'Report of the International Law Commission on the Work of its Sixty-First Session, 4 May to 5 June and 6 July to 7 August 2009', UN Doc A/64/10, 2009, Ch IV, paras 31–51, available at: http://legal.un.org/ilc/documentation/english/reports/a_64_10.pdf). It was also at the turn of the millennium that collections of essays on both the proliferation (see Blokker and Schermers (eds) (n 53)) and the legitimacy of intergovernmental organisations (Coicaud and Heiskanen (n 4)) appeared for the first time. The literature in this area has grown considerably since; see, eg, K Wellens, *Remedies against International Organizations* (Cambridge, Cambridge University Press, 2002); as well as the contributions to C de Cooker (ed), *Accountability, Investigation and Due Process in International Organizations* (Leiden, Martinus Nijhoff, 2005) and J Wouters, E Brems, S Smis and P Schmitt (eds), *Accountability for Human Rights Violations by International Organisations* (Cambridge, Intersentia, 2010).

[70] See, eg, recently the discussion in Wouters, Hachez and Schmitt (n 12).

[71] See M Hirsch, *Responsibility of International Organizations Towards Third Parties: Some Basic Principles* (Dordrecht, Martinus Nijhoff, 1995).

[72] M Koskenniemi, 'What is International Law for?' in M Evans (ed), *International Law*, 4th edn (Oxford, Oxford University Press, 2014) 29, at 39–42.

On the one hand, institutionalisation is seen as necessary to remedy the perceived weaknesses or deficiencies of a decentralised international legal order, to restrain arbitrary political power and therefore achieve agreed-upon global objectives. On the other hand, the more 'effective' this institutionalisation has become, the more the rule of law appears threatened by the perceived weakening or circumventing of the formal structure of the international legal system.[73] This ambivalence surrounding the phenomenon of global governance is thus helpful in better framing the stakes of a perceived legitimacy crisis, which appears constantly to threaten or undermine the coherence of international law in the contemporary era.

With this frame in mind, then, we must move beyond overly simplistic, teleological explanations of international law's structural change, which tend to overemphasise hierarchy or centralisation, and instead focus upon the more fragmented, layered complexity of what we might still understand as 'post-Westphalian' international law. For instance, Joseph Weiler has suggested that a more plausible understanding of contemporary international law would try to capture its 'geological layering', a metaphor that goes some way towards unearthing many of the growing strains and tensions recounted above. This notion of layering is revealing for, as Weiler puts it himself: 'History emphasizes change; geology emphasizes accretion.'[74] According to this approach, the development of the international legal order now sees a thickening 'regulatory' or 'governance' layer (developed through complex institutional regimes) atop a 'communitarian' (that is, constitutional and legislative) layer, itself atop an original base of Westphalian ('transactional') international law. However, none of these layers displaces the other:

> Change … would not be adequately described as a shift from, say, bilateralism to multilateralism. What had changed was the stratification. Bilateralism persists and even thrives as an important stratum of international law throughout the century till this day. Thus, geology allows us to speak not so much about transformations but of layering, of change which is part of continuity, of new strata which do not replace earlier ones, but simply layer themselves alongside.[75]

According to Weiler, this layering has thus not so much transformed the nature of the law as complicated it, giving rise to tensions within and between the layers on the basis of the ever more expansive normative and institutional demands placed on the international legal order overall. For example, he notes that the 'communitarian' layer is distinct from classic transactionalism not only because of the kinds of interests it aims to protect,

[73] We can, in some ways, relate this to what Slaughter labels the 'globalization paradox', ie, the increasing need for, yet growing fear of, international governance. See Slaughter (n 49) 8.

[74] Weiler (n 1) 549.

[75] ibid 551.

but also because most community interests—whether conceived in terms of human rights, trade, development etc—tend to be negotiated on a 'take it or leave it' basis, with the institutional arrangements that follow also often departing from the formal 'secondary rules' of international treaty law (for example, in the case of specific provisions on reservations to human rights regimes).[76] This problem is intensified by the realisation that withdrawal from many organisations is simply not an option. As José Alvarez notes, for most states, participation in organisations is as much about guaranteeing as it is restricting or limiting their sovereignty—a clear sign of 'the very success of the Grotian consensus that led to their establishment, proliferation, and growing legal clout'.[77]

As such, Weiler sees it as somewhat of a fiction to understand many of these norms as expressly adopted through, or given continued legitimisation on the basis of, state consent.[78] At the same time, however, he argues that neither can these structures be legitimised in any direct, participatory way: the individuals, or groups of individuals, are the ultimate addressees of the purported values, but remain objects of regulation rather than the embodiment of legislative will. Thus, in line with the argument developed in the previous chapter, it seems that the 'deep structure' underlying the protection of communitarian interests seems to sit uneasily with the substance of the interests themselves. Weiler gives the example of the regulation of international human rights law to illustrate this point:

> The surface language of international legal rights discourse may be neo-Kantian. Its deep structure is utterly pre-modern. It is a rights notion that resembles the Roman Empire which regards individuals as an object on which to bestow

[76] ibid 557–58. This concern arises in particular from the jurisprudence of the European Court of Human Rights, which has attempted to construct the Convention as an 'objective' regime by departing from the standard treaty rules on the basis of the special nature of the Convention and the particular 'constitutional' position of the Court. See in particular *Belilos v Switzerland*, Decision of 29 April 1988, 1988 ECHR, Series A, No 132 and *Loizidou v Turkey*, Preliminary Objections, 23 March 1995, 1995 ECHR, Series A, No 310, in both of which the Court rejected the validity of reservations entered into by the respondent countries. The UN Human Rights Committee has made a similar observation with regard to reservations to the International Covenant on Civil and Political Rights. See General Comment No 24: 'Issues relating to reservations made upon ratification or accession to the Covenant or the Optional Protocols thereto, or in relation to declarations under article 41 of the Covenant', 4 November 1994, in CCPR/C/21/Rev.1/Add.6, available at: http://tbinternet.ohchr.org/_layouts/treatybodyexternal/Download.aspx?symbolno=CCPR%2FC%2F21%2FRev.1%2FAdd.6&Lang=en. However, note that this position has been rejected by, inter alia, the UK and the US. See Report of the Human Rights Committee, UN Doc A/50/40 (1995), Annex VI, available at: www.un.org/documents/ga/docs/50/plenary/a50-40.htm.

[77] Alvarez, 'International Organizations: Then and Now' (n 5) 343.

[78] See also in this respect R Wolfrum, 'Legitimacy of International Law from a Legal Perspective: Some Introductory Considerations' in Wolfrum and Röben (n 14) 1, at 10–19.

> or recognize rights, not as agents from whom emanates the power to do such bestowing. It is a vision of the individual as an object or, at best, as a consumer of outcomes, but not as an agent of process ... The individual in international law seen, structurally, only as an object of rights but not as the source of authority, is not different from women in the pre-emancipation societies, or indeed of slaves in Roman times whose rights were recognized—at the grace of others.[79]

On the one hand, therefore, this kind of protection of rights appears to undermine them to some degree; it reveals itself as inadequate as a means of securing the kinds of interests it seeks to protect. On the other hand, it also runs the risk of undermining the values underpinning the rights where their 'enforcement' through multilateral action occurs. In fact, in line with the analysis of the previous section, one can easily see how rights become instrumentalised simply as triggers for managing problems, for example, through military intervention,[80] or as a form of conditionality in economic governance,[81] as rights holders themselves become side-lined in the ensuing governance arrangements.[82]

More troubling still, however, is the idea of governance through Weiler's 'regulatory' layer. The effect of this form of global governance may in fact be very direct, where international norms essentially replace domestic norms as governing principles: most obviously, as noted above,[83] in the post-conflict administration of territories by international organisations;[84] or more indirect regulation, whether through trade prohibitions (such as in Article 16 of the WTO Agreement),[85] Security Council prescriptions (many of which increasingly address individuals and non-state actors directly

[79] Weiler (n 1) 558.

[80] See, eg, M Koskenniemi, 'International Law in Europe: Between Tradition and Renewal' (2005) 16 *European Journal of International Law* 113, at 123.

[81] L Bartels, *Human Rights Conditionality in the EU's International Agreements* (Oxford, Oxford University Press, 2005); and for critical engagements, see P Leino-Sandberg, 'Particularity as Universality: The Politics of Human Rights in the European Union' (2005) *The Erik Castrén Institute Research Reports 15/2005*, available at: http://ethesis.helsinki.fi/julkaisut/oik/erikc/vk/leino-sandberg/particul.pdf.

[82] F Kratochwil, 'Has the "Rule of Law" Become a "Rule of Lawyers"? An Inquiry into the Use and Abuse of an Ancient *Topos* in Contemporary Debates' in G Palombella and N Walker (eds), *Relocating the Rule of Law* (Oxford, Hart Publishing, 2009) 171, at 185–86.

[83] See Knoll (n 44).

[84] The literature on post-conflict state reconstruction and administration is particularly extensive, but for perhaps the most damning critique from an accountability perspective, see R Wilde, *International Territorial Administration: How Trusteeship and the Civilizing Mission Never Went Away* (Oxford, Oxford University Press, 2008); and for a good overview of the literature generally, see S Chesterman, 'International Territorial Administration and the Limits of Law' (2009) 23 *Leiden Journal of International Law* 23.

[85] See in particular art 16(3) and (4), which requires, respectively, for the WTO Agreement to prevail in a case of conflict with other multilateral trade agreements and that '[e]ach Member shall ensure the conformity of its laws, regulations and administrative procedures with its obligations' under the GATT and other annexed agreements.

through targeted sanctions,[86] or require widespread regulatory measures to be implemented at the domestic level in the fight against terrorism),[87] or more subtly through economic conditionality,[88] or forms of soft governance through reputational assessments or indicators,[89] which, despite their 'softness', have significant regulatory impacts at the domestic level. It is hardly surprising, therefore, that when such decisions are taken by international actors away from the intergovernmental layer (whilst at the same time impacting internally within states without any means of democratic mediation), their legitimacy will be brought into question.[90]

Weiler's framework is particularly insightful in this respect as, by avoiding the kind of 'transitional' language in more teleological explanations of recent changes, he is able to develop a more nuanced account of how different kinds of interests and values pull in different directions and thereby give rise to legitimacy deficits. However, his approach also suffers from a tendency towards over-simplification insofar as he seems to ignore any importance attached to international law's underlying legal form itself—each layer is simply defined by its substantive character, function or effects. To explain more clearly, in treating the different geological strata as various, distinct typologies of international law, and in so doing suggesting that 'transactionalism' finds its justification *only* in an outdated philosophical commitment to state freedom,[91] he overlooks, or perhaps deliberately dismisses, the idea of the transactional layer as in some sense structural and foundational—it becomes only one more stratum existing alongside others. However, it is far too easy to portray this basal layer simply as an outdated philosophical commitment to national interest and unrestrained sovereignty, and in that sense merely an older species of international law, occupying an uneasy space with a more modern, dynamic, communitarian and, indeed, more 'public' international law. However, as I have sought to show thus far, but particularly in Chapter 7, the basal—transactional—layer represents the legal form

[86] See, eg, SC Res 1975 of 30 March 2001 against the former incumbent leader of the Ivory Coast, Laurent Gbagbo. Most obviously, such targeted sanctions have been applied in the fight against international terrorism: see, eg, SC Res 1267 of 15 October 1999 and a series of further resolutions in relation to the Taliban and Al-Qaeda. For a discussion of the human rights implications of these and other resolutions, see M Bothe, 'Security Council's Targeted Sanctions against Presumed Terrorists: The Need to Comply with Human Rights Standards' (2008) 6 *Journal of International Criminal Justice* 541.

[87] See, eg, SC Res 1540 of 28 April 2004; for a discussion of this and other measures, see LMH Martínez, 'The Legislative Role of the Security Council in its Fight against Terrorism: Legal, Political and Practical Limits' (2008) 57 *International and Comparative Law Quarterly* 333.

[88] See, eg, Anghie (n 7) at 224–29 in particular.

[89] See, eg, KE Davis, B Kingsbury and SE Merry, 'Indicators as a Technology of Governance' (2012) 46 *Law and Society Review* 71.

[90] Weiler (n 1) 559–60.

[91] ibid 552–53.

which has allowed states and other actors to give effect to the other layers. If, as I have argued, there remain strong normative reasons for retaining international law's decentralised structural form, then the 'transactionalism' of Westphalian international law, as Weiler puts it, plays an important foundational role in supporting the other 'layers'—it cannot simply be categorised in the same way, however much it seems to be straining under the weight of that which has been built upon it.

This is a point perhaps better captured in Antonio Cassese's metaphor, where he describes the decentralised structural form of international law as being 'like a human skeleton that can only be seen on an X-ray being covered by flesh and skin and clothes. Though momentarily concealed, it is still very much there, constituting the framework on which all the rest is based'.[92] Looking at it this way—as the legal form upon which the more complex edifice of modern international law is constructed—does not in any way prejudice the nature, substance or function of the rules, structures or institutions of this constructed legal order.[93] It does, however, help us to better come to terms with the reason for the apparent legitimacy crisis that has emerged as a result of the phenomenon of post-national governance, insofar as it highlights the growing structural tension between the contemporary functioning of the international legal system and its underlying legal form, and mirrors our competing conceptions—or different sides of—the international rule of law.

We can imagine the implications of this tension by placing competing legitimacy claims on two linked axes. International law's *formal* legitimacy comes from the sense that it is *structured* on a horizontal axis, as a pluralistic order existing between sovereign-equal states (according to the premises of something like the *Discontinuity Thesis* outlined in Chapter 7). However, increasingly, insofar as contemporary international law is seen as a purposive practice aimed at securing certain communitarian values (eg, human rights, welfare concerns or other 'public goods' that were traditionally conceived to lie within the domestic realm of states),[94] its legitimacy is also measured *functionally*, on a vertical axis, by reference to the capacity of the law to penetrate state sovereignty to achieve sovereign restraint.

[92] A Cassese, *International Law in a Divided World* (Oxford, Clarendon Press, 1986) 32.

[93] For a similar point, though aimed at a slightly different issue, see Klabbers (n 29) 179–81.

[94] See, eg, E Jouannet, 'What is the Use of International Law? International Law as a 21st Century Guardian of Welfare' (2008) 28 *Michigan Journal of International Law* 815. This concern seems most pronounced perhaps in the continuing debates over the legitimacy of the international criminal law regime, where the primacy of political considerations seemingly inherent in a decentralised legal order, as well as reliance on customary law principles, seems to raise some concerns from the perspective of the rule of law: see, eg, R Cryer, *Prosecuting International Crimes: Selectivity and the International Criminal Law Regime* (Cambridge, Cambridge University Press, 2005) 194–99 and 241–42 respectively.

On this basis, we can see how the competing legitimacy claims sit uneasily with one another: on the one hand, international law's decentralised legal form—its 'transactionalism', on Weiler's terms—takes its legitimacy from its openness and ability to be put to use for a number of cooperative purposes; on the other, the increasingly 'communitarian' focus of many of these collective interests is seen as necessitating more effective, more interventionist institutional solutions—hence the need to develop a more 'regulatory' institutional layer. However, it becomes increasingly difficult to maintain the legitimacy of these community interests, expressed through regulatory architecture, the more removed they are from the intergovernmental nature of the system from which they are brought into being—at least those possessing some formal treaty base. As such, in the absence of appeal to some a priori legitimacy or in the absence of any other mediatory form of direct accountability (beyond the intergovernmental), the kind of institutional autonomy that pushes on the 'vertical' axis will necessarily invoke counter-pulls on the 'horizontal' axis.[95] As Friedrich Kratochwil puts it, 'legitimisation deficits will appear in all instances of institutionalised inter-state cooperation that go beyond the classical alliance patterns or ad hoc limited purpose arrangements'.[96]

III. RE-INVENTING THE INSTITUTIONAL PROBLEM: INTERNATIONAL LAW AS PUBLIC LAW?

If, as I have suggested, this apparent legitimacy crisis arises from a tension ingrained into the structural condition of international law itself, how might we respond to it? Unsurprisingly perhaps, few have advocated a simple retreat 'back to Westphalia'. Insofar as any such retreat is seen as simply a concession to sovereignty or to state consent, it remains deeply unpopular (though it does have some adherents in the 'neo-sovereigntist' approach advocated by some US academics).[97] Weiler, for instance, is explicit that there is no going back to a transactional paradigm that places emphasis on the consent of states. At the same time, he sees limited potential in any sort of mediatory democratic legitimacy at the global level.[98] Whilst there

[95] This perhaps goes some way towards explaining what Klabbers terms a 'changing image' of international organisations since the mid-1990s: Klabbers (n 5).

[96] Kratochwil (n 82) 171, at 178.

[97] This threat was perceived particularly acutely from the mid-1990s in the wake of US opposition to an international criminal court. See, for instance, LF Damrosch, '"Sovereignty" and International Organizations' (1997) 3 *UC Davis Journal of International Law and Policy* 159; J Bolton, 'Should We Take Global Governance Seriously?' (2000) 1 *Chicago Journal of International Law* 220; and for a critical discussion of these positions, see GW Brown, 'The Idea of Autonomy: Accountability, Self-determinism and What Normative Claims about Institutional Autonomy in Global Governance Should Mean' in Collins and White (n 12) 104–19.

[98] Weiler (n 1) 561–2.

have been well-meaning attempts to find some means of democratic legitimisation at the international level (though perhaps more amongst political scientists than international lawyers),[99] many of these proposals remain far from persuasive.[100] With direct forms of political representation at the universal level being something of a chimera, the only plausible prospect appears to be to enhance the participatory role and normative influence of NGOs and other non-state actors as a nascent form of 'global civil society'.[101] Nevertheless, with long-standing concerns about the accountability and representative credentials of many NGOs,[102] the idea that this nascent civil society could serve to legitimise the kind of authority claimed by many global actors seems to drain democracy of much of its meaning, ultimately premised on a decidedly 'pre-modern' idea of constituent power.[103]

In its place, then, Weiler urges more thinking about 'alternative legitimating devices which would make up for the non-applicability of some of the classical institutions of democracy where that is not possible'.[104] The question this invokes, of course, is whether any such compensatory approach is possible (and desirable) beyond the kind of specific institutional mechanisms, briefly outlined above, aimed simply at enhancing accountability in particular institutional contexts. I remain somewhat sceptical, especially given the kind of proposals on the table. In the main, international lawyers have tended to respond to this challenge by reverting to public law analogies and principles again, in order to find some universal vocabulary by which it might be possible to bring order to disunity and to restrain the exercise of arbitrary political power.[105] As diverse as these many approaches are in themselves, they can be understood together as an attempt to restrain or control institutionalisation rather than to advance it against the sovereignty of states. They are, in other words, a response to the perceived

[99] See, eg, D Held, *Models of Democracy*, 3rd edn (Cambridge, Polity Press, 2006) 275–81, 304–08; though for a push for a deliberative democratic approach to international law, see S Wheatley, *The Democratic Legitimacy of International Law* (Oxford, Hart Publishing, 2010); see also A von Bogdandy, 'Globalization and Europe: How to Square Democracy, Globalization, and International Law' (2004) 15 *European Journal of International Law* 885, at 904–05 (and references included therein at fns 98–101).

[100] See, eg, Weiler (n 1) 560–61.

[101] See, eg, the discussion of JA Scholte, 'Civil Society and Democratically Accountable Global Governance' (2004) 39 *Government and Opposition* 211.

[102] See, eg, J Friedrichs, 'The Neomedieval Renaissance: Global Governance and International Law in the New Middle Ages' in Dekker and Werner (n 34) 3, at 11–16.

[103] A Somek, 'The Owl of Minerva: Constitutional Discourse before its Conclusion' (2008) 71 *Modern Law Review* 473, at 487–89.

[104] Weiler (n 1) 561.

[105] See, eg, Koskenniemi (n 19) 18; Dunoff and Trachtman, 'A Functional Approach to International Constitutionalization', above n 55, 5–6. N Krisch, 'Global Administrative Law and the Constitutional Ambition' in P Dobner and M Loughlin (eds), *The Twilight of Constitutionalism?* (Oxford, Oxford University Press, 2010) 245, at 246. I discuss this further in R Collins, 'Constitutionalism as Liberal-Juridical Consciousness: Echoes from International Law's Past' (2009) 22 *Leiden Journal of International Law* 251.

erosion of sovereignty caused by global governance—or, rather, caused by its perceived externalities: the above-noted threats of deformalisation and fragmentation.[106]

Of the various strands of this 'public law' ambition, the most value-laden, arguably, has been an explicitly 'constitutionalist' agenda, which aims to find some means of balancing expressions of public authority with underlying public law values, procedures or accountability mechanisms.[107] In contrast to the kind of approach castigated by Arangio-Ruiz in the previous chapter, however, this kind of constitutional discourse is less 'architectural' in its ambition.[108] It acts as a 'compensatory' discourse[109] intended as 'a desirable reaction to visible de-constitutionalization on the domestic level'.[110] Whilst much of the empirical analysis in the constitutionalist literature is sophisticated and insightful, acknowledging many of the accountability deficits and structural tensions outlined above, its more normative ambition is nonetheless beset by a certain incoherence. In particular, insofar as it advocates a less formal approach to legal normativity, based around certain constitutional principles, as a response—at least in part—to the threat of deformalisation, one might accuse international or global constitutionalists of attempting to fight fire with fire. In other words, in order to re-imagine international law as already (potentially) regulated by some constitutional rationality, much of this response has

[106] See, eg, the recent project on developing the 'publicness' of public international law under the auspices of the *Max Planck Institute of Comparative Public Law and Public International Law*: A von Bogdandy, P Dann and M Goldmann, 'Developing the Publicness of Public International Law: Towards a Legal Framework for Global Governance Activities' (2008) 9 *German Law Journal* 1375, as well as the various contributions in the rest of the symposium that follows. On the recurrence of public law rhetoric as a means of constructing system in international law, see D Kennedy, 'The Mystery of Global Governance' in Dunoff and Trachtman (n 20) 43–54.

[107] The literature on constitutionalism within, and constitutionalisation of, international law is growing and somewhat diverse; for a good summary of the debates, however, see most recently J Klabbers, A Peters and G Ulfstein, *The Constitutionalization of International Law* (Oxford, Oxford University Press, 2010); and the collections of essays by R Macdonald and DM Johnston (eds), *Towards World Constitutionalism: Issues in the Legal Ordering of the World Community* (Leiden, Martinus Nijhoff, 2005); and Dunoff and Trachtman (n 20).

[108] Koskenniemi (n 19) at 18.

[109] See, eg, Dunoff and Trachtman, 'A Functional Approach to International Constitutionalization' (n 55) 9. And see further A Peters, 'Compensatory Constitutionalism: The Function and Potential of Fundamental International Norms and Structures' (2006) 19 *Leiden Journal of International Law* 579; BO Bryde, 'International Democratic Constitutionalism' in Macdonald and Johnston (n 107) 103, at 115–21; as well as M Kumm, 'The Legitimacy of International Law: A Constitutionalist Framework of Analysis' (2004) 15 *European Journal of International Law* 907.

[110] Peters (n 109) 580. And for similar ambition, see Paulus (n 20) 71; and A O'Donoghue, 'International Constitutionalism and the State' (2013) 11 *International Journal of Constitutional Law* 1021. On the distinction between these two modes of constitutionalism, see Collins (n 105) 252 (in fn 4); see further the useful classifications deployed by CEJ Schwöbel, 'Organic Global Constitutionalism' (2010) 23 *Leiden Journal of International Law* 529, at 530–33.

tended to advocate reading into international law necessary functional distinctions, normative hierarchies and procedural principles, which jar uneasily with its non-hierarchical institutional form.[111] As Jeffrey Dunoff and Joel Trachtman argue: 'A functionalist approach permits conceptual analysis that is not premised upon a definition setting forth a group of necessary and sufficient conditions which determine whether a given order is constitutional or not.'[112] Similarly, rather than looking for formal institutional hierarchies in international law, Andreas Paulus reflects 'on whether and how the international legal order fulfils the background principles of a constitutional order worthy of that name in a constitutional tradition'.[113] In this model, the constitutional character of particular norms is not derived from their source (or, rather, higher entrenchment)—*as the rule of law would seem to require*—but merely their substance or overall effect.[114] Anne Peters makes this point most explicitly:

> Since a unified constitutional charter is missing and because a normative hierarchy within the international legal order is present—if at all—only in relation to the small subset of *jus cogens*, the option of establishing a clear distinction based on formal characteristics is foreclosed. It remains possible to distinguish according to the substance of the norms in question. Only those norms which have 'something fundamental' to them may be duly qualified as constitutional norms ... *But this distinction is inevitably blurry and contestable.*[115] (emphasis added, footnote omitted)

The logic here is curious. The motivation behind this constitutionalist reading is to respond, in part, to the effect that deformalisation (and fragmentation) has on achieving rule of law values. As we have seen, however, in Chapter 7 particularly, the rule of law depends for its coherence on the formalism of law's source; it suggests the arbitrariness of reading legal norms according to their substance or particular effects. As quoted above, Peters herself admits that such a substantive reading relies on necessarily 'blurry and contestable' distinctions. As such, to suggest that norms can be assessed on the basis of their relative importance is to re-state the problem to which something like the rule of law purports to respond. Matthias Kumm's analysis of constitutionalism seen as a means to respond to the apparent legitimacy crisis outlined above seems to result in much the same problem.

111 See, eg, Peters (n 109) 585.

112 Dunoff and Trachtman, 'A Functional Approach to International Constitutionalization' (n 55) 6.

113 Paulus (n 20) 71. Mattias Kumm refers to something similar as the 'practice conception' of constitutionalism: see M Kumm, 'The Best of Times and the Worst of Times: Between Constitutional Triumphalism and Nostalgia' in Dobner and Loughlin (n 105) 201, at 212–8.

114 See, eg, Peters (n 109) 588; and see the criticisms of A Somek, 'From the Rule of Law to the Constitutionalist Makeover: Changing European Conceptions of Public International Law' (2011) 18 *Constellations* 567, at 579.

115 Peters (n 109) 599.

Whilst he acknowledges the legitimacy of formal source-based criteria for legality, following many of the concerns outlined previously, he suggests now that such formal criteria are not enough on their own to ensure the legitimacy of contemporary international law. Instead, he argues, this prima facie legitimacy may be rebutted where other factors such as 'subsidiarity', 'process legitimacy' and—albeit with some reservations—'outcome legitimacy' undermine the rational acceptance of a particular legal norm.[116] Again, this suggests that a subjective, evaluative determination is necessary in assessing the validity of the legal norm: *one kind of deformalisation is merely replaced with another.*

This problem is only intensified once we move to the concrete level, where constitutional 'norm-balancing' is demanded of particular institutions or regimes.[117] As noted above, even if there is agreement on values and principles in the abstract such that clashes between particular normative areas are capable of resolution, the result of the normative balancing will inevitably be influenced by the particular structural bias of any given institutional decision-maker. This concern has arisen in institutions seen as having an inherently limited remit, such as the WTO, with its narrow market-based focus,[118] but the inevitable fragmentary effect seems to apply in any institutional context. In this respect, constitutionalist discourse seems to have the paradoxical effect of heightening fragmentation concerns. The EU, for instance, seems increasingly to be asserting its autonomy from the broader international legal order by stressing the constitutional nature of its treaty base[119] or by noting the importance of certain fundamental rights which override other international obligations.[120] Even the European Court of

[116] Kumm (n 109) 918–27.

[117] The most obvious context being the EU: see, eg, JHH Weiler and M Wind (eds), *European Constitutionalism Beyond the State* (Cambridge, Cambridge University Press, 2003); though the same claim is applied to distinctly more 'intergovernmental' bodies such as the WTO, on which see, eg, DZ Cass, *The Constitutionalization of the World Trade Organization* (Oxford, Oxford University Press, 2005). For a critical reflection, see J Klabbers, 'Constitutionalism Lite' (2004) 1 *International Organizations Law Review* 31.

[118] This is by now a well-trodden critique of the idea of constitutionalism in the WTO. See, eg, the criticisms of R Howse, 'From Politics to Technocracy—and Back Again: The Fate of the Multilateral Trading Regime' (2002) 96 *American Journal of International Law* 94, at 106–07; R Howse, 'Human Rights in the WTO: Whose Rights, What Humanity? Comment on Petersmann' (2002) 13 *European Journal of International Law* 651, at 655; JL Dunoff, 'Constitutional Conceits: The WTO's "Constitution" and the Discipline of International Law' (2006) 17 *European Journal of International Law* 647, at 665; R Howse and K Nicolaidis, 'Enhancing WTO Legitimacy: Constitutionalization or Global Subsidiarity?' (2003) 16 *Governance* 73, at 75; P Alston, 'Resisting the Merger and Acquisition of Human Rights by Trade Law: A Reply to Petersmann' (2002) 13 *European Journal of International Law* 815, at 826.

[119] For an extremely clear conceptual study of the EU's claimed autonomy in this respect, see N Tsagourias, 'Conceptualizing the Autonomy of the European Union' in Collins and White (n 12) 339–52.

[120] For example, in the famous *Kadi* and *Yusuf* cases: Case T-306/01, *Yusuf and Al Barakaat International Foundation v Council and Commission*, 21 September 2005 [2005] ECR II-3533; Case T-315/01, *Kadi v Council and Commission*, 21 September 2005 [2005] ECR II-3649.

Human Rights has in some senses separated the operation of the Convention regime from broader rules of international treaty law by stressing its constitutional nature.[121] By bolstering the constitutionality of the particular regime, the institution can seemingly isolate itself from the restraining conditions of the constitutive rules of the international legal order upon which it is built.[122]

In response to these more institution-specific constitutional ambitions, some have suggested the need for a broader systemic approach. In particular, Paulus argues that further normative integration within particular institutions, bringing particular goals into normative conflict with other values outside of the internal legal order, will inevitably prompt decision-makers to look outside the institution to reason according to overarching systemic rules.[123] Again, however, this merely re-states the same structural problem: the concern is not the existence of a background system in the abstract; in fact, to reason according to systemic logic in this way merely serves to bolster the particular authority of any given institution, thus in turn adding to the apparent fragmentation and deformalisation of international law overall. As Eyal Benvenisti comments:

> This [systemic] legal discourse empowers primarily judges ... The vision of international law as a legal system rather than a mix of discrete treaties allows them to interpret, deduct, draw inferences and resolve conflicts not only by resorting to the specific treaties at hand but also by relying on the basic principles of the system and its underlying norms.[124]

In the absence of any overarching hierarchy of courts, these systemic-constitutionalist readings of international law may only be used to strengthen the autonomy of the institution in question, whilst paradoxically reinforcing the disunity of the international legal order:

> If a treaty establishes institutions, the courts will bolster those institutions, strengthening their authority internally and externally. At the internal level of that institution, the court will reinforce an institution's authority and impact vis-à-vis state parties beyond what the negotiators intended. At the external level, the court will recognize the institution's status as a 'subject' of international law that must be treated and recognized as such by non-member states.[125]

121 See, eg, *Belilos v Switzerland* (n 76) and *Loizidou v Turkey* (n 76) at paras 67 and 72 in particular, distinguishing the special characteristics of the Convention on the basis of its object and purpose rather than its legal form in the law of treaties. See the discussion to this effect in Koskenniemi and Leino (n 19) 567–69.

122 See, eg, the discussion in Paulus (n 20) 82–87.

123 ibid 70, 84–85. See further JP Trachtman, 'The Constitutions of the WTO' (2006) 17 *European Journal of International Law* 623, at 624–25.

124 E Benvenisti, 'The Conception of International Law as a Legal System' (2008) 50 *German Yearbook of International Law* 393, at 396.

125 ibid 397–98.

Despite its more limited ambition and rejection of the constitutionalist vocabulary of global values, one sees a similar problem in the 'global administrative law' (GAL) project.[126] In line with the analysis above, GAL addresses the increasingly informal means of governance through international organisations, informal networks or other non-state actors, attempting to come to terms with:

> [T]he legal mechanisms, principles, and practices, along with supporting social understandings, that promote or otherwise affect the *accountability* of global administrative bodies, in particular by ensuring these bodies meet adequate standards of transparency, consultation, participation, rationality, and legality, and by providing effective review of the rules and decisions these bodies make.[127]

However, as before, to understand this broad sweep of practices as giving rise to or being regulated by law requires an evaluative judgement on the substance or effects of legal norms rather than their simple conformity with source-based criteria. Perhaps the leading proponent of the GAL approach, Benedict Kingsbury, makes this point explicitly in his (well-reasoned) account of the concept of law underpinning the GAL project.[128] As he notes, the term 'global' is employed to note the broader sweep proposed under this project, aimed at including the 'informal institutional arrangements … and other normative practices and sources that are not encompassed within standard conceptions of "international law"' and which go beyond the kind of norms included in standard sources doctrine. As he continues:

> The term GAL is applied to shared sets of norms and norm-guided practices that are in some cases regarded as obligatory, and in many cases are given some weight, even where they are not obviously part of national (state) law or standard interstate law. The analysis is further complicated because global administrative law is practised at multiple sites, so GAL norms are also meshed with other sources of obligation applicable to that site … If a claim to 'law' is made in applying the label GAL in some of these situations, *it is a claim that diverges from, and can be sharply in tension with the classical models of consent based inter-state international law* and most models of national law.[129] (emphasis added)

[126] The literature here is now somewhat voluminous, but as an introduction, see principally N Krisch and B Kingsbury, 'Introduction: Global Governance and Global Administrative Law in the International Legal Order' (2006) 17 *European Journal of International Law* 1; and see the symposium which follows at 1–278 of the same edition; B Kingsbury, N Krisch and R Stewart, 'The Emergence of Global Administrative Law' (2005) 68 *Law and Contemporary Problems* 15 and the rest of the symposium in the same issue, at 1–377.

[127] B Kingsbury, N Krisch, RB Stewart and JB Wiener, 'Foreword: Global Governance as Administration—National and Transnational Approaches to Global Administrative Law' (2005) 68 *Law and Contemporary Problems* 1, at 5.

[128] B Kingsbury, 'The Concept of "Law" in Global Administrative Law' (2009) 20 *European Journal of International Law* 23.

[129] ibid 25–26.

Kingsbury's approach tries to avoid a distinctly subjective, value or content-based analysis of the law—in fact, he refers to it as explicitly positivist, stressing its social factuality—but at the same time, he attempts to move away from binary distinctions in order to encompass the idea that different standards or norms (formal or otherwise) have different compliance pulls or legal effects.[130] A similar approach also seems to underpin Alvarez's recent study on the law-making activities of international organisations, as he attempts to legally situate, and re-orient focus upon, what he sees as the evident normative force of the 'legislative' activities of institutions. In order to capture this, he suggests one measures the 'normative ripples' of a particular output rather than its conformity with formal sources.[131] Similarly, Nigel White argues that one must 'relativise' legality to some degree in order to capture and respond to the normative output of many global institutions:

> An understanding of the nature and impact of the legal output of international organizations is not achieved by simply considering the issue as a matter of the traditional sources of international law. By widening the context to encompass ideas drawn from international relations, we are able to see that institutional law-making is much more influential than a strictly legal approach would allow for.[132]

A similar trend seems apparent for the group of scholars behind the Max Planck Institute for Comparative Public Law and International Law's (MPIL) project on 'International Public Authority', which aims to adopt a similarly relative, 'external effects' based approach,[133] in judging the legitimate authority of a range of formal and informal decision-making bodies by reference to a standard of 'publicness'.[134]

Interestingly, Kingsbury explains the rationale behind this more expansive approach to normativity he advocates in terms of a response to the kind of perceived constitutional deficiency outlined previously. In the absence of centralised authorities, he places emphasis on the role of subjects, actors or participants themselves in assigning 'weight' to normative standards.

[130] ibid 27.

[131] Alvarez (n 5) 122–45.

[132] ND White, 'Separate But Connected: Inter-governmental Organizations and International Law' (2008) 5 *International Organizations Law Review* 175, at 187.

[133] Von Bogdandy, Dann and Goldmann (n 106). A distinctive but still effects-based approach is also employed by Dekker and Wessel, relying on a 'speech act' approach: Dekker and Wessel (n 34) 218–19 ff.

[134] See most recently M Goldmann, 'A Matter of Perspective: Global Governance and the Distinction between Public and Private Authority (and Not Law)' (4 November 2013), http://ssrn.com/abstract=2260293, in which legitimate international public authority is identified (at 18) on the basis of whether 'the actor may reasonably claim to act on behalf of a community of which the affected person or entity is a member, or a member of such member'. A similar though not identical approach is taken in A von Bogdandy and I Venzke, *In Whose Name? A Public Law Theory of International Adjudication* (Oxford, Oxford University Press, 2014).

As he puts it: 'Law is a social practice, and it is a feature of the particular social practices involved in GAL that both validity and weight are important.'[135] As such, in the absence of a unifying rule of recognition able to capture the full extent of the authority exercised by global institutions, the two criteria are combined together—weight and validity—as part of an overall 'gatekeeper' standard based on the 'publicness' of the normative authority exercised. Publicness, in essence, is somewhat similar to Lon Fuller's evaluative standard of 'legality', but goes beyond the procedural requirements of the rule of law in order to recognise substantive public goods, such as the protection of human rights.[136]

Once again, this is curious reasoning bearing in mind the motivation which drives the desire to bring order to the apparently disordered 'global administrative space'. Kingsbury openly admits that his approach is partly conceptual and partly political—indeed, that it aims to amalgamate political concerns within conceptual analysis—but in so doing, he seems to disregard, or devalue, the potential legitimising effects of such value-laden legalism, which are surely only accentuated by the structural condition of the international legal order. To move beyond formal source-based criteria to make determinations based upon evaluative judgement merely offers up a deeply subjective standard for decision-makers to justify their conduct. As Alexander Somek argues:

> The problem that arises for the GAL project is that owing to its practical ambition it is inclined to describe processes which do not give rise to legally binding acts as though they were constituted by administrative law, while these very same processes can equally plausibly also be described as mere instances of permissible conduct.[137]

Although GAL and other public law-based approaches set themselves up against constitutionalist rhetoric by attempting to avoid the inherent subjectivity of values, by employing a similarly evaluative approach to legal normativity, they seem to risk precisely the same kind of deformalisation of rule of law standards.[138] If this subjectivism is admitted, this leads us back to the question of who decides: either it is the administrators this approach purports to bind or it requires some form of adjudicatory model, the lack of which prompted Kingsbury (and it seems many others) to read the normativity of GAL in this way in the first place. As such, it seems that the auto-interpretation of international law by states is simply replaced by the auto-application of law by functional decision-makers; the former may appear inefficient and imperfect, but the latter is hardly an improvement.

[135] Kingsbury (n 128) 27.
[136] ibid 31–33.
[137] A Somek, 'The Concept of "Law" in Global Administrative Law: A Reply to Benedict Kingsbury' (2009) 20 *European Journal of International Law* 985, at 987.
[138] ibid.

In summary, I am sceptical about such attempts at functional compensation based on public law values. As before, there is a failure to adequately appreciate the importance of international law's decentralised legal form and the agnostic, open indeterminacy which is seen as an important aspect of its core legitimacy. If, as I have argued, the legitimacy crisis arises precisely because functional institutional autonomy has emerged (and been encouraged) in a way which sits uneasily with the formal criteria of this system, then no means of functional compensation is likely to alleviate that tension; indeed, it is likely only to exacerbate it. As Jan Klabbers notes, this attempt at reading international law's normative effects in functional terms requires, in the end, some medium for distinguishing law and non-law,[139] which prompts us either to decry the illegality of certain normative influences where they occur or else admit that they simply fall outside of international law's reach. Jean d'Aspremont makes a similar point, ultimately pointing to the self-defeating nature of the argument that the criteria for ascertaining international law can be deformalised and expanded to address these perceived accountability deficits:

> International actors have consciously and purposely placed such a normative activity outside the traditional framework of international law with a view to eluding … the mechanisms of accountability provided by international law. If legal scholars, analysts, or theorists were to succeed in their attempt to bring these forms of the exercise of public authority in the remit of international law it can be anticipated that international actors would in turn, again create new normative tools and use other norm-making channels which allow them to evade accountability.[140]

As always, the problem is more structural; the system is designed to defer back to the values and vices, the politics and prejudices and, ultimately, the responsibility of its constituent members. If we try to imagine an international legal world capable of securing accountability by reference to these kinds of expanded criteria, it seems almost impossible to secure anything like a functioning international rule of law. In such a model, as Somek claims, 'there is neither system nor centre, merely family resemblancess among different processes'.[141] By moving away from formal criteria and concentrating on legitimacy rather than legality per se, we seem to give up on law's autonomy, and the limited accountability it brings with it, in any form.[142] In other words, there is a benefit to retaining a formalist,

[139] J Klabbers, 'Law-Making and Constitutionalism' in Klabbers, Peters and Ulfstein (n 107) 81, at 102.

[140] J d'Aspremont, *Formalism and the Sources of International Law: A Theory of the Ascertainment of Legal Norms* (Oxford, Oxford University Press, 2011) 136.

[141] A Somek, 'Administration without Sovereignty' in P Dobner and M Loughlin (eds), *The Twilight of Constitutionalism?* (Oxford, Oxford University Press, 2010) 267, at 272.

[142] J Klabbers, 'The Relative Autonomy of International Law or the Forgotten Politics of Interdisciplinarity' (2005) 1 *Journal of International Law & International Relations* 35.

'doctrinal' perspective as a mirror against which we can highlight the contingent nature of, as well as power imbalances potentially perpetuated by, much of the rule-making, standard-setting and more indirect normative influence of this increasingly post-national political space.[143]

IV. CONCLUSION

This might seem a somewhat conservative—indeed, potentially unfashionable—conclusion to a chapter concerned very much with evolution and change in contemporary international law. Nevertheless, I believe that there remain good reasons for excluding certain types of normative influence from international law's formal criteria of validity. To the extent that many of these practices remain contested and controversial, the ability to decry their 'non-legality' (if not illegality) by reference to some agreed-upon formal criteria (ie, criteria which do not invoke the very same values which might be the source of conflict in the first place) still seems important to the legitimate authority of the system overall. Whether, and to what extent, such norms have other normative influence and whether they fall within some other 'global' mode of legality[144] may well depend on a range of non-formal considerations, necessarily implicating the evaluative judgement of states and other actors in the increasingly fragmented and complex international legal order. My point, however, is that the judgement required in making such determinations—whether in terms of fairness, legitimacy, 'publicness' or some other standard—is not susceptible to being publicly promulgated without a concomitant acceptance of some prior-agreed procedure or institution with the ability to determine authoritatively what such values might mean in any given situation; that is, precisely the kind of centralised authority which is not only absent, but arguably incompatible with the very idea of international law.

This conclusion, however, is not to ignore these more informal modes of authority and normative influence as somehow irrelevant to international law. Rather, it seems to me that these innovative governance solutions remain important in securing some cooperation towards common ends when agreement to formal legal rules is likely only to prevent action or limit its practical purport. Nevertheless, by retaining the formal legality-illegality binary and thereby side-lining the normative influence of much of this global governance activity, we retain some ability to evaluate it on its own terms, that is, we refuse to grant it any a priori legitimacy of the type

[143] See on this point Somek (n 137) 993–94.

[144] See, eg, recently the impressive empirical survey of typologies of 'global law' in Ch 3 of N Walker, *Intimations of Global Law* (Cambridge, Cambridge University Press, 2014).

bestowed by formal legality. In other words, the authority of this post-national form of global governance remains 'content-*dependent*', not independent, leaving assessments of its normative force susceptible to being measured by some more value-based framework as the need arises. Indeed, following the argument developed in this part so far, it may well be the case that this very act of formal exclusion is the most important consequence of the attempt to secure the rule of law at the global level.

Conclusion

I BEGAN THIS book with a question posed by the late Arthur Watts as to the importance of international law in the conduct of international affairs. It might be worth now briefly recalling Watts' own response to this question as his argument reflects familiar themes developed in this work so far. He acknowledged, for instance—as did Henkin—that for the most part, most rules of international law are obeyed most of the time.[1] He equally noted—as did Hart and, indeed, many international lawyers—that international law's objective validity as such can be understood to follow simply from the fact that actors in the international system recognise a set (*or system*) of rules as binding upon them. In doing so, he argued that a 'climate of legality' clearly pertains at the international level—that states believe in 'the general notion of law as a basis for their behaviour'.[2]

The reference to 'legality' here recalls the problem of an international rule of law, which I have outlined at length in Chapter 7. For Watts, the existence of a climate of 'legality' in the limited sense I have defended was not sufficient to secure any form of order in international affairs—a goal which he saw as intimately related to the very existence of international law itself. Whilst he therefore argued that the 'rule of law' in a strict sense 'has not yet been firmly established', the 'self-evident' benefits of rule of law compliance still 'exert a powerful positive influence'.[3] Watts' analysis—perhaps unwittingly—draws out the fundamental ambiguities surrounding the idea of an international rule of law, of achieving a condition of 'legality' in international relations. He noted how 'State practice is replete with acknowledgements of the importance of international law as a system, and of the need to observe particular rules of the system', but he was equally aware of how the aura of legality acts instrumentally as a powerful legitimising force, facilitating states' (and other actors') unilateral actions to the detriment of a just, ordered international society.[4]

Unsurprisingly, Watts' tone became more cautionary as his focus shifted to the problem of how international law could secure order and justice at

[1] A Watts, 'The Importance of International Law' in M Byers (ed), *The Role of Law in International Politics: Essays in International Relations and International Law* (Oxford, Oxford University Press, 2000) 5, at 8–9.

[2] ibid 6.

[3] ibid 7.

[4] ibid.

the same time. The former seems to presuppose an institutional framework for mediating between the imbalances of power prevalent in any political community; the latter some form of institutional intervention, to secure certain purposive, communitarian ends as agreed upon within these institutional frameworks. Whilst at the time of his writing—at the turn of the new millennium—he saw that international law had made progress in improving its institutional structure, particularly through the introduction of more effective international adjudication, Watts still saw that the consensual nature of such jurisdiction remained problematic from the point of view of the international rule of law. Similarly, he noted how international law had evolved at the substantive level: as a system, it was capable of securing legal change to reflect community interests, particularly through the negotiation of new treaty regimes, but at the basal level of the system itself, its customary character still made the process of legal change slow and inefficient, and indeed more likely to reflect the existing balances of power in international relations.[5]

As such, Watts' essay is revealing of familiar disciplinary concerns: recognising the importance of the rule of law in international affairs, whilst at the same time expressing concern over how international law's institutional condition prevents the full realisation of this goal. It is also revealing in its particular disciplinary context. His desire to answer the question of the importance of international law, and to do so in a volume of essays aimed at a notoriously sceptical political audience, reflects an all too familiar disciplinary self-defensiveness. At the beginning of Part I, I sought to show how the modern discipline emerged as an attempt to prove the relevance of international law as a positive, systemic legal order on much the same terms as Watts—and, indeed, against similarly sceptical voices. I argued that this view of international law presupposed a condition of legal autonomy which seemed prima facie incompatible with the decentralised institutional order of international law, and therefore arguably undermined the ambitions of those who see in the rule of law the potential for legal rules to restrain the worst excesses of sovereign political freedom. The question that this left open, and to which the book has tried to respond, is how we should therefore react to this apparent *institutional problem*.

In response, I have sought to do two things. The first is to attempt to re-orient this problem, to show that insofar as there has long been perpetuated a view of international law as somehow constitutionally deficient, defective or primitive, that this view is built on unsustainable presumptions: not only about international law's potential and scope in international relations, but *most importantly* about the role and function of law in any political community. In this respect, I have engaged with the dominant analytical

[5] ibid 13–16.

tradition in jurisprudence to show how within descriptive explanations of constitutive features of legal order, there remain a number of presumptions about the necessary governance functions of law and therefore a resultant need for institutional hierarchy. I have argued that these claims are not only methodologically problematic, but in substance misunderstand the contingent nature of law's institutional form—particularly insofar as this form seeks to give structure to the political relations that pertain in any given society. As such, applying this reasoning to international law, I have defended its decentralised institutional form as important to the legitimacy of legal rules in international society. This form is not only facilitative in advancing agreed-upon objectives, but acts as an important basis for inter-subjective accountability in the agnostic, pluralistic society of states.

My second ambition, therefore, was to engage in a form of imminent critique of what I believe has been an unhelpful tendency to overlook or disregard the international legal form in an effort to read into international law certain functional substitutes for the kind of constitutional or governance functions seen as necessary to law's perceived role in bringing order to international society. Rather than seeing in the international rule of law an important basis for formal association under conditions of political plurality, which itself therefore facilitates the possibility of more cooperative and purposive forms of institutional association, it has often been seen simply as a goal to be achieved through the transformation of international law by way of a more interventionist institutional structure. By showing not only the theoretical difficulties of reading existing international institutions in this way, but also the practical impacts and legitimacy concerns raised by the intensification of global governance activity, I have sought to demonstrate the limitations of trying to overcome the institutional problem in this way. In fact, the problem has arguably only resurfaced in a more 'postmodern' form, with growing disciplinary unease over the normative reach and influence of an increasingly autonomous range of regimes and institutions, precipitating anxieties over the fragmentation and deformalisation of the international legal system. However, the point is that these impacts are the inevitable result of the institutionalisation of a decentralised legal order. By also showing some of the theoretical and practical difficulties of reading any actor—state or institution—as authoritatively representing universal interests or fulfilling 'official' functions in international law, I have instead suggested that the effect of international law's institutionalisation has been to complicate contemporary international law, creating a quite noticeable strain and tension between its functional operation on the one hand and its formal decentralised structure on the other. However, it is within the push and pull of these different claims to legitimacy that we can perhaps find space for continued political engagement with any claim to universal legitimacy or authority, that is, to leave open the possibility of genuinely universal values, interests and ambitions, whilst continuing to subject such claims to scrutiny and contestation.

If the 'institutional problem' is therefore a problem after all, it surely relates to the question of how best to secure this balance: how to leave open this space for authentically international expressions of solidarity, whilst continuing to resist international law's complete instrumentalisation towards more particular political ends.

Bibliography

Abbott, KW, and Snidal, D, 'Hard and Soft Law in International Governance' (2000) 54 *International Organization* 421

Abi-Saab, G, 'Cours général de droit international public' (1987-VII) 207 *Recueil des Cours* 9

—— 'Whither the International Community?' (1998) 9 *European Journal of International Law* 248

Ackerman, BA, 'Transformative Appointments' (1988) 101 *Harvard Law Review* 1164

—— 'Constitutional Politics/Constitutional Law' (1989) 99 *Yale Law Journal* 453

Ago, R, 'Positive Law and International Law' (1957) 51 *American Journal of International Law* 691

Akehurst, M, 'Custom as a Source of International Law' (1974–75) 47 *British Yearbook of International Law* 1

Allott, P, 'The Concept of International Law' (1999) 10 *European Journal of International Law* 31

—— 'The Myopia of the Handmaidens: International Lawyers and Globalization' (1997) 8 *European Journal of International Law* 435

Alston, P, 'Resisting the Merger and Acquisition of Human Rights by Trade Law: A Reply to Petersmann' (2002) 13 *European Journal of International Law* 815

Alvarez, JE, 'The New-Dispute Settlers: (Half) Truths and Consequences' (2003) 38 *Texas International Law Journal* 405

—— *International Organizations as Law-Makers* (Oxford, Oxford University Press, 2005)

—— 'International Organizations: Then and Now' (2006) 100 *American Journal of International Law* 324

Anand, RP, 'The Role of Individual and Dissenting Opinions in International Adjudication' (1965) 14 *International and Comparative Law Quarterly* 788

—— 'Enhancing the Acceptability of Compulsory Procedures of International Dispute Settlement' (2001) 5 *Max Planck Yearbook of United Nations Law* 1

Anghie, A, 'International Financial Institutions' in C Reus-Smit (ed), *The Politics of International Law* (Oxford, Oxford University Press, 2004) 217–37

—— *Imperialism, Sovereignty and the Making of International Law* (Cambridge, Cambridge University Press, 2005)

Anzilotti, D, *Corso di Diritto Internazionale*, 4th edn (Padua, CEDAM, 1955)

—— *Scritti di Diritto Internazionale* (Padua, CEDAM, 1957)

Arajärvi, N, *The Changing Nature of Customary International Law: Methods of Interpreting the Concept of Custom in International Criminal Tribunals* (Abingdon, Routledge, 2014)

Arangio-Ruiz, G, *The UN Declaration on Friendly Relations and the System of the Sources of International Law* (Alphen aan den Rijn, Sijthoff & Noordhoff, 1979)

Arendt, H, 'What is Freedom?' in *Between Past and Future: Eight Exercises in Political Thought* (New York, Penguin, 1977) 143–72
—— *On Revolution* (New York, Penguin, 2006)
Astorino, S, 'The Impact of Sociological Jurisprudence on International Law in the Inter-War Period: The American Experience' (1996) 34 *Duquesne Law Review* 277
Austin, J, *The Province of Jurisprudence Determined* (London, John Murray, 1832)
—— *Lectures on Jurisprudence or the Philosophy of Positive Law*, 4th edn, revised and edited by R Campbell (London, John Murray, 1873)
Barnett, M, and Finnemore, M, 'The Politics, Power, and Pathologies of International Organizations' (1999) 53 *International Organization* 699
—— *Rules for the World: International Organizations in Global Politics* (Ithaca, Cornell University Press, 2004)
Bartels, L, *Human Rights Conditionality in the EU's International Agreements* (Oxford, Oxford University Press, 2005)
Beaulac, S, 'The Rule of Law in International Law Today' in G Palombella and N Walker (eds), *Relocating the Rule of Law* (Oxford, Hart Publishing, 2009) 197–223
Beckett, J, 'The Hartian Tradition in International Law' (2008) 1 *The Journal Jurisprudence* 51
Bederman, D, 'The Souls of International Organizations: Legal Personality and the Lighthouse at Cape Spartel' (1996) 36 *Virginia Journal of International Law* 275
Bedjaoui, M, 'General Introduction' in M Bedjaoui (ed), *International Law: Achievements and Prospects* (Dordrecht, Martinus Nijhoff, 1991) 1–18
Bentham, J, *An Introduction to the Principles of Morals and Legislation* (JH Burns and HLA Hart (eds), London, Athlone Press, 1970)
Benvenisti, E 'The Conception of International Law as a Legal System' (2008) 50 *German Yearbook of International Law* 393
Berman, HJ, 'World Law Transcendent' (2005) 54 *Emory Law Journal* 53
Berman, N, 'A Perilous Ambivalence: Nationalist Desire, Legal Autonomy, and the Limits of the Interwar Framework' (1992) 33 *Harvard International Law Journal* 353
—— '"But the Alternative is Despair": European Nationalism and the Modernist Renewal of International Law' (1993) 106 *Harvard Law Review* 1792
Bernstorff, J von, 'Sisyphus was an International Lawyer. On Martti Koskenniemi's "From Apology to Utopia" and the Place of Law in International Politics' (2006) 7 *German Law Journal* 1015
—— *The Public International Law Theory of Hans Kelsen: Believing in Universal Law* (Cambridge, Cambridge University Press, 2010)
—— 'Georg Jellinek and the Origins of Liberal Constitutionalism in International Law' (2012) 4 *Goettingen Journal of International Law* 659
Besson, S, 'Theorizing the Sources of International Law' in S Besson and J Tasioulas (eds), *The Philosophy of International Law* (Oxford, Oxford University Press, 2010) 163–85
Besson, S, and Tasioulas, J, 'Introduction' in S Besson and J Tasioulas (eds), *The Philosophy of International Law* (Oxford, Oxford University Press, 2010) 1–27
Bia, JJ, 'The Relations between Treaties and Custom' (2010) 9 *Chinese Journal of International Law* 81

Bianchi, A, 'Ad-Hocism and the Rule of Law' (2002) 13 *European Journal of International Law* 263
—— 'Assessing the Effectiveness of the UN Security Council's Anti-terrorism Measures: The Quest for Legitimacy and Cohesion' (2007) 17 *European Journal of International Law* 881
—— 'Looking Ahead: International Law's Main Challenges' in D Armstrong (ed), *Routledge Handbook of International Law* (Abingdon, Routledge, 2009) 392–409
Bianchi, A, Peat, A, and Windsor, M (eds), *Interpretation in International Law* (Oxford, Oxford University Press, 2015)
Bingham, T, *The Rule of Law* (London, Penguin, 2010)
Bix, BH, 'Law as an Autonomous Discipline' in P Cane and M Tushnet (eds), *The Oxford Handbook of Legal Studies* (Oxford, Oxford University Press, 2003) 975–87
Blokker, NM, and Schermers, HG (eds), *Proliferation of International Organizations: Legal Issues* (The Hague, Kluwer, 2001)
Blum, G, 'Bilateralism, Multilateralism, and the Architecture of International Law' (2008) 48 *Harvard International Law Journal* 323
Bluntschli, JC, *The Theory of the State*, English translation from the 6th German edn (Oxford, Clarendon Press, 1885)
—— *Le Droit International Codifié*, 5th edn (Paris, Guillaumin, 1895)
Bogdandy, A von, 'Law and Politics in the WTO: Strategies to Cope with a Deficient Relationship' (2001) 5 *Max Planck Yearbook of United Nations Law* 609
—— 'Globalization and Europe: How to Square Democracy and Globalization' (2004) 15 *European Journal of International Law* 885
Bogdandy, A von, Dann, P, and Goldmann, M, 'Developing the Publicness of Public International Law: Towards a Legal Framework for Global Governance Activities' (2008) 9 *German Law Journal* 1375
Bogdandy, A von, and Goldmann, M, 'The Exercise of International Public Authority through National Policy Assessments: The OECD's PISA Policy as a Paradigm for a New Standard Instrument' (2008) 5 *International Organizations Law Review* 241
Bogdandy, A von, and Venzke, I, *In Whose Name? A Public Law Theory of International Adjudication* (Oxford, Oxford University Press, 2014)
Bolton, J, 'Should We Take Global Governance Seriously?' (2000) 1 *Chicago Journal of International Law* 220
Bothe, M, 'Security Council's Targeted Sanctions against Presumed Terrorists: The Need to Comply with Human Rights Standards' (2008) 6 *Journal of International Criminal Justice* 541
Boucher, D, and Kelly, PJ (eds), *The Social Contract from Hobbes to Rawls* (Abingdon, Routledge, 2005)
Boyle, A, 'Soft Law in International Law-Making' in M Evans (ed), *International Law*, 4th edn (Oxford, Oxford University Press, 2014) 118–36
Boyle, A, and Chinkin, C, *The Making of International Law* (Oxford, Oxford University Press, 2007)
Boyle, FA, *World Politics and International Law* (Durham, NC, Duke University Press, 1985)
Brierly, JL, 'The "*Lotus*" Case' (1928) 174 *Law Quarterly Review* 154

—— *The Law of Nations: An Introduction to the International Law of Peace*, 2nd edn (Oxford, Oxford University Press, 1936)

—— *The Outlook for International Law* (Oxford, Clarendon Press, 1944)

—— 'The Basis of Obligation in International Law' in H Lauterpacht and CHM Waldock (eds), *The Basis of Obligation in International Law and Other Papers by the Late James Leslie Brierly* (Oxford, Clarendon Press, 1958) 1–67

—— 'The Shortcomings of International Law' in H Lauterpacht and CHM Waldock (eds), *The Basis of Obligation in International Law and Other Papers by the Late James Leslie Brierly* (Oxford, Clarendon Press, 1958) 68–80

Brölmann, C, 'Law-Making Treaties: Form and Function in International Law' (2005) 74 *Nordic Journal of International Law* 383

—— *The Institutional Veil in Public International Law: International Organizations and the Law of Treaties* (Oxford, Hart Publishing, 2007)

Broude, T, 'Fragmentation(s) of International Law: On Normative Integration as Authority Allocation' in T Broude and Y Shany (eds), *The Shifting Allocation of Authority in International Law: Considering Sovereignty, Supremacy and Subsidiarity* (Oxford, Hart Publishing, 2008) 99–120

Brown, GW, 'The Idea of Autonomy: Accountability, Self-determinism and What Normative Claims about Institutional Autonomy in Global Governance Should Mean' in R Collins and ND White (eds), *International Organizations and the Idea of Autonomy: Institutional Independence in the International Legal Order* (Abingdon, Routledge, 2011) 104–19

Brownlie, I, 'The United Nations as a Form of Government' in JES Fawcett and R Higgins (eds), *International Organization: Law in Movement (Essays in Honour of John McMahon)* (Oxford, Oxford University Press, 1974) 26–36

—— 'The Reality and Efficacy of International Law' (1981) 52 *British Yearbook of International Law* 1

—— *The Rule of Law in International Affairs: International Law at the 50th Anniversary of the United Nations* (The Hague, Martinus Nijhoff, 1998)

Brunnée, J, and Toope, SJ, *Legitimacy and Legality in International Law: An Interactional Account* (Cambridge, Cambridge University Press, 2010)

Bryde, BO, 'International Democratic Constitutionalism' in R St J Macdonald and DM Johnston (eds), *The Structure and Process of International Law: Essays in Legal Philosophy, Doctrine, and Theory* (The Hague, Martinus Nijhoff, 1983) 103–23

Buchanan, A, and Keohane, RO, 'The Legitimacy of Global Governance Institutions' (2006) 20 *Ethics and International Affairs* 405

Buchanan, RM, 'Protesting the WTO in Seattle: Transnational Citizen Action, International Law, and the Event' in F Johns, R Joyce and S Pahuja (eds), *Events: The Force of International Law* (Abingdon, Routledge, 2011) 221–33

Bull, H, *The Anarchical Society: A Study of Order in World Politics*, 4th edn (Basingstoke, Palgrave Macmillan, 2012)

Byers, M, *Custom, Power and the Power of Rules: International Relations and Customary International Law* (Cambridge, Cambridge University Press, 1999)

Campbell, A, 'International Law and Primitive Law' (1988) 8 *Oxford Journal of Legal Studies* 169

Campbell, T, *The Legal Theory of Ethical Positivism* (Aldershot, Dartmouth, 1996)

Capaldo, GZ, *The Pillars of Global Law* (Aldershot, Ashgate, 2008)
Capps, P, 'The Rejection of the Universal State' in N Tsagourias (ed), *Transnational Constitutionalism* (Cambridge, Cambridge University Press, 2007) 17–43
—— *Human Dignity and the Foundations of International Law* (Oxford, Hart Publishing, 2009)
—— 'Lauterpacht's Method' (2012) 82 *British Yearbook of International Law* 248
Cardwell, PJ, and French, D, 'Who Decides? The ECJ's Judgment on Jurisdiction in the MOX Plant Dispute' (2007) 19 *Journal of Environmental Law* 121
Carr, EH, *The Twenty Years' Crisis 1919–1939: An Introduction to the Study of International Relations*, 2nd edn (London, MacMillan, 1946)
Carty, A, *The Decay of International Law: A Reappraisal of the Limits of Legal Imagination in International Affairs* (Manchester, Manchester University Press, 1986)
—— 'Why Theory?—The Implications for International Law Teaching' in P Allott et al, *Theory and International Law: An Introduction* (London, British Institute of International and Comparative Law, 1991) 75–99
Casanovas, O, *Unity and Pluralism in Public International Law* (The Hague, Martinus Nijhoff, 2001)
Cass, DZ, *The Constitutionalization of the World Trade Organization* (Oxford, Oxford University Press, 2005)
Cassese, A, *International Law in a Divided World* (Oxford, Clarendon Press, 1986)
—— 'Remarks on Scelle's Theory of "Role Splitting" (*dédoublement fonctionnel*) in International Law' (1990) 1 *European Journal of International Law* 210
—— 'The *Nicaragua* and *Tadic* Tests Revisited in Light of the ICJ Judgment on Genocide in Bosnia' (2007) 18 *European Journal of International Law* 649
—— *International Law*, 2nd edn (Oxford, Oxford University Press, 2005)
Charney, JL, 'Universal International Law' (1993) 87 *American Journal of International Law* 529
Charnovitz, S, 'Nongovernmental Organizations and International Law' (2006) 100 *American Journal of International Law* 348
Cherif Bassiouni, M, 'The Philosophy and Policy of International Criminal Justice' in LC Vorah et al (eds), *Man's Inhumanity to Man: Essays on International Law in Honour of Antonio Cassese* (Leiden, Martinus Nijhoff Publishers, 2003) 65–126
Chesterman, S, 'An International Rule of Law?' (2008) 56 *American Journal of Comparative Law* 331
—— 'International Territorial Administration and the Limits of Law' (2009) 23 *Leiden Journal of International Law* 23
Chimni, BS, 'International Institutions Today: An Imperial Global State in the Making' (2004) 15 *European Journal of International Law* 1
Chinkin, C, 'Normative Development in the International Legal System' in D Shelton (ed), *Commitment and Compliance: The Role of Non-binding Norms in the International Legal System* (Oxford, Oxford University Press, 2003) 21–42
Christiano, T, 'Authority' in EN Zalta (ed), *The Stanford Encyclopedia of Philosophy* (spring 2013 edn), available at: http://plato.stanford.edu/archives/spr2013/entries/authority
Churchill, R, and Ulfstein, G, 'Autonomous Institutional Arrangements in Multilateral Environmental Agreements: A Little-Noticed Phenomenon in International Law' (2000) 94 *American Journal of International Law* 623

Claude, Jr IL, *Swords into Plowshares: The Problems and Progress of International Organization*, 4th edn (New York, Random House, 1971)

Coleman, J, 'Incorporationism, Conventionality, and the Practical Difference Thesis' in J Coleman (ed), *Hart's Postscript: Essays on the Postscript to the* Concept of Law (Oxford, Oxford University Press, 2001) 99–147

—— *The Practice of Principle: In Defence of a Pragmatist Approach to Legal Theory* (Oxford, Oxford University Press, 2001)

Collins, R, 'Constitutionalism as Liberal-Juridical Consciousness: Echoes from International Law's Past' (2009) 22 *Leiden Journal of International Law* 251

—— 'Modernist-Positivism and the Problem of Institutional Autonomy in International Law' in R Collins and ND White (eds), *International Organizations and the Idea of Autonomy: Institutional Independence in the International Legal Order* (Abingdon, Routledge, 2011) 22–47

—— 'Non-state Actors in International Institutional Law: Non-state, Inter-state or Supra-state? The Peculiar Identity of the Intergovernmental Organization' in J d'Aspremont (ed), *Participants in the International Legal System: Multiple Perspectives on Non-state Actors in International Law* (Abingdon, Routledge, 2011) 311–25

—— 'Classical Legal Positivism in International Law Revisited' in J d'Aspremont and J Kammerhofer (eds), *International Legal Positivism in a Postmodern World* (Cambridge, Cambridge University Press, 2014) 23–49

—— 'No Longer at the Vanishing Point? International Law and the Analytical Tradition in Jurisprudence' (2014) 5 *Jurisprudence* 265

—— 'The Rule of Law and the Quest for Constitutional Substitutes in International Law' (2014) 83 *Nordic Journal of International Law* 87

—— 'Mapping the Terrain of Institutional "Lawmaking": Form and Function in International Law' in E Fahey (ed), *The Actors of Postnational Rule-Making: Contemporary Challenges of European and International Law* (Abingdon, Routledge, 2015) 27–46

—— 'The Problematic Concept of the International Legal Official' (2015) 3-4 *Transnational Legal Theory* 608

—— 'The Progressive Conception of International Law: Brierly and Lauterpacht in the *Interbellum* Period' in R McCorquodale and J-P Gauci (eds), *British Influences on International Law 1915–2015* (Leiden, Brill, forthcoming, 2016)

Collins, R, and Bohm, A, 'International Law as Professional Practice: The Bounds of Legal Autonomy' in A Nollkaemper, J d'Aspremont, W Werner and T Gazzini (eds), *International Law as a Profession* (Cambridge, Cambridge University Press, 2016, forthcoming)

Collins, R, and White, ND (eds), *International Organizations and the Idea of Autonomy: Institutional Independence in the International Legal Order* (Abingdon, Routledge, 2011)

Cooker, C de (ed), *Accountability, Investigation and Due Process in International Organizations* (Leiden, Martinus Nijhoff, 2005)

Cotterrell, R, *The Politics of Jurisprudence: A Critical Introduction to Legal Philosophy*, 2nd edn (Oxford, Oxford University Press, 2003)

Coyle, S, 'Positivism as a Statist Philosophy of Law' (2008) 59 *Northern Ireland Legal Quarterly* 49

—— 'The Ideality of Law' (2009) 6 *Journal of Moral Philosophy* 521
—— 'Legality and the Liberal Order' (2013) 76 *Modern Law Review* 401
Craig, P, 'Formal and Substantive Conception of the Rule of Law: An Analytical Framework' (1997) *Public Law* 467
Crawford, J, 'International Law and the Rule of Law' (1993) 24 *Adelaide Law Review* 3
—— 'The Charter of the United Nations as a Constitution' in H Fox (ed), *The Changing Constitution of the United Nations* (London, British Institute of International and Comparative Law, 1997) 3–16
Cryer, R, *Prosecuting International Crimes: Selectivity and the International Criminal Law Regime* (Cambridge, Cambridge University Press, 2005)
Cryer, R, and White, ND, 'The International Criminal Court and the Security Council: An Uncomfortable Relationship' in J Doria, H-P Gasser and M-C Bassiouni (eds), *The Legal Regime of the International Criminal Court: Essays in Memory of Igor Blishchenko* (Leiden, Martinus Nijhoff, 2009) 455–84
Culver, K and Giudice, M, *Legality's Borders: An Essay in General Jurisprudence* (Oxford, Oxford University Press, 2010)
d'Amato, A, 'The Neo-positivist Concept of International Law' (1965) 59 *American Journal of International Law* 321
—— *The Concept of Custom in International Law* (Ithaca, NY, Cornell University Press, 1971)
—— 'Is International Law Really "Law"?' (1985) 79 *Northwestern University Law Review* 1293
—— 'Trashing Customary International Law' (1987) 81 *American Journal of International Law* 101
Damrosch, LF, '"Sovereignty" and International Organizations' (1997) 3 *UC Davis Journal of International Law and Policy* 159
Danilenko, GM, *Law-Making in the International Community* (Dordrecht, Martinus Nijhoff, 1993)
d'Aspremont, J, 'Softness in International Law: A Self-Serving Quest for New Legal Materials' (2008) 19 *European Journal of International Law* 1075
—— *Formalism and the Sources of International Law: A Theory of the Ascertainment of Legal Norms* (Oxford, Oxford University Press, 2011)
—— 'Formalism versus Flexibility in the Law of Treaties' in CJ Tams, A Tzanakopoulos, A Zimmerman and AE Richford (eds), *Research Handbook on the Law of Treaties* (Cheltenham, Edward Elgar, 2014) 257–84
—— 'Herbert Hart in Today's International Legal Scholarship' in J d'Aspremont and J Kammerhofer (eds), *International Legal Positivism in a Postmodern World* (Cambridge, Cambridge University Press, 2014) 114–50
David, E, 'Primary and Secondary Rules' in J Crawford, A Pellet and S Olleson (eds), *The Law of International Responsibility* (Oxford, Oxford University Press, 2010) 27–33
Davis, KE, Kingsbury, B, and Merry, SE, 'Indicators as a Technology of Governance' (2012) 46 *Law and Society Review* 71
de Wet, E, *The Chapter VII Powers of the United Nations Security Council* (Oxford, Hart Publishing, 2004)
Dekker, IF, and Wessel, RA, 'Governance by International Organisations: Rethinking the Source and Normative Force of International Decisions' in IF Dekker and

WG Werner (eds), *Governance and International Legal Theory* (Leiden, Martinus Nijhoff, 2004) 215–36

Delbruck, J, 'Prospects for a "World (Internal) Law?" Legal Developments in a Changing International System' (2002) 9 *Indiana Journal of Global Legal Studies* 401

Dickson, J, *Evaluation and Legal Theory* (Oxford, Hart Publishing, 2001)

—— 'Methodology in Jurisprudence: A Critical Survey' (2004) 10 *Legal Theory* 117

—— 'Is the Rule of Recognition Really a Conventional Rule?' (2007) 27 *Oxford Journal of Legal Studies* 373

Dinstein, Y, 'The ICRC Customary International Humanitarian Law Study' (2006) 36 *Israel Yearbook of Human Rights* 1

Dixon, M, *Textbook on International Law*, 6th edn (Oxford, Oxford University Press, 2007)

Duncanson, IW, 'The Strange World of English Jurisprudence' (1979) 30 *Northern Ireland Legal Quarterly* 207

Dunoff, JL, 'Constitutional Conceits: The WTO's "Constitution" and the Discipline of International Law' (2006) 17 *European Journal of International Law* 647

Dunoff, JL, and Trachtman, JP, 'A Functional Approach to International Constitutionalization' in JL Dunoff and JP Trachtman (eds), *Ruling the World? Constitutionalism, International Law, and Global Governance* (Cambridge, Cambridge University Press, 2009) 3–36

Dupuy, P-M, 'The Constitutional Dimension of the Charter of the United Nations Revisited' (1997) 1 *Max Planck Yearbook of United Nations Law* 1

—— 'L'unité de l'ordre juridique international: cours général de droit international public' (2002) 297 *Recueil des Cours* 9

Dworkin, R, *Taking Rights Seriously* (Cambridge, MA, Harvard University Press, 1978)

—— *Freedom's Law: The Moral Reading of the American Constitution* (Cambridge, MA, Harvard University Press, 1996)

—— *Law's Empire* (Oxford, Hart Publishing, 2004, first published in 1986)

Dyzenhaus, D, 'Why Positivism is Authoritarian' (1992) 37 *American Journal of Jurisprudence* 83

Ehrenberg, KM, 'The Anarchist Official: A Problem for Legal Positivism' (2011) 36 *Australian Journal of Legal Philosophy* 89

Elias, O, 'The Nature of the Subjective Element in Customary International Law' (1995) 44 *International and Comparative Law Quarterly* 501

Elias, OA, and Lim, CL, *The Paradox of Consensualism in International Law* (The Hague, Kluwer Law International, 1998)

Escorihuela, AL, 'Alf Ross: Towards a Realist Critique and Reconstruction of International Law' (2003) 14 *European Journal of International Law* 703

Falk, R, 'The Reality of International Law' (1962) 14 *World Politics* 353

Farrell, I, 'H.L.A. Hart and the Methodology of Jurisprudence' (2006) 84 *Texas Law Review* 983

Fassbender, B, 'Pressure for Security Council Reform' in D Malone (ed), *The UN Security Council: From the Cold War to the 21st Century* (Boulder, CO, Lynne Rienner, 2004) 341–71

Fassbender, B, *The United Nations Charter as the Constitution of the International Community* (Leiden, Martinus Nijhoff, 2009)

Finnis, J, 'Revolutions and Continuity of Law' in AWB Simpson (ed), *Oxford Essays in Jurisprudence: Second Series* (Oxford, Clarendon Press, 1971) 44–76
—— 'The Truth in Legal Positivism' in RP George (ed), *The Autonomy of Law: Essays on Legal Positivism* (Oxford, Oxford University Press, 1996) 195–214
—— 'On Hart's Ways: Law as Reason and as Fact' (2007) 52 *American Journal of Jurisprudence* 25
—— *Natural Law and Natural Rights*, 2nd edn (Oxford, Oxford University Press, 2011)
Fiore, P, *International Law Codified and its Legal Sanction; or the Legal Organization of the Society of States* (translated from the 5th Italian edn by Edwin M Borchard) (New York, Baker, Voorhis & Company, 1918)
Fitzmaurice, GG, 'The Foundations of the Authority of International Law and the Problem of Enforcement' (1956) 19 *Modern Law Review* 1
—— 'Some Problems Regarding the Formal Sources of International Law' in *Symbolae Verzijl* (The Hague, Martinus Nijhoff, 1958) 153–76
Franck, TM, 'Some Observations on the ICJ's Procedural and Substantive Innovations (in Appraisals of the ICJ's Decision in Nicaragua vs. United States (Merits))' (1987) 81 *American Journal of International Law* 116
—— 'Legitimacy in the International System' (1988) 82 *American Journal of International Law* 705
—— *The Power of Legitimacy among Nations* (New York, Oxford University Press, 1990)
—— 'United Nations Based Prospects for a New Global Order' (1990) 22 *New York University Journal of International Law and Politics* 601
—— 'Fairness in the International Legal and Institutional System: General Course on Public International Law' (1993-III) 240 *Recueil des Cours* 9
—— *Fairness in International Law and Institutions* (Oxford, Oxford University Press, 1995)
French, D, 'Autonomy in International Environmental Law and Governance: A Case Study of the Actual (Somewhere between the Fable and the Threat)' in R Collins and ND White (eds), *International Organizations and the Idea of Autonomy: Institutional Independence in the International Legal Order* (Abingdon, Routledge, 2011) 366–79
French, D, Saul, M, and White, ND (eds), *International Law and Dispute Settlement: New Problems and Techniques* (Oxford, Hart Publishing, 2010)
Friedmann, W, 'National Sovereignty, International Cooperation, and the Reality of International Law' (1962–63) 10 *UCLA Law Review* 739
—— *The Changing Structure of International Law* (London, Stevens & Sons, 1964)
—— 'General Course in Public International Law' (1969-II) 127 *Recueil des Cours* 39
—— 'The Reality of International Law—A Reappraisal' (1971) 10 *Columbia Journal of International Law* 46
Friedrichs, J, 'The Meaning of New Medievalism' (2001) 4 *European Journal of International Relations* 475
—— 'The Neomedieval Renaissance: Global Governance and International Law in the New Middle Ages' in IF Dekker and WG Werner (eds), *Governance and International Legal Theory* (Leiden, Martinus Nijhoff, 2004) 3–36

Frowein, JA, and Krisch, N, 'Introduction to Chapter VII' in B Simma (ed), *The Charter of the United Nations: A Commentary*, 2nd edn (Oxford, Oxford University Press, 2002) 701–16

Fukuyama, F, *The End of History and the Last Man* (New York: Avon Books, 1992)

Fuller, L, *The Morality of Law*, revised edn (New Haven, CT, Yale University Press, 1969)

Gaja, G, 'Positivism and Dualism in Dinisio Anzilotti' (1992) 3 *European Journal of International Law* 123

Gazzini, T, 'The Relationship between International Legal Personality and the Autonomy of International Organizations' in R Collins and ND White (eds), *International Organizations and the Idea of Autonomy: Institutional Independence in the International Legal Order* (Abingdon, Routledge, 2011) 196–212

George, RP (ed), *The Autonomy of Law: Essays on Legal Positivism* (Oxford, Oxford University Press, 1996)

Georgiev, D, 'Politics or Rule of Law: Deconstruction and Legitimacy in International Law' (1993) 4 *European Journal of International Law* 1

Goldmann, M, 'A Matter of Perspective: Global Governance and the Distinction between Public and Private Authority (and Not Law)' (4 November 2013), available at: http://ssrn.com/abstract=2260293

Goldsmith, JL, and Posner, EA, *The Limits of International Law* (Oxford, Oxford University Press, 2005)

Goldstein, J, et al (eds), *Legalization and World Politics* (Cambridge, MA, MIT Press, 2001)

Gourgourinis, A, 'General/Particular International Law and Primary/Secondary Rules: Unitary Terminology of a Fragmented System' (2011) 22 *European Journal of International Law* 993

Green, L, 'The Concept of Law Revisited' (1996) 94 *Journal of Legal Studies* 1687

—— 'Positivism and Conventionalism' (1999) 12 *Canadian Journal of Law and Jurisprudence* 35

—— 'Legal Positivism' in EN Zalta (ed), *The Stanford Encyclopedia of Philosophy* (Fall 2009 Edition), available at: http://plato.stanford.edu/archives/fall2009/entries/legal-positivism

—— 'Legal Obligation and Authority' in EN Zalta (ed), *The Stanford Encyclopedia of Philosophy* (Winter 2012 edn), available at: http://plato.stanford.edu/archives/win2012/entries/legal-obligation

Grewe, WG, *The Epochs of International Law* (Berlin, Walter de Gruyter, 2000)

Griffith, J, 'Is Law Important?' (1979) 54 *New York University Law Review* 339

Guggenheim, P, 'The Birth of Autonomous International Law' in *International Law in a Changing World* (Dobbs Ferry, NY, Oceana, 1963)

Gur, N, 'Are Legal Rules Content-Independent Reasons?' (2011) 5 *Problema* 175

Hall, WE, *A Treatise on International Law*, 2nd edn (Oxford, Clarendon Press, 1884)

Hampton, J, *Hobbes and the Social Contract Tradition* (Cambridge, Cambridge University Press, 1986)

Hart, HLA 'Scandinavian Realism' (1959) 17 *Cambridge Law Journal* 233

—— 'Comment' in R Gavison (ed), *Issues in Contemporary Legal Philosophy: The Influence of HLA Hart* (Oxford, Clarendon Press, 1987) 35–42

—— *The Concept of Law*, 3rd edn (Oxford, Clarendon Press, 2012)
Hegel, GWF, *Grundlinien der Philosophie des Rechts* (G Lasson(ed)) (Leipzig, Felix Meiner, 1911, originally published in 1821)
Held, D, *Models of Democracy*, 3rd edn (Cambridge, Polity Press, 2006)
Held, D, and McGrew, A (eds), *The Global Transformation Reader: An Introduction to the Globalization Debate*, 2nd edn (Cambridge, Polity Press, 2003)
Henkin, L, *How Nations Behave: Law and Foreign Policy*, 2nd edn (New York, Columbia University Press, 1979)
Hernandez, G, *The International Court of Justice and the Judicial Function* (Oxford, Oxford University Press, 2014)
Higgins, R, *The Development of International Law through the Political Organs of the United Nations* (Oxford, Oxford University Press, 1963)
Hirsch, M, *Responsibility of International Organizations Towards Third Parties: Some Basic Principles* (Dordrecht, Martinus Nijhoff, 1995)
Hirst, P, and Thompson, G, *Globalization in Question*, 2nd edn (Cambridge, Polity Press, 2000)
Hobbes, T, *Leviathan* (CB Macpherson (ed), London, Penguin, 1968, first published in 1651)
Holland, TE, *Studies in International Law* (Oxford, Clarendon Press, 1898)
—— *Elements of Jurisprudence*, 9th edn (Oxford, Oxford University Press, 1900)
Holls, FW, *The Peace Conference at the Hague, and its Bearing on International Law and Policy* (New York, MacMillan, 1900)
Hoof, GJH van, *Rethinking the Sources of International Law* (Deventer, Kluwer, 1983)
Howse, R, 'The Legitimacy of the World Trade Organization' in J-M Coicaud and V Heiskanen (eds), *The Legitimacy of International Organizations* (Tokyo, United Nations University Press, 2001) 355–407
—— 'From Politics to Technocracy—and Back Again: The Fate of the Multilateral Trading Regime' (2002) 96 *American Journal of International Law* 94
—— 'Human Rights in the WTO: Whose Rights, What Humanity? Comment on Petersmann' (2002) 13 *European Journal of International Law* 651
Howse, R, and Nicolaidis, K, 'Enhancing WTO Legitimacy: Constitutionalization or Global Subsidiarity?' (2003) 16 *Governance* 73
Hudson, MO, 'The Development of International Law since the War' (1928) 22 *American Journal of International Law* 330
—— *Progress in International Organization* (Stanford, CA, Stanford University Press; London, Oxford University Press, 1932)
Hueck, IJ, 'The Discipline of the History of International Law—New Trends and Methods on the History of International Law' (2001) 3 *Journal of the History of International law* 194
Hurd, I, 'The International Rule of Law and the Domestic Analogy' (2015) 4 *Global Constitutionalism* 365
Jain, N, 'A Separate Law for Peacekeepers: The Clash between the Security Council and the International Criminal Court' (2005) 16 *European Journal of International Law* 239
Janis, MW, 'Jeremy Bentham and the Fashioning of 'International Law'' (1984) 78 *American Journal of International Law* 405

Jellinek, G, *Die Rechtliche Natur der Staatenverträge* (Vienna, A Hölder, 1880)
Jenks, CW, 'The Conflict of Law-Making Treaties' (1953) 30 *British Yearbook of International Law* 401
—— 'Craftsmanship in International Law' (1956) 50 *American Journal of International Law* 32
—— *The Common Law of Mankind* (London, Stevens and Sons, 1958)
Jennings, RY, 'What is International Law and How Do We Tell it When We See it?' (1981) 37 *Schweitzerisches Jahrbuch für Internationales Recht* 59
Jessup, PC, *A Modern Law of Nations: An Introduction* (New York, Macmillan, 1952)
Johnston, DM, 'Functionalism in the Theory of International Law' (1988) 26 *Canadian Yearbook of International Law* 3
Jouannet, E, 'What is the Use of International Law? International Law as a 21st Century Guardian of Welfare' (2008) 28 *Michigan Journal of International Law* 815
—— 'A Century of French International Legal Scholarship' (2009) 61 *Maine Law Review* 83
Kammerhofer, J, 'Uncertainty in the Formal Sources of International Law: Customary International Law and Some of its Problems' (2004) 15 *European Journal of International Law* 523
—— *Uncertainty in International Law: A Kelsenian perspective* (Abingdon, Routledge, 2011)
Kazansky, P, 'Théorie de l'administration internationale' (1902) IX *Revue Générale de Droit International Public* 366
Kelsen, H, *Law and Peace in International Relations: The Oliver Wendell Holmes Lectures, 1940–41* (Cambridge, MA, Harvard University Press, 1942)
—— *General Theory of Law and State* (Cambridge, MA, Harvard University Press, 1945)
—— *Principles of International Law* (New York, Rinehart & Co, 1952)
—— 'Théorie du droit international public' (1953-III) 84 *Recueil des Cours* 1
—— *Pure Theory of Law* (Berkeley, University of California Press, 1967)
Kennedy, D, 'The Move to Institutions' (1987) 8 *Cardozo Law Review* 841
—— 'International Law and the Nineteenth Century: History of an Illusion' (1997) 17 *Quinnipiac Law Review* 99
—— 'The Mystery of Global Governance' in JL Dunoff and JP Trachtman (eds), *Ruling the World? Constitutionalism, International Law, and Global Governance* (Cambridge, Cambridge University Press, 2009) 37–68
Kingsbury, B, 'Legal Positivism as Normative Politics: International Society, Balance of Power and Lassa Oppenheim's Positive International Law' (2002) 13 *European Journal of International Law* 401
—— 'The Concept of "Law" in Global Administrative Law' (2009) 20 *European Journal of International Law* 23
Kingsbury, B, Krisch, N, and Stewart, R, 'The Emergence of Global Administrative Law' (2005) 68 *Law and Contemporary Problems* 15
Kingsbury, B, Krisch, N, Stewart, RB, and Wiener, JB, 'Foreword: Global Governance as Administration—National and Transnational Approaches to Global Administrative Law' (2005) 68 *Law and Contemporary Problems* 1

Kirgis Jr, FL, 'Custom on a Sliding Scale' (1987) 81 *American Journal of International Law* 146

Klabbers, J, *The Concept of Treaty in International Law* (The Hague, Kluwer International, 1996)

—— 'The Redundancy of Soft Law' (1996) 65 *Nordic Journal of International Law* 167

—— 'Clinching the Concept of Sovereignty: Wimbledon Redux' (1998) 3 *Austrian Review of International and European Law* 345

—— 'The Changing Image of International Institutions' in J-M Coicaud and V Heiskanen (eds), *The Legitimacy of International Organizations* (Tokyo, United Nations University Press, 2001) 221–55

—— 'The Life and Times of International Organizations' (2001) 70 *Nordic Journal of International Law* 287

—— 'Constitutionalism Lite' (2004) 1 *International Organizations Law Review* 3

—— 'The Concept of Legal Personality' (2005) 11 *Ius Gentium* 35

—— 'The Relative Autonomy of International Law or the Forgotten Politics of Interdisciplinarity' (2005) 1 *Journal of International Law & International Relations* 35

—— 'Possible Islands of Predictability: The Legal Thought of Hannah Arendt' (2007) 20 *Leiden Journal of International Law* 1

—— 'Reluctant *Grundnormen*: Articles 31(3)(c) and 41 of the Vienna Convention on the Law of Treaties and the Fragmentation of International Law' in M Craven, M Fitzmaurice and M Vogiatzi (eds), *Time, History and International Law* (Leiden: Martinus Nijhoff, 2007) 141–61

—— *An Introduction to International Institutional Law*, 2nd edn (Cambridge, Cambridge University Press, 2009)

—— 'Setting the Scene' in J Klabbers, A Peters and G Ulfstein, *The Constitutionalization of International Law* (Oxford, Oxford University Press, 2010) 1–44

—— 'Law-Making and Constitutionalism' in J Klabbers, A Peters and G Ulfstein, *The Constitutionalization of International Law* (Oxford, Oxford University Press, 2010) 81–126

—— 'Autonomy, Constitutionalism and Virtue in International Institutional Law' in R Collins and ND White (eds), *International Organizations and the Idea of Autonomy: Institutional Independence in the International Legal Order* (Abingdon, Routledge, 2011) 120–40

Klabbers, J, Peters, A, and Ulfstein, G, *The Constitutionalization of International Law* (Oxford, Oxford University Press, 2010)

Knoll, B, *The Legal Status of Territories Subject to Administration by International Organizations* (Cambridge, Cambridge University Press, 2008)

Koh, HH, 'Why Do Nations Obey International Law?' (1997) 106 *Yale Law Journal* 2599

Kolb, R, 'Politis and Sociological Jurisprudence of Inter-War International Law' (2012) 23 *European Journal of International Law* 233

Koskenniemi, M, 'The Politics of International Law' (1990) 1 *European Journal of International Law* 4

—— 'The Police in the Temple. Order, Justice and the UN: A Dialectical View' (1995) 6 *European Journal of International Law* 325

—— 'Lauterpacht: The Victorian Tradition in International Law' (1997) 8 *European Journal of International Law* 215

—— 'Repetition as Reform: Repetition as Reform: Georges Abi-Saab Cours Général de droit international public' (1998) 9 *European Journal of International Law* 405

—— 'Carl Schmitt, Morgenthau, and the Image of Law in International Relations' in M Byers (ed), *The Role of Law in International Politics: Essays in International Relations and International Law* (Oxford, Oxford University Press, 2000) 17–34

—— *The Gentle Civilizer of Nations: The Rise and Fall of International Law 1870–1960* (Cambridge, Cambridge University Press, 2001)

—— 'Global Governance and Public International Law' (2004) 37 *Kritische Justiz* 241

—— 'Why History of International Law Today?' (2004) *Rechtsgeschichte* 61

—— *From Apology to Utopia: The Structure of International Legal Argument* (Cambridge, Cambridge University Press, 2005)

—— 'International Law in Europe: Between Tradition and Renewal' (2005) 16 *European Journal of International Law* 113

—— 'International Legislation Today: Limits and Possibilities' (2005) 23 *Wisconsin International Law Journal* 61

—— 'Constitutionalism as Mindset: Reflections on Kantian Themes about International Law and Globalization' (2007) 8 *Theoretical Inquiries in Law* 9

—— 'The Fate of Public International Law: Between Technique and Politics' (2007) 70 *Modern Law Review* 1

—— 'Legacy of the Nineteenth Century' in D Armstrong (ed), *Routledge Handbook of International Law* (Abingdon, Routledge, 2009) 141–53

—— 'Miserable Comforters: International Relations as New Natural Law' (2009) 15 *European Journal of International Relations* 395

—— 'What is International Law for?' in M Evans (ed), *International Law*, 4th edn (Oxford, Oxford University Press, 2014) 29–52

Koskenniemi, M, and Leino, P, 'Fragmentation of International Law? Postmodern Anxieties' (2002) 15 *Leiden Journal of International Law* 553

Kramer, M, 'The Rule of Misrecognition in the Hart of Jurisprudence' (1988) 8 *Oxford Journal of Legal Studies* 401

Kramer, MH, Grant, C, Colburn, B, and Hatzistavrou, A (eds), *The Legacy of H.L.A. Hart: Legal, Political, and Moral Philosophy* (Oxford, Oxford University Press, 2008)

Kratochwil, F, 'The Limits of Contract' (1994) 5 *European Journal of International Law* 465

—— 'How do Norms Matter?' in M Byers (ed), *The Role of Law in International Politics: Essays in International Relations and International Law* (Oxford, Oxford University Press, 2000) 35–68

—— 'Has the "Rule of Law" Become a "Rule of Lawyers"? An Inquiry into the Use and Abuse of an Ancient *Topos* in Contemporary Debates' in G Palombella and N Walker (eds), *Relocating the Rule of Law* (Oxford, Hart Publishing, 2009) 171–96

Krisch, N, 'International Law in Times of Hegemony: Unequal Power and the Shaping of the International Legal Order' (2005) 16 *European Journal of International Law* 369

—— 'Global Administrative Law and the Constitutional Ambition' in P Dobner and M Loughlin (eds), *The Twilight of Constitutionalism?* (Oxford, Oxford University Press, 2010) 245–66

Krisch, N, and Kingsbury, B, 'Introduction: Global Governance and Global Administrative Law in the International Legal Order' (2006) 17 *European Journal of International Law* 1

Kumm, M, 'International Law in National Courts: The International Rule of Law and the Limits of the Internationalist Model' (2003–04) 44 *Virginia Journal of International Law* 19

—— 'The Legitimacy of International Law: A Constitutionalist Framework of Analysis' (2004) 15 *European Journal of International Law* 907

—— 'The Best of Times and the Worst of Times: Between Constitutional Triumphalism and Nostalgia' in P Dobner and M Loughlin (eds), *The Twilight of Constitutionalism?* (Oxford, Oxford University Press, 2010) 201–19

Kunz, J, 'On the Theoretical Basis of the Law of Nations' (1924) 10 *Transactions of the Grotius Society* 115

Kyritsis, D, 'The Normativity of the Practice of Officials: A Philosophical Programme' in S Bertea and G Pavlakos (eds), *New Essays on the Normativity of Law* (Oxford, Hart Publishing, 2011) 177–95

Lachs, M, 'Some Reflections on Substance and Form in International Law' in W Friedmann, L Henkin and O Lissitzyn (eds), *Transnational Law in a Changing Society: Essays in Honour of Philip C Jessup* (New York, Columbia University Press, 1972) 99–112

Landauer, C, 'J. L. Brierly and the Modernization of International Law' (1993) 25 *Vanderbilt Journal of International Law* 881

Lasson, A, *Princip und Zukunft des Völkerrechts* (Berlin, Hertz, 1871)

Lauterpacht, H, 'Westlake and Present Day International Law' (1925) 5 *Economica* 307

—— *Private Law Sources and Analogies of International Law (with Special Reference to International Arbitration)* (London, Longmans, 1927)

—— 'The Nature of International Law and General Jurisprudence' (1932) 37 *Economica* 301

—— *The Function of Law in the International Community* (Oxford, Clarendon Press, 1933)

—— 'The Covenant as the Higher Law' (1936) 17 *British Yearbook of International Law* 54

—— 'The Grotian Tradition in International Law' (1946) 23 *British Yearbook of International Law* 1

—— *The Development of International Law by the International Court* (London, Stevens and Sons, 1958)

—— 'The Definition and Nature of International Law and its Place in Jurisprudence' in E Lauterpacht (ed), *International Law, Being the Collected Papers of Hersch Lauterpacht*, vol 1 (Cambridge, Cambridge University Press, 1970) 9–49

—— 'Kelsen's Pure Science of International Law' in E Lauterpacht (ed), *International Law, Being the Collected Papers of Hersch Lauterpacht*, vol 1 (Cambridge, Cambridge University Press, 1970) 424–29

—— 'The Place of International Law in Jurisprudence' in E Lauterpacht (ed), *International Law, Being the Collected Papers of Hersch Lauterpacht*, vol 1 (Cambridge, Cambridge University Press, 1970) 193–215

—— 'The Nature of International Law and General Jurisprudence' in E Lauterpacht (ed), *International Law: Being the Collected Papers of Hersch Lauterpacht—Volume 2: The Law of Peace, Pt 1* (Cambridge, Cambridge University Press, 1975) 3–21

Lavranos, N, 'The *MOX Plant* and *IJzeren Rijn* Disputes: Which Court is the Supreme Arbiter?' (2006) 19 *Leiden Journal of International Law* 223

Lawrence, TJ, *Essays on Some Disputed Questions in Modern International Law* (Cambridge, Deighton, Bell and Co, 1885)

—— *A Handbook of Public International Law* (Cambridge, D Bell & Co, 1898)

—— *The Principles of International Law*, 7th edn (London, MacMillan, 1923)

Leben, C, 'Hans Kelsen and the Advancement of International Law' (1998) 9 *European Journal of International Law* 287

Lefkowitz, D, '(Dis)solving the Chronological Paradox in Customary International Law: A Hartian Approach' (2008) 21 *Canadian Journal of Law and Jurisprudence* 129

Leino-Sandberg, P, 'Particularity as Universality: The Politics of Human Rights in the European Union' (2005) *The Erik Castrén Institute Research Reports 15/2005*, available at: http://ethesis.helsinki.fi/julkaisut/oik/erikc/vk/leino-sandberg/particul.pdf

Lev, A, 'The Transformation of International Law in the 19th Century' in A Orakhelashvili (ed), *Research Handbook on the Theory and History of International Law* (Cheltenham, Edward Elgar, 2011) 111–42

Lim, CL, and Elias, OA, *The Paradox of Consensualism in International Law* (The Hague, Martinus Nijhoff, 1998)

Linderfalk, U, 'Is the Hierarchical Structure of Articles 31 and 32 of the Vienna Convention Real or Not? Interpreting the Rules of Interpretation' (2007) 65 *Netherlands International Law Review* 133

Livoja, R, 'The Scope of the Supremacy Clause of the United Nations Charter' (2008) 58 *International and Comparative Law Quarterly* 583

Llewellyn, KN, 'The Normative, the Legal, and the Law-Jobs: The Problem of Juristic Method' (1940) 49 *Yale Law Journal* 1355

Lobban, M, 'English Approaches to International Law in the Nineteenth Century' in M Craven, M Fitzmaurice and M Vogiatzi (eds), *Time, History and International Law* (Leiden, Martinus Nijhoff, 2007) 65–90

Locke, J, *Two Treatises of Government: A Critical Edition with an Introduction and Apparatus Criticus by Peter Laslett* (Cambridge, Cambridge University Press, 1967)

Lorimer, J, *The Institutes of the Law of Nations: A Treatise on the Jural Relations of Separate Political Communities*, vol II (Edinburgh, William Blackwood and Sons, 1884)

Lowe, V, 'The Politics of Law-Making: Are the Method and Character of Norm Creation Changing?' in M Byers (ed), *The Role of Law in International Politics: Essays in International Relations and International Law* (Oxford, Oxford University Press, 2000) 207–26

Luhmann, N, 'Operational Closure and Structural Coupling: The Differentiation of the Legal System' (1992) 13 *Cardozo Law Review* 1419

MacCormick, N, *Legal Reasoning and Legal Theory* (Oxford, Clarendon Press, 1978)

—— 'A Moralistic Case for A-Moralistic Law?' (1985–86) 20 *Valparaiso University Law Review* 1

—— 'The Concept of Law and "*The Concept of Law*"' (1994) 14 *Oxford Journal of Legal Studies* 1

—— 'The Concept of Law and *The Concept of Law*' in RP George (ed), *The Autonomy of Law: Essays on Legal Positivism* (Oxford, Oxford University Press, 1996) 163–93

—— 'Norms, Institutions, and Institutional Facts' (1998) 17 *Law and Philosophy* 301

—— *Institutions of Law: An Essay in Legal Theory* (Oxford, Oxford University Press, 2007)

—— *H. L. A. Hart*, 2nd edn (Stanford, CA, Stanford University Press, 2008)

Macdonald, R St J, 'The International Community as a Legal Community' in R St J Macdonald and DM Johnston (eds), *Towards World Constitutionalism: Issues in the Legal Ordering of the World Community* (Leiden, Martinus Nijhoff, 2005) 853–909

Macdonald, R St J, and Johnston, DM, 'International Legal Theory: New Frontiers of the Discipline' in R St J Macdonald and DM Johnston (eds), *The Structure and Process of International Law: Essays in Legal Philosophy, Doctrine, and Theory* (The Hague, Martinus Nijhoff, 1983) 1–14

Macdonald, R St J, and Johnston, DM (eds), *Towards World Constitutionalism: Issues in the Legal Ordering of the World Community* (Leiden, Martinus Nijhoff, 2005)

Maine, HS, *Ancient Law: Its Connection with the Early History of Society, and its Relations to Modern Ideas* (London, John Murray, 1861)

—— *International Law*, 2nd edn (London, John Murray, 1894)

Marks, S, 'The End of History? Reflections on Some International Legal Theses' (1997) 8 *European Journal of International Law* 449

Marmor, A, 'Legal Conventionalism' in J Coleman (ed), *Hart's Postscript: Essays on the Postscript to the Concept of Law* (Oxford, Oxford University Press, 2001) 195–217

—— *Positive Law and Objective Values* (Oxford, Oxford University Press, 2001)

—— 'The Conventional Foundations of Law' in S Bertea and G Pavlakos (eds), *New Essays on the Normativity of Law* (Oxford, Hart Publishing, 2011) 143–57

Martin, M, 'Raz's The Morality of Freedom: Two Models of Authority' (2010) 1 *Jurisprudence* 63

—— *Judging Positivism* (Oxford, Hart Publishing, 2014)

Martínez, LMH, 'The Legislative Role of the Security Council in its Fight against Terrorism: Legal, Political and Practical Limits' (2008) 57 *International and Comparative Law Quarterly* 333

McNair, A, 'The Functions and Differing Legal Character of Treaties' (1930) 11 *British Yearbook of International Law* 100

—— 'International Legislation' (1933–34) 19 *Iowa Law Review* 177

—— *The Law of Treaties* (Oxford, Clarendon Press, 1961, first published in 1938)

Mendelson, M, 'Are Treaties Merely a Source of Obligation?' in WE Butler (ed), *Perestroika and International Law* (Dordrecht, Martinus Nijhoff, 1990) 81–88

Meron, T, 'International Law in the Age of Human Rights: General Course on Public International Law' (2003) 301 *Recueil des Cours* 9

Merrills, JG, *Anatomy of International Law*, 2nd edn (London, Sweet & Maxwell, 1981)

Millar, AJ, 'Legal Aspects of Stopping Sexual Exploitation and Abuse in U.N. Peacekeeping Operations' (2006) 39 *Cornell International Law Journal* 71

Morgenthau, H, 'Positivism, Functionalism, and International Law' (1940) 34 *American Journal of International Law* 260

—— *Scientific Man vs Power Politics* (Chicago, University of Chicago Press, 1946)

—— *Politics among Nations* (New York, Knopf, 1949)

Morison, WL, 'The Schools Revisited' in R St J Macdonald and DM Johnston (eds), *The Structure and Process of International Law: Essays in Legal Philosophy, Doctrine, and Theory* (The Hague, Martinus Nijhoff, 1983) 131–76

Mulligen, A van, 'Framing Deformalisation in Public International Law' (2015) 3–4 *Transnational Legal Theory* 635

Nardin, T, *Law, Morality, and the Relations of States* (Princeton, NJ, Princeton University Press, 1983)

Neff, S, 'A Short History of International Law' in M Evans (ed), *International Law*, 4th edn (Oxford, Oxford University Press, 2014) 3–28

—— *Justice among Nations: A History of International Law* (Cambridge, MA, Harvard University Press, 2014)

Nijman, JE, *The Concept of International Legal Personality: An Inquiry into the History and Theory of International Law* (The Hague, TMC Asser Press, 2004)

Nippold, O, *The Development of International Law after the War* (Oxford, Clarendon Press, 1923, originally published in German in 1917)

Nollkaemper, A, *National Courts and the International Rule of Law* (Oxford, Oxford University Press, 2011)

Noortmann, M, 'The International Law Association and Non-state Actors: Professional Network, Public Interest Group or Epistemic Community?' in J d'Aspremont (ed), *Participants in the International Legal System* (Abingdon, Routledge, 2011) 233–47

Nussbaum, A, *A Concise History of the Law of Nations* (New York, Macmillan, 1954)

O'Donoghue, A, 'International Constitutionalism and the State' (2013) 11 *International Journal of Constitutional Law* 1021

Olsen, HP, and Toddington, S, 'Legal Idealism and the Autonomy of Law' (1999) 12 *Ratio Juris* 286

—— *Law in its Own Right* (Oxford, Hart Publishing, 1999)

Oppenheim, L, 'The Science of International Law: Its Task and Method' (1908) 2 *American Journal of International Law* 313

—— *The League of Nations and its Problems: Three Lectures* (London, Longmans, Green & Co, 1919)

—— *International Law: A Treatise*, vol 1, 3rd edn (London, Longmans, Green & Co. 1920)

—— *Future of International Law* (Oxford, Clarendon Press, 1921)

Orakhelashvili, A, 'The Impact of Peremptory Norms on Interpretation and Application of the UN Security Council Resolutions' (2005) 16 *European Journal of International Law* 59

Orford, A, 'Locating the International: Military and Monetary Interventions after the Cold War' (1997) 38 *Harvard International Law Journal* 443

—— 'The Gift of Formalism' (2004) 15 *European Journal of International Law* 179

Palombella, G, 'The Rule of Law and its Core' in G Palombella and N Walker (eds), *Relocating the Rule of Law* (Oxford, Hart Publishing, 2009) 17–42

—— 'The Rule of Law as an Institutional Ideal' in L Morlino and G Palombella (eds), *Rule of Law and Democracy: Internal and External Issues* (Leiden, Brill, 2010) 3–40

Palombella, G, and Walker, N, 'Introduction' in G Palombella and N Walker (eds), *Relocating the Rule of Law* (Oxford, Hart Publishing, 2009) xi-xv

Paulus, A, 'From Territoriality to Functionality? Towards a Legal Methodology of Globalization' in IF Dekker and WG Werner (eds), *Governance and International Legal Theory* (Leiden, Martinus Nijhoff, 2004) 59–95

—— 'International Law and International Community' in D Armstrong (ed), *Routledge Handbook of International Law* (Abingdon, Routledge, 2009) 44–54

—— 'The International Legal System as a Constitution' in JL Dunoff and JP Trachtman (eds), *Ruling the World? Constitutionalism, International Law, and Global Governance* (Cambridge, Cambridge University Press, 2009) 69–112

Paulus, A, and Simma, B, 'Responsibility of Individuals for Human Rights Abuses in Internal Conflicts: A Positivist View' (1999) 93 *American Journal of International Law* 302

Pauwelyn, J, *Conflict of Norms in Public International Law: How WTO Law Relates to Other Rules of International Law* (Cambridge, Cambridge University Press, 2003)

Payandeh, M, 'The Concept of International Law in the Jurisprudence of H. L. A. Hart' (2011) 21 *European Journal of International Law* 967

Pellet, A, 'Brief Remarks on the Unilateral Use of Force' (2000) 11 *European Journal of International Law* 385

Perry, SR, 'Hart's Methodological Positivism' in J Coleman (ed), *Hart's Postscript: Essays on the Postscript to the* Concept of Law (Oxford, Oxford University Press, 1994) 311–54

—— 'Hart on Social Rules and the Foundations of Law: Liberating the Internal Point of View' (2006) 75 *Fordham Law Review* 1171

Peters, A, 'Compensatory Constitutionalism: The Function and Potential of Fundamental International Norms and Structures' (2006) 19 *Leiden Journal of International Law* 579

Phillimore, R, *Commentaries upon International Law*, 3rd edn (London, Butterworths, 1879)

Pillet, A, 'Recherches sur les Droits Fondamentaux des États dans l'Ordre des Rapports Internationaux et sur la Solution des Conflits qu'ils Font Naitre' (1898) 5 *Revue Générale de Droit International* 503

Politis, N, *The New Aspects of International Law* (Washington DC, Carnegie Endowment for International Peace, 1928)

Poole, T, 'Sovereign Indignities: International Law as Public Law' (2011) 22 *European Journal of International Law* 351

Portmann, R, *Legal Personality in International Law* (Cambridge, Cambridge University Press, 2008)

Postema, G, 'Coordination and Convention at the Foundations of Law' (1982) 11 *Journal of Legal Studies* 165

—— *Bentham and the Common Law Tradition* (Oxford, Clarendon Press, 1986)

—— 'Law's Autonomy and Public Practical Reasoning' in RP George (ed), *The Autonomy of Law: Essays on Legal Positivism* (Oxford, Clarendon Press, 1996) 79–118

—— 'Jurisprudence as Practical Philosophy' (1998) 4 *Legal Theory* 329

—— 'Norms, Reasons, and Law' (1998) 51 *Current Legal Problems* 149

Pound, R, 'Philosophical Theory and International Law' (1923) 1 *Bibliotheca Visseriana* 1

Prost, M, *The Concept of Unity in Public International Law* (Oxford, Hart Publishing, 2012)

Prost, M, and Clark, PK, 'Unity, Diversity and the Fragmentation of International Law' (2004) 5 *Chinese Journal of International Law* 341

Pulkowski, D, 'Structural Paradigms of International Law' in T Broude and Y Shany (eds), *The Shifting Allocation of Authority in International Law: Considering Sovereignty, Supremacy and Subsidiarity* (Oxford, Hart Publishing, 2008) 51–77

Rawls, J, *A Theory of Justice*, revised edn (Cambridge, MA, Harvard University Press, 1999)

—— *The Law of Peoples* (Cambridge, MA, Harvard University Press, 2001)

Raz, J, *Practical Reason and Norms* (Oxford, Oxford University Press, 1975)

—— 'The Institutional Nature of Law' (1975) 38 *Modern Law Review* 489

—— 'The Rule of Law and its Virtue' (1977) 93 *Law Quarterly Review* 195

—— *The Concept of a Legal System*, 2nd edn (Oxford, Clarendon Press, 1980)

—— *Ethics in the Public Domain: Essays in the Morality of Law and Politics*, revised edn (Oxford, Clarendon Press, 1994)

—— 'Postema on Law's Autonomy and Public Practical Reasons: A Critical Comment' (1998) 4 *Legal Theory* 1

—— *Practical Reason and Norms* (Oxford, Oxford University Press, 1999)

—— *The Authority of Law: Essays on Law and Morality*, 2nd edn (Oxford, Oxford University Press, 2009)

Reinalda, B, and Verbeek, B, 'Policy Autonomy of Intergovernmental Organizations' in R Collins and ND White (eds), *International Organizations and the Idea of Autonomy: Institutional Independence in the International Legal Order* (Abingdon, Routledge, 2011) 87–103

Reinsch, PS, 'International Administrative Law and National Sovereignty' (1909) 3 *American Journal of International Law* 1

Reus-Smit, C, 'The Constitutional Structure of International Society and the Nature of Fundamental Institutions' (1997) 51 *International Organization* 555

—— *'The Moral Purpose of the State: Culture, Social Identity, and Institutional Rationality in International Relations* (Princeton, NJ, Princeton University Press, 1999)

—— 'The Politics of International Law' in C Reus-Smit (ed), *The Politics of International Law*, (Cambridge, Cambridge University Press, 2004) 14–44

Ripstein, A, *Force and Freedom: Kant's Legal and Political Philosophy* (Cambridge, MA, Harvard University Press, 2009)
Roberts, AE, 'Traditional and Modern Approaches to Customary International Law: A Reconciliation' (2001) 95 *American Journal of International Law* 757
Rodriguez-Blanco, V, 'The Moral Puzzle of Legal Authority: A Commentary on Shapiro's Planning Theory of Law' in S Bertea and G Pavlakos (eds), *New Essays on the Normativity of Law* (Oxford, Hart Publishing, 2011) 86–106
Rolin-Jaecquemyns, G, 'De l'étude de la législation comparée et de droit international' (1869) 1 *Revue de Droit International* 11
Romano, C, 'International Organizations and the International Judicial Process: An Overview' in L Boisson de Chazournes, C Romano and R MacKenzie (eds), *International Organizations and International Dispute Settlement: Trends and Prospects* (Ardsley on Hudson, Transnational Publishers, 2002) 3–36
Romano, CPR, 'The Shift from the Consensual to the Compulsory Paradigm in International Adjudication: Elements for a Theory of Consent' (2007) 39 *New York University Journal of International Law and Politics* 791
Root, E, 'The Sanction of International Law' (1908) 2 *American Journal of International Law* 451
Rosenau, JN, 'Governance, Order, and Change in World Politics' in JN Rosenau and E-O Czempiel (eds), *Governance without Government: Order and Change in World Politics* (Cambridge, Cambridge University Press, 1992) 1–29
Ross, A, *On Law and Justice* (Berkeley, University of California Press, 1959)
Rousseau, JJ, *The Social Contract and Other Later Political Writings*, V Gourevitch (ed) (Cambridge, Cambridge University Press, 1997)
Ryngaert, C, Molenaar, EJ, and Nouwen, SMH (eds), *What's Wrong with International Law?: Liber Amicorum A.H.A. Soons* (Leiden, Brill, Nijhoff, 2015)
Scelle, G, 'Essai de systématique de droit international (Plan d'un cours de droit international public)' (1923) 30 *Revue Générale de Droit International Public* 116
—— *Précis de droit des gens: principes et systématique. Pt.2, Droit constitutionnel international* (Paris, Sirey, 1934)
—— *Manuel de droit international public* (Paris, Domat-Montchrestien, 1948)
—— 'Le phénomène juridique du dédoublement fonctionnel' in W Schatzel and H-J Schlochauer (eds), *Rechtsfragen der Internationalen Organisation—Festschrift für H. Wehberg* (Frankfurt am Main, Klostermann, 1956) 324–42
Schachter, O, 'The Nature and Process of Legal Development in International Society' in R St J Macdonald and DM Johnston (eds), *The Structure and Process of International Law: Essays in Legal Philosophy, Doctrine, and Theory* (The Hague, Martinus Nijhoff, 1983) 745–808
—— *International Law in Theory and Practice* (Dordrecht, Martinus Nijhoff, 1991)
Schaubroeck, 'Legal Normativity and the Instrumental Principle' in S Bertea and G Pavlakos (eds), *New Essays on the Normativity of Law* (Oxford, Hart Publishing, 2011) 107–40
Schauer, F, 'Formalism' (1988) 97 *Yale Law Journal* 509
—— 'The Limited Domain of the Law' (2004) 90 *Virginia Law Review* 1909
Schmoeckel, M, 'The Internationalist as a Scientist and Herald: Lassa Oppenheim' (2000) 11 *European Journal of International Law* 699

—— 'Consent and Caution: Lassa Oppenheim and His Reaction to World War I' in R Lessafer (ed), *Peace Treaties and International Law in European History: From the Late Middle Ages to World War One* (Cambridge, Cambridge University Press, 2004) 270–88

Scholte, JA, 'Civil Society and Democratically Accountable Global Governance' (2004) 39 *Government and Opposition* 211

Schücking, W, *The International Union of the Hague Conferences*, Charles G Fenwick (trans) (Oxford, Oxford University Press, 1918)

Schwarzenberger, G, 'The Rule of Law and the Disintegration of the International Society' (1939) 33 *American Journal of International law* 56

Schwöbel, CEJ, 'Organic Global Constitutionalism' (2010) 23 *Leiden Journal of International Law* 529

Scobbie, I, 'A View of Delft: Some Thoughts about Thinking about International Law' in M Evans (ed), *International Law*, 4th edn (Oxford, Oxford University Press, 2014) 53–88

Shany, Y, 'No Longer a Weak Department of Power? Reflections on the Emergence of a New International Judiciary' (2009) 20 *European Journal of International Law* 73

Shapiro, S, 'On Hart's Way Out' in J Coleman (ed), *Hart's Postscript: Essays on the Postscript to the* Concept of Law (Oxford, Oxford University Press, 1994) 149–92

—— 'What is the Rule of Recognition (and Does it Exist)?' in M Alder and K Himma (eds), *The Rule of Recognition and the U.S. Constitution* (Oxford, Oxford University Press, 2009) 235–68

—— *Legality* (Cambridge, MA, Harvard University Press, 2011)

Shaw, M, *International Law*, 7th edn (Cambridge, Cambridge University Press, 2014)

Shelton, D, 'Normative Hierarchy in International Law' (2006) 100 *American Journal of International Law* 291

—— 'International Law and "Relative Normativity"' in M Evans (ed), *International Law*, 4th edn (Oxford, Oxford University Press, 2014) 137–65

Simma, B, 'International Crimes: Injury and Countermeasures: Comments on Part 2 of the ILC Work on State Responsibility' in JHH Weiler, A Cassese and M Spinedi (eds), *International Crimes of State: A Critical Analysis of the ILC's Draft Article 19 on State Responsibility* (Berlin, De Gruyter, 1989) 283–315

—— 'From Bilateralism to Community Interest in International Law' (1994-VI) 250 *Recueil des Cours* 221

Simma, B, and Paulus, A, 'The 'International Community': Facing the Challenge of Globalization' (1998) 9 *European Journal of International Law* 266

Simmonds, N, 'Between Positivism and Idealism' (1991) 50 *Cambridge Law Journal* 308

—— *Law as a Moral Idea* (Oxford, Oxford University Press, 2007)

—— 'Reflexivity and the Idea of law' (2010) 1 *Jurisprudence* 1

Simpson, G, *Great Powers and Outlaw States: Unequal Sovereigns in the International Legal Order* (Cambridge, Cambridge University Press, 2004)

Skouteris, T, *The Notion of Progress in International Law Discourse* (The Hague, TMC Asser Press, 2010)

Slaughter, A-M, *A New World Order* (Princeton, NJ, Princeton University Press, 2004)

Somek, A, 'Kelsen Lives!' (2007) 18 *European Journal of International Law* 409

—— Somek, A, 'The Owl of Minerva: Constitutional Discourse before its Conclusion' (2008) 71 *Modern Law Review* 473

—— 'The Concept of "Law" in Global Administrative Law: A Reply to Benedict Kingsbury' (2009) 20 *European Journal of International Law* 985

—— 'Administration without Sovereignty' in P Dobner and M Loughlin (eds), *The Twilight of Constitutionalism?* (Oxford, Oxford University Press, 2010) 267–87

—— 'From the Rule of Law to the Constitutionalist Makeover: Changing European Conceptions of Public International Law' (2011) 18 *Constellations* 567

Stavropoulos, N, 'Legal Interpretivism' in EN Zalta (ed), *The Stanford Encyclopedia of Philosophy* (Summer 2014 edn), available at: http://plato.stanford.edu/archives/sum2014/entries/law-interpretivist

Stein, E, 'International Integration and Democracy: No Love at First Sight' (2001) 95 *American Journal of International Law* 489

Suganami, H, *The Domestic Analogy and World Order Proposals* (Cambridge, Cambridge University Press, 1989)

Sylvest, C, 'International Law in Nineteenth-Century Britain' (2005) 75 *British Yearbook of International Law* 9

Tamanaha, BZ, *A General Jurisprudence of Law and Society* (Oxford, Oxford University Press, 2001)

—— *On the Rule of Law: History, Politics, Theory* (Cambridge, Cambridge University Press, 2004)

Tasioulas, J, 'The Legitimacy of International Law' in S Besson and J Tasioulas (eds), *The Philosophy of International Law* (Oxford, Oxford University Press, 2010) 97–116

Thirlway, H, *International Customary Law and Codification: An Examination of the Continuing Role of Custom in the Present Period of Codification of International Law* (Leiden, AW Sijthoff, 1972)

—— *The Sources of International Law* (Oxford, Oxford University Press, 2014)

Thürer, D, 'Max Huber: A Portrait in Outline' (2007) 18 *European Journal of International Law* 69

Tomlins, C, 'How Autonomous is Law?' (2007) 3 *Annual Review of Law and Social Science* 45

Tomuschat, C, 'Obligations Arising for States Without or against their Will' (1993-IV) 241 *Recueil des Cours* 195

—— 'International Law: Ensuring the Survival of Mankind on the Eve of a New Century, General Course on Public International Law' (1999) 281 *Recueil des Cours* 9

Trachtman, JP, 'The Constitutions of the WTO' (2006) 17 *European Journal of International Law* 623

Triepel, H, *Völkerrecht und Landesrecht* (Leipzig, CL Hirschfeld, 1899)

—— *Droit international et droit interne* (Paris, A Pedone, 1920)

Tsagourias, N, 'Conceptualizing the Autonomy of the European Union' in R Collins and ND White (eds), *International Organizations and the Idea of Autonomy: Institutional Independence in the International Legal Order* (Abingdon, Routledge, 2011) 339–52

Tunkin, GI, *Theory of International Law* (Cambridge, MA, Harvard University Press, 1974)
Twining, W, 'A Post-Westphalian Conception of Law' (2003) 37 *Law & Society Review* 199
—— *General Jurisprudence: Understanding Law from a Global Perspective* (Cambridge, Cambridge University Press, 2009)
Twiss, T, *The Law of Nations Considered as Independent Political Communities* (Oxford, Oxford University Press, 1861)
Unger, R, *Law in Modern Society* (New York, Free Press, 1976)
Verdross, A, 'Le fondement du droit International' (1927-I) 16 *Recueil des Cours* 247
Verdross, A, and Simma, B, *Universelles Völkerrecht: Theorie und Praxis*, 3rd edn (Berlin, Duncker & Humblot, 1984)
Vignes, D, 'The Impact of International Organizations on the Development and Application of Public International Law' in R St J Macdonald and DM Johnston (eds), *The Structure and Process of International Law: Essays in Legal Philosophy, Doctrine, and Theory* (The Hague, Martinus Nijhoff, 1983) 809–55
Villa, V, 'Neil MacCormick's Legal Positivism' in M del Mar and Z Bankowski (eds), *Law as Institutional Normative Order* (Farnham, Ashgate, 2009) 45–64
Villalpando, S, 'The Legal Dimension of the International Community: How Community Interests are Protected in International Law' (2010) 21 *European Journal of International Law* 387
Vinogradoff, P, *The Teaching of Sir Henry Maine: An Inaugural Lecture*, (London, Henry Frowde, 1904)
Waldron, J, 'The Irrelevance of Moral Objectivity' in RP George (ed), *Natural Law Theory* (Oxford, Clarendon Press, 1992)
—— 'Kant's Legal Positivism' (1996) 109 *Harvard Law Review* 1535
—— 'Normative (or Ethical) Positivism' in J Coleman (ed), *Hart's Postscript: Essays on the Postscript to the* Concept of Law (Oxford, Oxford University Press, 2001) 411–33
—— 'The Concept and the Rule of Law' (2008–09) 43 *Georgia Law Review* 1
—— 'Judges as Moral Reasoners' (2009) 7 *International Journal of Constitutional Law* 2
—— 'International Law: "A Relatively Small and Unimportant" Part of Jurisprudence?' in L Duarte d'Almeida, J Edwards and A Dolcetti (eds), *Reading HLA Hart's 'The Concept of Law'* (Oxford, Hart Publishing, 2013) 209–26
Walker, N, 'Beyond Boundary Disputes and Basic Grids: Mapping the Global Disorder of Normative Orders' (2008) 3 *International Journal of Constitutional Law* 373
—— *Intimations of Global Law* (Cambridge, Cambridge University Press, 2014)
Warbrick, C, 'The Theory of International Law: Is There an English Contribution?' in P Allott et al, *Theory and International Law: An Introduction* (London, British Institute of International and Comparative Law, 1991) 47–71
—— 'Brownlie's *Principles of Public International Law*: An Assessment' (2000) 11 *European Journal of International Law* 621
Warbrick, C, and Tierney, S (eds), *Towards an International Legal Community? Sovereignty of States and the Sovereignty of International Law* (London, British Institute of International and Comparative Law, 2006)

Watts, A, 'The International Rule of Law' (1993) 36 *German Yearbook of International Law* 15

—— 'The Importance of International Law' in M Byers (ed), *The Role of Law in International Politics: Essays in International Relations and International Law* (Oxford, Oxford University Press, 2000) 5–16

Weber, M, *Theory of Social and Economic Organization* (New York, Oxford University Press, 1947)

—— *Economy and Society* (New York, Free Press, 1964)

Weil, P, 'Towards Normative Relativity in International Law?' (1983) 77 *American Journal of International Law* 413

—— 'Le droit international en quête de son identité (Cours général de droit international public)' (1992) 237 *Recueil des cours* 9

Weiler, JHH, 'The Geology of International Law—Governance, Democracy and Legitimacy' (2004) 64 *Zeitschrift für Ausländisches Öffentliches Recht und Völkerrecht* 547

Weiler, JHH, and Wind, M (eds), *European Constitutionalism Beyond the State* (Cambridge, Cambridge University Press, 2003)

Weinrib, EJ, 'Legal Formalism: On the Imminent Rationality of Law' (1988) 97 *Yale Law Journal* 949

Wellens, K, *Remedies against International Organizations* (Cambridge, Cambridge University Press, 2002)

—— 'Solidarity as a Constitutional Principle: Its Expanding Role and Inherent Limitations' in R St J Macdonald and DM Johnston (eds), *Towards World Constitutionalism: Issues in the Legal Ordering of the World Community* (Leiden, Martinus Nijhoff, 2005) 775–807

Weller, M, 'Undoing the Global Constitution: UN Security Council Action on the International Criminal Court' (2002) 78 *International Affairs* 693

Werner, WG, 'The Never-Ending Closure: Constitutionalism and International Law' in N Tsagourias (ed), *Transnational Constitutionalism: International and European Perspectives* (Cambridge, Cambridge University Press, 2007) 329–67

Westlake, J, *Chapters on the Principles of International law* (Cambridge, Cambridge University Press, 1894)

—— *International Law: Part I, Peace* (Cambridge, Cambridge University Press, 1904)

—— 'Chapters on International Law' in L Oppenheim (ed), *The Collected Papers of John Westlake on International Law* (Cambridge, Cambridge University Press, 1914, originally published in 1894) 13–282

Wheatley, S, *The Democratic Legitimacy of International Law* (Oxford, Hart Publishing, 2010)

White, ND, 'The United Nations System: Conference, Contract or Constitutional Order?' (2000) 4 *Singapore Journal of International and Comparative Law* 281

—— 'Discerning Separate Will' in WP Heere (ed), *From Government to Governance: The Growing Impact of Non-state Actors on the International and European Legal System* (The Hague, TMC Asser Press, 2004) 31–33

—— *The Law of International Organisations*, 2nd edn (Manchester, Manchester University Press, 2006)

—— 'Separate But Connected: Inter-governmental Organizations and International Law' (2008) 5 *International Organizations Law Review* 175

Whittuck, EA, 'Professor Oppenheim' (1920–21) 1 *British Yearbook of International Law* 1

Wilde, R, *International Territorial Administration: How Trusteeship and the Civilizing Mission Never Went Away* (Oxford, Oxford University Press, 2008)

Williams, G, 'International Law and the Controversy Concerning the Word "Law"' (1945) 22 *British Yearbook of International Law* 146

Williams, JF, *Aspects of Modern International Law: An Essay* (London, Oxford University Press, 1939)

Wolfrum, R, 'Legitimacy of International Law from a Legal Perspective: Some Introductory Considerations' in R Wolfrum and V Röben (eds), *Legitimacy in International Law* (New York, Springer, 2008) 1–24

Wolfrum, R, and Röben, V (eds), *Legitimacy in International Law* (New York, Springer, 2008)

Wouters, J, Brems, E, Smis, S, and Schmitt, P, (eds), *Accountability for Human Rights Violations by International Organisations* (Cambridge, Intersentia, 2010)

Wouters, J, Hachez, N, and Schmitt, P, 'Managerial Accountability: What Impact on International Organizations' Autonomy?' in R Collins and ND White (eds), *International Organizations and the Idea of Autonomy: Institutional Independence in the International Legal Order* (Abingdon, Routledge, 2011) 230–56

Zimmern, A, *The League of Nations and the Rule of Law, 1918–1935* (London, MacMillan and Co, 1936)

Zolo, D, 'International Peace through International Law' (1998) 9 *European Journal of International Law* 306

Index